McGraw-Hill
Mathematics

Gary G. Bitter

Carole E. Greenes

Shirley A. Hill

Evan M. Maletsky

Linda Schulman

Gwen Shufelt

Max A. Sobel

Linda L. Thompson

Consulting Editor
Max A. Sobel

Webster Division,
McGraw-Hill
Book Company

New York   St. Louis   San Francisco

Authors

Gary G. Bitter
Professor of Computer and Mathematics Education
Arizona State University

Carole E. Greenes
Associate Professor of Education
Boston University

Shirley A. Hill
Professor of Mathematics and Education
University of Missouri at Kansas City

Evan M. Maletsky
Professor of Mathematics & Computer Science
Montclair State College

Linda Schulman
Associate Professor of Mathematics
Lesley College

Gwen Shufelt
Director Educational Microcomputing Unit
University of Missouri at Kansas City

Max A. Sobel
Professor of Mathematics & Computer Science
Montclair State College

Linda L. Thompson
Consultant
Arizona State Department of Education

Editorial Development

Joanne E. Kane, Dominic Costa, Linda Nicholson, Patricia Kijak, Pat Hunter-Hicklin

Editing and Styling: Linda Richmond

Art and Design: Rosemary O'Connell, Clint Anglin, Valerie Greco, Terry Harmon, Kay Wanous

Photo Editing: Suzanne V. Skloot, Nancy Dyer, Safra Nimrod, Nancy Grimes, Ilene Cherna

Production Manager: Angela Biola

Special Assistant: Vivian Alessi

Series Design: Donald R. Long Design

Cover Design: Group 4, Inc.

This book was set in 12 point Helvetica Light by York Graphic Services. The color separation was done by York Graphic Services.

ISBN 0–07–012625–9

2 3 4 5 6 7 8 9 10 DOWDOW 95 94 93 92 91 90 89 88 87 86

CONTENTS

 Numeration

 Addition and Subtraction

 Multiplication

4 Division by 1-Digit Numbers

5 Division by 2-Digit Numbers

6 Measurement

Fractions: Addition and Subtraction

Decimals: Addition and Subtraction

Decimals: Multiplication and Division

10 Geometry and Measurement

11 More about Fractions

12 Ratio and Percent

1

NUMERATION

Thousands

■ These digits name the numbers in our number system:

0, 1, 2, 3, 4, 5, 6, 7, 8, 9

| 1 thousand | 2 hundreds | 5 tens | 8 ones |

Thousands	Hundreds	Tens	Ones
1	2	5	8

The digit 1 means 1 thousand, or 1,000.
The digit 2 means 2 hundreds, or 200.
The digit 5 means 5 tens, or 50.
The digit 8 means 8 ones, or 8.

Write: 1,258
Read: one thousand, two hundred fifty-eight

> *The comma separates the thousands and the hundreds.*

■ You can also write the number in **expanded form**.

1,258 = 1,000 + 200 + 50 + 8

Try These

Write each number.

1.

2.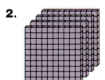

3. 8 thousands 2 hundreds 6 tens 5 ones

4. 7 thousands 8 tens 3 ones

What does the digit 7 mean in each number?

5. 7,318   **6.** 9,672   **7.** 1,746   **8.** 6,237   **9.** 173

Write each number in expanded form.

10. 3,927   **11.** 475   **12.** 5,163   **13.** 728   **14.** 8,172

Exercises

Write each number.

1.

2.

3. 2 thousands 7 hundreds 6 tens 9 ones

4. 4 thousands 8 hundreds 0 tens 5 ones

5. 6 hundreds 4 tens 8 ones

6. 9 thousands 0 hundreds 1 ten 3 ones

7. five thousand, one hundred sixty-two

8. three thousand, six hundred twelve

9. two hundred forty-nine

10. nine thousand, twenty-five

What does the digit 5 mean in each number?

11. 8,135 **12.** 1,520 **13.** 5,417 **14.** 4,657 **15.** 2,510

16. 5,802 **17.** 9,658 **18.** 3,125 **19.** 6,549 **20.** 7,051

Write each number in expanded form.

21. 1,286 **22.** 3,715 **23.** 383 **24.** 5,872 ★ **25.** 9,040

Write each number.

26. 3 tens
5 ones
2 hundreds
8 thousands

27. 4 ones
8 hundreds
0 tens

28. 3 hundreds
1 thousand
9 tens
0 ones

29. 4 thousands
2 tens
7 ones
1 hundred

Solve each problem.

A carton of tacks contains 1,000 tacks. A box of tacks contains 100 tacks. Write the number of tacks on each shelf.

30. On one shelf, there are 4 cartons, 7 boxes, and 23 extra tacks.

31. Another shelf has 3 cartons and 6 boxes of tacks.

★ **32.** On another shelf, there are 5 cartons and 8 extra tacks.

More about Thousands

■ In large numbers, the digits are grouped into **periods**. Each period is a group of three digits. Commas separate the periods.

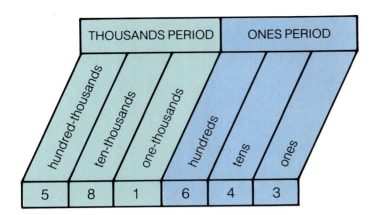

The digit 5 means 5 hundred-thousands, or 500,000.
The digit 8 means 8 ten-thousands, or 80,000.
The digit 1 means 1 thousand, or 1,000.

Write: 581,643
Read: five hundred eighty-one thousand, six hundred forty-three

Another way to read large numbers
is to think about the periods: 581 thousand 643

■ In expanded form:
      581,643 = 500,000 + 80,000 + 1,000 + 600 + 40 + 3

Try These

What does the digit 3 mean in each number?

1. 46,379   **2.** 3,218   **3.** 36,495   **4.** 235,510   **5.** 327,019

Write each number.

6. 32 thousand 841   **7.** 142 thousand 856   **8.** 105 thousand 32

Write each number in expanded form.

9. 392,458   **10.** 64,172   **11.** 835,916   **12.** 26,743   **13.** 71,285

Exercises

What does the digit 7 mean in each number?

1. 3,719   **2.** 1,473   **3.** 17,291   **4.** 84,207   **5.** 79,845

6. 42,976   **7.** 520,967   **8.** 798,160   **9.** 672,018   **10.** 443,749

Use 429,386. Write the digit that is in each place.

11. ones place   **12.** ten-thousands place   **13.** hundreds place

14. thousands place   **15.** hundred-thousands place   **16.** tens place

Write each number.

17. 18 thousand 472   **18.** 453 thousand 193   **19.** 62 thousand 25

20. 36 thousand 81   **21.** 932 thousand 148   **22.** 22 thousand 17

23. 67 thousand 321   **24.** 42 thousand 616   **25.** 131 thousand 9

26. two hundred seventy-five thousand, six hundred fifty-two

27. one hundred ten thousand, six hundred seventy

28. five thousand, twenty-nine

29. thirty-five thousand, eight hundred twelve

30. two thousand, seven hundred sixty

31. fourteen thousand, six hundred nineteen

32. eight hundred two thousand, three hundred one

Write each number in expanded form.

33. 8,294   **34.** 41,532   **35.** 162,317   **36.** 329,568   ★ **37.** 605,420

 Enter each number in your calculator. Turn the calculator upside down. What word do you spell?

38. three thousand, forty-five

39. seven thousand, one hundred five

40. five thousand, three hundred six

41. three thousand, five hundred four

42. fifty-seven thousand, seven hundred thirty-nine

43. five hundred seventy-seven thousand, three hundred forty-five

44. thirty-five thousand, six

45. four thousand, six hundred fifteen

Comparing and Ordering

You can compare numbers with the same number of digits by starting at the left and comparing the digits in each place.

■ Compare 19,726 and 19,426.

Line up the digits.

Compare the ten-thousands.

1 9 , 7 2 6
1 9 , 4 2 6
same

Compare the thousands.

1 9 , 7 2 6
1 9 , 4 2 6
same

Compare the hundreds.

1 9 , 7 2 6
1 9 , 4 2 6

7 **is greater than** 4
7 > 4
so
19,726 > 19,426

■ Compare 6,438 and 6,458.

6 , 4 3 8
6 , 4 5 8
same

6 , 4 3 8
6 , 4 5 8
same

6 , 4 3 8
6 , 4 5 8

3 **is less than** 5
3 < 5
so
6,438 < 6,458

■ Write 4,739; 618; and 4,826 in order from least to greatest.

4 , 7 3 9
   6 1 8   618 is the least.
4 , 8 2 6

Compare 4,739 and 4,826.

4 , 7 3 9
4 , 8 2 6   4,739 < 4,826

The order from least to greatest is 618; 4,739; 4,826.

Try These

Write >, <, or =.

1. 217 ▨ 210
2. 785 ▨ 87
3. 100 ▨ 110
4. 365 ▨ 365
5. 2,762 ▨ 2,652
6. 4,870 ▨ 869
7. 2,500 ▨ 25,000
8. 36,999 ▨ 39,699
9. 561,070 ▨ 560,170

Write in order from least to greatest.

10. 497   4,927   6,013
11. 7,851   7,862   9,503   8,946

Exercises

Write >, <, or =.

1. 127 ▨ 137
2. 612 ▨ 62
3. 187 ▨ 187
4. 3,122 ▨ 3,123
5. 8,720 ▨ 7,306
6. 433 ▨ 4,331
7. 26,840 ▨ 26,842
8. 98,859 ▨ 98,860
9. 68,248 ▨ 68,247
10. 43,273 ▨ 4,273
11. 16,402 ▨ 16,402
12. 8,765 ▨ 87,659
13. 314,212 ▨ 34,212
14. 419,671 ▨ 41,867
15. 924,868 ▨ 924,868

Write in order from least to greatest.

16. 278   265   283   290
17. 8,432   872   8,341   4,782
18. 5,381   5,830   5,380   5,038
19. 6,000   36,000   43,000   5,000
20. 16,243   5,376   8,234   16,342
21. 37,818   38,781   38,188   31,718

Find the greatest digit to make each sentence true.

★ 22. 3,6▨5 > 3,685
★ 23. 9,▨38 < 9,235
★ 24. 37,▨45 < 37,136

Solve each problem.

25. The diameter of Mercury is 4,878 kilometers. The diameter of Venus is 12,100 kilometers. Which planet has a greater diameter?

26. The diameter of Earth is 12,756 kilometers. The diameter of Jupiter is 142,700 kilometers. Which planet has a smaller diameter?

27. The diameter of Mars is 6,790 kilometers. Is the diameter of Mercury greater than or less than the diameter of Mars?

Rounding Numbers

You can round numbers to tell about how many.
A number line can help you to round numbers.

■ Round 132 to the nearest ten.

132 is between 130 and 140.
132 is nearer to 130.
132 rounds down to 130.

■ Round 647 to the nearest ten.

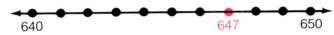

647 is between 640 and 650.
647 is nearer to 650.
647 rounds up to 650.

■ Round 365 to the nearest ten.

365 is between 360 and 370.
365 is halfway between 360 and 370.
365 rounds up to 370.

■ Round 850 to the nearest hundred.

850 is between 800 and 900.
850 is halfway between 800 and 900.
850 rounds up to 900.

■ Round 5,473 to the nearest thousand.

5,473 is between 5,000 and 6,000.
5,473 is nearer to 5,000
5,473 rounds down to 5,000.

Try These

Round to the nearest ten.

1. 98   **2.** 105   **3.** 112   **4.** 115   **5.** 94

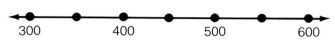

Round to the nearest hundred.

6. 521   **7.** 486   **8.** 450   **9.** 309   **10.** 567

Round to the nearest thousand.

11. 7,125   **12.** 6,500   **13.** 5,475   **14.** 6,900   **15.** 5,238

Exercises

Round to the nearest ten.

1. 92   **2.** 118   **3.** 96   **4.** 104   **5.** 75

Round to the nearest hundred.

6. 326   **7.** 480   **8.** 575   **9.** 703   **10.** 385

Round to the nearest thousand.

11. 7,500   **12.** 6,420   **13.** 5,006   **14.** 6,918   ★ **15.** 9,915

Solve each problem.

16. How long is Lookout Trail?

17. Which bicycle trail is longest?

18. Which bicycle trail is shortest?

19. Round the length of each trail to the nearest 10 kilometers.

Bicycle Trail	Length of Trail in Kilometers
Lookout	56
Waterfall	34
Everett	128
Cabin	109

Rules for Rounding

■ You can use this rule for rounding numbers.

> To round a number, find the place you are rounding to. Look at the digit to the right. If the digit is less than 5, round down. If the digit is 5 or greater, round up.

Round 6,473 to the nearest thousand.

Look at the digit in the hundreds place.
6 , ④ 7 3   Compare this digit with 5.
4 < 5   Round down.

6,473 to the nearest thousand is 6,000.

■ Round 235,817 to the nearest ten-thousand.

Look at the digit in the thousands place.
2 3 ⑤ , 8 1 7   Compare this digit with 5.
5 = 5   Round up.

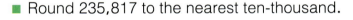

235,817 to the nearest ten-thousand is 240,000.

■ Round 382,973 to the nearest hundred-thousand.

Look at the digit in the ten-thousands place.
3 ⑧ 2 , 9 7 3   Compare this digit with 5.
8 > 5   Round up.

382,973 to the nearest hundred-thousand is 400,000.

■ To round money to the nearest dollar, look at the cents. If the number of cents is $.50 or more, round up to the next dollar.

Round $6.54 to the nearest dollar.

$6 . ⑤④ $.54 > $.50

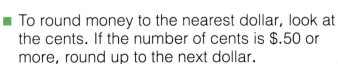

$6.54 rounds up to $7.00.

Try These

Round to the nearest thousand.

1. 1,246   **2.** 4,849   **3.** 7,516   **4.** 18,387   **5.** 376,872

Round to the nearest hundred-thousand.

6. 325,867   **7.** 681,009   **8.** 758,243   **9.** 437,158   **10.** 591,436

Exercises

Round to the nearest ten-thousand.

1. 24,125   **2.** 37,890   **3.** 81,045   **4.** 65,260   **5.** 79,150
6. 143,455   **7.** 358,925   **8.** 422,859   **9.** 763,500   **10.** 547,342

Round to the nearest hundred-thousand.

11. 326,019   **12.** 518,246   **13.** 681,015   **14.** 815,869   **15.** 237,308
16. 865,359   **17.** 467,199   **18.** 155,515   **19.** 341,425   **20.** 744,321

Round each number to the nearest ten, hundred, and thousand.

21. 1,292   **22.** 6,574   **23.** 8,549   ★ **24.** 4,086   ★ **25.** 19,951

Round to the nearest dollar.

26. $14.25

28. $4.98

30. $7.19

27. $.99

29. $5.75

Solve each problem.

31. The number to the nearest hundred is 700. The number to the nearest ten is 720. The digits read the same forward or backward. What is the number?

32. The number to the nearest hundred is 400. The number to the nearest ten is 430. The sum of the digits is 9. What is the number?

Problem Solving: Strategies

LOGICAL REASONING

Why did Joel decide that the population figure was not exactly correct?

Joel used the following conditions to decide whether or not the population figure was exactly correct.

IF the sign is changed every day, THEN it is likely to be correct.

IF the sign is changed every week, THEN it is a little less likely to be correct.

IF the sign is changed every month, THEN it is less likely to be correct. He would need information on when the sign was last changed.

IF the sign is changed every year, THEN it is unlikely to be correct.

Using the Strategy

Joel and Meg stopped at the city hall in Crossville. They asked how often the sign is changed. They found out that the sign is changed every 5 years.

Year	Population
1983	3,598
1984	3,607
1985	3,615
1986	3,621
1987	3,624

The table shows the population figures for 5 years.

1. When was the sign last changed?

2. What year has the lowest population figure?

3. What year has the highest population figure?

4. Is the population of Crossville increasing or decreasing?

IF the population figure is rounded, THEN it would be more accurate for a 5-year period.

5. Round each figure in the table to the nearest ten, hundred, and thousand.

6. Rounding to which places gives the same population figures for the 5-year period.

7. Look at the answer to exercise 6. Rounding to which place gives the more exact population figure?

★ 8. IF a new industry moves to Crossville, THEN what might happen to the population? Why?

ACTIVITY

USING REFERENCES

Go to the library or to your city hall. Find some information about the population of your city or town.

1. What is the population of your city or town?

2. Find out what a **census** is.

3. Find out how often a census is taken.

4. Find the population figures from the last four census counts in your area.

5. Is the population of your city increasing or decreasing?

6. What rounded population figure would be most correct on a population sign? To what place did you round the population figure?

Millions

■ Earth is about this many kilometers from the sun:

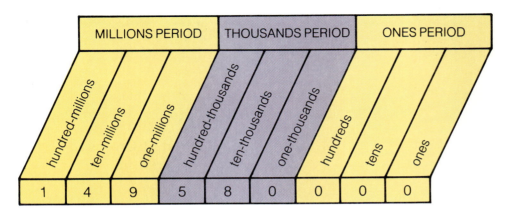

MILLIONS PERIOD			THOUSANDS PERIOD			ONES PERIOD		
hundred-millions	ten-millions	one-millions	hundred-thousands	ten-thousands	one-thousands	hundreds	tens	ones
1	4	9	5	8	0	0	0	0

The digit 1 means 1 hundred-million, or 100,000,000.
The digit 4 means 4 ten-millions, or 40,000,000.
The digit 9 means 9 millions, or 9,000,000.

Write: 149,580,000
Read: 149 million 580 thousand

■ Venus is about 108,230,000 kilometers from the sun.
Compare 149,580,000 and 108,230,000.

$$1\,4\,9{,}5\,8\,0{,}0\,0\,0 \quad 4 > 0, \text{ so}$$
$$1\,0\,8{,}2\,3\,0{,}0\,0\,0 \quad 149{,}580{,}000 > 108{,}230{,}000$$

■ Jupiter is 778,400,000 kilometers from the sun.
778,400,000 rounded to the nearest million is 778,000,000.

Try These

What does the digit 8 mean in each number?

1. 4,285,150   **2.** 187,642,259   **3.** 8,054,076   **4.** 822,740,000

Write each number.

5. 6 million 124 thousand 607   **6.** 12 million 83 thousand 5

Write >, <, or =.

7. 464,809 ■ 3,404,687   **8.** 5,218,147 ■ 5,208,147

Exercises

What does the digit 5 mean in each number?

1. 4,523,187
2. 15,674,000
3. 850,227,113

Use 482,190,673. Write the digit that is in each place.

4. hundred-millions place
5. hundred-thousands place

Write each number.

6. 7 million 125 thousand 549
7. 18 million 320 thousand 75
8. one hundred fifty-one million, nine hundred forty-five

Write >, <, or =.

9. 6,329,185 ▩ 6,328,185
10. 187,143,176 ▩ 186,147,213

Round to the nearest million.

11. 1,046,320
12. 31,246,000
13. 712,840,120
★ **14.** 299,890,000

Solve each problem.

15. Which of these planets is closest to the sun?

16. Which planet is farthest from the sun?

★ **17.** Which planet is closest to Earth?

Planet	Distance from the Sun in Kilometers
Venus	108,230,000
Earth	149,580,000
Mars	227,720,000
Jupiter	778,400,000

KEEPING IN SHAPE

What does the digit 4 mean in each number?

1. 347
2. 54,962
3. 415,973
4. 364,217,900

Write >, <, or =.

5. 567 ▩ 657
6. 14,526 ▩ 8,975
7. 325,967 ▩ 325,967

Billions

■ The United States produced this many eggs in 1 year:

BILLIONS PERIOD			MILLIONS PERIOD			THOUSANDS PERIOD			ONES PERIOD		
hundred-billions	ten-billions	one-billions	hundred-millions	ten-millions	one-millions	hundred-thousands	ten-thousands	one-thousands	hundreds	tens	ones
	6	9	6	3	6	0	0	0	0	0	0

The digit 6 means 6 ten-billions, or 60,000,000,000.
The digit 9 means 9 billions, or 9,000,000,000.

Write: 69,636,000,000
Read: 69 billion 636 million

■ Alabama produced 3,095,000,000 eggs. North Carolina produced 3,078,000,000 eggs.
Compare 3,095,000,000 and 3,078,000,000.

3,0**9**5,0 0 0,0 0 0   9 > 7, so
3,0**7**8,0 0 0,0 0 0   3,095,000,000 > 3,078,000,000

■ California produced 8,400,000,000 eggs.
8,400,000,000 to the nearest billion is 8,000,000,000.

Try These

What does the digit 3 mean in each number?

1. 36,945,000,000   2. 145,236,000,000   3. 3,788,000,000

Write each number.

4. 9 billion 365 million 472 thousand 808
5. 62 billion 76 million 95 thousand 5

Write >, <, or =.

6. 5,219,165,827 ■ 5,291,165,827   7. 86,275,500,075 ■ 86,275,005,075

Exercises

Use 498,321,576,000. Write the digit that is in each place.

1. millions place
2. hundred-billions place
3. billions place

What does the digit 6 mean in each number?

4. 6,320,125,000
5. 464,300,100,000
6. 129,643,000,083

Write each number.

7. 352 billion 139 million 917 thousand 429
8. 15 billion 452 million
9. 108 billion 26 million 103 thousand 98

Write >, <, or =.

10. 87,326,125,000 ■ 87,325,125,000
11. 9,000,128,000 ■ 9,001,128,000

Round to the nearest billion.

12. 2,327,000,000
13. 6,892,000,140
★ **14.** 9,999,999,001

Write in order from least to greatest.

15. 63,200,321   62,310,321   62,210,321   63,310,321
16. 133,386,124,011   133,286,124,011   133,276,124,011

THINK AND TRY

EXPLORING PLACE VALUE

Count the number of hundreds in 28,500. Start at the left. Read all the digits to the hundreds place.

$$28,500 = 285 \text{ hundreds}$$

Copy and complete.

1. 290 = ■ tens
2. 2,750 = ■ tens
3. 5,000 = ■ hundreds
4. 1,000,000 = ■ thousands
5. 5,000,000,000 = ■ millions

Write the number.

6. 13 tens
7. 200 tens
8. 19 hundreds
9. 10 thousands
10. 35 hundreds
11. 23 millions

Problem Solving: Applications

USING A TABLE

The Admiral Company wants to build a microcomputer factory. The company is looking for a site for the factory. It wants to build in a city with a population between 500,000 and 800,000. Should Dallas be considered as a site for the factory?

READ   Find cities with a population between 500,000 and 800,000. Is Dallas one of these cities?

PLAN   Compare to find out if Dallas meets the conditions:
greater than 500,000
less than 800,000

DO   The population of Dallas is 904,078.

$904,078 > 500,000$ meets the first condition

$904,078 > 800,000$ does not meet the second condition

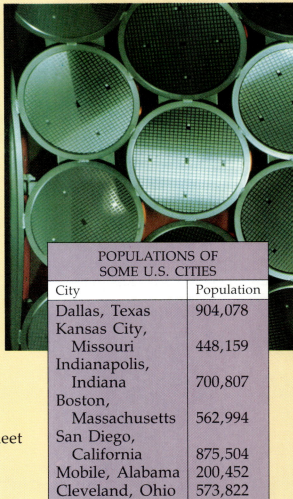

POPULATIONS OF SOME U.S. CITIES	
City	Population
Dallas, Texas	904,078
Kansas City, Missouri	448,159
Indianapolis, Indiana	700,807
Boston, Massachusetts	562,994
San Diego, California	875,504
Mobile, Alabama	200,452
Cleveland, Ohio	573,822

CHECK   Did you read the table correctly?
Did you compare the correct numbers?

The population of Dallas is too large. It will not be considered as a site for the microcomputer factory.

Try These

Which of these cities should be considered as a site for the microcomputer factory? Write *yes* or *no*.

1. Kansas City, Missouri
2. Indianapolis, Indiana
3. Boston, Massachusetts
4. San Diego, California
5. Mobile, Alabama
6. Cleveland, Ohio

Exercises

Solve each problem.

The Admiral Company received bids from five construction companies. This table shows the price each company would charge for building the new factory.

BIDS ON COST OF FACTORY	
Company	Cost
DV Construction	$3,485,900
Adel Builders	3,996,750
Brookby, Inc.	3,123,800
CKM Construction	3,800,000
Build-Rite, Inc.	3,650,000
Forever Construction	4,128,000

1. Which company had the highest bid?

2. Which company had the lowest bid?

3. Which company made a bid of $3,650,000?

Which companies should be considered if the Admiral Company has a budget between $3,000,000 and $3,750,000? Write *yes* or *no*.

4. DV Construction

5. Adel Builders

6. Brookby, Inc.

7. CKM Construction

8. Build-Rite, Inc.

9. Forever Construction

This table shows the quantities of some parts produced by the Admiral Company. This table shows production for last year and expected production for this year.

PRODUCTION OF MICROCOMPUTER PARTS		
Name	Number Produced Last Year	Expected Production This Year
discs	50,984	74,000
chips	280,000	300,000
keyboards	120,000	155,000
circuits	78,650	65,000
screens	136,409	98,750
printers	95,090	102,400

10. Is the production of discs increasing or decreasing?

11. Is the production of screens increasing or decreasing?

12. Which parts were produced in quantities of more than 100,000 last year?

13. Which parts are expected to be produced in quantities of more than 100,000 this year?

14. Which parts were produced in quantities of more than 50,000 but less than 100,000 last year?

CHAPTER CHECKPOINT

Write each number. (pp. 2–17)

1. 3 hundreds 2 tens 5 ones

2. 9 thousand 437

3. 13 million 817 thousand 425

4. 105 billion 18 million 465 thousand

5. 89 billion 725 million

6. 345 billion 9 million 15 thousand 8

7. four hundred sixty-eight

8. seven thousand, six hundred forty

9. sixteen thousand, three hundred thirty-nine

10. two million, one hundred twenty-five thousand, eighty-nine

11. eight hundred three million, four hundred thousand, fifty-six

12. forty-seven billion, five hundred fourteen million, eight hundred

13. three hundred twenty billion, six hundred ten million, six hundred four

14. five hundred four billion, three million, eight thousand, two hundred seven

Write each number in expanded form. (pp. 2–5)

15. 476

16. 4,916

17. 15,287

18. 65,375

19. 86,439

20. 729,816

What does the digit 3 mean in each number? (pp. 2–17)

21. 635

22. 1,347

23. 58,203

24. 327,628

25. 435,628

26. 3,657,204

27. 103,789,096

28. 23,876,054,000

29. 576,309,215,496

Use 35,642,178,900. Write the digit that is in each place. (pp. 2–17)

30. hundreds place

31. tens place

32. ten-thousands place

33. millions place

34. thousands place

35. ten-millions place

36. billions place

37. ten-billions place

38. hundred-millions place

Write >, <, or =. (pp. 6–17)

39. 395 ▨ 415 **40.** 6,842 ▨ 6,840 **41.** 7,803 ▨ 783
42. 86,418 ▨ 86,418 **43.** 4,676 ▨ 40,766 **44.** 164,233 ▨ 64,232
45. 36,196 ▨ 406,125 **46.** 2,550,050 ▨ 550,050 **47.** 471,638,900 ▨ 471,683,900

Write in order from least to greatest. (pp. 6–17)

48. 318 286 381 268 **49.** 2,516 1,575 1,868 2,615

50. 4,281 4,820 4,280 4,082 **51.** 75,694 75,496 57,964 59,674

52. 808,247 880,742 808,742 880,472

53. 5,370,619 5,730,619 5,307,916 5,703,196

Round each number. (pp. 8–17)

54. 86 to the nearest ten **55.** 782 to the nearest ten
56. 350 to the nearest hundred **57.** 6,721 to the nearest hundred
58. 4,896 to the nearest thousand **59.** 326,504 to the nearest thousand

60. 621,843 to the nearest hundred-thousand
61. 737,760,080 to the nearest million
62. 9,315,000,000 to the nearest billion

Solve each problem. (pp. 2–19)

63. What is the population of West Virginia?

64. Which state has the greatest population?

65. Which state has the least population?

66. Is the population of Massachusetts greater than or less than the population of Maryland?

67. Make another table. Put the states in order from the greatest population to the least population.

Population of Some States in 1980	
Delaware	594,317
Maryland	4,216,975
Alaska	401,851
Illinois	11,426,518
West Virginia	1,950,279
Pennsylvania	11,863,895
Massachusetts	5,737,037
New Hampshire	920,610

COMPUTERS AND PROBLEM SOLVING

■ Three BASIC statements that a computer recognizes are PRINT, LET, and GOTO. Two BASIC system commands are NEW and RUN. See how many other BASIC words and symbols you remember by doing the activity below.

Match these columns.

1. It causes an output.	**a.** 12−3
2. It assigns a value to a variable.	**b.** Logo
3. This language is for turtle graphics.	**c.** LET
4. It changes the order in which a computer does things.	**d.** variable
	e. PRINT
5. It is where values are stored.	**f.** GOTO
6. It causes a computer to carry out the instructions in a program.	**g.** 8/9
7. It erases everything in a computer's memory.	**h.** NEW
	i. 5×3
8. This language uses numbered lines.	**j.** RUN
9. It is a multiplication in BASIC.	**k.** 6∗4
10. It is a division in BASIC.	**l.** BASIC

■ INPUT is a powerful BASIC statement. It lets you give the computer new values without writing a new program.

Read these programs.

```
NEW                    NEW
10   LET A=5           10   INPUT A
20   LET B=7           20   INPUT B
30   PRINT A ∗ B       30   PRINT A ∗ B
40   END               40   END
```

When the first program is run, the computer will print 35.

When the second program is run, the computer will reach line 10 and stop. The screen will look like this.

```
] RUN
?▓
```

The computer is waiting for the user to type in, or input, a value for A. If you type 5 and press <Return>, the screen will look like this.

```
] RUN
?5
?▓
```

The computer will have reached line 20 and will be waiting for the user to input a value for B. If you type 7, the screen will look like this.

```
] RUN
?5
?7
35
]▓
```

The product of A and B has been printed.

Solve each problem.

1. What makes the second program more powerful than the first?

2. Why is this program more powerful than either of the others?

```
NEW
10   INPUT A
20   INPUT B
30   PRINT A * B
35   GOTO 10
40   END
```

ENRICHMENT

ROMAN NUMERALS

Hundreds of years ago, the Romans used symbols to write numbers. Each symbol always had the same value.

These are symbols the Romans used to write the numbers from 1 to 1,000.

Our Number	1	5	10	50	100	500	1,000
Roman Numeral	I	V	X	L	C	D	M

To name other numbers, they used addition.

Add the value of each symbol to find the number.

III means 1 + 1 + 1, or 3.
VI means 5 + 1, or 6.
MM means 1,000 + 1,000, or 2,000.
LX means 50 + 10, or 60.

They also used subtraction to name numbers. When a symbol for a smaller number is written before a symbol for a larger number, subtract.

IV means 5 − 1, or 4.   XC means 100 − 10, or 90.

Write our number.

1. XXVI **2.** XXIV **3.** XXVII **4.** XXXV
5. LIII **6.** LIV **7.** LXXII **8.** CLXXXIV
9. MD **10.** DCL **11.** MCM **12.** MCMLXXXIV

Write the Roman numeral.

13. 7 **14.** 41 **15.** 88 **16.** 137
17. 502 **18.** 1,005 **19.** 2,069 **20.** 1,987
21. 99 **22.** 449 **23.** 2,206 **24.** 3,473

Write the Roman numeral that comes next.

25. XX **26.** VIII **27.** LXIV **28.** DCXLIX

Write each number.

1. 5 hundreds 3 tens 8 ones
2. 4 thousand 253
3. 86 thousand 281
4. 129 million 856 thousand 940

5. three hundred twenty-seven
6. fourteen thousand, two hundred nine
7. nine hundred fifteen thousand, two hundred seventy-five
8. six hundred four million, five hundred thousand, eighteen
9. nine hundred twelve billion, three hundred sixty million, two hundred ten

What does the digit 7 mean in each number?

10. 875
11. 48,237
12. 347,956
13. 57,183,516
14. 706,000,942
15. 675,203,150,924

Use 5,768,324,000. Write the digit that is in each place.

16. hundreds place
17. ten-thousands place
18. billions place
19. thousands place
20. hundred-millions place
21. ten-millions place

Write >, <, or =.

22. 256 ▧ 276
23. 3,245 ▧ 3,243
24. 6,962 ▧ 8,262
25. 54,896 ▧ 54,698
26. 46,816 ▧ 406,861
27. 206,421 ▧ 206,421

28. 5,120,090 ▧ 5,102,090
29. 281,743,500 ▧ 281,473,900

Write in order from least to greatest.

30. 215   251   125   225
31. 6,846   4,866   8,468   4,686

Round each number.

32. 782 to the nearest ten
33. 450 to the nearest hundred
34. 4,938 to the nearest thousand
35. $8.43 to the nearest dollar

36. 656,281 to the nearest hundred-thousand
37. 432,857,269 to the nearest million

SKILLS CHECK

Choose the correct answer.

1. In 649, what does the digit 4 mean?

   a. 4 ones
   b. 4 tens
   c. 40 tens
   d. 4 hundreds

2. 2 hundreds 4 tens 5 ones is which number?

   a. 245
   b. 254
   c. 542
   d. NG

3. In 27,341, which digit is in the thousands place?

   a. 2
   b. 3
   c. 4
   d. NG

4. Which number is less than 268,433?

   a. 268,429
   b. 268,531
   c. 269,431
   d. 278,531

5. Which sentence is correct?

   a. 24,356 > 24,336
   b. 24,356 < 24,336
   c. 24,356 = 24,336

6. What is 365 rounded to the nearest ten?

   a. 300
   b. 360
   c. 370
   d. 400

7. What is 24,697 rounded to the nearest thousand?

   a. 20,000
   b. 24,000
   c. 24,700
   d. 25,000

8. Which is the number for twenty-nine dollars and eight cents?

   a. $29.08
   b. $29.80
   c. $29.8
   d. NG

9. What is $16.79 rounded to the nearest dollar?

   a. $16.00
   b. $16.70
   c. $16.80
   d. $17.00

10. Which is the number for fourteen million, nine hundred one thousand, six hundred seventy-two?

    a. 1,491,672
    b. 14,672,901
    c. 14,901,672
    d. 149,001,672

11. What is 17,398,060,452 rounded to the nearest billion?

    a. 10,000,000,000
    b. 17,000,000,000
    c. 17,400,000,000
    d. 18,000,000,000

12. Which number is greater than 2,487,100,369?

    a. 2,478,100,369
    b. 2,487,010,369
    c. 2,748,100,369
    d. NG

2

ADDITION AND
SUBTRACTION

Addition Facts

- There are 9 test tubes and 3 flasks in the science room. How many pieces of equipment are there in all?

  Add 9 and 3 to find how many in all.

  $$\begin{array}{r} 9 \\ +3 \\ \hline 12 \end{array}$$

  There are 12 pieces of equipment in all.

- Here are two ways you can write an addition fact.

  $$\begin{array}{r} 9 \\ +5 \\ \hline 14 \end{array}$$ addends · sum

  $9 + 5 = 14$
  addends · sum

- Addition has some special properties that can help you add mentally.

ORDER
You can change the order of the addends. The sum is the same. You can use the order property to check addition.

$9 + 7 = 16$

$7 + 9 = 16$

GROUPING
You can change the grouping of the addends. The sum is the same. The parentheses mean *do this first*.

$(6 + 4) + 2$
$\quad\downarrow$
$\;10 \quad + 2 = 12$

$6 + (4 + 2)$
$\qquad\downarrow$
$6 + \quad 6 \quad = 12$

ZERO
If one addend is 0, the sum is the other addend.

$0 + 5 = 5$

$5 + 0 = 5$

Try These

Add.

1. $\begin{array}{r} 7 \\ +4 \\ \hline \end{array}$

2. $\begin{array}{r} 8 \\ +7 \\ \hline \end{array}$

3. $\begin{array}{r} 4 \\ +0 \\ \hline \end{array}$

4. $\begin{array}{r} 6 \\ +9 \\ \hline \end{array}$

5. $\begin{array}{r} 3 \\ +8 \\ \hline \end{array}$

6. $\begin{array}{r} 7 \\ +7 \\ \hline \end{array}$

7. $\begin{array}{r} 9 \\ +2 \\ \hline \end{array}$

8. $5 + 4$

9. $0 + 6$

10. $(3 + 6) + 9$

11. $5 + 6$

Exercises

Add.

1. 6	2. 5	3. 6	4. 7	5. 8	6. 7	7. 9
+2	+8	+5	+6	+2	+0	+8

8. 1	9. 0	10. 9	11. 4	12. 9	13. 3	14. 7
+9	+3	+3	+3	+9	+3	+5

15. 4	16. 0	17. 8	18. 5	19. 8	20. 7	21. 4
+4	+8	+9	+5	+8	+9	+8

22. 8 + 3   **23.** 3 + 7   **24.** 6 + 6   **25.** 9 + 0

26. 6 + 8   **27.** 7 + 7   **28.** 0 + 6   **29.** 8 + 4

Add. Do as many as you can mentally.

30. (2 + 3) + 4   **31.** 2 + (3 + 4)   **32.** (4 + 1) + 8

33. 8 + (2 + 0)   **34.** (8 + 2) + 0   **35.** 5 + (2 + 7)

36. 5 + 9 + 1   **37.** 4 + 5 + 3   **38.** 2 + 6 + 8

39. 3 + 8 + 2 + 5   **40.** 6 + 4 + 8 + 2 + 3   **41.** 5 + 4 + 8 + 3 + 7

Find the missing addend.

★ **42.** 2 + ■ = 7   ★ **43.** 3 + ■ = 6   ★ **44.** 8 + ■ = 15

★ **45.** ■ + 9 = 18   ★ **46.** ■ + 5 = 13   ★ **47.** ■ + 6 = 6

Copy and complete each arrow train.

48. 4 $\xrightarrow{+3}$ ■ $\xrightarrow{+8}$ ■   **49.** 5 $\xrightarrow{+4}$ ■ $\xrightarrow{+7}$ ■   **50.** 3 $\xrightarrow{+2}$ ■ $\xrightarrow{+6}$ ■

51. Make an arrow train from 6 to 13. Use only $\xrightarrow{+2}$ and $\xrightarrow{+3}$ arrows.

★ **52.** Try to make an arrow train from 6 to 13 using only $\xrightarrow{+2}$.
Explain what happens.

Solve each problem.

53. There are 6 test tubes in a rack. Ed puts 8 more test tubes in the rack. How many test tubes are there altogether?

54. Ed has 3 flasks filled with water. He fills 9 more flasks with water before starting an experiment. How many flasks are filled with water?

Adding 2-Digit Numbers

■ The school had a puppet show. There were 41 fifth graders in the show. There were 34 fourth graders in the show. How many students were in the show altogether?

To find how many altogether, add 41 and 34.

Add the ones.

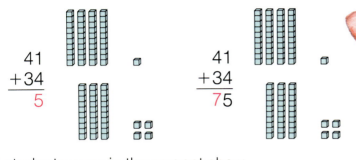

$$\begin{array}{r} 41 \\ +34 \\ \hline 5 \end{array}$$

Add the tens.

$$\begin{array}{r} 41 \\ +34 \\ \hline 75 \end{array}$$

75 students were in the puppet show.

■ Sometimes you need to regroup ones.

Add: 38 + 26

Add the ones. Regroup.

$$\begin{array}{r} \overset{1}{3}8 \\ +26 \\ \hline 4 \end{array}$$

Add the tens.

$$\begin{array}{r} \overset{1}{3}8 \\ +26 \\ \hline 64 \end{array}$$

Check.

$$\begin{array}{r} 26 \\ +38 \\ \hline 64 \end{array} \checkmark$$

14 ones is 1 ten 4 ones.

■ Sometimes you need to regroup ones and tens.

Add: 74 + 39

Add the ones. Regroup.

$$\begin{array}{r} \overset{1}{7}4 \\ +39 \\ \hline 3 \end{array}$$

Add the tens. Regroup.

$$\begin{array}{r} \overset{1}{7}4 \\ +39 \\ \hline 113 \end{array}$$

Check.

$$\begin{array}{r} 39 \\ +74 \\ \hline 113 \end{array} \checkmark$$

11 tens is 1 hundred 1 ten.

Try These

Add. Check each answer.

1. 13 +17	**2.** 26 +15	**3.** 37 +89	**4.** 46 + 4	**5.** 64 +89	**6.** 75 +13

7. 36 + 14   **8.** 84 + 7   **9.** 75 + 19   **10.** 25 + 8

Exercises

Add.

1. 67 +12	**2.** 45 +23	**3.** 36 +13	**4.** 42 +18	**5.** 94 + 9	**6.** 92 +14
7. 47 +19	**8.** 36 +48	**9.** 75 + 8	**10.** 25 +14	**11.** 87 +62	**12.** 88 + 6
13. 84 + 6	**14.** 64 +25	**15.** 68 + 8	**16.** 54 +42	**17.** 96 +17	**18.** 49 + 8
19. 72 + 9	**20.** 36 +36	**21.** 82 + 4	**22.** 86 +18	**23.** 49 +16	**24.** 86 +37

25. 57 + 22   **26.** 85 + 7   **27.** 67 + 39   **28.** 49 + 6

29. 88 + 11   **30.** 74 + 16   **31.** 60 + 85   **32.** 53 + 28

33. 51 + 93   **34.** 26 + 40   **35.** 73 + 18   **36.** 48 + 25

Solve each problem.

37. How many fourth graders bought tickets?

38. How many third graders bought tickets?

39. Which grade bought more tickets, the fifth grade or the sixth grade?

40. How many tickets were bought by fourth and fifth graders altogether?

41. How many tickets were bought by third and sixth graders altogether?

PUPPET-SHOW TICKET SALES	
Grade	Number of Tickets
3	35
4	27
5	23
6	36

★ **42.** How many tickets were sold for the puppet show in all?

Adding 3-Digit Numbers

■ Farmers buy equipment from a farm-supply store. There are 248 pails in the store. A shipment of 137 more arrives. How many pails are there now?

To find the answer, add.

Add the ones. Regroup.	Add the tens.	Add the hundreds.
1 248 +137 ‾‾5	1 248 +137 ‾85	1 248 +137 ‾385

There are now 385 pails.

■ Sometimes you need to regroup more than once.

Add: 563 + 749

Add the ones. Regroup.	Add the tens. Regroup.	Add the hundreds. Regroup.	Check.
1 563 +749 ‾‾2	1 1 563 +749 ‾12	1 1 563 +749 ‾1,312	749 +563 ‾1,312 ✔

13 hundreds is
1 thousand 3 hundreds.

■ You add money the same way you add **whole numbers.** Whole numbers are the numbers 0, 1, 2, 3, 4, and so on.

Add: $4.57 + $.89

1 1 457 + 89 ‾546	1 1 $4.57 + .89 ‾$5.46

Remember: Write the $ and the . in the answer.

32   Chapter 2

Try These

Add. Check each answer.

1. $\begin{array}{r} 284 \\ +105 \\ \hline \end{array}$
2. $\begin{array}{r} 615 \\ +268 \\ \hline \end{array}$
3. $\begin{array}{r} 846 \\ +175 \\ \hline \end{array}$
4. $\begin{array}{r} 807 \\ +296 \\ \hline \end{array}$
5. $\begin{array}{r} 374 \\ +838 \\ \hline \end{array}$
6. $\begin{array}{r} \$2.49 \\ + 6.73 \\ \hline \end{array}$

7. 672 + 88   8. 607 + 193   9. 314 + 97   10. $6.55 + $2.49

Exercises

Add.

1. $\begin{array}{r} 103 \\ +514 \\ \hline \end{array}$
2. $\begin{array}{r} 142 \\ +348 \\ \hline \end{array}$
3. $\begin{array}{r} 275 \\ +606 \\ \hline \end{array}$
4. $\begin{array}{r} 909 \\ + 98 \\ \hline \end{array}$
5. $\begin{array}{r} 127 \\ +157 \\ \hline \end{array}$
6. $\begin{array}{r} \$7.92 \\ + 1.96 \\ \hline \end{array}$

7. $\begin{array}{r} 479 \\ + 87 \\ \hline \end{array}$
8. $\begin{array}{r} 75 \\ +26 \\ \hline \end{array}$
9. $\begin{array}{r} 347 \\ +456 \\ \hline \end{array}$
10. $\begin{array}{r} 452 \\ +199 \\ \hline \end{array}$
11. $\begin{array}{r} 672 \\ +449 \\ \hline \end{array}$
12. $\begin{array}{r} \$5.98 \\ + 2.15 \\ \hline \end{array}$

13. $\begin{array}{r} 623 \\ +516 \\ \hline \end{array}$
14. $\begin{array}{r} 261 \\ +891 \\ \hline \end{array}$
15. $\begin{array}{r} 974 \\ + 87 \\ \hline \end{array}$
16. $\begin{array}{r} 34 \\ +49 \\ \hline \end{array}$
17. $\begin{array}{r} 624 \\ +158 \\ \hline \end{array}$
18. $\begin{array}{r} \$8.71 \\ + 6.95 \\ \hline \end{array}$

19. $\begin{array}{r} 196 \\ + 38 \\ \hline \end{array}$
20. $\begin{array}{r} 315 \\ +284 \\ \hline \end{array}$
21. $\begin{array}{r} \$7.05 \\ + 6.29 \\ \hline \end{array}$
22. $\begin{array}{r} 27 \\ +29 \\ \hline \end{array}$
23. $\begin{array}{r} \$9.20 \\ + 7.86 \\ \hline \end{array}$
24. $\begin{array}{r} 314 \\ +958 \\ \hline \end{array}$

25. 45 + 198   26. 329 + 486   27. 95 + 18   28. $8.25 + $3.79

29. 204 + 57   30. 65 + 107   31. $6.86 + $2.48   32. 938 + 756

Solve each problem.

Stock clerks keep records of items received and stock on hand. They add what is received to the total.

33. On 6/1, there were 324 feeding troughs on hand. On 6/10, the store received 144 more troughs. Is the total 468 correct?

★ 34. Add the number received on 6/21 to the total to get a new total.

★ 35. Copy and complete the rest of the card.

STOCK-RECORD CARD

Stock Item Received: Feeding Troughs			
6/1 Number on Hand: 324			
Date	Order	Received	Total
6/10	B-150	144	468
6/21	B-342	288	
6/24	B-351	144	
Total items in:			

More Than Two Addends

■ The school cafeteria served 293 lunches on Monday. On Tuesday, 325 lunches were served. 349 lunches were served on Wednesday. How many lunches were served in the 3 days?

Add to find how many lunches were served.

Add the ones.
Regroup.

```
  1
  293
  325
+ 349
    7
```

Add the tens.
Regroup.

```
 1 1
  293
  325
+ 349
   67
```

Add the hundreds.

```
 1 1
  293
  325
+ 349
  967
```

The school cafeteria served 967 lunches in the 3 days.

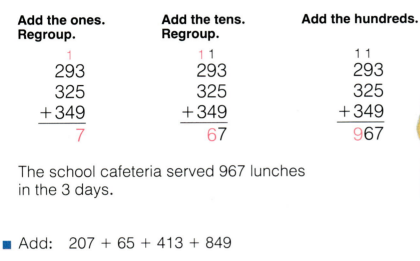

■ Add: $207 + 65 + 413 + 849$

```
 1 1
  207
   65
  413
+ 849
1,534
```

Check.

```
  849
  413
   65
+ 207
1,534 ✔
```

Try These

Add. Check each answer.

1.	**2.**	**3.**	**4.**	**5.**	**6.**
261	365	518	360	891	309
318	254	906	523	68	264
+175	+527	+267	+181	125	75
				+217	+487

7. $154 + 206 + 387$

8. $124 + 697 + 78 + 486$

Exercises

Add.

1.	367 121 +316	**2.**	563 436 +219	**3.**	804 162 +575	**4.**	582 96 +154	**5.**	219 508 +126	**6.**	821 916 + 87

7.	189 75 +684	**8.**	835 207 +154	**9.**	718 37 +268	**10.**	767 189 +215	**11.**	204 419 +197	**12.**	429 495 +103

13.	586 109 76 +215	**14.**	125 316 827 +146	**15.**	375 192 96 +533	**16.**	506 85 236 +888	**17.**	815 345 106 + 45	**18.**	720 683 404 +267

19. 183 + 97

20. 687 + 104 + 84

21. 671 + 923 + 130

22. 874 + 251 + 533

23. 104 + 78 + 239 + 318

24. 551 + 875 + 209 + 343

Solve each problem.

25. The cafeteria manager orders 120 bananas, 250 apples, and 300 oranges. How many pieces of fruit does the cafeteria manager order?

26. The cafeteria manager ordered utensils. She ordered 860 forks, 650 knives, and 780 spoons. How many utensils did she order in all?

27. One carton of napkins costs $6.89. One carton of paper plates costs $9.25. The cafeteria manager orders one carton of each item. What is the total cost?

★ **28.** The cafeteria manager needs 1,000 cups. She has 150 red plastic cups, 290 blue plastic cups, 375 white paper cups, and 160 yellow paper cups. Does she have enough cups?

KEEPING IN SHAPE

Write >, <, or =.

1. 743 ■ 734

2. 1,068 ■ 1,608

3. 491,753 ■ 491,753

4. 12,337 ■ 12,377

5. 3,072,448 ■ 3,702,484

6. 97,285,364 ■ 97,285,346

7. 3,752 ■ 3,725

8. 815,643 ■ 815,643

9. 26,437 ■ 26,374

Adding Greater Numbers

■ One week 6,978 people went to see the opera. The same week 8,542 people went to hear the symphony orchestra. How many people attended the performances altogether?

To find how many people attended the performances, add 6,978 and 8,542.

Add the ones. Regroup.	Add the tens. Regroup.	Add the hundreds. Regroup.	Add the thousands. Regroup.
1	1 1	1 1 1	1 1 1
6,978	6,978	6,978	6,978
+8,542	+8,542	+8,542	+8,542
0	20	520	15,520

15,520 people attended the performances.

■ You can **estimate** mentally to check whether or not your answer is reasonable.

Add: 394,685 + 45,709

```
 1 1 1   1
 394,685
+  45,709
 440,394
```

Estimate to check.

Circle the first digit in each addend. Round each addend to the circled place. Add.

$$\begin{array}{r} ③94,685 \longrightarrow 400,000 \\ +\ ④5,709 \longrightarrow +\ 50,000 \\ \hline 450,000 \end{array}$$

The sum seems reasonable since 440,394 is close to 450,000.

Try These

Add. Estimate to check.

1. 2,834	**2.** 9,367	**3.** 15,604	**4.** 16,825	**5.** 485,374
+3,729	+4,096	+ 3,513	+54,976	+286,968

6. 8,365 + 7,069   **7.** 43,462 + 8,559

8. 296,538 + 86,914   **9.** 17,468 + 396,572

Exercises

Add. Estimate to check.

1. 3,645
    +1,248

2. $64.26
    +   1.93

3. 40,368
    +17,927

4. 76,854
    + 2,639

5. 83,642
    +86,375

6. 73,894
    +15,356

7. 715,785
    +962,549

8. 175,323
    + 32,647

9. 66,887
    +34,652

10. 619,307
    +127,283

11. 12,206
    + 4,318

12. $640.19
    + 178.53

13. 312,487
    + 23,624

14. $5,221.46
    + 2,837.58

15. 865
    +279

16. 52,146
    2,175
    +16,381

17. $ 3.75
    15.83
    + 132.57

18. 172,153
    68,508
    +536,512

19. 243,155
    172,435
    465,251
    +631,434

20. 846,718
    154,563
    7,576
    + 45,891

21. 4,278 + 5,899

22. 297 + 368 + 27 + 829

23. 35,156 + 51,314

24. $412.08 + $65.14

25. 433,157 + 581,675

26. 5,324 + 16,308 + 31,507

Solve each problem.

27. Mr. and Mrs. Holmes went to the concert. Their tickets cost $35.50. They bought programs and snacks for $17.75. How much did they spend altogether?

28. The weekly attendance at three concerts was 31,226; 27,475; and 29,260 people. What was the total attendance for all three concerts?

29. The manager of the concert hall hires 52 ushers, 86 musicians, 33 maintenance workers, 8 ticket sellers, 4 secretaries, and 12 stagehands. How many people work at the concert hall?

30. The management spent $897 to replace the curtain on the stage. It cost $1,475 to fix some broken seats. How much did the management spend on these improvements?

Problem Solving: Strategies

FINDING INFORMATION

A **double bar graph** shows information. It can help you solve problems. This double bar graph shows high and low temperatures in Atlanta, Georgia, for 5 days in January.

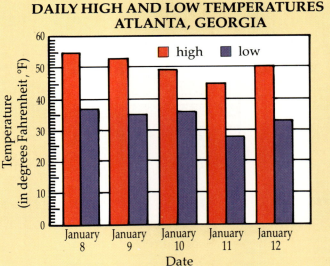

DAILY HIGH AND LOW TEMPERATURES ATLANTA, GEORGIA

Find the key for the bars. The red bar shows the high temperature for the day. The purple bar shows the low temperature for the day.

Along the bottom of the graph is the date. Along the left side of the graph is the temperature scale.

What were the high and low temperatures in Atlanta on January 9th? Find the bars for January 9th.

> The red bar shows the high temperature.
> Read from the top of the red bar to the temperature scale.

The high temperature was 53°F.

> The purple bar shows the low temperature.
> Read from the top of the purple bar to the temperature scale.

The low temperature was 35°F.

Using the Strategy

Use the double bar graph to find the high and low temperatures on each of these days.

1. January 8

2. January 10

3. January 11

4. January 12

5. On which day was the temperature highest?

6. On which day was the temperature lowest?

7. Which day had the highest low temperature?

8. Which day had the lowest high temperature?

This double bar graph shows the normal temperature in some cities during January and July.

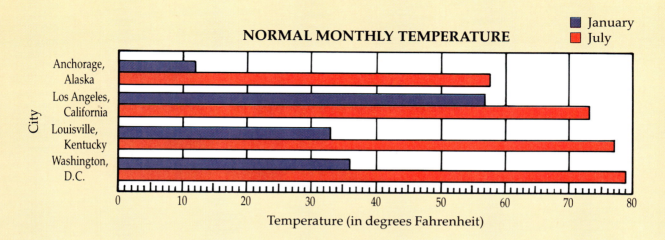

NORMAL MONTHLY TEMPERATURE

■ January
■ July

Find the normal temperature during January and during July in each city.

9. Anchorage, Alaska

10. Los Angeles, California

11. Louisville, Kentucky

12. Washington, D.C.

13. Which of these cities has the lowest temperature in January?

14. Which of these cities has the highest temperature in January?

15. Which of these cities has the lowest temperature in July?

16. Which of these cities has the highest temperature in July?

ACTIVITY

MAKING A DOUBLE BAR GRAPH

1. Use the information in the table to make a double bar graph.

2. Keep a record of the high and low temperatures in your city for a week. You may find this information in a newspaper or during a weather report on television or radio. Make a double bar graph to show your temperature record.

DAILY HIGH AND LOW TEMPERATURES OF KANSAS CITY, MISSOURI		
Date	High (°F)	Low (°F)
Jan. 8	24	13
Jan. 9	29	18
Jan. 10	35	19
Jan. 11	40	23
Jan. 12	38	20

Subtraction Facts

■ There are 15 runners in a race. 8 of them have finished the race. How many runners are left?

Subtract to find how many are left.

$$\begin{array}{r} 15 \\ -\ 8 \\ \hline 7 \end{array}$$

7 runners are left.

■ Here are two ways you can write a subtraction fact.

$$\begin{array}{r} 14 \\ -\ 9 \\ \hline 5 \end{array} \leftarrow \textbf{difference}$$

$$14 - 9 = 5$$
$$\uparrow$$
$$\textbf{difference}$$

■ These patterns in subtraction can help you find differences mentally.

When you subtract a number from itself, the difference is 0.

$$4 - 4 = 0$$
$$9 - 9 = 0$$

When you subtract 0 from a number, the difference is that number.

$$5 - 0 = 5$$
$$7 - 0 = 7$$

■ Addition and subtraction are related. If you know an addition fact, then you know two subtraction facts.

$$\begin{array}{r} 5 \\ +7 \\ \hline 12 \end{array} \quad \text{so} \quad \begin{array}{r} 12 \\ -\ 7 \\ \hline 5 \end{array} \quad \text{and} \quad \begin{array}{r} 12 \\ -\ 5 \\ \hline 7 \end{array}$$

Because of this relationship, you can use addition to check subtraction.

You can write four sentences using 5, 7, and 12.

addition sentences: $5 + 7 = 12$ $7 + 5 = 12$
subtraction sentences: $12 - 7 = 5$ $12 - 5 = 7$

Try These

Subtract. Check each answer.

1. 8
    −3

2. 3
    −3

3. 5
    −0

4. 15
    − 7

5. 13
    − 4

6. 16
    − 9

7. 9
    −4

8. 6 − 5

9. 12 − 3

10. 8 − 6

11. 9 − 7

Exercises

Subtract.

1. 15
    − 9

2. 8
    −8

3. 12
    − 6

4. 9
    −5

5. 4
    −1

6. 8
    −3

7. 14
    − 8

8. 9
    −0

9. 11
    − 3

10. 6
    −1

11. 15
    − 8

12. 6
    −6

13. 5
    −2

14. 10
    − 5

15. 20 − 4

16. 11 − 6

17. 6 − 3

18. 8 − 4

19. 14 − 7

20. 14 − 9

21. 11 − 4

22. 13 − 9

Copy and complete.

23. 4 + 3 = ▦
    3 + 4 = ▦
    7 − 3 = ▦
    7 − 4 = ▦

24. 9 + 5 = ▦
    5 + 9 = ▦
    14 − 5 = ▦
    14 − 9 = ▦

25. 8 + 9 = ▦
    9 + 8 = ▦
    17 − 9 = ▦
    17 − 8 = ▦

26. 9 + 2 = ▦
    2 + 9 = ▦
    11 − 2 = ▦
    11 − 9 = ▦

Write two addition and two subtraction sentences using the three numbers.

★ **27.** 1, 8, 9

★ **28.** 6, 9, 15

★ **29.** 3, 7, 10

★ **30.** 6, 8, 14

Subtracting 2-Digit Numbers

■ Joan Williams is a food technologist. She is trying to find a new way to preserve vegetables. In experiment A, she preserved 56 grams of carrots. In experiment B, she preserved 42 grams of carrots. How many more grams of carrots were preserved in experiment A?

Subtract to find how many more.

Subtract the ones.

$$\begin{array}{r} 56 \\ -42 \\ \hline 4 \end{array}$$

Subtract the tens.

$$\begin{array}{r} 56 \\ -42 \\ \hline 14 \end{array}$$

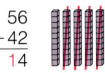

14 more grams were preserved in experiment A.

■ Sometimes you need to regroup tens.

Subtract: 62 − 37

Not enough ones. Regroup.	**Subtract the ones.**	**Subtract the tens.**	**Check.**
$\begin{array}{r} \overset{5}{\cancel{6}}\,\overset{12}{\cancel{2}} \\ -3\ 7 \\ \hline \end{array}$	$\begin{array}{r} \overset{5}{\cancel{6}}\,\overset{12}{\cancel{2}} \\ -3\ 7 \\ \hline 5 \end{array}$	$\begin{array}{r} \overset{5}{\cancel{6}}\,\overset{12}{\cancel{2}} \\ -3\ 7 \\ \hline 2\ 5 \end{array}$	$\begin{array}{r} 2\ 5 \\ +3\ 7 \\ \hline 6\ 2 \end{array}$ ✔

6 tens 2 ones is
5 tens 12 ones.

Try These

Subtract. Check each answer.

1. $\begin{array}{r} 57 \\ -23 \\ \hline \end{array}$
2. $\begin{array}{r} 97 \\ -\ 4 \\ \hline \end{array}$
3. $\begin{array}{r} 62 \\ -43 \\ \hline \end{array}$
4. $\begin{array}{r} 75 \\ -\ 8 \\ \hline \end{array}$
5. $\begin{array}{r} 87 \\ -49 \\ \hline \end{array}$
6. $\begin{array}{r} 43 \\ -26 \\ \hline \end{array}$

7. 69 − 23   8. 67 − 58   9. 75 − 9   10. 51 − 18

Exercises

Subtract.

1. 88 −76	**2.** 48 − 3	**3.** 73 −16	**4.** 25 −17	**5.** 42 − 9	**6.** 32 − 4
7. 61 −18	**8.** 45 −44	**9.** 41 −15	**10.** 87 −14	**11.** 86 −29	**12.** 41 −36
13. 65 −26	**14.** 50 −30	**15.** 27 − 5	**16.** 98 −89	**17.** 27 −18	**18.** 64 −57
19. 16 −12	**20.** 48 −39	**21.** 45 − 9	**22.** 63 − 7	**23.** 52 −18	**24.** 77 − 7

25. 36 − 14 **26.** 89 − 9 **27.** 45 − 15 **28.** 86 − 19

29. 57 − 49 **30.** 77 − 69 **31.** 23 − 5 **32.** 37 − 26

Add or subtract.

33. 34 + 18 **34.** 62 − 29 **35.** 71 − 56 **36.** 28 + 86

37. (59 + 25) − 37 **38.** (76 − 28) + 94 **39.** 217 + (83 − 69) **40.** 84 − (31 + 48)

Solve each problem.

Ms. Williams is helping to develop a B-complex vitamin. Here is a list of some of the ingredients.

Each Capsule Contains:	
Vitamin B_1	20 mg
Vitamin B_2	16 mg
Vitamin B_6	8 mg
Vitamin B_{12}	32 mg

41. How many milligrams of vitamin B_{12} are contained in each B-complex vitamin?

42. How many more milligrams of B_{12} are there than B_2 in each capsule?

43. How many fewer milligrams of B_6 are there than B_1 in each capsule?

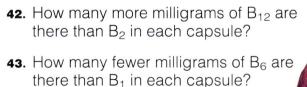

Subtracting 3-Digit Numbers

■ Robert works in a greenhouse. A customer wants 367 zinnia plants. Robert has only 185 plants in stock. How many more plants does he need to fill the order?

To find how many more are needed, subtract.

Subtract the ones.	**Regroup. Subtract the tens.**	**Subtract the hundreds.**
367 −185 ―――― 2	2 16 3̸ 6̸ 7 −1 8 5 ―――― 8 2	2 16 3̸ 6̸ 7 −1 8 5 ―――― 1 8 2
	3 hundreds 6 tens is 2 hundreds 16 tens.	

Robert needs 182 more plants to fill the order.

■ Sometimes you need to regroup more than once.

Subtract: 653 − 186

Regroup. Subtract the ones.	**Regroup. Subtract the tens.**	**Subtract the hundreds.**	**Check.**
4 13 6 5̸ 3̸ −1 8 6 ―――― 7	14 5 4̸ 13 6̸ 5̸ 3̸ −1 8 6 ―――― 6 7	14 5 4̸ 13 6̸ 5̸ 3̸ −1 8 6 ―――― 4 6 7	4 6 7 +1 8 6 ―――― 6 5 3 ✔

■ You subtract money the same way you subtract whole numbers.

Subtract: $9.75 − $7.96

16 8 6̸ 15 9̸ 7̸ 5̸ −7 9 6 ―――― 1 7 9	16 8 6̸ 15 $9̸.7̸ 5̸ − 7.9 6 ―――― $1.7 9	*Remember: Write the $ and the . in the answer.*

Try These

Subtract. Check each answer.

1. $\begin{array}{r} 467 \\ -158 \end{array}$

2. $\begin{array}{r} 675 \\ -485 \end{array}$

3. $\begin{array}{r} 531 \\ -257 \end{array}$

4. $\begin{array}{r} 643 \\ -245 \end{array}$

5. $\begin{array}{r} 889 \\ -476 \end{array}$

6. $\begin{array}{r} \$7.32 \\ -\ 4.63 \end{array}$

7. $980 - 170$

8. $821 - 738$

9. $216 - 79$

10. $\$6.14 - \$2.28$

Exercises

Subtract.

1. $\begin{array}{r} 312 \\ -101 \end{array}$

2. $\begin{array}{r} 795 \\ -463 \end{array}$

3. $\begin{array}{r} 674 \\ -208 \end{array}$

4. $\begin{array}{r} 821 \\ -730 \end{array}$

5. $\begin{array}{r} 368 \\ -\ 79 \end{array}$

6. $\begin{array}{r} \$5.26 \\ -\ 1.89 \end{array}$

7. $\begin{array}{r} 124 \\ -\ 94 \end{array}$

8. $\begin{array}{r} 365 \\ -187 \end{array}$

9. $\begin{array}{r} 43 \\ -29 \end{array}$

10. $\begin{array}{r} \$4.72 \\ -\ 1.86 \end{array}$

11. $\begin{array}{r} 254 \\ -\ 65 \end{array}$

12. $\begin{array}{r} 429 \\ -136 \end{array}$

13. $\begin{array}{r} \$3.25 \\ -\ 1.04 \end{array}$

14. $\begin{array}{r} 917 \\ -328 \end{array}$

15. $\begin{array}{r} \$1.36 \\ -\ .49 \end{array}$

16. $\begin{array}{r} 74 \\ -56 \end{array}$

17. $\begin{array}{r} 337 \\ -175 \end{array}$

18. $\begin{array}{r} \$8.72 \\ -\ 4.79 \end{array}$

19. $422 - 304$

20. $316 - 74$

21. $581 - 272$

22. $\$9.26 - \$.78$

23. $62 - 49$

24. $612 - 123$

25. $\$2.64 - \$1.85$

26. $726 - 258$

Solve each problem.

27. A greenhouse has 132 boxes of zinnias. A class buys 95 boxes to sell at a fund-raising fair. How many boxes of zinnias are left?

28. A customer wants to buy 224 tulip bulbs. A greenhouse has 169 bulbs in stock. How many more bulbs are needed to fill the order?

29. Mr. Mayer goes to a greenhouse to buy supplies for his garden. He buys fertilizer for $5.98, potting soil for $2.25, and clay pots for $6.40. How much does Mr. Mayer spend?

★ 30. A greenhouse has 158 packets of seeds. It receives 3 boxes of seeds. Each box contains 35 packets of seeds. How many packets of seeds does the greenhouse have now?

Zeros in Subtraction

- On Saturday, 158 people rode their bicycles through the park.
On Sunday, 302 people rode their bicycles through the park.
How many more people rode through the park on Sunday?

To find how many more, subtract.

There are no tens. Regroup hundreds first.	Regroup tens.	Subtract.	Check.
2 10 3 Ø 2 −1 5 8	9 2 10 12 3 Ø 2 −1 5 8	9 2 10 12 3 Ø 2 −1 5 8 1 4 4	1 4 4 +1 5 8 3 0 2 ✔

144 more people rode through the park on Sunday.

- Subtract: 500 − 67

Regroup hundreds first.	Regroup tens.	Subtract.
4 10 5 Ø 0 − 6 7	9 4 10 10 5 Ø Ø − 6 7	9 4 10 10 5 Ø Ø − 6 7 4 3 3

Try These

Subtract. Check each answer.

1. 407
   −238

2. 300
   −152

3. $8.01
   − .75

4. 700
   −623

5. 604
   −186

6. 200
   − 92

7. 304 − 87

8. $6.00 − $1.84

9. 140 − 83

10. 600 − 357

Exercises

Subtract.

1. 602 − 124

2. 500 − 146

3. $8.40 − 3.59

4. 206 − 48

5. 301 − 157

6. $1.03 − .96

7. 100 − 54

8. 900 − 895

9. 643 − 287

10. $6.00 − .25

11. 702 − 654

12. 555 − 87

13. $3.04 − 1.26

14. 814 − 679

15. 700 − 286

16. 901 − 146

17. 500 − 396

18. $4.00 − 1.65

19. 370 − 152

20. $2.80 − $1.45

21. 675 − 126

22. 570 − 65

23. 300 − 182

24. 500 − 167

25. $4.05 − $2.69

26. 462 − 378

Add or subtract.

27. 326 − 123

28. $17.53 + 5.89

29. 927 + 816

30. 609 − 402

31. 804 + 328

32. 802 − 76

33. (406 − 398) + 572

34. 812 − (265 + 437)

35. 3,094 + (604 − 129)

Solve each problem.

36. There are 500 contestants in a bicycle race. The race is completed by 367 contestants. How many did not complete the race?

37. The second-place contestant completed the race in 103 minutes. The winner finished 6 minutes sooner. How long did it take the winner to complete the race?

THINK AND TRY

SOLVING EQUATIONS

Use the relationship between addition and subtraction to tell how to find each answer.

1. ■ + 8 = 13

2. 19 + ■ = 35

3. ■ − 6 = 5

4. 73 − ■ = 37

5. 90 − ■ = 57

6. ■ + 62 = 103

Problem Solving: Applications

READ
PLAN
DO
CHECK

USING A DOUBLE BAR GRAPH

The Johnson Seed Company studies four varieties of tomato plants. This double bar graph shows the stem growth and root growth after 2 months.

How much more is the stem growth of Red Bell compared to the stem growth of Grow Home?

Subtract to find how much more.

Red Bell has a stem growth of 120 centimeters.
Grow Home has a stem growth of 95 centimeters.

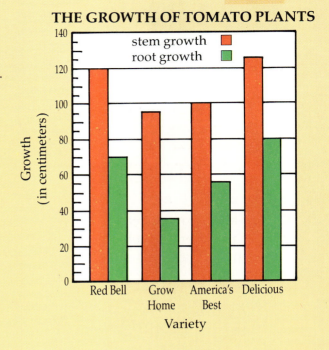

THE GROWTH OF TOMATO PLANTS

$$\begin{array}{r} \overset{11}{} \\ 0\ \overset{1}{\cancel{1}}\ 10 \\ \cancel{1}\ \cancel{2}\ \cancel{0} \\ -\ \ 9\ 5 \\ \hline 2\ 5 \end{array}$$

The stem growth of Red Bell is 25 centimeters more than the stem growth of Grow Home.

Try These

Solve each problem.

1. Which variety had the most root growth?

2. Which variety had the least stem growth?

3. How much more is the root growth of America's Best compared to the root growth of Grow Home?

4. Mr. Cregan wants a tomato plant with a stem growth between 80 centimeters and 100 centimeters. Which plants could he buy?

Exercises

Solve each problem.

This graph compares the number of tomatoes produced by three varieties of tomato plants when grown in the garden and in pots.

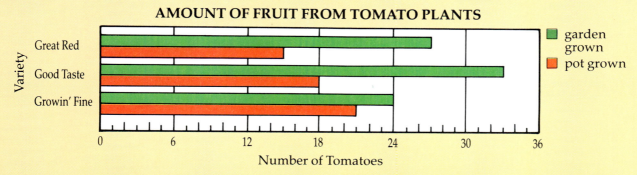

AMOUNT OF FRUIT FROM TOMATO PLANTS

Variety / Number of Tomatoes

■ garden grown
■ pot grown

1. Which variety produces the greatest number of tomatoes when grown in the garden?

2. Which variety produces almost the same number of tomatoes regardless of where it is grown?

3. About how many more tomatoes are produced by Great Red when grown in the garden than when grown in a pot?

4. About how many fewer tomatoes are produced by Good Taste when grown in a pot than when grown in the garden?

5. Pat bought 3 Great Red plants for her garden. How much fruit should she expect to have?

★ 6. Peggy grew 2 Growin' Fine plants in pots. Joel grew 2 Good Taste plants in pots. Who should have more tomatoes? How many more?

This graph compares the sales of three varieties of tomato seeds this year and last year.

7. During which year did Great Red have the greatest sales?

8. During which year did sales of Good Taste go over $7,000?

9. What were the total sales of Great Red for the two years shown?

★ 10. How much more were the total sales of Growin' Fine last year than the total sales this year?

★ 11. What were the total sales for all three varieties last year? How much more was that than this year's total sales?

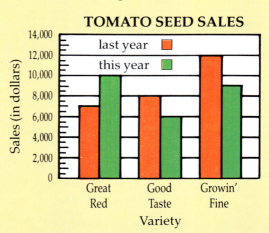

TOMATO SEED SALES

Sales (in dollars) / Variety

■ last year
■ this year

Subtracting Greater Numbers

■ Fran Hope works for a computer company. In May, she traveled 5,035 miles. In June, she traveled 3,476 miles. How many more miles did she travel in May than in June?

Subtract to find how many more miles she traveled in May.

Regroup.
Subtract the ones.

```
    2 15
5,0 3̸ 5̸
-3,4 7 6
        9
```

Regroup.
Subtract the tens.

```
      9  12
  4  10̸ 2̸ 15
5,0 3̸ 5̸
-3,4 7 6
      5 9
```

Subtract
the hundreds.

```
      9  12
  4  10̸ 2̸ 15
5̸,0̸ 3̸ 5̸
-3,4 7 6
    5 5 9
```

Subtract
the thousands.

```
      9  12
  4  10̸ 2̸ 15
5̸,0̸ 3̸ 5̸
-3,4 7 6
  1,5 5 9
```

She traveled 1,559 more miles in May than in June.

■ You can estimate mentally to check whether or not your answer is reasonable.

Subtract: 720,468 − 37,519

```
      11  9
  6  1̸ 10̸ 14 5 18
7̸ 2̸ 0̸,4̸ 6̸ 8̸
 −   3 7,5 1 9
  6 8 2,9 4 9
```

Estimate to check.

Circle the first digit in each number. Round each number to the circled place. Subtract.

```
⑦20,468 ⟶     700,000
− ③7,519 ⟶   −  40,000
                660,000
```

The difference seems reasonable since 682,949 is close to 660,000.

Try These

Subtract. Estimate to check.

1. 4,827 −1,628	**2.** 3,602 − 843	**3.** 61,924 − 5,036	**4.** 45,216 −19,491	**5.** 817,423 −613,895

6. 3,362 − 208

7. 64,309 − 15,875

Exercises

Subtract. Estimate to check.

1. 5,314
      −2,728

2. 6,432
      −2,257

3. $61.03
      − 12.36

4. 73,682
      −21,798

5. 86,014
      −18,256

6. 64,205
      − 7,138

7. 26,478
      −15,139

8. $575.49
      − 125.98

9. 954,700
      −368,125

10. 6,201
       − 465

11. 26,423
       −18,534

12. 92,045
       − 3,788

13. 156,314
       − 1,417

14. $26.15
       − 19.69

15. 605,109
       − 37,857

16. 1,745 − 846

17. $47.02 − $40.96

18. 12,005 − 986

19. 125,010 − 16,975

Solve.

20. (1,620 − 389) + 849

21. 42,000 − (6,432 + 9,387)

22. (2,027 + 3,148) − 4,586

23. 35,026 − (4,197 + 28,536)

24. (2,466 − 897) + 13,654

25. 42,579 + (3,604 − 2,981)

**Do each of these subtractions.
Look for a pattern.**

26. 30,000
       −   1

27. 30,000
       −   11

28. 30,000
       −   111

29. 30,000
       − 1,111

30. Make up some other patterns. Guess the answer. Then check with a calculator.

Solve each problem. You may choose paper and pencil or a calculator.

31. Fran was given $600 to cover the cost of traveling expenses for one month. She spent $479.75. How much money does she have left?

32. In July, Fran traveled 2,364 miles. In August, she traveled 3,156 miles. How many miles did she travel altogether in July and August?

33. The computer company sold 12,368 units one year. It sold 15,215 units the next year. How many more units did it sell the second year than the first year?

★ 34. Fran sold 3,167 personal computers and 1,817 desktop computers. Steve sold 2,618 personal computers and 1,924 desktop computers. How many fewer computers did Steve sell?

Making Change

■ Some cash registers show the amount of change you should receive.

Elena spent $2.94 at Nature's Den. She paid with $10. What is her change?

$$\begin{array}{r} \$10.00 \\ -2.94 \\ \hline \$7.06 \end{array}$$

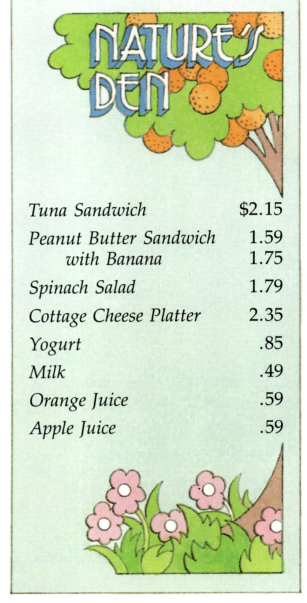

Count out Elena's change. Start with the largest possible bill.

$5 bill and 2 $1 bills is $7.
$7 and 1 nickel is $7.05.
$7.05 and 1 penny is $7.06.

Elena's change is one $5 bill, two $1 bills, one nickel, and one penny.

■ Some cash registers show only the amount you spent.

Alex spent $2.38 at Nature's Den. He paid with $10. What is his change?

Count up from $2.38 to find Alex's change. Start with the smallest coins.

$2.38 and 2 pennies is $2.40.
$2.40 and 1 dime is $2.50.
$2.50 and 2 quarters is $3.
$3 and 2 $1 bills is $5.
$5 and 1 $5 bill is $10.

Alex's change is one $5 bill, two $1 bills, two quarters, one dime, and two pennies.

Tuna Sandwich	$2.15
Peanut Butter Sandwich	1.59
with Banana	1.75
Spinach Salad	1.79
Cottage Cheese Platter	2.35
Yogurt	.85
Milk	.49
Orange Juice	.59
Apple Juice	.59

Try These

Solve each problem.

1. Kim spent $.85. She paid with $5. The cash register shows that Kim should receive $4.15 change. Count out Kim's change.

2. Patrick spent $3.23. He paid with $10. Count up to find the change he should receive.

Exercises

Solve each problem.

1. Clara spent $2.34. She paid with $5. The cash register shows that Clara should receive $2.66 change. Count out Clara's change.

2. Bruce bought a tuna sandwich for $2.15. He paid with $10. Count up to find the change he should receive.

3. Juan spent $3.19. He paid with $5. The cash register shows that Juan should receive $1.81 change. Count out Juan's change.

4. Earl spent $3.49 on a tuna sandwich, yogurt, and milk. He paid with $10. Count up to find the change he should receive.

5. A spinach salad and apple juice cost $2.39. Cathy paid with $5. Count up to find the change Cathy should receive.

6. Linda and her sister spent $5.02 at Nature's Den. Linda paid with $10. Count up to find the change she should receive.

★ 7. Anne bought a cottage cheese platter and apple juice. She paid with $10. What is her change?

★ 8. The Anderson family bought a tuna sandwich, a spinach salad, a peanut butter sandwich, and 3 apple juices. Mr. Anderson paid with $20. What is his change?

Copy and complete the table. Use the fewest number of coins and bills.

	Spent	Given	Penny	Nickel	Dime	Quarter	$1 Bill	$5 Bill	$10 Bill
9.	$4.50	$5							
10.	$1.28	$5							
11.	$4.69	$10							
12.	$8.10	$10							
13.	$5.95	$20							
14.	$14.23	$20							
15.	$3.70	$20							

Problem Solving: Applications

ESTIMATING SUMS AND DIFFERENCES

■ Janice Smith is a truck driver. She delivers farm vegetables to a packing plant in Center City. About how far is it from a farm in Brownsville to Center City?

To find the answer, estimate the sum.

Circle the first digit in each addend.
Round each addend to the circled place.
Then add to estimate the sum.

$$
\begin{array}{r}
①18 \longrightarrow 100 \\
②14 \longrightarrow 200 \\
+②85 \longrightarrow +300 \\
\hline
600
\end{array}
$$

It is about 600 kilometers to Center City.

■ Janice sells a crate of pears for $21.85. A crate of apples costs $12.39. About how much more does a crate of pears cost?

To find about how much more, estimate the difference.

Circle the first digit in each amount.
Round each amount to the circled place.
Then subtract to estimate the difference.

$$
\begin{array}{r}
\$②1.85 \longrightarrow \$20 \\
- ①2.39 \longrightarrow - 10 \\
\hline
\$10
\end{array}
$$

A crate of pears costs about $10 more.

Try These

Estimate to solve each problem.

1. The packing plant orders 56 crates of red cabbage and 102 crates of green cabbage. About how many more crates of green cabbage are ordered?

2. On a trip to Endicott Bay, Janice stopped for three meals. She spent $2.85 for breakfast, $3.25 for lunch, and $6.79 for dinner. About how much did Janice spend on meals?

Exercises

Choose estimation, paper and pencil, or a calculator to solve.

1. The packing plant orders 275 crates of tomatoes, 318 crates of potatoes, and 180 crates of carrots. About how many crates were ordered in all?

2. Janice drove 288 kilometers in the morning and 318 kilometers in the afternoon. About how far did Janice drive that day?

3. A crate of cantaloupes sells for $14.80. A crate of honeydew melons sells for $22.35. How much more does a crate of honeydew melons cost?

4. In August, Janice traveled 11,816 kilometers. In September, she traveled 8,425 kilometers. About how many more kilometers did she travel in August?

5. The packing plant manager spent $1,898 to replace a conveyor belt and $4,148 to replace a packing machine. How much did the plant manager spend on these improvements?

6. There are two shifts of workers at the plant. There are 184 employees working the day shift. There are 92 employees working the night shift. About how many employees are there in all?

7. Janice drives round-trip from Mt. Holly to Center City. About how many kilometers does she drive?

8. About how many kilometers must Janice drive if she makes a delivery to Center City from Bradley and then returns to Rangeville?

★ 9. Janice sold 178 bunches of carrots for $71.20. She also sold 310 heads of cabbage for $77.50 and 215 bunches of broccoli for $75.25. Estimate Janice's total sales in dollars.

★ 10. This year the packing plant canned 6,825 cases of crushed tomatoes and 4,140 cases of whole tomatoes. Last year, 5,218 cases of crushed tomatoes and 3,675 cases of whole tomatoes were canned. About how many fewer cases of tomatoes were canned last year?

Distance to Center City from:	Kilometers
Rangeville	178
Bradley	296
Mt. Holly	321

Problem Solving: Applications

TOO MUCH INFORMATION

In some problems, there is more information than you need. You must find the needed information before solving the problem.

Bob North is a car salesman. In the first 2 weeks of the month, he sold $32,254 worth of cars. His commission on the sales was $493.58. The next 2 weeks he sold $45,856 worth of cars. His commission was $627.84. What was his total commission for the month?

Find the information you need:
Bob North's commissions were $493.58 and $627.84.

Add to find the total commission for the month.

```
      111 1
$   493.58
+   627.84
 $1,121.42
```

Bob North had a total commission of $1,121.42 for the month.

Try These

Solve each problem.

1. Chris sells for a tire company. One week he took 15 orders for a total of $3,642. The next week he took 12 orders for a total of $4,286. How many orders did he take for the 2 weeks?

2. Mr. Posley drove 1,290 miles in September and used 68 gallons of gasoline. He drove 918 miles in October. He drove for 18 hours in October. How many more miles did he drive in September?

Exercises

Solve each problem.

1. Susan sold one car that had gone 16,479 miles for $2,580. She sold another car that had gone 24,005 miles for $1,976. What was the total price for the two cars?

2. Ms. Chin drove 6,420 miles and used 310 gallons of gasoline. For the next 5,972 miles, she used 276 gallons of gasoline. How many miles did she drive in all?

3. A gas station sold 9,125 gallons of regular gasoline. It sold 12,342 gallons of unleaded gasoline. It sold 432 tires. How many more gallons of unleaded gasoline did the station sell?

4. One month DC Motors received $24,056 from new-car sales, $18,250 from used-car sales, and $14,905 from car repairs. How much did DC Motors receive from car sales that month?

5. In 1983, Century Motors made a profit of $125,264. In 1984, its profit was $216,417. How much more was its profit in 1984?

6. In June, Jim sold 18 cars for a total of $39,568. In July, he sold 23 cars for a total of $42,959. How many more cars did he sell in July?

7. One week a car wash used 4,590 gallons of water to clean 129 cars. The next week 5,264 gallons of water were used to clean 186 cars. How many cars were cleaned in the 2 weeks?

8. The repair shop used 250 cans of oil and 18 fan belts one month. The next month it used 189 cans of oil and 48 oil filters. How many cans of oil did the shop use in the 2 months?

9. During one hour, 5,350 cars, 872 trucks, and 216 buses went over the bridge. The toll for cars is $2. The toll for buses is $3.50. About how many vehicles went over the bridge that hour?

10. Mrs. Abels paid $11,465 for her car. The first year she spent $285.19 on repairs. The second year she spent $419.78 on repairs. How much more did she spend on repairs the second year?

11. The base price of a new car is $10,565. An air conditioner costs $425, and an AM-FM radio costs $185. What is the total price of the car if you order an air conditioner?

★ 12. Jim drives to work 5 days a week. He pays $4 each day in tolls. How much money does Jim spend in tolls in 4 weeks?

CHAPTER CHECKPOINT

Add. (pp. 28–37)

1. $\begin{array}{r} 6 \\ +9 \\ \hline \end{array}$	**2.** $\begin{array}{r} 7 \\ +5 \\ \hline \end{array}$	**3.** $\begin{array}{r} 29 \\ +37 \\ \hline \end{array}$	**4.** $\begin{array}{r} 46 \\ +86 \\ \hline \end{array}$	**5.** $\begin{array}{r} 75 \\ +\ 8 \\ \hline \end{array}$
6. $\begin{array}{r} 362 \\ +137 \\ \hline \end{array}$	**7.** $\begin{array}{r} 483 \\ +171 \\ \hline \end{array}$	**8.** $\begin{array}{r} 657 \\ +787 \\ \hline \end{array}$	**9.** $\begin{array}{r} \$5.68 \\ +\ \ .79 \\ \hline \end{array}$	**10.** $\begin{array}{r} 4{,}216 \\ +8{,}793 \\ \hline \end{array}$
11. $\begin{array}{r} 42{,}675 \\ +47{,}218 \\ \hline \end{array}$	**12.** $\begin{array}{r} 207 \\ 865 \\ +927 \\ \hline \end{array}$	**13.** $\begin{array}{r} 504 \\ 196 \\ +375 \\ \hline \end{array}$	**14.** $\begin{array}{r} 175{,}107 \\ 89{,}218 \\ +\ 76{,}974 \\ \hline \end{array}$	**15.** $\begin{array}{r} 27{,}175 \\ 986 \\ 9{,}218 \\ +45{,}977 \\ \hline \end{array}$

16. $0 + 6$

17. $4 + 5 + 8$

18. $86 + 8$

19. $248 + 97$

20. $\$15.25 + \$9.67$

21. $1{,}467 + 375 + 4{,}698$

Subtract. (pp. 40–47, 50–51)

22. $\begin{array}{r} 13 \\ -\ 4 \\ \hline \end{array}$	**23.** $\begin{array}{r} 16 \\ -\ 9 \\ \hline \end{array}$	**24.** $\begin{array}{r} 86 \\ -32 \\ \hline \end{array}$	**25.** $\begin{array}{r} 72 \\ -38 \\ \hline \end{array}$	**26.** $\begin{array}{r} 44 \\ -\ 9 \\ \hline \end{array}$
27. $\begin{array}{r} 463 \\ -186 \\ \hline \end{array}$	**28.** $\begin{array}{r} 821 \\ -575 \\ \hline \end{array}$	**29.** $\begin{array}{r} \$9.25 \\ -\ 7.89 \\ \hline \end{array}$	**30.** $\begin{array}{r} 400 \\ -186 \\ \hline \end{array}$	**31.** $\begin{array}{r} 607 \\ -479 \\ \hline \end{array}$
32. $\begin{array}{r} \$3.00 \\ -\ 1.78 \\ \hline \end{array}$	**33.** $\begin{array}{r} 4{,}016 \\ -1{,}747 \\ \hline \end{array}$	**34.** $\begin{array}{r} 36{,}821 \\ -\ 9{,}976 \\ \hline \end{array}$	**35.** $\begin{array}{r} 95{,}017 \\ -26{,}758 \\ \hline \end{array}$	**36.** $\begin{array}{r} 407{,}244 \\ -275{,}187 \\ \hline \end{array}$

37. $11 - 7$

38. $9 - 9$

39. $92 - 77$

40. $527 - 286$

41. $\$25.04 - \$19.75$

42. $8{,}018 - 5{,}679$

Add or subtract. Estimate to check. (pp. 36–37, 50–51)

43. $\begin{array}{r} 608 \\ +180 \\ \hline \end{array}$	**44.** $\begin{array}{r} 1{,}567 \\ +2{,}132 \\ \hline \end{array}$	**45.** $\begin{array}{r} 670 \\ -220 \\ \hline \end{array}$	**46.** $\begin{array}{r} 3{,}260 \\ -1{,}480 \\ \hline \end{array}$	**47.** $\begin{array}{r} 4{,}816 \\ +2{,}104 \\ \hline \end{array}$
48. $\begin{array}{r} 4{,}830 \\ +1{,}670 \\ \hline \end{array}$	**49.** $\begin{array}{r} 2{,}315 \\ -1{,}251 \\ \hline \end{array}$	**50.** $\begin{array}{r} \$45.24 \\ -\ 36.89 \\ \hline \end{array}$	**51.** $\begin{array}{r} 65{,}196 \\ +26{,}750 \\ \hline \end{array}$	**52.** $\begin{array}{r} \$10.55 \\ +\ \ 9.85 \\ \hline \end{array}$

Solve each problem. (pp. 28–57)

53. Two bookstores merge. The first bookstore has 10,586 books. The second bookstore has 24,362 books. What will the total number of books in the new store be?

54. In April, 10,250 copies of a new spy novel were printed. After 2 weeks, 3,794 books were sold. About how many copies of the book were left?

55. A bookstore sold 29 cat calendars at $8.95 each. It sold 56 dog calendars at $7.50 each. How many calendars did it sell?

56. Amy bought a book for $7.49. She gave the clerk $10. Count up to find the change she should receive.

57. Jim bought a health book for $12. He bought a travel book for $7.95 and a pet care book for $5.29. How much did he spend in all?

58. There are 144 bookmarks in one box. There are 65 bookmarks in another box. How many more bookmarks are in the first box?

This graph shows the number of calendars sold in December of two different years.

59. Which type of calendar was most popular in 1986?

60. Which type of calendar was least popular in 1985?

61. How many cat calendars were sold in December 1985?

62. Which types of calendar sold fewer than 50 copies each? In which year?

63. How many horse calendars were sold in the two years altogether?

64. How many more cat calendars than dog calendars were sold in 1985?

65. How many lake calendars were sold in the two years altogether?

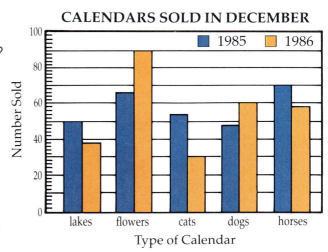

CALENDARS SOLD IN DECEMBER

■ 1985 ■ 1986

Number Sold

lakes flowers cats dogs horses

Type of Calendar

COMPUTERS AND PROBLEM SOLVING

■ A **flow chart** can help you to plan a computer program. Here is a flow chart for a familiar activity.

Each step has been placed inside a rectangle. The START and END positions are in ovals.

Solve each problem.

1. The flow chart for brushing teeth is incomplete. Add five more steps. One of them should be *opening the toothpaste tube*. Be sure to put all the steps in the correct shapes and in the correct order.

2. Name three more steps that could have been included.

3. Redraw the flow chart so it includes *all* the steps.

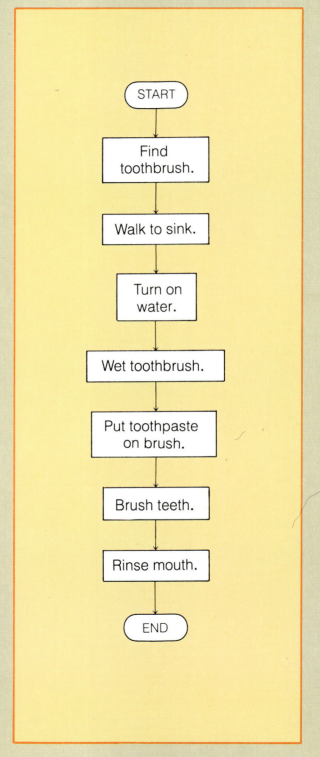

START

Find toothbrush.

Walk to sink.

Turn on water.

Wet toothbrush.

Put toothpaste on brush.

Brush teeth.

Rinse mouth.

END

■ The flow chart below shows the steps for adding
5 + 8 + 9 in your head. It shows that when you add three
numbers in your head, it is only possible to add
two numbers at a time.

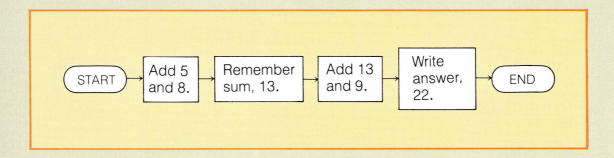

START → Add 5 and 8. → Remember sum, 13. → Add 13 and 9. → Write answer, 22. → END

Solve each problem.

1. The flow chart for adding numbers could also include steps such as *adding the ones together when combining 13 + 9*. Think of two other flow charts to map out the answer to 5 + 8 + 9. Draw one of them.

2. Draw a flow chart for adding 27 + 35 + 58. Include steps that show adding the tens and the ones.

3. Draw a flow chart that could be used as a map for doing your laundry. Start by picking up your clothes. End with putting away the folded clothes.

ENRICHMENT

PARENTHESES AND BRACKETS

Parentheses are used in a number sentence that has more than one addition or subtraction. Sometimes there are two sets of parentheses in a number sentence. Work inside each set of parentheses first.

$$(18 - 3) + (36 + 14)$$
$$15 + 50 = 65$$

Brackets are used in a number sentence that also has parentheses. Work inside the parentheses. Then work inside the brackets.

$$25 + [40 - (18 - 6)]$$
$$25 + [40 - 12]$$
$$25 + 28 = 53$$

Solve.

1. $(13 + 5) - (10 + 6)$

2. $(26 - 18) - (46 - 39)$

3. $(75 + 38) + (192 - 146)$

4. $(292 - 257) + (346 + 801)$

5. $98 + [36 + (87 - 79)]$

6. $164 - [(101 + 18) + 9]$

7. $[(846 + 457) - 215] - 1{,}009$

8. $[1{,}479 - (735 - 268)] - 69$

Put in parentheses, or parentheses and brackets, to make each sentence true.

9. $10 - 4 + 6 = 12$

10. $67 - 7 - 42 + 18 = 0$

11. $45 - 53 - 37 - 25 = 4$

12. $87 + 29 + 34 - 15 = 135$

13. $66 - 27 + 83 - 49 = 73$

14. $159 + 701 - 386 + 243 = 717$

PROBLEM SOLVING: SITUATIONS

PLANNING AN AFTER-SCHOOL PROGRAM

You are a recreational director with $2,000 to spend on an after-school program. How will you budget the money?

Some Questions to Explore
- What activities will you plan and how much will each cost?
- How will you schedule the activities?
- How will you advertise the after-school program?

Some Strategies to Explore
Consider the first question. One strategy you might use is to work backward. Remember, you have $2,000.

- Decide what activities you will have and the number of instructors needed.
- Decide how much you will pay each instructor.
- Determine the supplies needed and the cost of each.

What strategies will you use to answer the other questions above? What other questions and strategies do you need to explore? List them. Then use them to solve the problem.

SKILLS CHECK

Choose the correct answer.

1. In 258,147, which digit is in the ten-thousands place?

   a. 2
   b. 4
   c. 5
   d. 8

2. What is the number for ten million, six hundred twelve thousand, three hundred seven?

   a. 10,612,307
   b. 10,612,370
   c. 100,612,307
   d. 10,600,123,007

3. Which number is greater than 71,625?

   a. 70,629
   b. 71,530
   c. 71,630
   d. 71,614

4. What is 7,386 rounded to the nearest hundred?

   a. 7,000
   b. 7,300
   c. 7,390
   d. 7,400

5. $(3 + 0) + 6$

   a. 9
   b. 10
   c. 36
   d. NG

6. $\begin{array}{r} 43 \\ +25 \\ \hline \end{array}$

   a. 67
   b. 68
   c. 78
   d. 79

7. $\begin{array}{r} 46,952 \\ +20,376 \\ \hline \end{array}$

   a. 66,328
   b. 76,238
   c. 67,328
   d. 77,228

8. $\begin{array}{r} 46 \\ -26 \\ \hline \end{array}$

   a. 66
   b. 72
   c. 60
   d. NG

9. $\begin{array}{r} 634 \\ -297 \\ \hline \end{array}$

   a. 437
   b. 363
   c. 337
   d. 463

10. There are about 1,250,000 wild African elephants. There are about 15,000 wild Asiatic elephants. How many wild elephants are left in the world altogether?

   a. 1,250,015 elephants
   b. 1,265,000 elephants
   c. 1,400,000 elephants
   d. 2,750,000 elephants

11. Male African elephants weigh about 12,000 pounds. Male Asiatic elephants weigh about 8,500 pounds. How much heavier are the male African elephants?

   a. 3,500 pounds
   b. 4,000 pounds
   c. 20,000 pounds
   d. NG

3

MULTIPLICATION

Multiplication Facts

■ There are 5 packages of postcards. There are 4 postcards in each package. How many postcards are there in all?

There are 5 groups of 4. Multiply to find how many in all.

$$\begin{array}{r} 4 \\ \times 5 \\ \hline 20 \end{array}$$

There are 20 postcards in all.

■ Here are two ways you can write a multiplication fact.

$$\begin{array}{r} 6 \\ \times 3 \\ \hline 18 \end{array}\leftarrow \text{factors}$$
$18 \leftarrow$ **product**

$3 \times 6 = 18$

factors   **product**

■ Multiplication has some special properties that can help you multiply mentally.

ORDER
You can change the order of the factors. The product is the same.

$7 \times 4 = 28$
$4 \times 7 = 28$

GROUPING
You can change the grouping of the factors. The product is the same. The parentheses mean *do this first*.

$(3 \times 2) \times 4 \qquad 3 \times (2 \times 4)$
$\qquad\; 6 \quad \times 4 = 24 \quad 3 \times \quad 8 \quad = 24$

ONE
If one factor is 1, the product is the other factor.

$1 \times 6 = 6$
$6 \times 1 = 6$

ZERO
If one factor is 0, the product is 0.

$0 \times 5 = 0$
$5 \times 0 = 0$

Try These

Multiply.

1. $\begin{array}{r} 2 \\ \times 7 \\ \hline \end{array}$
2. $\begin{array}{r} 7 \\ \times 2 \\ \hline \end{array}$
3. $\begin{array}{r} 8 \\ \times 5 \\ \hline \end{array}$
4. $\begin{array}{r} 5 \\ \times 4 \\ \hline \end{array}$
5. $\begin{array}{r} 7 \\ \times 0 \\ \hline \end{array}$
6. $\begin{array}{r} 5 \\ \times 6 \\ \hline \end{array}$
7. $\begin{array}{r} 2 \\ \times 9 \\ \hline \end{array}$

8. 1×3
9. 6×0
10. 5×3
11. $(1 \times 8) \times 3$

Exercises

Multiply.

1. $\begin{array}{r} 3 \\ \times 6 \\ \hline \end{array}$
2. $\begin{array}{r} 6 \\ \times 2 \\ \hline \end{array}$
3. $\begin{array}{r} 9 \\ \times 7 \\ \hline \end{array}$
4. $\begin{array}{r} 4 \\ \times 3 \\ \hline \end{array}$
5. $\begin{array}{r} 9 \\ \times 1 \\ \hline \end{array}$
6. $\begin{array}{r} 5 \\ \times 9 \\ \hline \end{array}$
7. $\begin{array}{r} 0 \\ \times 8 \\ \hline \end{array}$

8. $\begin{array}{r} 8 \\ \times 2 \\ \hline \end{array}$
9. $\begin{array}{r} 9 \\ \times 3 \\ \hline \end{array}$
10. $\begin{array}{r} 4 \\ \times 7 \\ \hline \end{array}$
11. $\begin{array}{r} 6 \\ \times 5 \\ \hline \end{array}$
12. $\begin{array}{r} 7 \\ \times 7 \\ \hline \end{array}$
13. $\begin{array}{r} 1 \\ \times 6 \\ \hline \end{array}$
14. $\begin{array}{r} 3 \\ \times 5 \\ \hline \end{array}$

15. $\begin{array}{r} 5 \\ \times 5 \\ \hline \end{array}$
16. $\begin{array}{r} 0 \\ \times 4 \\ \hline \end{array}$
17. $\begin{array}{r} 5 \\ \times 8 \\ \hline \end{array}$
18. $\begin{array}{r} 8 \\ \times 8 \\ \hline \end{array}$
19. $\begin{array}{r} 8 \\ \times 9 \\ \hline \end{array}$
20. $\begin{array}{r} 7 \\ \times 3 \\ \hline \end{array}$
21. $\begin{array}{r} 6 \\ \times 7 \\ \hline \end{array}$

22. 9×9
23. 7×5
24. 9×6
25. 7×8
26. 5×0
27. 7×1
28. 4×6
29. 5×2

Multiply. Do as many as you can mentally.

30. $4 \times (2 \times 2)$
31. $(4 \times 2) \times 2$
32. $2 \times (3 \times 3)$
33. $2 \times 5 \times 3$
34. $0 \times 8 \times 5$
35. $1 \times 7 \times 4$

Copy and complete each arrow train.

36. $3 \xrightarrow{\times 2} \blacksquare \xrightarrow{\times 2} \blacksquare$

37. $8 \xrightarrow{\times 1} \blacksquare \xrightarrow{\times 6} \blacksquare$

38. $4 \xrightarrow{\times 0} \blacksquare \xrightarrow{\times 3} \blacksquare$

Name the arrow.

39. $5 \longrightarrow 10$
40. $4 \longrightarrow 12$
41. $2 \longrightarrow 2$

42. $0 \longrightarrow 0$ Is there just one name?

43. Compare these two trains. Name the property illustrated.
$5 \xrightarrow{\times 3} \blacksquare$ and $3 \xrightarrow{\times 5} \blacksquare$

Solve each problem.

44. A minibus picks up 9 tourists in front of the Washington Monument. Then it picks up 8 tourists in front of the Jefferson Memorial. How many tourists are on the minibus?

45. Janet and Frank give tours of the Capitol building. Janet's tour had 8 people. Frank's tour had 4 times as many people. How many people were in Frank's tour?

46. There are 15 tourists on a minibus. At the Lincoln Memorial, 6 tourists get off. How many tourists are left on the minibus?

47. Eve gives 7 tours of the Smithsonian each day. Each tour group has 8 people. How many people have Eve as a tour guide?

Multiples and Common Multiples

■ Multiply any two whole numbers.
The product is a **multiple** of each number.

$2 \times 3 = 6$
6 is a multiple of 2.
6 is a multiple of 3.

Some multiples of 2 are:

0, 2, 4, 6, 8, 10, 12, 14, 16, 18, 20

Some multiples of 3 are:

0, 3, 6, 9, 12, 15, 18, 21, 24, 27, 30

0 is a multiple of any number.

Some numbers (other than 0) are multiples of both 2 and 3.
6, 12, and 18 are multiples of both 2 and 3.

6, 12, and 18 are **common multiples** of 2 and 3.
6 is the **least common multiple** of 2 and 3.

■ Multiples of 2 are called **even numbers**.
All other whole numbers are called **odd numbers**. Even numbers end in 0, 2, 4, 6, or 8. Odd numbers end in 1, 3, 5, 7, or 9.

Try These

Copy and complete.

1. multiples of 7: 0, 7, 14, 21, ■, ■, ■

2. multiples of 9: 0, 9, 18, 27, ■, ■, ■

3. multiples of 6: 0, 6, 12, 18, ■, ■, ■

4. multiples of 8: 0, 8, 16, ■, ■, ■

Solve.

5. List the first fourteen multiples of 3.
List the first ten multiples of 4.
List four common multiples of 3 and 4.
What is the least common multiple of 3 and 4 (other than 0)?
Is the least common multiple even or odd?

6. List the first eleven multiples of 3.
List the first seven multiples of 5.
List three common multiples of 3 and 5.
What is the least common multiple of 3 and 5 (other than 0)?
Is the least common multiple even or odd?

Exercises

Solve.

1. List the first ten multiples of 8.
List the first seven multiples of 12.
List four common multiples of 8 and 12.
What is the least common multiple of 8 and 12 (other than 0)?
Is the least common multiple even or odd?

Find the least common multiple (other than 0).

2. 2 and 7   **3.** 3 and 6   **4.** 5 and 10   **5.** 7 and 5

6. 2 and 9   **7.** 7 and 3   **8.** 4 and 5   **9.** 6 and 8

10. 6 and 9   **11.** 5 and 8   **12.** 6 and 7   **13.** 4 and 10

14. 4 and 12   **15.** 6 and 10   **16.** 7 and 9   **17.** 9 and 12

★ **18.** List six multiples of 10 and twelve multiples of 5.
Are *all* the multiples of 10 also multiples of 5?
Are *all* the multiples of 5 also multiples of 10?

Copy and complete each table. Then answer each question.

19. Multiplication Table of Even Numbers

×	0	2	4	6	8
0	0				0
2			8		
4					
6				36	
8					

Is the product of two even numbers even or odd?

20. Multiplication Table of Odd Numbers

×	1	3	5	7	9
1					
3					
5					
7					
9					

Is the product of two odd numbers even or odd?

Solve each problem.

21. For the Craft Shop, Pat wants to order the same number of quilt kits as pillow kits. What is the smallest number of boxes of each she should order?

Kit	Quilts	Pillows
number per box	6	8

22. Pat wants to display the same number of packages of green yarn and yellow yarn. What is the smallest number of boxes of each she should display?

Yarn	Green	Yellow
packages per box	12	20

Multiplying 2-Digit Numbers

■ Mark Delaney is a stock clerk in a sporting goods store. He is counting the number of tennis rackets in stock. There are 43 tennis rackets on each shelf. How many tennis rackets are on 2 shelves?

To find the number of tennis rackets, multiply 2 times 43.

Multiply the ones by 2.

$$\begin{array}{r} 43 \\ \times\ 2 \\ \hline 6 \end{array}$$

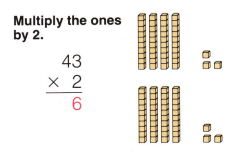

Multiply the tens by 2.

$$\begin{array}{r} 43 \\ \times\ 2 \\ \hline 86 \end{array}$$

There are 86 tennis rackets.

■ Sometimes you need to regroup ones.

Multiply: 3 × 24

Multiply the ones by 3. Regroup.

$$\begin{array}{r} \overset{1}{2}4 \\ \times\ 3 \\ \hline 2 \end{array}$$

12 ones is 1 ten 2 ones.

Multiply the tens by 3. Add the regrouped ten.

$$\begin{array}{r} \overset{1}{2}4 \\ \times\ 3 \\ \hline 72 \end{array}$$

■ Sometimes you need to regroup ones and tens.

Multiply: 6 × 38

Multiply the ones by 6. Regroup.

$$\begin{array}{r} \overset{4}{3}8 \\ \times\ 6 \\ \hline 8 \end{array}$$

Multiply the tens by 6. Add the regrouped tens.

$$\begin{array}{r} \overset{4}{3}8 \\ \times\ 6 \\ \hline 228 \end{array}$$

22 tens is
2 hundreds 2 tens.

Try These

Multiply.

1. 24
× 2

2. 36
× 2

3. 47
× 5

4. 18
× 3

5. 21
× 4

6. 92
× 6

7. 6 × 54

8. 3 × 33

9. 7 × 29

10. 8 × 81

Exercises

Multiply.

1. 34
× 2

2. 23
× 3

3. 42
× 4

4. 82
× 3

5. 63
× 3

6. 52
× 5

7. 14
× 4

8. 86
× 2

9. 43
× 5

10. 34
× 4

11. 13
× 6

12. 75
× 5

13. 64
× 7

14. 89
× 9

15. 37
× 9

16. 78
× 5

17. 64
× 7

18. 90
× 7

19. 2 × 43

20. 6 × 51

21. 9 × 63

22. 5 × 83

23. 4 × 16

24. 5 × 53

25. 8 × 79

26. 8 × 78

Solve.

27. 7 × (13 + 8)

28. (4 × 36) − 59

29. 6 × (42 − 19)

Solve each problem.

30. There are 15 football helmets in each box. There are 5 boxes. How many helmets are there?

31. One box has 15 tennis rackets. A second box has 8 tennis rackets. How many rackets are there in all?

★ **32.** There are 8 boxes with 24 golf balls in each box. Another box has 15 golf balls in it. How many golf balls are there in all?

★ **33.** There are 6 boxes of baseballs with 24 balls in each. There are 9 boxes of basketballs with 14 balls in each. Are there more baseballs or basketballs? How many more?

Multiplication   71

Multiplying 3-Digit Numbers

■ Each section in a bookstore holds 243 books. There are 5 sections in the bookstore. How many books can these sections hold?

Multiply 5 times 243 to find the answer.

Multiply the ones by 5. Regroup.

```
  1
 243
×  5
────
   5
```

Multiply the tens by 5. Add the regrouped ten.

```
 2 1
 243
×  5
────
  15
```

Multiply the hundreds by 5. Add the regrouped hundreds.

```
 2 1
 243
×  5
────
1,215
```

12 hundreds is
1 thousand 2 hundreds.

The sections can hold 1,215 books.

■ You multiply money the same way you multiply whole numbers.

Multiply: 4 × $1.09

```
  3
 109
×  4
────
 436
```

```
  3
$1.09
×   4
─────
$4.36
```

> *Remember: Write the $ and the . in the answer.*

Try These

Multiply.

1. 423 × 4	**2.** 202 × 6	**3.** 642 × 5	**4.** $5.43 × 3	**5.** $4.96 × 7	**6.** 517 × 8

7. 7 × 807　　　　**8.** 9 × 384　　　　**9.** 6 × $8.24　　　　**10.** 5 × 196

Exercises

Multiply.

1. $\begin{array}{r} 200 \\ \times\ \ 4 \\ \hline \end{array}$	**2.** $\begin{array}{r} 134 \\ \times\ \ 2 \\ \hline \end{array}$	**3.** $\begin{array}{r} 712 \\ \times\ \ 5 \\ \hline \end{array}$	**4.** $\begin{array}{r} \$2.67 \\ \times\ \ 3 \\ \hline \end{array}$	**5.** $\begin{array}{r} 518 \\ \times\ \ 4 \\ \hline \end{array}$	**6.** $\begin{array}{r} 213 \\ \times\ \ 3 \\ \hline \end{array}$
7. $\begin{array}{r} \$2.12 \\ \times\ \ 4 \\ \hline \end{array}$	**8.** $\begin{array}{r} 214 \\ \times\ \ 3 \\ \hline \end{array}$	**9.** $\begin{array}{r} 312 \\ \times\ \ 5 \\ \hline \end{array}$	**10.** $\begin{array}{r} 84 \\ \times\ \ 3 \\ \hline \end{array}$	**11.** $\begin{array}{r} \$1.47 \\ \times\ \ 5 \\ \hline \end{array}$	**12.** $\begin{array}{r} 453 \\ \times\ \ 6 \\ \hline \end{array}$
13. $\begin{array}{r} 507 \\ \times\ \ 3 \\ \hline \end{array}$	**14.** $\begin{array}{r} \$2.22 \\ \times\ \ 7 \\ \hline \end{array}$	**15.** $\begin{array}{r} 608 \\ \times\ \ 4 \\ \hline \end{array}$	**16.** $\begin{array}{r} 748 \\ \times\ \ 3 \\ \hline \end{array}$	**17.** $\begin{array}{r} 645 \\ \times\ \ 4 \\ \hline \end{array}$	**18.** $\begin{array}{r} 889 \\ \times\ \ 2 \\ \hline \end{array}$

19. 8×25

20. $6 \times \$4.05$

21. $9 \times \$5.98$

22. 2×981

23. 7×432

24. 8×653

25. $5 \times \$9.30$

26. 6×705

Solve.

27. $(234 + 79) - 64$

28. $(6 \times 123) + 196$

29. $475 - (8 \times 56)$

30. $9 \times (204 - 88)$

31. $(647 + 753) - 521$

32. $2,605 + (3 \times 819)$

Solve each problem.

33. Carla buys 3 paperback books. Each book costs $2.95. How much does Carla pay for the books?

34. There were 144 book covers in stock. 19 book covers were sold. How many book covers are left?

35. The bookstore received a shipment of 6 cartons of books. Each carton holds 115 books. How many books were in the shipment?

36. Jason places an order at the bookstore for 8 computer textbooks. Each textbook costs $9.79. How much does Jason's order come to?

37. A display rack holds 24 copies of a new cookbook. There are 6 copies of the new cookbook in a window display. How many copies of the cookbook are there?

38. The bookstore sells puzzles. There are 78 puzzles on display. There are 140 puzzles in the stockroom. How many more puzzles are in the stockroom than on display?

39. A company printed 15,850 books about architecture. It printed 21,600 books about Italian cooking. The company also printed 34,250 books about American cooking. How many books about cooking were printed?

★ **40.** Wildlife calendars are packed 12 to a box. Sports calendars are packed 15 to a box. The manager wants to display the same number of each calendar. What is the smallest number of boxes of each he should order?

Multiplying Greater Numbers

■ Each section in a stadium has 4,632 seats. There are 9 sections. How many seats are there in the stadium?

To find the number of seats in the stadium, multiply.

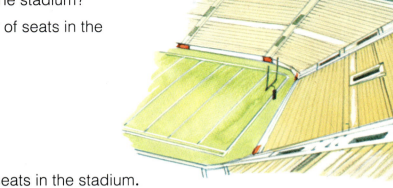

$$\begin{array}{r} {\scriptstyle 5\ 2\ 1} \\ 4{,}632 \\ \times\qquad 9 \\ \hline 41{,}688 \end{array}$$

There are 41,688 seats in the stadium.

■ Multiply: 827,065 × 3

$$\begin{array}{r} 3 \\ \times 827{,}065 \end{array}$$

Use the order property to rewrite this example.

$$\begin{array}{r} {\scriptstyle 2\quad 1\ 1} \\ 827{,}065 \\ \times\qquad\quad 3 \\ \hline 2{,}481{,}195 \end{array}$$

■ You can estimate mentally to check whether or not your answer is reasonable.

Multiply: 6 × 47,058

Estimate to check.

$$\begin{array}{r} {\scriptstyle 4\quad 3\,4} \\ 47{,}058 \\ \times\qquad 6 \\ \hline 282{,}348 \end{array}$$

Circle the first digit in the top factor. Round the factor to the circled place. Multiply.

$$\begin{array}{r} ④7{,}0\,5\,8 \longrightarrow 50{,}000 \\ \times\qquad\quad 6 \longrightarrow \times\qquad 6 \\ \hline 300{,}000 \end{array}$$

The product seems reasonable since 282,348 is close to 300,000.

Try These

Multiply. Estimate to check.

1. $\begin{array}{r} 3{,}126 \\ \times\quad 4 \end{array}$
2. $\begin{array}{r} 34{,}057 \\ \times\quad 6 \end{array}$
3. $\begin{array}{r} 9{,}863 \\ \times\quad 2 \end{array}$
4. $\begin{array}{r} 27{,}608 \\ \times\quad 8 \end{array}$
5. $\begin{array}{r} 187{,}120 \\ \times\quad 3 \end{array}$

6. 5 × 1,239
7. 34,875 × 9
8. 7 × 660,942
9. 446,719 × 3

Exercises

Multiply. Estimate to check.

1. 4,132
    × 2

2. 23,126
    × 4

3. 2,156
    × 3

4. 540,237
    × 5

5. $14.59
    × 6

6. 12,180
    × 5

7. 53,456
    × 7

8. 614,258
    × 8

9. $8.95
    × 4

10. 1,275
     × 5

11. 902,748
     × 2

12. $115.48
     × 7

13. 17,608
     × 6

14. 26,470
     × 3

15. $4,165.18
     × 8

16. 6 × 7,826

17. 98 × 3

18. 3 × 586

19. 2 × 465,298

20. $61.72 × 8

21. 5 × $150.49

22. 46,510 × 9

23. 8 × 376,915

Solve each problem.

24. The team made 4 round-trips in a year. Each trip was about 5,860 miles. How many miles did the team travel that year?

25. In March, two scoreboards were installed in the stadium. One scoreboard cost $12,500. The other scoreboard cost $17,196. How much was spent for scoreboards?

26. During one month, 6 games were played. At each game, all 41,688 seats of the stadium were occupied. How many people attended the games in the one month?

27. Pennants sell for $3.25 each at the stadium. At each of 3 games, the pennant stand made $7,198.75. How much money did the pennant stand make during the 3 games?

 KEEPING IN SHAPE

1. 3,769
    +17,826

2. 965,340
    −187,257

3. $203.05
    − 98.79

4. $4,573.02
    + 7,947.68

5. $2,170.15
    − 967.86

6. 65,134 − 927

7. 6,481 + 33,257

8. $27.53 + $941.68

9. 28,530 − 1,467

Problem Solving: Applications

TWO-STEP PROBLEMS

In a library, there are 12 tables with 6 chairs at each table. A class of 28 students visits the library. How many extra chairs are there?

Step 1   To find out how many chairs there are, multiply 6 times 12.

$$\begin{array}{r} 12 \\ \times\ 6 \\ \hline 72 \end{array}$$

Step 2   Then subtract 28 from the total number of chairs.

$$\begin{array}{r} 72 \\ -28 \\ \hline 44 \end{array}$$

There are 44 extra chairs in the library.

Try These

Solve each problem.

1. One day 3 classes of 28 students and 1 class of 32 students visited the library. How many students visited the library that day?

2. The librarian orders 4 dictionaries that cost $39.75 each. He also orders an atlas for $27.98. What is the total cost of the order?

3. The card catalog contains 9 drawers of 355 cards each. There are 977 cards for fiction books. How many of the cards are for nonfiction books?

4. 13 bookcases are on the first floor. 15 bookcases are on the second floor. If there are 42 bookcases in all, how many are in the rest of the library?

Exercises

Solve each problem. Explain the way you solved each problem.

1. 3 classes of 32 students visited the library. Each student borrowed 2 books. How many books were borrowed from the library?

2. The library has $4,000 to spend on furniture. The librarian bought 8 round tables for $259.75 each. How much money is left?

3. The library subscribes to 3 magazines that are published 52 times a year. The library has received these magazines for 5 years. How many of the magazines does the library have?

4. There are 163 books in the social studies section. 78 books are about American history, and 46 books are about European history. How many social studies books are about other topics?

5. The library contains 7,345 books. One day 264 books are borrowed and 176 books are returned. How many books are in the library at the end of the day?

6. In the science section, there are 8 shelves holding 23 books each. 109 of the books are about living things. How many science books are not about living things?

7. In the reference section, there are 4 encyclopedias that have 24 volumes each. There are also 3 dictionaries and 2 atlases. How many books are in the reference section?

★ 8. Fay Li, the librarian, is paid $9.60 an hour. She works 6 hours a day, 5 days a week. How much does she make in 2 weeks?

Multiplying by Multiples of 10

■ Multiply: 10 × 8

You can use the order property to find this product.

$$10 \times 8 = 8 \times 10$$
$$8 \times 10 = 80$$
$$\text{so, } 10 \times 8 = 80$$

Notice the pattern when you multiply by 10.

7	29	436	7,853
×10	×10	× 10	× 10
70	290	4,360	78,530

■ You can use this pattern to multiply by 10 mentally.

Multiply: 10 × 358

```
  358
×  10
3,580
```

To multiply by 10, write a 0 in the ones place. Then multiply by 1.

■ You can use this rule to multiply by multiples of 10.

Multiply: 30 × 2,786

Write the 0 in the ones place.

```
 2,786
×    30  ← 3 × 10
     0  ← shows multiplying
          by 10
```

Multiply by 3.

```
 2,786
×    30
83,580
        └ 3 × 2,786
```

Try These

Multiply. Do as many as you can mentally.

1. 46
  ×10

2. 52
  ×30

3. 483
  × 20

4. 395
  × 10

5. 4,578
  ×   40

6. 10 × 148

7. 37 × 60

8. 90 × 4,607

9. 3,617 × 10

Exercises

Multiply. Do as many as you can mentally.

1. 23
× 10

2. 431
× 30

3. 16
× 40

4. 947
× 60

5. 1,792
× 20

6. 1,453
× 60

7. 8,729
× 10

8. 562
× 8

9. 75
× 90

10. $4.89
× 20

11. 621
× 30

12. 4,659
× 40

13. $5.06
× 60

14. 7,514
× 50

15. $92.63
× 70

16. 3,219
× 7

17. 509
× 50

18. 2,918
× 30

19. $8.65
× 20

20. $4,927
× 80

21. 10 × 86
22. 60 × 513
23. 6 × 721
24. 94 × 40
25. 30 × 435
26. 7,314 × 20
27. 10 × 603
28. 4,186 × 9
29. 4,309 × 20
30. 50 × $62
31. 80 × $64.57
32. 5,216 × 80

Write >, <, or =.

33. 80 × 60 ▓ 8 × 600
34. 20 × 200 ▓ 20 × 20
35. 90 × 900 ▓ 9 × 9,000
36. 600 × 7 ▓ 70 × 600
37. 70 × 500 ▓ 50 × 70
38. 850 × 20 ▓ 2 × 8,500

Solve each problem mentally or with paper and pencil.

Canoeists on a lake make about 30 paddle strokes per minute.

39. How many strokes is that in 1 hour (60 minutes)?

40. How many strokes can a canoeist make in 2 hours?

41. It takes about 300 strokes to go 1 kilometer. About how many strokes does it take to go 9 kilometers?

★ 42. Could a canoeist go 9 kilometers in 2 hours?

Multiplying by 2-Digit Numbers

■ Roger Fairchild works as an auto mechanic. He earns $12 an hour. One week he worked 42 hours. How much did Roger earn?

Multiply to find how much Roger earned.

Think: 42 = 40 + 2

Multiply by 2.

$$\begin{array}{r} \$12 \\ \times\ 42 \\ \hline 24 \end{array} \leftarrow 2 \times 12$$

Multiply by 40.

$$\begin{array}{r} \$12 \\ \times\ 42 \\ \hline 24 \\ 480 \end{array} \leftarrow 40 \times 12$$

Add the products.

$$\begin{array}{r} \$12 \\ \times\ 42 \\ \hline 24 \\ 480 \\ \hline \$504 \end{array}$$

Roger earned $504 that week.

■ Be sure you add the right number when you multiply by the tens.

Multiply: 36 × 58

Think: 36 = 30 + 6

Multiply by 6.

$$\begin{array}{r} 4 \\ 58 \\ \times 36 \\ \hline 348 \end{array} \leftarrow 6 \times 58$$

Multiply by 30.

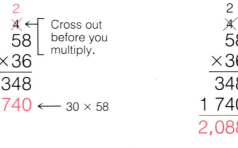

$$\begin{array}{r} \overset{2}{\cancel{4}} \\ 58 \\ \times 36 \\ \hline 348 \\ 1\,740 \end{array} \leftarrow 30 \times 58$$

Cross out before you multiply.

Add the products.

$$\begin{array}{r} \overset{2}{\cancel{4}} \\ 58 \\ \times 36 \\ \hline 348 \\ 1\,740 \\ \hline 2{,}088 \end{array}$$

■ Multiply: 25 × 843

Think: 25 = 20 + 5

$$\begin{array}{r} 2\,1 \\ 843 \\ \times\ \ 25 \\ \hline 4\,215 \\ 16\,860 \\ \hline 21{,}075 \end{array} \begin{array}{l} \leftarrow 5 \times 843 \\ \leftarrow 20 \times 843 \end{array}$$

Try These

Multiply.

1. $\begin{array}{r} 61 \\ \times 36 \\ \hline \end{array}$ **2.** $\begin{array}{r} 72 \\ \times 43 \\ \hline \end{array}$ **3.** $\begin{array}{r} \$34 \\ \times \ 67 \\ \hline \end{array}$ **4.** $\begin{array}{r} 293 \\ \times \ 28 \\ \hline \end{array}$ **5.** $\begin{array}{r} \$635 \\ \times \ \ 64 \\ \hline \end{array}$ **6.** $\begin{array}{r} 346 \\ \times \ 39 \\ \hline \end{array}$

7. 32×13 **8.** 46×18 **9.** $\$609 \times 35$ **10.** 175×48

Exercises

Multiply.

1. $\begin{array}{r} 93 \\ \times 12 \\ \hline \end{array}$ **2.** $\begin{array}{r} 430 \\ \times \ 94 \\ \hline \end{array}$ **3.** $\begin{array}{r} 57 \\ \times 40 \\ \hline \end{array}$ **4.** $\begin{array}{r} 824 \\ \times \ 46 \\ \hline \end{array}$ **5.** $\begin{array}{r} 63 \\ \times 58 \\ \hline \end{array}$ **6.** $\begin{array}{r} 358 \\ \times \ 14 \\ \hline \end{array}$

7. $\begin{array}{r} \$5.84 \\ \times \ \ \ 37 \\ \hline \end{array}$ **8.** $\begin{array}{r} 69 \\ \times 80 \\ \hline \end{array}$ **9.** $\begin{array}{r} 480 \\ \times \ 54 \\ \hline \end{array}$ **10.** $\begin{array}{r} \$476 \\ \times \ \ 89 \\ \hline \end{array}$ **11.** $\begin{array}{r} 279 \\ \times \ 83 \\ \hline \end{array}$ **12.** $\begin{array}{r} 807 \\ \times \ \ 9 \\ \hline \end{array}$

13. $\begin{array}{r} 132 \\ \times \ 32 \\ \hline \end{array}$ **14.** $\begin{array}{r} \$256 \\ \times \ \ 14 \\ \hline \end{array}$ **15.** $\begin{array}{r} 27 \\ \times \ 6 \\ \hline \end{array}$ **16.** $\begin{array}{r} \$4.12 \\ \times \ \ \ 7 \\ \hline \end{array}$ **17.** $\begin{array}{r} 274 \\ \times \ 15 \\ \hline \end{array}$ **18.** $\begin{array}{r} 873 \\ \times \ 50 \\ \hline \end{array}$

19. 41×89 **20.** 654×9 **21.** 89×730 **22.** 218×76
23. 38×76 **24.** $88 \times \$64$ **25.** $\$3.97 \times 27$ **26.** 384×55

Solve.

27. $(15 + 28) \times 30$ **28.** $(19 \times 37) - 82$ **29.** $56 \times (97 - 69)$
30. $32 \times (51 - 37)$ **31.** $(45 + 18) \times 36$ **32.** $(21 \times 39) - 147$

Solve each problem.

33. Roger is paid at the end of each week. His weekly checks for the month were $420, $564, $480, and $468. How much money did Roger earn that month?

34. Roger repaired the radiators of 86 cars this year. He repaired the mufflers of 214 cars this year. How many more mufflers did he repair than radiators?

35. The auto repair shop where Roger works has auto supplies in stock. The stock includes 24 gas filters worth $2.79 each. The stock also includes 74 spark plugs worth $1.85 each. How much is this stock worth in all?

★ **36.** Roger worked on Mrs. Harper's car. The car needed 5 cans of oil that cost $2.89 each. It needed 6 spark plugs that cost $1.98 each. Roger also installed a new oil filter that cost $4.95. What was Mrs. Harper's total bill?

Multiplying Greater Numbers

■ Abdul runs 2,366 meters each day. He runs 24 days each month. How many meters does he run each month?

To find the answer, multiply 24 times 2,366.

Think: 24 = 20 + 4

Multiply by 4.

$$\begin{array}{r} 2{,}366 \\ \times \quad 24 \\ \hline 9\ 464 \end{array}$$ ← 4 × 2,366

Multiply by 20.

$$\begin{array}{r} 2{,}366 \\ \times \quad 24 \\ \hline 9\ 464 \\ 47\ 320 \end{array}$$ ← 20 × 2,366

Add the products.

$$\begin{array}{r} 2{,}366 \\ \times \quad 24 \\ \hline 9\ 464 \\ 47\ 320 \\ \hline 56{,}784 \end{array}$$

Abdul runs 56,784 meters each month.

■ Multiply: 27 × 2,195

Think: 27 = 20 + 7

$$\begin{array}{r} 2{,}1\,9\,5 \\ \times \quad 2\,7 \\ \hline 1\,5\,3\,6\,5 \\ 4\,3\,9\,0\,0 \\ \hline 5\,9{,}2\,6\,5 \end{array}$$

15365 ← 7 × 2,195
43900 ← 20 × 2,195

Estimate to check.

Circle the first digit in each factor. Round each factor to the circled place. Multiply.

$$\begin{array}{r} ②,\,1\,9\,5 \longrightarrow 2{,}000 \\ \times \quad ②7 \longrightarrow \times \quad 30 \\ \hline 60{,}000 \end{array}$$

The product seems reasonable since 59,265 is close to 60,000.

Try These

Multiply. Estimate to check.

1. $\begin{array}{r} 1{,}613 \\ \times \quad 54 \end{array}$

2. $\begin{array}{r} 4{,}895 \\ \times \quad 68 \end{array}$

3. $\begin{array}{r} 7{,}906 \\ \times \quad 34 \end{array}$

4. $\begin{array}{r} 6{,}583 \\ \times \quad 79 \end{array}$

5. $\begin{array}{r} 4{,}489 \\ \times \quad 26 \end{array}$

6. 51 × 8,742

7. 6,458 × 87

8. 36 × 1,275

9. 3,718 × 44

Exercises

Multiply. Estimate to check.

1.	4,273 × 32	**2.**	6,307 × 24	**3.**	$32.05 × 26	**4.**	2,134 × 32	**5.**	1,525 × 43
6.	2,136 × 74	**7.**	5,204 × 38	**8.**	1,382 × 46	**9.**	$37.05 × 48	**10.**	264 × 60
11.	$41.20 × 25	**12.**	107 × 34	**13.**	1,072 × 56	**14.**	$26.50 × 6	**15.**	2,069 × 75

16. 36 × 7,431   **17.** 48 × $72.98   **18.** 1,678 × 54   **19.** 875 × 9

20. 7,832 × 62   **21.** 43 × 529   **22.** 52 × $75.55   **23.** 2,416 × 30

Solve each problem.

24. Juan is training for a track meet. He runs 5,640 meters a day. How many meters does he run in 15 days?

25. Janice ran 37,462 meters this week. Lee ran 33,944 meters. How many meters more did Janice run?

26. There were 19 schools represented at a track meet. Each team had 28 runners. How many runners were at the track meet?

27. Charles ran 4,625 meters on Monday, 4,795 meters on Tuesday, and 4,487 meters on Friday. How many meters did he run in all?

 THINK AND TRY

FORMING A RULE

Look at the multiplication table. Study the squares below. Find the products of the numbers on the diagonal.

10 × 18 = ■
15 × 12 = ■

1. What is true about these products?

2. Try other squares. Is this rule always true?

×	0	1	2	3	4	5	6	7	8	9
0	0	0	0	0	0	0	0	0	0	0
1	0	1	2	3	4	5	6	7	8	9
2	0	2	4	6	8	10	12	14	16	18
3	0	3	6	9	12	15	18	21	24	27
4	0	4	8	12	16	20	24	28	32	36
5	0	5	10	15	20	25	30	35	40	45
6	0	6	12	18	24	30	36	42	48	54
7	0	7	14	21	28	35	42	49	56	63
8	0	8	16	24	32	40	48	56	64	72
9	0	9	18	27	36	45	54	63	72	81

Problem Solving: Strategies

GENERALIZING

Fallsbrook is a planned city. There are 18 avenues running east and west. There are 23 streets running north and south. How many intersections are there?

Simplifying the problem is a strategy you can use. Suppose there were only 3 avenues and 2 streets.

Draw a diagram.

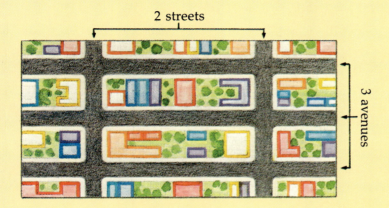

You can count the number of intersections. Or you can multiply to find the number of intersections.

3 avenues × 2 streets = 6 intersections

How many intersections are there in Fallsbrook?

18 × 23 = 414

There are 414 intersections in Fallsbrook.

Using the Strategy

Solve each problem.

1. The members of the Fallsbrook Community Center grow tomatoes. They plant 15 rows. Each row has 21 tomato plants. They get about 25 tomatoes from each plant. About how many tomatoes do they get altogether?

2. Tom Baker owns a supermarket. He wants to find the number of cans on a shelf without counting them. The shelf in his store has 20 cans across, 6 cans deep, and 4 cans high. How many cans are on the shelf?

3. The city council wants to plant flowers in the Fallsbrook parks. There are 12 parks. The Garden Club suggests planting 150 tulips and 97 daffodils in each park. How many flowers will be planted altogether?

4. The board of education bought school furniture and supplies. They spent $105,885 on supplies. Twice that plus $163,480 was spent on furniture. How much was spent for furniture? How much was spent altogether?

5. Lisa Harmon owns a hardware store. She is counting her stock. She has 105 boxes of nails and screws. She has 6 times more boxes of nails than screws. She has 15 boxes of screws. How many boxes of nails does Lisa have?

6. The Runners' Society is sponsoring a race. They expect each runner to eat 1 orange about every 5 miles. There are 263 runners. The race is 10 miles long. How many oranges do they need?

7. The traffic department wants to paint crosswalks at 214 intersections. It takes 45 gallons of paint to do each intersection. A gallon of paint costs $15. How much will it cost to paint all the crosswalks?

8. The Fallsbrook Bank has 27 rolls of quarters in the vault. There are 40 quarters in a roll. The bank has 32 rolls of pennies in the vault. There are 50 pennies in a roll. What is the value of this money?

ACTIVITY

FINDING PATTERNS

Look at any three diagonal numbers.

5
 7
  9

The sum is 21, or 3 × 7.
↑——— the middle number

6
 8
  10

The sum is 24, or 3 × 8.
↑———the middle number

+	1	2	3	4	5	6	7	8	9
1	2	3	4	5	6	7	8	9	10
2	3	4	5	6	7	8	9	10	11
3	4	5	6	7	8	9	10	11	12
4	5	6	7	8	9	10	11	12	13
5	6	7	8	9	10	11	12	13	14
6	7	8	9	10	11	12	13	14	15
7	8	9	10	11	12	13	14	15	16
8	9	10	11	12	13	14	15	16	17
9	10	11	12	13	14	15	16	17	18

1. Find the sum of any three numbers in a row. Is it 3 times the middle number?

2. Try 5 numbers in a row. Is the sum 5 times the middle number? Try 5 diagonal numbers. Is the sum 5 times the middle number?

3. What other patterns can you find?

Multiplying by Multiples of 100

■ Notice the pattern when you multiply by 100.

$$\begin{array}{r} 24 \\ \times 100 \\ \hline 2,400 \end{array} \qquad \begin{array}{r} 356 \\ \times 100 \\ \hline 35,600 \end{array} \qquad \begin{array}{r} 1,654 \\ \times\ \ \ 100 \\ \hline 165,400 \end{array}$$

You can use this pattern to multiply by 100 mentally.

$$\begin{array}{r} 3,692 \\ \times\ \ \ 100 \\ \hline 369,200 \end{array}$$

> To multiply by 100, write a 0 in the ones place and in the tens place. Then multiply by 1.

■ You can use this rule to multiply by multiples of 100.

Multiply: 600 × 3,241

Write a 0 in the ones place and in the tens place.

$$\begin{array}{r} 3,241 \\ \times\ \ \ 600 \longleftarrow 6 \times 100 \\ \hline 00 \longleftarrow \text{shows multiplying by 100} \end{array}$$

Multiply by 6.

$$\begin{array}{r} 3,241 \\ \times\ \ \ 600 \\ \hline 1,944,600 \end{array}$$
6 × 3,241

Try These

Multiply. Do as many as you can mentally.

1. $\begin{array}{r} 65 \\ \times 100 \\ \hline \end{array}$	**2.** $\begin{array}{r} 3,427 \\ \times\ \ \ 300 \\ \hline \end{array}$	**3.** $\begin{array}{r} 518 \\ \times 200 \\ \hline \end{array}$	**4.** $\begin{array}{r} 317 \\ \times 500 \\ \hline \end{array}$	**5.** $\begin{array}{r} 1,976 \\ \times\ \ \ 100 \\ \hline \end{array}$

6. 400 × 375   **7.** 100 × 684   **8.** 3,609 × 600

Exercises

Multiply. Do as many as you can mentally.

1.	700 × 100	2.	370 × 700	3.	2,676 × 100	4.	6,823 × 500	5.	$9.14 × 300

6.	800 × 400	7.	3,500 × 500	8.	$639 × 100	9.	4,265 × 200	10.	8,943 × 7

11.	428 × 100	12.	773 × 900	13.	1,047 × 300	14.	6,503 × 80	15.	$2,959 × 200

16.	1,582 × 400	17.	$5.42 × 10	18.	2,836 × 200	19.	335 × 84	20.	$3,645 × 500

21. 100 × 475

24. 4,687 × 100

22. 2,694 × 400

25. 800 × 146

23. 50 × $8.06

26. 900 × $60.38

★ 27. ▧ × 864 = 86,400

★ 29. ▧ × 2,807 = 2,807,000

★ 28. ▧ × 945 = 9,450

★ 30. ▧ × 4,518 = 451,800,000

Solve each problem mentally or with paper and pencil.

31. Everglow Candle Company packs 200 red candles in each case. How many red candles are in 625 cases?

32. Wick N' Stem orders 1,450 white candles and 700 gold candles. How many more white candles do they order?

33. A box of small candles costs Wick N' Stem $4.95. How much does Wick N' Stem pay for 300 boxes?

★ 34. Everglow Candle Company packs 100 scented candles in each case. Wick N' Stem orders 60 cases of bayberry-scented candles and 175 cases of strawberry-scented candles. How many scented candles does Wick N' Stem order?

Multiplying by 3-Digit Numbers

■ Ms. Fusco's class wanted to know how much 1 million is. They tried to collect 1 million bottle caps. On the first day, they collected 624 bottle caps. There were only 176 school days left. At that rate, could they collect 1 million bottle caps?

Multiply 176 times 624 to find the number of bottle caps.

Think: 170 = 100 + 70 + 6

Multiply by 6.

$$
\begin{array}{r}
624 \\
\times 176 \\
\hline
3\,744 \leftarrow 6 \times 624
\end{array}
$$

Multiply by 70.

$$
\begin{array}{r}
624 \\
\times 176 \\
\hline
3\,744 \\
43\,680 \leftarrow 70 \times 624
\end{array}
$$

Multiply by 100. Add the products.

$$
\begin{array}{r}
624 \\
\times 176 \\
\hline
3\,744 \\
43\,680 \\
62\,400 \leftarrow 100 \times 624 \\
\hline
109{,}824
\end{array}
$$

No. They would not be able to collect 1 million bottle caps at that rate.

■ Multiply: 296 × 3,048

Think: 296 = 200 + 90 + 6

$$
\begin{array}{r}
3{,}048 \\
\times \quad 296 \\
\hline
18\,288 \leftarrow 6 \times 3{,}048 \\
274\,320 \leftarrow 90 \times 3{,}048 \\
609\,600 \leftarrow 200 \times 3{,}048 \\
\hline
902{,}208
\end{array}
$$

Estimate to check.

Circle the first digit in each factor. Round each factor to the circled place. Multiply.

$$
\begin{array}{r}
③{,}048 \longrightarrow 3{,}000 \\
\times \quad ②96 \longrightarrow \times \quad 300 \\
\hline
900{,}000
\end{array}
$$

The product seems reasonable since 902,208 is close to 900,000.

Try These

Multiply. Estimate to check.

1.
$$
\begin{array}{r}
728 \\
\times 479
\end{array}
$$

2.
$$
\begin{array}{r}
623 \\
\times 324
\end{array}
$$

3.
$$
\begin{array}{r}
609 \\
\times 276
\end{array}
$$

4.
$$
\begin{array}{r}
7{,}426 \\
\times \quad 368
\end{array}
$$

5.
$$
\begin{array}{r}
9{,}534 \\
\times \quad 816
\end{array}
$$

6. 528 × 271

7. 164 × 349

8. 258 × 5,012

Exercises

Multiply. Estimate to check.

1. 234
  ×317

2. 502
  ×236

3. 1,621
  × 354

4. 6,543
  × 212

5. 643
  ×314

6. 276
  ×523

7. 8,215
  × 312

8. 643
  ×145

9. $45.34
  × 127

10. 4,458
  × 300

11. $610
  × 437

12. 5,924
  × 738

13. 890
  × 92

14. 274
  ×365

15. 6,320
  × 154

16. 425
  ×381

17. 1,728
  × 60

18. 869
  ×463

19. $50.86
  × 47

20. $9.00
  × 578

21. 323 × 909

22. 700 × 5,392

23. 6,504 × 59

24. 684 × 239

25. $7.24 × 958

26. $81.54 × 782

27. 827 × 349

28. 65 × 3,861

29. 965 × 81

30. 200 × 7,095

31. 57 × $130.68

32. 125 × 800

 When you are at rest, your heart beats about 72 times every minute.

33. How many times does your heart beat in 1 hour? In 1 day? In 1 year?

34. Can a calculator show about how many times your heart has beat in your lifetime? Try it.

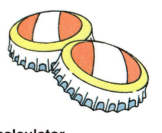

Solve each problem. You may choose paper and pencil or a calculator.

35. The center recycles 130 tons of paper each month. How much paper is recycled in a year?

36. The school year is 180 days long. Each school day is 6 hours long. How many hours do the students attend school in a year?

37. The class took 392 bottles to the recycling center in October. In November, the class took 425 bottles to be recycled. How many bottles did the class take to be recycled in the two months?

★ 38. The Glendale School is having a recycling drive. There are 465 students in the school. Each student collects 4 cans per day. How many cans could be collected in 165 days?

More about Multiplying

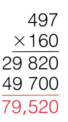

■ Mr. Graham has a poultry farm. Each hen lays about 160 eggs. He has 497 hens. About how many eggs do the hens lay?

To find how many eggs, multiply 160 times 497.

Think: 160 = 100 + 60 + 0

There are no ones to multiply by. Multiply by 60.	Multiply by 100.	Add the products.
497 ×160 **29 820** ← 60 × 497	497 ×160 29 820 **49 700** ← 100 × 497	497 ×160 29 820 49 700 **79,520**

The hens lay about 79,520 eggs.

■ Multiply: 207 × 328

Think: 207 = 200 + 0 + 7

Multiply by 7.	There are no tens to multiply by. Multiply by 200.	Add the products.
328 ×207 **2 296** ← 7 × 328	328 ×207 2 296 **65 600** ← 200 × 328	328 ×207 2 296 65 600 **67,896**

Try These

Multiply.

1. 654
×280

2. 197
×560

3. 2,467
× 508

4. 825
×409

5. 4,537
× 240

6. 402 × 473

7. 350 × 219

8. 4,176 × 108

Exercises

Multiply.

1. 334×350

2. 113×408

3. $3{,}576 \times 680$

4. $3{,}289 \times 706$

5. $\$987 \times 310$

6. $4{,}386 \times 620$

7. $\$8.14 \times 502$

8. 527×908

9. $8{,}463 \times 37$

10. $\$24.56 \times 404$

11. 918×750

12. 575×608

13. $\$37.20 \times 50$

14. $2{,}650 \times 780$

15. $\$16.52 \times 901$

16. $450 \times 3{,}526$

17. $680 \times \$982$

18. $4{,}621 \times 705$

19. 802×775

20. $70 \times \$61.85$

21. 290×539

Add, subtract, or multiply.

22. $369 + 748$

23. 718×850

24. $8{,}641 - 2{,}974$

25. $358 - 199$

26. 937×204

Solve each problem.

27. Mr. Graham takes his eggs to a poultry market. A round-trip is 110 miles. He makes the trip 156 times a year. How many miles does he drive a year?

28. Mr. Graham collected 246 eggs in the morning and 307 eggs in the afternoon. How many eggs did he collect that day?

29. Mr. Graham receives $.48 for each dozen eggs. He brings 97 dozen eggs to the poultry market. How much is he paid for the eggs?

★ 30. There are 129 chickens in a coop. Each chicken eats 4 ounces of grain at each feeding. Each day there are 2 feedings. How many ounces of grain are used each day to feed the chickens?

Problem Solving: Applications

ESTIMATING PRODUCTS

■ In 1 week, the General Store sold 185 pairs of jeans. At that rate, about how many pairs could the store sell in 13 weeks?

To find out, estimate the product.

Circle the first digit in each factor. Round each factor to the circled place. Multiply to estimate the product.

$$
\begin{array}{r}
①85 \longrightarrow 200 \\
\times\ ①3 \longrightarrow \times\ 10 \\
\hline
2{,}000
\end{array}
$$

The store could sell about 2,000 pairs of jeans in 13 weeks.

■ The General Store manager orders 84 vests. Each vest costs $12.40. About how much is spent on vests?

To find about how much, estimate the product.

$$
\begin{array}{r}
\$①2.40 \longrightarrow \$10 \\
\times\ \ \ \ ⑧4 \longrightarrow \times\ 80 \\
\hline
\$800
\end{array}
$$

The General Store spends about $800 on vests.

Try These

Estimate to solve each problem.

1. There are 48 sweaters in a box. About how many sweaters are there in 28 boxes?

2. Joel earns $4.20 per hour. He works 18 hours each week. About how much does he earn each week?

Exercises

Choose estimation, paper and pencil, or a calculator to solve.

1. The General Store pays $12.85 for each sweater. An order is placed for 72 sweaters. About how much is spent on sweaters?

2. There are 18 sections in a display rack. 1 section holds 12 shirts. About how many shirts can be displayed?

3. There are 110 T-shirts in a box. How many T-shirts are there in 25 boxes?

4. Sales for a day were $945. At that rate, about how much would sales total in a month (27 working days)?

5. Each carton holds 184 sweaters. There are 13 cartons in the stock room. About how many sweaters are there altogether?

6. The cost of 1 display rack is $449.85. The manager of the General Store buys 6 racks. About how much is spent on display racks?

7. Mr. George orders 48 medium jackets, 72 large jackets, and 36 extra-large jackets. Each jacket costs $32.90. How much more is spent on large jackets than on extra-large jackets?

8. The General Store has belts in stock. The stock includes 36 vinyl belts worth $9.95 each. The store also has leather belts worth a total of $1,400. About how much is this stock worth?

9. The Washington Shirt Company packs 36 shirts in each case. The General Store ordered 36 cases. How many shirts did the General Store order?

10. A glee club places an order for jackets. The total cost of the jackets is $500. They also order 36 shirts for $16.95 each. About how much does the total order cost?

11. The General Store sells jeans. There are 95 pairs of children's jeans. There are 130 pairs of adults' jeans. About how many pairs of jeans are there in all?

★ 12. The General Store sold 22 scarves for $12.89 each. Each scarf costs the General Store $6.79. About how much profit did the store make?

★ 13. Angela is paid $5.85 per hour. She works 28 hours each week. About how much does she earn in 52 weeks?

Problem Solving: Applications

MORE THAN ONE WAY TO SOLVE

Alice Fields is redecorating her house. She has 4 boxes of tiles for one of the kitchen walls. Each box has 18 plain tiles and 6 patterned tiles. How many tiles does Alice have in all?

There is more than one way to solve this problem.

One Way: Add to find how many tiles are in each box.

$$\begin{array}{r} 18 \text{ plain tiles} \\ +\ 6 \text{ patterned tiles} \\ \hline 24 \text{ tiles in each box} \end{array}$$

Multiply to find the number of tiles in 4 boxes.

$$\begin{array}{r} 24 \\ \times\ 4 \\ \hline 96 \text{ tiles in 4 boxes} \end{array}$$

Another Way: Multiply to find the total number of plain tiles and the total number of patterned tiles.

$$\begin{array}{r} 18 \\ \times\ 4 \\ \hline 72 \text{ plain tiles} \end{array} \qquad \begin{array}{r} 6 \\ \times 4 \\ \hline 24 \text{ patterned tiles} \end{array}$$

Add to find the total number of plain and patterned tiles.

$$\begin{array}{r} 72 \\ +24 \\ \hline 96 \text{ tiles in 4 boxes} \end{array}$$

Alice has 96 tiles in all.

Try These

Solve each problem.

1. Alice hires Brian and Wayne to help her. She pays Brian $50 each day. She pays Wayne $60 each day. How much does Alice spend if Brian and Wayne work for 6 days?

2. Each roll of wallpaper is $9.85. When Alice takes 8 rolls to the cashier, she is told the wallpaper is on sale for $7.95. How much does Alice save on 8 rolls?

Exercises

Solve each problem. Explain the way you solved each problem.

1. Brian works for 3 hours each morning and 2 hours each afternoon. How many hours does Brian work in 6 days?

2. Wayne helps Alice redecorate for 4 hours each morning and 2 hours each evening. How many hours does Wayne work in 12 days?

3. Wayne is mixing beige paint for each room in Alice's house. He uses 1 can of brown paint and 3 cans of white paint for each room. How many cans of paint are used to paint 5 rooms?

4. Alice bought 20 cans of paint. Each can cost $11.25. There was a rebate coupon on each can. The paint company sent Alice $2.50 for each coupon. How much did Alice spend on paint?

5. Alice bought 3 rolls of striped wallpaper. She bought 5 rolls of floral print for the dining room. Each roll cost $14.60. How much did Alice spend on the wallpaper?

6. Alice bought 4 packages of picture-hanging kits. Each kit contained 3 small hooks and 5 large hooks. How many hooks did Alice buy?

7. New kitchen cabinet doors were delivered to Alice. Each carton contained 2 small cabinet doors and 2 large cabinet doors. 4 cartons were delivered. How many cabinet doors were delivered?

8. Each box of bathroom tiles is $24.65. When Alice takes 6 boxes to the cashier, she is told the tiles are on sale for $21.99. How much does Alice save on 6 boxes?

9. Alice hired a plumber and an electrician. The plumber charges $18.50 an hour. The electrician charges $22.75 an hour. Each of them worked 14 hours. How much more did the electrician earn for the 14 hours?

★ 10. Alice is making a stained-glass window for the front door. She works on it for 25 minutes each morning and 35 minutes each evening. How many hours does she spend on the window each week?

CHAPTER CHECKPOINT

Find the least common multiple (other than 0). (pp. 68–69)

1. 2 and 5 **2.** 3 and 7 **3.** 4 and 6 **4.** 2 and 10

Multiply. (pp. 66–67, 70–75)

5. 4 $\times 8$	**6.** 7 $\times 6$	**7.** 1 $\times 5$	**8.** 23 $\times\ 3$	**9.** 36 $\times\ 5$
10. 432 $\times\ \ 7$	**11.** \$5.36 $\times\ \ \ \ 5$	**12.** 5,086 $\times\ \ \ \ 9$	**13.** 68 $\times\ 7$	**14.** 6,532 $\times\ \ \ \ 4$
15. 376 $\times\ \ 6$	**16.** \$16.29 $\times\ \ \ \ \ 4$	**17.** 87,643 $\times\ \ \ \ \ \ 5$	**18.** 904,358 $\times\ \ \ \ \ \ \ 7$	**19.** 540,271 $\times\ \ \ \ \ \ \ 8$

20. $(4 \times 2) \times 3$ **21.** 0×8 **22.** $6 \times \$96.45$

Multiply. (pp. 78–83)

23. 24 $\times 21$	**24.** 431 $\times\ 52$	**25.** 4,835 $\times\ \ \ 47$	**26.** \$26.50 $\times\ \ \ \ 72$	**27.** 96 $\times 40$
28. 312 $\times\ 18$	**29.** 57 $\times 80$	**30.** \$16.85 $\times\ \ \ \ 25$	**31.** 34 $\times 65$	**32.** 874 $\times\ 60$

33. $45 \times 8,024$ **34.** $40 \times \$75.29$ **35.** 400×25

Multiply. (pp. 86–91)

36. 6,835 $\times\ \ \ 500$	**37.** 762 $\times 283$	**38.** 1,587 $\times\ \ \ 356$	**39.** 525 $\times 208$	**40.** \$82.75 $\times\ \ \ \ 904$
41. 847 $\times 235$	**42.** \$65.14 $\times\ \ \ \ 200$	**43.** 463 $\times 850$	**44.** \$75.49 $\times\ \ \ \ 643$	**45.** 8,647 $\times\ \ \ 502$

46. 467×265 **47.** $8,720 \times 461$ **48.** $926 \times \$8.75$

Estimate each product. (pp. 74–75, 82–83, 88–89)

49.	1,362 × 83	50.	139 × 64	51.	972 ×596	52.	5,601 × 7	53.	3,541 × 970

54.	2,609 × 9	55.	8,757 × 92	56.	2,978 × 287	57.	7,987 × 342	58.	953 ×685

59. 728×489
62. 265×34

60. 279×93
63. 134×733

61. $306 \times 2,794$
64. $3,516 \times 782$

Solve each problem. (pp. 66–95)

65. Michael bought a 3-speed bicycle, a horn, and a light. How much money did he spend?

66. Mr. and Mrs. Lopez bought a 10-speed bicycle for their daughter and a tricycle for their son. How much change did the Lopezes receive from $250?

Item	Price
standard bicycle	$75.25
3-speed bicycle	96.50
10-speed bicycle	174.99
tricycle	49.98
unicycle	31.75
horn	6.79
light	15.35
basket	9.60

67. The bicycle store sold 678 10-speed bicycles this year. How much money did the store make on these sales?

68. The Valley Bicycle Club ordered 14 horns and 1 basket. What is the cost of the order?

69. The bicycle store received a shipment of 15 unicycles. A circus bought 10 of the unicycles. How much did the circus spend on unicycles?

70. Each box contains 144 safety reflectors. There are 18 boxes in the stockroom. Estimate how many safety reflectors are in stock.

71. One month the bicycle store sold 107 standard bicycles, 85 3-speed bicycles, and 62 10-speed bicycles. How many bicycles did it sell altogether that month?

72. The bicycle store had 127 tires in stock. The store sold 58 tires and received a shipment of 42 tires. How many tires are now in stock?

COMPUTERS AND PROBLEM SOLVING

■ Computers have the ability to make logical decisions. The most powerful decision statement in the BASIC language is IF . . . THEN. The flow chart at right shows an IF . . . THEN statement at work.

The user will be asked to input two numbers. The diamond shape shows that a decision must be made. IF the product of the two numbers *is not* greater than 50, THEN the computer will print that product. IF the product *is* greater than 50, THEN the computer will print the message, TOO BIG!

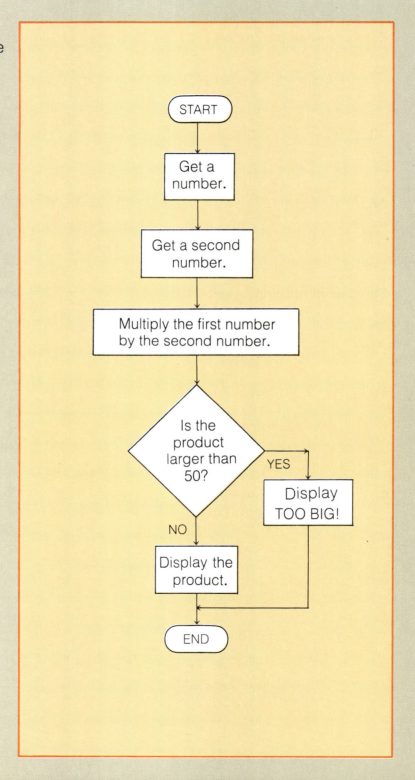

This BASIC program will do the same thing.

These are sample results of this program.

```
10   INPUT A
20   INPUT B
30   IF A * B>50 THEN GOTO 60
40   PRINT A * B
50   GOTO 70
60   PRINT "TOO BIG!"
70   END
```

```
] RUN
?5
?7
35
]▤
```

```
] RUN
?8
?64
TOO BIG!
]▤
```

Solve each problem.

1. Why does the NEW command come first?

2. What parts of the flow chart show what lines 10 and 20 of the program do?

3. Which program line does the same thing as the decision diamond in the flow chart?

4. What does line 50 do?

5. Draw a flow chart for a program that will ask for two numbers and will print the answer *only* if the product of those numbers is *greater* than 50. If the product is 50 or less, have the computer print TOO SMALL!

6. Change the flow chart so that the computer will ask for more numbers and will repeat the same process until <CTRL> <Reset> is pressed.

7. Write a program for this flow chart.

ENRICHMENT

EXPONENTS

This multiplication example uses the same number, 2, as a factor four times.

$$2 \times 2 \times 2 \times 2$$

There is a short way to write $2 \times 2 \times 2 \times 2$. Use an **exponent**. An exponent tells how many times a number is used as a factor.

$$2 \times 2 \times 2 \times 2 = 2^4$$

Read: 2 to the 4th power

The exponent 4 tells that 2 is used as a factor four times.

$$2 \times 2 \times 2 \times 2 = 16 \qquad \text{and} \qquad 2^4 = 16$$

Multiply to find 5^3.

$$5^3 = 5 \times 5 \times 5$$
$$= 125$$

Write each exponent.

1. $7 \times 7 = 7^{\blacksquare}$

2. $3 \times 3 \times 3 \times 3 \times 3 = 3^{\blacksquare}$

3. $4 \times 4 \times 4 = 4^{\blacksquare}$

4. $6 \times 6 \times 6 \times 6 = 6^{\blacksquare}$

Show each product using an exponent.

5. $3 \times 3 \times 3 \times 3$

6. $8 \times 8 \times 8$

7. $2 \times 2 \times 2 \times 2 \times 2 \times 2$

8. $10 \times 10 \times 10$

9. 17×17

10. $9 \times 9 \times 9 \times 9 \times 9$

Find each product.

11. 2^5 12. 3^2 13. 10^4 14. 4^3 15. 5^4 16. 6^4

17. 4^5 18. 2^6 19. 3^5 20. 9^3 21. 36^2 22. 18^3

CUMULATIVE REVIEW

Write each number.

1. 3 thousands 9 tens 2 ones
2. 36 million 15 thousand 8
3. nine billion, seventy-four thousand, twenty-eight
4. six hundred thousand, five hundred fifty

Use 84,019,254,785. Write the digit that is in each place.

5. ten-thousands place
6. billions place
7. hundred-millions place
8. hundreds place

What does the digit 7 mean in each number?

9. 207,514
10. 179,538,024
11. 4,710,293
12. 9,128,735

Write >, <, or =.

13. 236 ▧ 263
14. 904,784 ▧ 904,784
15. 68,432,207 ▧ 68,423,207
16. 4,527 ▧ 4,572
17. 2,761,054 ▧ 2,716,504
18. 273,409 ▧ 237,490

Round each number.

19. 874 to the nearest ten
20. 72,504 to the nearest thousand
21. 7,468 to the nearest hundred
22. 87,156,943 to the nearest million

Add or subtract.

23.
$$\begin{array}{r} 58 \\ +49 \\ \hline \end{array}$$

24.
$$\begin{array}{r} 365 \\ -76 \\ \hline \end{array}$$

25.
$$\begin{array}{r} 784 \\ -265 \\ \hline \end{array}$$

26.
$$\begin{array}{r} \$37.87 \\ +29.36 \\ \hline \end{array}$$

27.
$$\begin{array}{r} 62,109 \\ +18,467 \\ \hline \end{array}$$

28.
$$\begin{array}{r} 95 \\ -32 \\ \hline \end{array}$$

29.
$$\begin{array}{r} 325 \\ +184 \\ \hline \end{array}$$

30.
$$\begin{array}{r} 2,009 \\ -578 \\ \hline \end{array}$$

31.
$$\begin{array}{r} \$16.40 \\ -11.49 \\ \hline \end{array}$$

32.
$$\begin{array}{r} 9,427 \\ +7,646 \\ \hline \end{array}$$

33.
$$\begin{array}{r} 16,107 \\ -9,869 \\ \hline \end{array}$$

34.
$$\begin{array}{r} 21,893 \\ -4,765 \\ \hline \end{array}$$

35.
$$\begin{array}{r} \$259.75 \\ +149.90 \\ \hline \end{array}$$

36.
$$\begin{array}{r} 654 \\ 107 \\ +25 \\ \hline \end{array}$$

37.
$$\begin{array}{r} 179 \\ 367 \\ +1,985 \\ \hline \end{array}$$

(Continued)

Multiply.

38. $\begin{array}{r} 0 \\ \times 3 \\ \hline \end{array}$

39. $\begin{array}{r} 21 \\ \times\ 4 \\ \hline \end{array}$

40. $\begin{array}{r} 423 \\ \times\ \ 6 \\ \hline \end{array}$

41. $\begin{array}{r} \$89.12 \\ \times\ \ \ \ \ 8 \\ \hline \end{array}$

42. $\begin{array}{r} 47{,}306 \\ \times\ \ \ \ \ \ 7 \\ \hline \end{array}$

43. $\begin{array}{r} 75 \\ \times 10 \\ \hline \end{array}$

44. $\begin{array}{r} 80 \\ \times 70 \\ \hline \end{array}$

45. $\begin{array}{r} 3{,}852 \\ \times\ \ \ \ 40 \\ \hline \end{array}$

46. $\begin{array}{r} 78 \\ \times 29 \\ \hline \end{array}$

47. $\begin{array}{r} 246 \\ \times\ \ 35 \\ \hline \end{array}$

48. $\begin{array}{r} 109 \\ \times\ \ 68 \\ \hline \end{array}$

49. $\begin{array}{r} \$56.89 \\ \times\ \ \ \ \ 400 \\ \hline \end{array}$

50. $\begin{array}{r} 832 \\ \times 647 \\ \hline \end{array}$

51. $\begin{array}{r} 2{,}419 \\ \times\ \ \ 187 \\ \hline \end{array}$

52. $\begin{array}{r} \$47.19 \\ \times\ \ \ \ 368 \\ \hline \end{array}$

Add, subtract, or multiply. Estimate to check.

53. $\begin{array}{r} 4{,}679 \\ +1{,}986 \\ \hline \end{array}$

54. $\begin{array}{r} 504 \\ -187 \\ \hline \end{array}$

55. $\begin{array}{r} 67 \\ \times\ 9 \\ \hline \end{array}$

56. $\begin{array}{r} 89 \\ \times 21 \\ \hline \end{array}$

57. $\begin{array}{r} 308 \\ \times\ \ 49 \\ \hline \end{array}$

58. $654 + 107 + 25$

59. $75{,}010 - 15{,}423$

60. $832 \times 6{,}479$

61. $2{,}004 - 689$

62. 246×35

63. $\$189.75 + \$75.98$

64. $48 \times 2{,}873$

65. $46{,}195 + 27{,}830$

66. $29{,}143 - 6{,}798$

Solve each problem.

67. A carpenter earns $12.50 an hour. She works 45 hours. How much money does she make?

68. Carol buys 3 books. Each book costs $5.98. How much does Carol spend?

69. There were 88 people on a bus when it left Pine Woods. 29 got off in Racine. How many went on to the next stop?

70. One day 47,968 people took buses to work. The same day 35,209 people took trains to work. How many people took public transportation that day?

71. Mrs. Richmond spent $6.50 for vegetables, $4.59 for dairy products, and $12.45 for meat. How much did she spend altogether?

72. The hardware store sold 2,190 tools in December. In January, 975 tools were sold. About how many more tools were sold in December?

4

DIVISION BY 1-DIGIT NUMBERS

Division Facts

■ Mr. Lucas has 18 tomato plants in his garden. There are 3 plants in each row. How many rows of tomato plants are there?

Divide 18 by 3 to find how many rows.

$$3\overline{)18}^{6}$$

Mr. Lucas has 6 rows of tomato plants.

■ Here are two ways you can write a division fact.

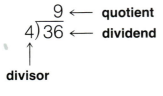

9 ←— **quotient**
4)36 ←— **dividend**
↑
divisor

36 ÷ 4 = 9 ←— **quotient**
↑   ↑
dividend **divisor**

■ These patterns in division can help you find quotients mentally.

When you divide by 1, the quotient is the same as the dividend.

$7 \div 1 = 7$
$4 \div 1 = 4$

When you divide a number other than 0 by itself, the quotient is 1.

$5 \div 5 = 1$
$9 \div 9 = 1$

When you divide 0 by a number other than 0, the quotient is 0.

$0 \div 9 = 0$
$0 \div 6 = 0$

O IS NEVER A DIVISOR.

■ Multiplication and division are related. If you know a multiplication fact, then you know two division facts.

$6 \times 8 = 48$ so $48 \div 6 = 8$

and

$48 \div 8 = 6$

Because of this relationship, you can use multiplication to check division.

Try These

Use each multiplication fact to divide.

1. 2 × 7
  14 ÷ 7
  14 ÷ 2

2. 3 × 4
  12 ÷ 4
  12 ÷ 3

3. 5 × 4
  20 ÷ 4
  20 ÷ 5

4. 9 × 3
  27 ÷ 3
  27 ÷ 9

Divide.

5. 6)30 **6.** 7)56 **7.** 1)9 **8.** 4)0 **9.** 8)8 **10.** 6)42

Exercises

Divide.

1. 7)14 **2.** 4)12 **3.** 4)20 **4.** 5)30 **5.** 9)18 **6.** 3)18

7. 6)54 **8.** 7)21 **9.** 8)32 **10.** 5)45 **11.** 9)63 **12.** 7)7

13. 9)0 **14.** 2)12 **15.** 4)8 **16.** 5)10 **17.** 3)9 **18.** 4)32

19. 2)18 **20.** 8)72 **21.** 1)6 **22.** 8)64 **23.** 4)28 **24.** 3)0

25. 36 ÷ 6 **26.** 7 ÷ 7 **27.** 45 ÷ 9 **28.** 16 ÷ 4
29. 14 ÷ 2 **30.** 20 ÷ 5 ★ **31.** 723 ÷ 1 ★ **32.** 0 ÷ 146

Write two related division sentences.

33. 3 × 2 **34.** 8 × 3 **35.** 7 × 9 **36.** 5 × 8

Copy and complete.

37. 15 ÷ ■ = 3 **38.** 35 ÷ ■ = 5 **39.** 40 ÷ ■ = 8
40. ■ ÷ 9 = 3 **41.** ■ ÷ 5 = 1 **42.** ■ ÷ 6 = 7

Solve each problem.

43. Mr. Lucas has 32 pepper plants in his garden. There are 8 plants in each row. How many rows of pepper plants are there?

44. Mr. Lucas planted 6 eggplants. Each plant produced 3 eggplants. How many eggplants did Mr. Lucas have in all?

45. Mr. Lucas fertilizes his garden. The first time he used 35 pounds of fertilizer. The second time he used 10 pounds. How many more pounds did he use the first time?

46. In July, Mrs. Lucas made 16 jars of strawberry jam. In August, she made 8 jars of blueberry jam. How many more jars of strawberry jam did Mrs. Lucas make?

Problem Solving: Applications

INTERPRETING DIVISION

Division is used to answer two kinds
of questions.

> How many groups?
> How many in each group?

■ **How many groups?**

There are 24 scouts in a troop. They
are going on a camping trip. Each tent
sleeps 4. How many tents are needed?

To find how many groups of 4 there
are, divide.

$$4)\overline{24}^{\ 6}$$

The scouts need 6 tents.

■ **How many in each group?**

To protect the plant life, the 24 scouts
use 3 separate campsites. The same
number of scouts camp at each site.
How many scouts are at each
campsite?

To find how many scouts are in each
group, divide.

$$3)\overline{24}^{\ 8}$$

There are 8 scouts at each campsite.

Try These

Read each problem. Decide whether each question asks *How many in each group?* or *How many groups?* Then answer the question.

1. There are 24 scouts going canoeing. There are 6 canoes. How many scouts go in each canoe?

2. The scouts buy 36 drinks. There are 6 drinks in each carton. How many cartons did the scouts buy?

3. The scouts need 72 apples for a picnic. There are 8 apples in each bag. How many bags of apples do the scouts need?

4. There are 28 scouts at a meeting. The leader forms 7 teams for a treasure hunt. How many scouts are in each team?

Exercises

Solve each problem.

1. The scouts need 48 containers of orange juice. Each carton holds 6 containers. How many cartons do they need?

2. There are 24 scouts at a meeting. The scout leader has given 9 scouts their assignments. How many more scouts need their assignments?

3. The scout leader unpacks 2 boxes of scout badges. Each box contains 12 badges. He then puts the badges into packages of 3. How many packages does he make?

4. The scouts eat dried fruit for their snacks. Herschel unpacks 18 bags of dried apricots, 16 bags of dried pineapple, and 8 bags of dried apples. How many bags of dried fruit did Herschel unpack?

5. The scouts have to set up 12 tents. They have already set up 5 of them. How many more tents do the scouts have to set up?

6. A first aid kit costs $7.58. A compass costs $16.50. This scout troop buys 4 first aid kits. How much money do they spend on kits?

7. There are 8 boys in Mr. Carey's Cub Scout den. There are 6 boys in Ms. Horton's den. How many boys are in these dens altogether?

★ 8. There are 24 scouts on a camping trip. Each of the scouts will eat 2 eggs for each breakfast. How many dozens of eggs are needed for 4 breakfasts?

★ 9. There are 36 trail markers in a case. The scout leader puts 4 trail markers in each bag. How many bags does he need for 5 cases?

Division with Remainders

■ Marsha has 17 shells. She wants to share them equally with each of her two friends. How many shells does each person get? How many shells are left?

Divide to find how many shells each person gets.

Find the quotient.

Think: ▓ × 3 = 17
Try 5.

$$
\begin{array}{r}
5 \\
3\overline{)17} \\
\underline{15} \quad \longleftarrow \text{ Multiply: } 5 \times 3 \\
2 \quad \longleftarrow \text{ Subtract: } 17 - 15
\end{array}
$$

Show the remainder.

$$
\begin{array}{r}
5 \text{ R2} \\
3\overline{)17} \\
\underline{15} \\
2
\end{array}
$$
← The remainder tells how many are left.

Each person gets 5 shells. There are 2 shells left.

■ To check division, multiply the quotient and the divisor. Then add the remainder. The answer should be the dividend.

Division

quotient ⟶ $\quad$ 5 R2 ← remainder
divisor ⟶ $3\overline{)17}$ ← dividend
$\qquad \underline{15}$
$\qquad \quad 2$

Check

$$
\begin{array}{r}
5 \quad \longleftarrow \text{ quotient} \\
\times 3 \quad \longleftarrow \text{ divisor} \\
\hline
15 \\
+ \quad 2 \quad \longleftarrow \text{ remainder} \\
\hline
17 \quad \longleftarrow \text{ dividend}
\end{array}
$$

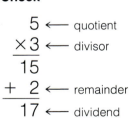

Try These

Divide. Check each answer.

1. $3\overline{)13}$ $\qquad$ 2. $5\overline{)21}$ $\qquad$ 3. $6\overline{)5}$ $\qquad$ 4. $6\overline{)26}$ $\qquad$ 5. $2\overline{)17}$ $\qquad$ 6. $4\overline{)18}$

7. $16 \div 3$ $\qquad$ 8. $23 \div 8$ $\qquad$ 9. $17 \div 5$ $\qquad$ 10. $11 \div 5$

Exercises

Divide.

1. $2\overline{)13}$
2. $4\overline{)9}$
3. $5\overline{)12}$
4. $3\overline{)10}$
5. $6\overline{)50}$
6. $4\overline{)3}$

7. $5\overline{)25}$
8. $3\overline{)24}$
9. $7\overline{)37}$
10. $5\overline{)27}$
11. $5\overline{)40}$
12. $6\overline{)45}$

13. $9\overline{)39}$
14. $8\overline{)48}$
15. $7\overline{)30}$
16. $8\overline{)60}$
17. $9\overline{)44}$
18. $6\overline{)36}$

19. $5\overline{)48}$
20. $8\overline{)7}$
21. $9\overline{)85}$
22. $7\overline{)68}$
23. $8\overline{)55}$
24. $8\overline{)66}$

25. $7\overline{)60}$
26. $6\overline{)54}$
27. $9\overline{)75}$
28. $7\overline{)43}$
29. $3\overline{)16}$
30. $7\overline{)51}$

31. $6\overline{)52}$
32. $4\overline{)24}$
33. $8\overline{)52}$
34. $9\overline{)38}$
35. $5\overline{)45}$
36. $3\overline{)11}$

37. $12 \div 7$
38. $64 \div 7$
39. $49 \div 5$
40. $42 \div 7$

41. $75 \div 8$
42. $57 \div 8$
43. $81 \div 9$
44. $61 \div 8$

Use this division.

$$\begin{array}{r} 7 \text{ R3} \\ 6\overline{)45} \\ 42 \\ \hline 3 \end{array}$$

45. Which number is the divisor?
46. Which number is the quotient?
47. Which number is the dividend?
48. Which number is the remainder?

Solve each problem.

49. Marsha collected scallop shells so she could make necklaces. She collected 27 scallop shells. She needs 6 shells for each necklace. How many necklaces can she make? How many shells are left?

50. There were 64 people on the ferry from Hyannis Port to Nantucket Island. 9 people were returning to Hyannis Port that evening. How many people stayed on Nantucket Island?

  KEEPING IN SHAPE

1. $\begin{array}{r} 23 \\ \times\ 3 \\ \end{array}$
2. $\begin{array}{r} 18 \\ \times\ 6 \\ \end{array}$
3. $\begin{array}{r} 59 \\ \times\ 4 \\ \end{array}$
4. $\begin{array}{r} \$1.75 \\ \times\ 8 \\ \end{array}$
5. $\begin{array}{r} 682 \\ \times\ 9 \\ \end{array}$

6. $\begin{array}{r} 15 \\ \times 26 \\ \end{array}$
7. $\begin{array}{r} 97 \\ \times 48 \\ \end{array}$
8. $\begin{array}{r} 408 \\ \times\ 16 \\ \end{array}$
9. $\begin{array}{r} \$4.96 \\ \times\ 37 \\ \end{array}$
10. $\begin{array}{r} 539 \\ \times\ 68 \\ \end{array}$

Dividing 2-Digit Numbers

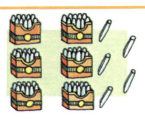

■ There are 6 boxes of chalk. There are 10 pieces of chalk in each box. There are 5 extra pieces.

In all, there are 65 pieces of chalk. The chalk is divided equally among 3 classes. How many pieces of chalk does each class get?

Each gets 2 boxes of 10.   **Each gets 1 extra piece.**   **There are 2 pieces left.**

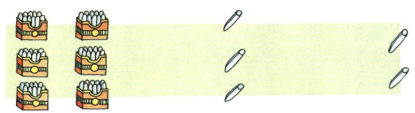

You can also divide to find the answer.

Divide: 3)65   Think: Are there enough tens to divide?
Yes, because 3 < 6. The quotient has two digits.

Find the tens.

Think: 3)6

$$
\begin{array}{r}
2 \\
3\overline{)6\;5} \\
6
\end{array}
$$
6 ← Multiply: 2 × 3
5 ← Subtract: 6 − 6
   Bring down the 5.

Find the ones.

Think: 3)5

$$
\begin{array}{r}
2\;1 \\
3\overline{)6\;5} \\
6 \\
5
\end{array}
$$
3 ← Multiply: 1 × 3
2 ← Subtract: 5 − 3
   Nothing to bring down.

Show the remainder.

$$
\begin{array}{r}
2\;1\;\text{R2} \\
3\overline{)6\;5} \\
6 \\
5 \\
3 \\
2
\end{array}
$$

Each class gets 21 pieces of chalk. There are 2 pieces of chalk left.

■ Sometimes there is a 0 in the ones place.

Divide: 4)43   Think: Are there enough tens to divide?
Yes, because 4 = 4. The quotient has two digits.

Find the tens.

$$
\begin{array}{r}
1 \\
4\overline{)4\;3} \\
4 \\
3
\end{array}
$$

Find the ones.

$$
\begin{array}{r}
1\;0 \\
4\overline{)4\;3} \\
4 \\
3 \\
0 \\
3
\end{array}
$$
3 ← There are not enough ones to divide.

Show the remainder.

$$
\begin{array}{r}
1\;0\;\text{R3} \\
4\overline{)4\;3} \\
4 \\
3 \\
0 \\
3
\end{array}
$$

Check.

$$
\begin{array}{r}
10 \\
\times\;4 \\
\hline
40 \\
+\;3 \\
\hline
43
\end{array}
$$ ✔

Try These

Divide. Check each answer.

1. $4\overline{)48}$ **2.** $3\overline{)96}$ **3.** $2\overline{)85}$ **4.** $6\overline{)67}$ **5.** $8\overline{)85}$ **6.** $4\overline{)80}$

7. $67 \div 3$ **8.** $82 \div 2$ **9.** $58 \div 5$ **10.** $62 \div 3$

Exercises

Divide.

1. $2\overline{)42}$ **2.** $2\overline{)68}$ **3.** $5\overline{)56}$ **4.** $7\overline{)79}$ **5.** $3\overline{)95}$ **6.** $3\overline{)38}$

7. $5\overline{)56}$ **8.** $8\overline{)89}$ **9.** $2\overline{)41}$ **10.** $7\overline{)75}$ **11.** $9\overline{)95}$ **12.** $3\overline{)62}$

13. $7\overline{)51}$ **14.** $2\overline{)66}$ **15.** $2\overline{)87}$ **16.** $6\overline{)64}$ **17.** $9\overline{)85}$ **18.** $8\overline{)88}$

19. $2\overline{)60}$ **20.** $4\overline{)43}$ **21.** $2\overline{)29}$ **22.** $6\overline{)36}$ **23.** $5\overline{)59}$ **24.** $7\overline{)75}$

25. $3\overline{)97}$ **26.** $2\overline{)29}$ **27.** $3\overline{)93}$ **28.** $2\overline{)49}$ **29.** $7\overline{)77}$ **30.** $3\overline{)98}$

31. $6\overline{)61}$ **32.** $4\overline{)37}$ **33.** $5\overline{)42}$ **34.** $5\overline{)40}$ **35.** $3\overline{)69}$ **36.** $8\overline{)80}$

37. $47 \div 4$ **38.** $66 \div 2$ **39.** $37 \div 3$ **40.** $39 \div 3$
41. $89 \div 4$ **42.** $50 \div 5$ **43.** $25 \div 3$ **44.** $34 \div 3$

Solve.

45. $(88 \div 8) \times 2$ **46.** $(93 - 27) \div 6$ **47.** $(12 + 24) \div 4$
48. $(49 + 17) \div 3$ **49.** $(48 \div 2) \times 9$ **50.** $(14 \times 6) \div 4$

Solve each problem.

51. There are 72 file folders in a shipment of school supplies. Each of the 7 teachers receives the same number of folders. How many folders does each teacher receive? How many folders are left?

52. Ms. Kwan's class received 26 sheets of poster board. Mrs. Emery's class received 18 sheets of poster board. How many more sheets of poster board did Ms. Kwan's class receive?

53. There are 18 red markers, 24 blue markers, and 20 black markers. There are 27 crayons. How many markers are there in all?

54. Mrs. Ames unpacks 44 packages of construction paper. There are 4 packages of each color. How many different colors are there?

Regrouping Tens

■ Mike and Tara have 42 chairs. They must put the same number of chairs in each of 3 classrooms. How many chairs should they put in each room?

To find how many chairs, divide 42 by 3.

Think: Are there enough tens to divide? Yes, because 3 < 4. The quotient has two digits.

Find the tens

$$3)\overline{4\ 2}$$
with 1 above, 3 below 4, 1 2

Find the ones.

$$3)\overline{4\ 2}$$
with 1 4 above, 3 below, 1 2, 1 2, 0

Regroup. 1 ten 2 ones is 12 ones.

They should put 14 chairs in each classroom.

■ Divide: 2)$\overline{57}$

Think: Are there enough tens to divide? Yes, because 2 < 5. The quotient has two digits.

Find the tens.

$$2)\overline{5\ 7}$$
2 above, 4 below 5, 1 7

Find the ones.

$$2)\overline{5\ 7}$$
2 8 above, 4 below, 1 7, 1 6, 1

Show the remainder.

$$2)\overline{5\ 7}$$
2 8 R1, 4, 1 7, 1 6, 1

Check.

$$
\begin{array}{r}
28 \\
\times\ \ 2 \\
\hline
56 \\
+\ \ 1 \\
\hline
57 \ ✔
\end{array}
$$

Try These

Divide. Check each answer.

1. 6)$\overline{71}$ **2.** 5)$\overline{62}$ **3.** 2)$\overline{36}$ **4.** 8)$\overline{97}$ **5.** 4)$\overline{92}$ **6.** 7)$\overline{88}$

7. 74 ÷ 3   **8.** 61 ÷ 4   **9.** 81 ÷ 5   **10.** 78 ÷ 4

Exercises

Divide.

1. $3\overline{)48}$ **2.** $2\overline{)34}$ **3.** $2\overline{)76}$ **4.** $3\overline{)72}$ **5.** $6\overline{)78}$ **6.** $5\overline{)65}$

7. $5\overline{)75}$ **8.** $7\overline{)91}$ **9.** $7\overline{)22}$ **10.** $4\overline{)76}$ **11.** $3\overline{)78}$ **12.** $4\overline{)64}$

13. $6\overline{)96}$ **14.** $9\overline{)98}$ **15.** $7\overline{)84}$ **16.** $5\overline{)80}$ **17.** $6\overline{)48}$ **18.** $6\overline{)98}$

19. $8\overline{)40}$ **20.** $5\overline{)89}$ **21.** $8\overline{)98}$ **22.** $3\overline{)39}$ **23.** $7\overline{)87}$ **24.** $4\overline{)89}$

25. $4\overline{)97}$ **26.** $8\overline{)97}$ **27.** $7\overline{)94}$ **28.** $5\overline{)99}$ **29.** $6\overline{)87}$ **30.** $3\overline{)59}$

31. $5\overline{)86}$ **32.** $4\overline{)38}$ **33.** $4\overline{)58}$ **34.** $7\overline{)99}$ **35.** $2\overline{)89}$ **36.** $8\overline{)95}$

37. $5\overline{)55}$ **38.** $6\overline{)69}$ **39.** $6\overline{)90}$ **40.** $8\overline{)99}$ **41.** $5\overline{)70}$ **42.** $7\overline{)97}$

43. $72 \div 4$ **44.** $66 \div 5$ **45.** $54 \div 2$ **46.** $72 \div 9$

47. $86 \div 6$ **48.** $27 \div 5$ **49.** $81 \div 3$ **50.** $78 \div 2$

Solve.

51. $(9 \times 6) \div 2$ **52.** $(18 + 6) \times 47$ **53.** $(21 \times 4) - 39$

54. $9 \times (84 \div 4)$ **55.** $(72 \div 8) \times 35$ **56.** $(27 + 19) \div 3$

57. $(107 + 36) - (24 + 58)$ **58.** $(24 - 19) \times (36 \div 2)$ **59.** $(93 \div 3) + (8 \times 74)$

Solve each problem.

60. Mike has 90 chairs. He wants to make 8 equal rows. How many chairs can he put in each row? Are there any chairs left?

61. Tara orders 4 cases of paper towels. There are 16 packages of paper towels in each case. How many packages of paper towels does Tara order?

62. A delivery of furniture arrives at the school. Mike unloads 8 tables for the library, 9 tables for the cafeteria, and 6 tables for the art room. How many tables does Mike unload?

63. Tara needs 60 new shelves for the library bookcases. There are 4 shelves in each carton. How many cartons should she order?

Factors and Common Factors

■ These multiplication sentences show the whole number factors of 6.

$$6 = 1 \times 6 \qquad 6 = 2 \times 3$$

1 is a factor of 6.   2 is a factor of 6.
6 is a factor of 6.   3 is a factor of 6.

The factors of 6 are 1, 2, 3, and 6.

To find the factors of 16:
    Write all the pairs of numbers
       that you can multiply to get 16.
    List the factors in order.
    List each factor only once.

$$16 = 1 \times 16$$
$$16 = 2 \times 8$$
$$16 = 4 \times 4$$

The factors of 16 are 1, 2, 4, 8, and 16.

■ To test for factors, divide. Then check the remainder.

Is 2 a factor of 38?

```
      19
  2) 38
     2
     ‾‾
     18
     18
     ‾‾
      0
```

The remainder is 0.
2 is a factor of 38.

Is 3 a factor of 38?

```
      12
  3) 38
     3
     ‾‾
      8
      6
     ‾‾
      2
```

The remainder is not 0.
3 is not a factor of 38.

■ Some numbers are factors of both 12 and 18.

The factors of 12 are 1, 2, 3, 4, 6, and 12.
The factors of 18 are 1, 2, 3, 6, 9, and 18.

1, 2, 3, and 6 are factors of both 12 and 18.

1, 2, 3, and 6 are **common factors** of 12 and 18.
6 is the **greatest common factor** of 12 and 18.

Try These

List the factors of each number.

1. 15   **2.** 9   **3.** 28   **4.** 5   **5.** 24

Solve.

6. List the factors of 10.
List the factors of 15.
List the common factors of 10 and 15.
What is the greatest common factor
of 10 and 15?

7. List the factors of 8.
List the factors of 12.
List the common factors of 8 and 12.
What is the greatest common factor
of 8 and 12?

Exercises

Solve.

1. List the factors of 18.
List the factors of 30.
List the common factors of 18 and 30.
What is the greatest common factor
of 18 and 30?

2. List the factors of 9.
List the factors of 15.
List the common factors of 9 and 15.
What is the greatest common factor
of 9 and 15?

Find the common factors.

3. 9 and 18   **4.** 7 and 4   **5.** 10 and 12   **6.** 14 and 21
7. 15 and 25   **8.** 24 and 15   **9.** 27 and 36   **10.** 16 and 40

Find the greatest common factor.

11. 6 and 12   **12.** 16 and 20   **13.** 3 and 5   **14.** 20 and 30
15. 18 and 27   **16.** 24 and 18   ★ **17.** 8, 12, and 20   ★ **18.** 6, 10, and 12

THINK AND TRY

USING LOGICAL REASONING

Use your list of factors to answer each question.

1. Do all numbers have an even number of factors?

2. If a number has an odd number of factors, what can
you say about that number?

3. Is there a number that has just *one* factor?

Problem Solving: Applications

READ
PLAN
DO
CHECK

INTERPRETING THE REMAINDER

When you solve a division problem,
be sure your answer is reasonable.

■ Loretta Miller owns a pet store. She
has 6 puppies for sale. There are 22
dog bones in the stockroom. How
many dog bones can each puppy
have?

$$\begin{array}{r} 3 \\ 6\overline{)22} \\ 18 \\ \hline 4 \end{array}$$

Loretta wants each puppy to
have the same number of bones.
Do not count the remainder.

Each puppy can have 3 dog bones.

■ Loretta receives a shipment of 22 canaries. She
puts 6 canaries in each cage. How many cages
does Loretta need?

$$\begin{array}{r} 3 \\ 6\overline{)22} \\ 18 \\ \hline 4 \end{array}$$

Loretta needs 3 cages plus 1 more
cage for the 4 remaining canaries.

Loretta needs 4 cages.

Try These

Solve each problem.

1. A pet supply company gives
Loretta 15 free posters. She gives
an equal number to each of her 4
employees. How many posters
should she give each employee?

2. Loretta receives a shipment of 11
kittens. She puts 3 kittens in each
cage. How many cages does
Loretta need?

3. One tank will hold 8 turtles. There
are 30 turtles. How many tanks are
needed?

4. Loretta has $75 to buy new feeding
trays. Each tray costs $4. How
many feeding trays can she buy?

Exercises

Solve each problem.

1. A salesperson was asked to box up 80 dog collars. 6 collars fit into each box. How many boxes should the salesperson use?

2. Loretta ordered 6 new cages. Each cage cost $46.80. She also ordered a water bowl for $48. How much did the order total?

3. The pet store had 32 scratching posts for cats. All but 9 were sold. How many posts were sold?

4. There is $50 budgeted for dog shampoo. Each bottle costs $3. How many bottles can be ordered?

5. Each shelf of a standing book rack holds 6 pet care books. There are 35 books to display. How many shelves are needed?

6. On Saturday, pet sales totaled $945.90, and supply sales totaled $414.85. What were the total sales for Saturday?

7. Bruce earns $4.15 each hour working at the pet store. One week he worked 24 hours. How much did he earn?

8. A customer purchases a cat for $135, a book for $9.75, and a feeding dish for $3.49. How much change should the customer receive from $160?

9. Judy bought a 50-ounce bag of dry cat food. She gives her cat 4 ounces of dry food each day. How many daily feedings will Judy get from a bag of food?

10. The pet store has toys for cats, dogs, and birds. There are 42 kinds of toys. There are 16 kinds for cats and 18 for dogs. How many kinds are there for birds?

11. A 50-gallon aquarium contains 86 goldfish. A 25-gallon aquarium contains 39 goldfish. How many goldfish are there altogether?

★ 12. A shipment of 24 bird cages and 18 fish tanks arrived. Each bird cage cost $8.75. Each fish tank cost $8.95. How much did this shipment cost?

★ 13. Loretta received a shipment of pet food. There were 24 cases of cans of cat food and 40 cases of cans of dog food. There are 24 cans in each case. How many cans of pet food were in the shipment?

Problem Solving: Strategies

GUESSING AND CHECKING

A farmer has cows and chickens. Altogether his animals have 40 legs. He has 2 more chickens than cows. How many cows and chickens does he have?

Make a guess.
Check.

Suppose the farmer has 1 cow.
1 cow has 4 legs.

$$40 \quad - \quad 4 \quad = 36$$

legs
altogether

legs of
cows

Chickens have 2 legs.

$$36 \div 2 = 18$$

1 cow
18 chickens

The difference between cows and chickens is too large.

Guess more cows.
Check.

Suppose the farmer has 8 cows.
8 cows have 32 legs.

$$40 - 32 = 8$$

$$8 \div 2 = 4$$

He would have 4 chickens.

8 cows
4 chickens

But the farmer is supposed to have more chickens than cows. 8 cows is too many.

Guess.
Check.

Suppose the farmer has 6 cows.
6 cows have 24 legs.

$$40 - 24 = 16$$

$$16 \div 2 = 8$$

He would have 8 chickens.

6 cows
8 chickens

There are 2 more chickens than cows.

The farmer has 6 cows and 8 chickens.

Using the Strategy

Solve each problem.

1. Mary has $.45. She has three coins. What are the coins?

2. Joe has $.50. He has eight coins. What are the coins?

3. What is the fewest number of coins that have a total value of $.70? Only one coin is a quarter.

4. Peggy has $1.19 in coins. Yet she cannot make change of $1. What coins does Peggy have?

5. Two numbers have a sum of 21 and a difference of 9. What are the numbers?

6. Two numbers have a product of 68 and a sum of 21. What are the numbers?

7. Two numbers have a product of 54 and a quotient of 6. What are the numbers?

8. Two numbers have a sum of 42 and a quotient of 6. What are the numbers?

 ACTIVITY

CLASSIFYING

When you divide a number by 5, you may have a remainder of 0, 1, 2, 3, or 4.

$$
\begin{array}{r} 7 \\ 5)\overline{35} \\ 35 \\ \hline 0 \end{array}
\quad
\begin{array}{r} 7 \\ 5)\overline{36} \\ 35 \\ \hline 1 \end{array}
\quad
\begin{array}{r} 7 \\ 5)\overline{37} \\ 35 \\ \hline 2 \end{array}
\quad
\begin{array}{r} 7 \\ 5)\overline{38} \\ 35 \\ \hline 3 \end{array}
\quad
\begin{array}{r} 7 \\ 5)\overline{39} \\ 35 \\ \hline 4 \end{array}
\quad
\begin{array}{r} 8 \\ 5)\overline{42} \\ 40 \\ \hline 2 \end{array}
$$

When divided by 5, 42 has the same remainder as 37. 42 is in the same remainder class as 37 for divisor 5.

Find two other numbers that are in the same remainder class as the numbers below when divided by 5.

1. 35 2. 36 3. 37 4. 38 5. 29 6. 57

7. What remainders are possible when the divisor is 7?

To which remainder class for divisor 7 does each of these numbers belong?

8. 45 9. 64 10. 40 11. 48 12. 35 13. 142

Dividing 3-Digit Numbers

■ A class has 2 booths for the school carnival. The class buys 279 prizes. Each booth will share the prizes equally. How many prizes should each booth get? Are there any prizes left?

Divide 279 by 2 to find the answer.

Think: Are there enough hundreds to divide? Yes, because 2 = 2. The quotient has three digits.

Find the hundreds.

```
  1 _ _
2)2 7 9
  2
  7
```

Find the tens.

```
  1 3 _
2)2 7 9
  2
  7
  6
  1 9
```

Find the ones. Show the remainder.

```
  1 3 9 R1
2)2 7 9
  2
  7
  6
  1 9
  1 8
    1
```

Each booth should get 139 prizes.
There is 1 prize left.

■ Sometimes there are not enough hundreds in the dividend to divide. Then there are no hundreds in the quotient.

Divide: 3)146

Think: Are there enough hundreds to divide? No, because 3 > 1.
Are there enough tens to divide? Yes, because 3 < 14.
The quotient has two digits.

Find the tens.

```
    4 _
3)1 4 6
  1 2
    2 6
```

Find the ones. Show the remainder.

```
    4 8 R2
3)1 4 6
  1 2
    2 6
    2 4
      2
```

Check.

```
    48
  × 3
   144
 +   2
   146 ✔
```

Try These

Divide. Check each answer.

1. 6)684   **2.** 3)156   **3.** 4)864   **4.** 2)174   **5.** 3)485   **6.** 3)639

7. 484 ÷ 4   **8.** 675 ÷ 5   **9.** 325 ÷ 6   **10.** 215 ÷ 3

Exercises

Divide.

1. 3)246   **2.** 3)693   **3.** 2)264   **4.** 2)166   **5.** 4)488   **6.** 3)196

7. 2)844   **8.** 4)116   **9.** 3)396   **10.** 4)484   **11.** 9)99   **12.** 6)549

13. 4)324   **14.** 7)798   **15.** 7)506   **16.** 4)936   **17.** 3)159   **18.** 4)152

19. 6)739   **20.** 2)59   **21.** 5)687   **22.** 6)426   **23.** 7)854   **24.** 8)985

25. 7)948   **26.** 4)166   **27.** 8)988   **28.** 6)978   **29.** 6)91   **30.** 5)976

31. 6)247   **32.** 7)800   **33.** 9)162   **34.** 6)803   **35.** 2)136   **36.** 5)916

37. 378 ÷ 5   **38.** 353 ÷ 8   **39.** 700 ÷ 8   **40.** 329 ÷ 4

41. 654 ÷ 7   **42.** 276 ÷ 4   **43.** 71 ÷ 6   **44.** 175 ÷ 2

45. 90 ÷ 9   **46.** 848 ÷ 4   **47.** 683 ÷ 3   **48.** 626 ÷ 2

Solve each problem.

49. There are 161 banners for the school carnival. Each class gets the same number of banners. There are 7 classes. How many banners does each class get?

50. The school band gave two concerts on the carnival grounds. 168 people attended the morning concert. 97 people attended the afternoon concert. How many people attended the concerts in all?

★ **51.** You are waiting in line for the Loop-a-Doop ride at the carnival. There are 55 people ahead of you. Every 4 minutes, 8 people are put into a car. The first group of 8 starts right now! How long will you have to wait? Check by completing the table.

Number of People	Elapsed Time (in minutes)
8	0
16	4
24	8

Zeros in the Quotient

■ Sometimes a quotient has a 0 in the tens place.

Divide: 3)627   Think: Are there enough hundreds to divide? Yes, because 3 < 6. The quotient has three digits.

Find the hundreds.

```
  2 _ _
3)6 2 7
  6
  ‾
  2
```

Find the tens.

```
  2 0 _
3)6 2 7
  6
  ‾
  2  ← ┌There are
  0    │not enough
  ‾    │tens to
  2 7  └divide.
```

Find the ones.

```
  2 0 9
3)6 2 7
  6
  ‾
  2
  0
  ‾
  2 7
  2 7
  ‾‾‾
    0
```

■ Sometimes a quotient has a 0 in the ones place.

Divide: 6)245   Think: Are there enough hundreds to divide? No, because 6 > 2. Are there enough tens to divide? Yes, because 6 < 24. The quotient has two digits.

Find the tens.

```
  4 _
6)2 4 5
  2 4
  ‾‾‾
    5
```

**Find the ones.
Show the remainder.**

```
  4 0 R5
6)2 4 5
  2 4
  ‾‾‾
    5  ← ┌There are
    0    │not enough
    ‾    └ones to divide.
    5
```

■ Sometimes a quotient has more than one 0.

Divide: 5)502

```
  1 0 0 R2
5)5 0 2
  5
  ‾
  0
  0
  ‾
  2
  0
  ‾
  2
```

Check.

```
    1 0 0
  ×     5
  ‾‾‾‾‾‾‾
    5 0 0
  +     2
  ‾‾‾‾‾‾‾
    5 0 2 ✔
```

Try These

Divide. Check each answer.

1. 3)632   2. 5)302   3. 6)361   4. 8)404   5. 6)300   6. 3)917

7. 431 ÷ 4   8. 652 ÷ 5   9. 601 ÷ 3   10. 801 ÷ 4

Exercises

Divide.

1. 2)414   2. 3)309   3. 4)420   4. 5)525   5. 6)636   6. 4)838

7. 3)62   8. 4)830   9. 7)842   10. 6)650   11. 5)321   12. 5)545

13. 7)709   14. 6)49   15. 3)242   16. 9)909   17. 8)969   18. 6)634

19. 9)830   20. 8)966   21. 8)904   22. 7)52   23. 7)714   24. 4)603

25. 4)546   26. 4)819   27. 5)510   28. 3)601   29. 3)147   30. 8)805

31. 8)960   32. 8)826   33. 3)149   34. 7)708   35. 4)923   36. 3)91

37. 807 ÷ 8   38. 630 ÷ 3   39. 827 ÷ 4   40. 700 ÷ 8
41. 889 ÷ 7   42. 163 ÷ 9   43. 81 ÷ 2   44. 624 ÷ 2

Solve each problem.

45. A vegetable casserole contains 810 calories. It contains 5 servings. How many calories are in each serving?

46. One apple contains 70 calories. One banana contains 87 calories. How many calories are there in 12 apples?

47. One package of cheese slices contains 840 calories. There are 8 slices in the package. How many calories are there in each slice?

48. One serving of beef liver contains 250 calories. One serving of calves liver contains 279 calories. How many more calories does the calves liver contain?

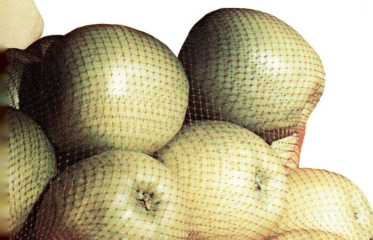

Dividing Greater Numbers

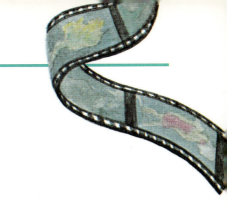

■ A photographic company has 5,734 cameras left in their warehouse. The cameras are divided equally among 4 stores. How many cameras does each store receive? How many cameras are left?

Divide 5,734 by 4 to find the answer.

Think: Are there enough thousands to divide? Yes, 4 < 5. The quotient has four digits.

Find the thousands.

```
  1 _ _ _
4)5,7 3 4
  4
  ‾‾
  1 7
```

Find the hundreds.

```
  1 4 _ _
4)5,7 3 4
  4
  ‾‾
  1 7
  1 6
  ‾‾‾
    1 3
```

Find the tens.

```
  1 4 3 _
4)5,7 3 4
  4
  ‾‾
  1 7
  1 6
  ‾‾‾
    1 3
    1 2
    ‾‾‾
      1 4
```

Find the ones. Show the remainder.

```
  1,4 3 3 R2
4)5,7 3 4
  4
  ‾‾
  1 7
  1 6
  ‾‾‾
    1 3
    1 2
    ‾‾‾
      1 4
      1 2
      ‾‾‾
        2
```

Each store receives 1,433 cameras. There are 2 cameras left.

■ You divide money the same way you divide whole numbers.

Divide: 8)$65.12

```
      8 1 4
8)6,5 1 2
  6 4
  ‾‾‾
    1 1
      8
    ‾‾‾
      3 2
      3 2
      ‾‾‾
        0
```

```
    $ 8.1 4
8)$6 5.1 2
  6 4
  ‾‾‾
    1 1
      8
    ‾‾‾
      3 2
      3 2
      ‾‾‾
        0
```

Remember: Write the $ and the . in the answer.

Try These

Divide. Check each answer.

1. $4\overline{)1{,}232}$ 2. $3\overline{)\$18.30}$ 3. $5\overline{)5{,}021}$ 4. $6\overline{)4{,}328}$ 5. $4\overline{)1{,}585}$

6. $1{,}870 \div 4$ 7. $\$25.40 \div 5$ 8. $2{,}480 \div 2$

Exercises

Divide.

1. $7\overline{)7{,}714}$ 2. $8\overline{)\$98.72}$ 3. $6\overline{)6{,}318}$ 4. $9\overline{)\$99.81}$ 5. $5\overline{)\$65.05}$

6. $3\overline{)9{,}324}$ 7. $7\overline{)7{,}035}$ 8. $2\overline{)90}$ 9. $2\overline{)4{,}653}$ 10. $3\overline{)5{,}406}$

11. $7\overline{)8{,}136}$ 12. $9\overline{)\$96.84}$ 13. $5\overline{)6{,}316}$ 14. $7\overline{)802}$ 15. $3\overline{)1{,}269}$

16. $7\overline{)\$35.98}$ 17. $3\overline{)850}$ 18. $5\overline{)\$25.95}$ 19. $8\overline{)6{,}496}$ 20. $6\overline{)300}$

21. $2\overline{)\$13.76}$ 22. $5\overline{)1{,}735}$ 23. $4\overline{)\$25.76}$ 24. $3\overline{)807}$ 25. $3\overline{)2{,}325}$

26. $3\overline{)204}$ 27. $6\overline{)1{,}951}$ 28. $7\overline{)2{,}104}$ 29. $8\overline{)1{,}682}$ 30. $5\overline{)1{,}356}$

31. $2{,}832 \div 2$ 32. $6{,}314 \div 3$ 33. $\$8.54 \div 7$
34. $\$23.08 \div 2$ 35. $1{,}842 \div 4$ 36. $\$16.14 \div 3$

Solve.

37. $(16 \times 9) \div 3$ 38. $9 \times (144 \div 3)$ 39. $(175 - 69) \div 2$
40. $(37 \times 25) \div 4$ 41. $(64 \times 18) \div 6$ 42. $6 \times (500 \div 2)$
43. $(86 \div 2) \times 5$ 44. $(275 + 886) \div 7$ 45. $(1{,}266 - 798) \div 3$

Copy and complete. Put in the signs that make each sentence true.

46. $(26 \blacksquare 53) \blacksquare 8 = 632$ 47. $(45 \blacksquare 9) \blacksquare 3 = 135$ 48. $(164 \blacksquare 2) \blacksquare 25 = 2{,}050$
49. $6 \blacksquare (18 \blacksquare 514) = 3{,}192$ 50. $(275 \blacksquare 189) \blacksquare 2 = 928$ 51. $8 \blacksquare (500 \blacksquare 4) = 133$
52. $(600 \blacksquare 175) \blacksquare 5 = 85$ 53. $9 \blacksquare (357 \blacksquare 186) = 1{,}539$ 54. $(406 \blacksquare 2) \blacksquare 795 = 998$

Solve each problem. You may choose paper and pencil or a calculator.

55. A customer spent $47.34 to have 6 rolls of film developed. How much did it cost for each roll of film?

★ 56. A store orders 8 cartons of film. There are 24 rolls of film in each carton. Each roll costs $2.86. What is the cost of this order?

Averages

■ Isabel runs an art gallery. The gallery is open 4 days a week. Each day, the number of people entering the gallery is counted. What was the **average** attendance at the art gallery each day?

Day	Attendance
Thursday	98
Friday	117
Saturday	247
Sunday	362

Add the attendance for each day.

```
  2 2
   98
  117
  247
+ 362
  824
```

Then divide the sum by the number of days, 4.

```
     206
  4)824
     8
     ‾
     2
     0
     ‾
     24
     24
     ‾‾
      0
```

The average daily attendance at the art gallery was 206 people.

■ Sometimes the sum is given.

The attendance at the art gallery for the past 4 weeks was 3,408 people. What was the average weekly attendance?

To find the weekly attendance, divide the total attendance by the number of weeks.

```
      852
  4)3,408
    3 2
    ‾‾
     20
     20
     ‾‾
      8
      8
      ‾
      0
```

The average weekly attendance was 852 people.

Try These

Find the average.

1. 54, 65, 70
2. 26, 43, 45
3. 8, 12, 10, 18
4. 12, 15, 22, 35
5. 105, 110, 124
6. 290, 292, 296, 294

Exercises

Find the average.

1. 36, 41, 46
2. 22, 30, 31, 35, 37
3. 95, 105, 106
4. 116, 118, 120
5. 336, 346, 350, 356
6. 152, 148, 131, 162, 122
7. 190, 193, 195, 197, 200
8. 37, 141, 30, 120, 62

Solve each problem. You may choose paper and pencil or a calculator.

9. Tours of the art gallery are available. In 4 weeks, 348 people paid for the tour. What was the average number of people who took the tour each week?

10. Isabel pays $86.36 to have 4 posters printed. She will sell the posters for $45 each. What is the average amount she pays for each poster?

11. Mr. Hadley represented the gallery at a convention. He drove 306 miles on 9 gallons of gas. What was the average number of miles per gallon?

12. Isabel attended an auction. She drove 182 miles on 7 gallons of gas. What was the average number of miles per gallon?

13. Isabel has an expense account. She spent $12.86 on Monday, $41.50 on Thursday, and $37.89 on Sunday. What is the average amount of her expenses?

14. Michelle worked as Isabel's assistant during her college break. She worked for 6 weeks. She earned $2,250. What were Michelle's average weekly earnings?

15. The gallery has three exhibit areas. There are 24 paintings in area A. There are 32 paintings in area B and 40 paintings in area C. What is the average number of paintings found in an exhibit area?

★ 16. Mr. Hadley mailed out membership cards. The first week he mailed out 110 cards. The second week he mailed out 96 cards. The third week he mailed out 88 cards. How many cards must he mail out the fourth week to have mailed an average of 100 cards per week?

Problem Solving: Applications

NOT ENOUGH INFORMATION

In some problems, there is not enough information. You cannot solve the problem because information is missing.

The Woodhaven School is having a field day. The students in the fifth grade are forming 5 groups for the games. How many students are in each group?

There are 5 groups of students. How many students in each group?

To solve the problem, you need to know how many students are in the fifth grade. This information is missing.

Missing information: There are 115 students in the fifth grade.

Divide to find how many students are in each group.

$$
\begin{array}{r}
23 \\
5{\overline{\smash{\big)}\,115}} \\
\underline{10} \\
15 \\
\underline{15} \\
0
\end{array}
$$

There are 23 students in each group.

Try These

If information is missing, tell what you need to know. If all the information is given, solve the problem.

1. Mr. Browne's class spends 30 minutes each day organizing the picnic. How many minutes are spent organizing the picnic?

2. There are 21 teachers. All but 6 teachers were in charge of a field day event. How many teachers were in charge of an event?

Exercises

If information is missing, tell what you need to know. If all the information is given, solve the problem.

1. Mrs. Rogers bought 20 packages of hamburger rolls for the picnic. There are 8 rolls in each package. How many rolls did she buy?

2. The music teacher was in charge of taking pictures at field day. He had 4 rolls of film. How many pictures could he take?

3. Each class stays at each field day event for 20 minutes. How long does it take for all the classes to participate in all 6 events?

4. The school is buying a megaphone to be used during field day. The students have saved $18.75. How much more do they need?

5. Each picnic table can seat 8 students. How many tables are needed to seat 75 students at the same time?

6. All but 9 of the students in Mr. Ryan's class are on the clean-up committee. How many students are on the clean-up committee?

7. Everett won first place in the softball throw. He threw the ball 2 meters farther than the student who finished in second place. The third-place winner threw the ball 12 meters. How far did Everett throw the softball?

8. The students sit in the auditorium to receive their field day awards. There are 3 sections in the auditorium. The first section has 165 seats. The second section has 48 seats. How many students can sit in the auditorium?

9. The Woodhaven School spent $356.19 on new equipment for field day. They also spent $75.14 on food. How much did the Woodhaven School spend in all?

10. A bag of apples contains about 9 apples. There are 356 students at the field day. How many bags of apples are needed?

11. There are 643 students in the school. 115 students are in the fifth grade. How many students are not in the fifth grade?

★ 12. Diane and Sue sold tickets to guests. Each ticket cost $1.50. Diane sold 5 more tickets than Sue sold. How much money did Diane collect in all?

Divide. (pp. 104–105, 108–113)

1. $8\overline{)56}$ 2. $4\overline{)32}$ 3. $9\overline{)45}$ 4. $1\overline{)6}$ 5. $4\overline{)0}$

6. $9\overline{)9}$ 7. $8\overline{)64}$ 8. $3\overline{)27}$ 9. $2\overline{)12}$ 10. $5\overline{)40}$

11. $8\overline{)49}$ 12. $6\overline{)37}$ 13. $9\overline{)75}$ 14. $2\overline{)11}$ 15. $3\overline{)13}$

16. $4\overline{)38}$ 17. $7\overline{)51}$ 18. $5\overline{)27}$ 19. $8\overline{)52}$ 20. $9\overline{)55}$

21. $3\overline{)36}$ 22. $4\overline{)48}$ 23. $2\overline{)84}$ 24. $3\overline{)38}$ 25. $4\overline{)82}$

26. $4\overline{)72}$ 27. $5\overline{)73}$ 28. $7\overline{)72}$ 29. $8\overline{)91}$ 30. $2\overline{)76}$

31. $8\overline{)97}$ 32. $6\overline{)79}$ 33. $4\overline{)89}$ 34. $7\overline{)99}$ 35. $5\overline{)64}$

36. $12 \div 3$ 37. $42 \div 6$ 38. $81 \div 9$
39. $26 \div 4$ 40. $42 \div 5$ 41. $50 \div 6$
42. $80 \div 4$ 43. $71 \div 2$ 44. $97 \div 5$

List the factors of each number. (pp. 114–115)

45. 21   46. 33   47. 30   48. 22

Find the greatest common factor. (pp. 114–115)

49. 6 and 9   50. 12 and 32   51. 4 and 10
52. 5 and 20   53. 8 and 28   54. 18 and 24

Divide. (pp. 120–125)

55. $7\overline{)850}$ 56. $3\overline{)363}$ 57. $4\overline{)335}$ 58. $6\overline{)126}$ 59. $5\overline{)697}$

60. $9\overline{)878}$ 61. $8\overline{)965}$ 62. $4\overline{)412}$ 63. $7\overline{)700}$ 64. $5\overline{)509}$

65. $3\overline{)3,210}$ 66. $9\overline{)\$92.70}$ 67. $5\overline{)6,316}$ 68. $2\overline{)2,407}$ 69. $6\overline{)7,991}$

70. $842 \div 2$ 71. $987 \div 7$ 72. $503 \div 5$
73. $246 \div 6$ 74. $805 \div 5$ 75. $691 \div 6$
76. $3,263 \div 8$ 77. $2,596 \div 8$ 78. $\$17.65 \div 5$

Find the average. (pp. 126–127)

79. 6, 8, 4

80. 26, 32, 35

81. 42, 45, 51

82. 118, 110, 98, 86

83. 125, 130, 120, 145

84. 215, 186, 197, 204, 198

85. 206, 315, 284, 299

86. 612, 593, 678, 704, 648

Solve each problem. If information is missing, tell what you need to know. (pp. 104–129)

87. Jan made 17 cups of peach yogurt. He shared them equally with 4 friends. How many cups does each person get? How many cups are left?

88. There are 63 people coming to a party. For each person, 2 drinks are needed. There are 6 drinks in each carton. How many cartons are needed?

89. There are 39 students going on a trip. Each car holds 5 students. How many cars are needed in all?

90. In 3 punts, Andy kicked a football 27 yards, 40 yards, and 32 yards. Find the average distance the football was kicked.

91. There are tickets to be sold by 4 classes. Each class receives the same number of tickets. How many tickets does each class get?

92. Joan and Sue work for 2 hours. They earn $8.06. They want to share the money equally. How much should each one get?

93. There are 630 chairs. Mr. Haynes wants to make 3 sections with the same number of chairs in each section. How many chairs should he put in each section?

94. Beth bought 525 sheets of notebook paper. It came in 3 packages. Each package held the same number of sheets. How many sheets were in each package?

95. In a long-jump contest, Kathy made jumps of 15 feet, 12 feet, and 9 feet. Find the average distance Kathy jumped.

96. A drugstore receives a shipment of shampoo. There are 16 cartons in the shipment. How many bottles of shampoo are in the shipment?

97. Melissa shapes clay into pottery. She has 35 pounds of clay. She uses 3 pounds of clay to make each bowl. How many bowls can Melissa make with the clay?

98. Linda takes skating lessons. She skates 2 days each week for 9 weeks. The total cost of the lessons is $198. How much do the lessons cost each week?

COMPUTERS AND PROBLEM SOLVING

■ Programmers call words or groups of words **strings**.

String variables are used to store strings. Any letter followed by a $ is a string variable. Use quotation marks to tell the computer where the string begins and ends. For example:

LET M$= "OUR CLASS"

If you ran a program with the instruction shown at the right, the computer would assign the value of 8 to the variable A.

```
] NEW
] 10 LET A = 8
```

What would happen if you ran a program with this instruction?

```
] NEW
] 10 LET A = "ROW"
```

The computer would stop and print this error message.

```
? TYPE MISMATCH
  ERROR IN 10
] ▓
```

How would you assign the string ROW to variable A?

```
] NEW
] 10 LET A$ = "ROW"
```

Solve each problem.

1. What would be the result of running this program?

```
NEW
10   LET A$="ROW"
20   PRINT A$
30   PRINT A$
40   PRINT A$
50   PRINT "YOUR BOAT"
60   PRINT "GENTLY DOWN THE STREAM . . ."
70   END
```

2. Move the END statement from line 70 to 130. Use lines 70 through 120 to write the statements that will make the computer print out:

```
MERRILY
MERRILY
MERRILY
MERRILY
LIFE IS BUT A DREAM.
```

3. Study the next program. Decide what the output will look like if you answer the computer's requests for inputs with 20 and 4.

```
NEW
10   LET Q$="THE QUOTIENT IS"
20   INPUT E
30   INPUT F
40   PRINT Q$
50   PRINT E/F
60   GOTO 20
70   END
```

4. Add 15 N$="YOUR NAME" to the program above. Use your name inside the quotation marks. Then add 55 PRINT N$ to the program. What will the program's output look like when it is run?

ENRICHMENT

DIVISIBILITY

One number **is divisible by** another if the remainder is 0.

$$3\overline{)9}$$
$$\underline{9}$$
$$0$$
(quotient 3)

$$2\overline{)9}$$
$$\underline{8}$$
$$1$$
(quotient 4 R1)

The remainder is 0.
9 is divisible by 3.

The remainder is not 0.
9 is not divisible by 2.

These are rules for divisibility.

DIVISIBILITY BY 2

A number is divisible by 2 if the ones digit is 0, 2, 4, 6, or 8.
These numbers are divisible by 2: 10, 32, 44, 56, 68.
All even numbers are divisible by 2.

DIVISIBILITY BY 5

A number is divisible by 5 if the ones digit is 0 or 5.
These numbers are divisible by 5: 30, 45, 60, 85.

DIVISIBILITY BY 10

A number is divisible by 10 if the ones digit is 0.
These numbers are divisible by 10: 50, 90, 170, 210.

Is the first number divisible by the second number?
Write *yes* or *no*.

1. 14, 7
2. 16, 3
3. 64, 4
4. 98, 9
5. 84, 7
6. 42, 2
7. 23, 2
8. 0, 5
9. 80, 10
10. 31, 5
11. 50, 2
12. 50, 5
13. 35, 10
14. 100, 10
15. 95, 5

Solve.

16. List the first 12 multiples of 10. Which of the numbers are divisible by both 2 and 5?

17. Find this 3-digit number. All three digits are the same. It can be divided (without a remainder) by 2, by 3, by 4, by 6, and by 8. What number is it?

Use 96,075,184,232. Write the digit that is in each place.

1. ten-thousands place

2. hundred-millions place

3. billions place

4. tens place

Write >, <, or =.

5. 467 ■ 476

6. 509 ■ 905

7. 4,216 ■ 4,126

8. 527,180 ■ 527,180

9. 2,571,497 ■ 2,517,497

10. 79,357 ■ 79,537

Round each number.

11. 821 to the nearest ten

12. 2,759 to the nearest hundred

13. 86,196 to the nearest thousand

14. 74,243,952 to the nearest million

Add or subtract.

15. 75	**16.** 227	**17.** 429	**18.** $35.12	**19.** 8,014
+86	− 89	−171	− 28.99	3,976
				+4,787

Multiply.

20. 31	**21.** 216	**22.** 90	**23.** 354	**24.** $15.95
× 3	× 4	×26	× 49	× 143

Estimate each answer.

25. 4,217	**26.** 507	**27.** 58	**28.** 87	**29.** 872
+1,975	− 189	× 5	×31	× 58

Solve each problem.

30. On Saturday, 325 adults paid $3.75 each to see the movie. 108 children went to see the movie. How many people saw the movie that day?

31. Janet baby-sat for 12 hours this week. She earned $2.50 each hour. How much did she make for the week?

SKILLS CHECK

Choose the correct answer.

1. In 94,071,862,135, which number is in the ten-billions place?

   a. 3
   b. 6
   c. 7
   d. 9

2. What is 1,347 rounded to the nearest hundred?

   a. 1,000
   b. 1,300
   c. 1,350
   d. 1,400

3. 35 + 18

   a. 43
   b. 44
   c. 52
   d. 53

4.
$$\begin{array}{r} 728 \\ +147 \\ \hline \end{array}$$

   a. 865
   b. 875
   c. 975
   d. NG

5.
$$\begin{array}{r} 76 \\ -18 \\ \hline \end{array}$$

   a. 52
   b. 58
   c. 62
   d. 68

6.
$$\begin{array}{r} 147 \\ \times\ 56 \\ \hline \end{array}$$

   a. 7,872
   b. 8,232
   c. 8,464
   d. NG

7. 6 × 30

   a. 5
   b. 150
   c. 180
   d. 1,800

8. $5 − $1.79

   a. $3.31
   b. $4.21
   c. $6.79
   d. NG

9. $7\overline{)155}$

   a. 20
   b. 21 R5
   c. 22 R1
   d. NG

10. Sam has 175 stamps. He buys 50 more stamps. How many stamps does he have altogether?

   a. 125 stamps
   b. 225 stamps
   c. 575 stamps
   d. NG

11. The travel budget for the movie was $350,000. So far, $218,560 has been spent. How much money is left?

   a. $101,440
   b. $121,650
   c. $130,540
   d. $131,440

12. Fred earns $4.80 each hour. He works for 22 hours. How much does he earn?

   a. $98.40
   b. $105.60
   c. $110.40
   d. $108.16

5

DIVISION BY 2-DIGIT NUMBERS

Dividing by Multiples of 10

■ Linda Flores unpacks new books for a bookstore display. There are 374 books. Each display rack holds 30 books. How many racks does she fill? How many books are left?

Divide 374 by 30 to find the answer.

Think: There are not enough hundreds to divide because 30 > 3.
The quotient has two digits.

Find the tens.

Think: 30)‾37‾

```
        1 _
30)3 7 4
   3 0
   7 4
```

Find the ones.

Think: 30)‾74‾

```
      1 2 R14
30)3 7 4
   3 0
   7 4
   6 0
   1 4
```

Check.

```
     1 2
   ×3 0
   3 6 0
 +  1 4
   3 7 4 ✔
```

Linda fills 12 racks. There are 14 books left.

■ Divide: 20)‾6,125‾

Think: There are not enough thousands to divide because 20 > 6.
The quotient has three digits.

Find the hundreds.

```
      3 _ _
20)6,1 2 5
   6 0
   1 2
```

Find the tens.

```
       3 0 _
20)6,1 2 5
   6 0
   1 2      ← There are not
    0         enough tens
  1 2 5       to divide.
```

Find the ones.

```
        3 0 6 R5
20)6,1 2 5
   6 0
   1 2
    0
  1 2 5
  1 2 0
      5
```

138   Chapter 5

Try These

Divide. Check each answer.

1. $20\overline{)40}$ **2.** $40\overline{)959}$ **3.** $30\overline{)4,507}$ **4.** $50\overline{)3,646}$ **5.** $60\overline{)237}$

6. $84 \div 10$ **7.** $479 \div 60$ **8.** $2,496 \div 80$

Exercises

Divide.

1. $30\overline{)90}$ **2.** $20\overline{)709}$ **3.** $30\overline{)807}$ **4.** $40\overline{)856}$ **5.** $30\overline{)675}$

6. $30\overline{)904}$ **7.** $50\overline{)150}$ **8.** $20\overline{)648}$ **9.** $6\overline{)914}$ **10.** $50\overline{)967}$

11. $40\overline{)619}$ **12.** $40\overline{)1,306}$ **13.** $40\overline{)83}$ **14.** $20\overline{)1,814}$ **15.** $70\overline{)9,549}$

16. $40\overline{)1,827}$ **17.** $8\overline{)1,675}$ **18.** $70\overline{)5,008}$ **19.** $60\overline{)5,909}$ **20.** $90\overline{)8,949}$

21. $80\overline{)5,264}$ **22.** $40\overline{)2,468}$ **23.** $50\overline{)2,054}$ **24.** $70\overline{)6,479}$ **25.** $30\overline{)7,864}$

26. $92 \div 30$ **27.** $820 \div 20$ **28.** $984 \div 70$

29. $271 \div 60$ **30.** $1,160 \div 50$ **31.** $9,578 \div 90$

32. $4,617 \div 30$ **33.** $8,280 \div 40$ **34.** $3,183 \div 30$

Solve each problem.

35. There are 950 books to display. Each shelf holds about 60 books. How many bookshelves are needed?

36. Denise unpacked 23 boxes of books. Each box held about 40 books. About how many books did she unpack?

37. The manager keeps a record of sales. One week the daily sales were $295, $103, $115, $407, and $520. What were the total sales for that week?

★ **38.** The bookstore received 8 boxes of new books. Each box had 30 books. Mike unpacked the books and loaded them on carts. If each cart held about 40 books, how many carts did he need?

Dividing by 2-Digit Numbers

■ Maria Amato is a pharmacist. She filled about 950 prescriptions in 21 weeks. About how many prescriptions did Maria fill each week?

To find how many prescriptions, divide 950 by 21.

Think: There are not enough hundreds to divide because 21 > 9.

Find the tens.

21 rounds to 20.
Think: $20\overline{)95}$

$$
\begin{array}{r}
4 \\
21\overline{)9\,5\,0} \\
\underline{8\,4} \\
1\,1\,0
\end{array}
$$

Find the ones.

Think: $20\overline{)110}$

$$
\begin{array}{r}
4\,5\ \text{R}5 \\
21\overline{)9\,5\,0} \\
\underline{8\,4} \\
1\,1\,0 \\
\underline{1\,0\,5} \\
5
\end{array}
$$

Check.

$$
\begin{array}{r}
4\,5 \\
\times\,2\,1 \\
\hline
4\,5 \\
9\,0\,0 \\
\hline
9\,4\,5 \\
+5 \\
\hline
9\,5\,0\ ✔
\end{array}
$$

Maria filled about 45 prescriptions each week.

■ Divide: $38\overline{)8{,}984}$

Think: There are not enough thousands to divide because 38 > 8.

Find the hundreds.

$$
\begin{array}{r}
2 \\
38\overline{)8{,}9\,8\,4} \\
\underline{7\,6} \\
1\,3\,8
\end{array}
$$

Find the tens.

$$
\begin{array}{r}
2\,3 \\
38\overline{)8{,}9\,8\,4} \\
\underline{7\,6} \\
1\,3\,8 \\
\underline{1\,1\,4} \\
2\,4\,4
\end{array}
$$

Find the ones.

$$
\begin{array}{r}
2\,3\,6\ \text{R}16 \\
38\overline{)8{,}9\,8\,4} \\
\underline{7\,6} \\
1\,3\,8 \\
\underline{1\,1\,4} \\
2\,4\,4 \\
\underline{2\,2\,8} \\
1\,6
\end{array}
$$

Try These

Divide. Check each answer.

1. $72\overline{)800}$ **2.** $48\overline{)1,752}$ **3.** $27\overline{)768}$ **4.** $39\overline{)2,475}$ **5.** $26\overline{)7,841}$

6. $936 \div 52$ **7.** $3,159 \div 68$ **8.** $7,968 \div 36$

Exercises

Divide.

1. $34\overline{)450}$ **2.** $29\overline{)909}$ **3.** $87\overline{)6,302}$ **4.** $79\overline{)6,000}$ **5.** $60\overline{)762}$

6. $39\overline{)440}$ **7.** $71\overline{)9,503}$ **8.** $40\overline{)196}$ **9.** $52\overline{)1,674}$ **10.** $42\overline{)336}$

11. $77\overline{)650}$ **12.** $22\overline{)176}$ **13.** $8\overline{)2,767}$ **14.** $39\overline{)8,980}$ **15.** $80\overline{)6,962}$

16. $59\overline{)8,873}$ **17.** $60\overline{)758}$ **18.** $42\overline{)8,569}$ **19.** $32\overline{)9,276}$ **20.** $19\overline{)760}$

21. $42\overline{)1,700}$ **22.** $9\overline{)645}$ **23.** $64\overline{)2,176}$ **24.** $50\overline{)9,427}$ **25.** $51\overline{)1,530}$

26. $845 \div 35$ **27.** $511 \div 26$ **28.** $365 \div 59$

29. $6,080 \div 20$ **30.** $8,526 \div 21$ **31.** $4,863 \div 92$

32. $7,450 \div 31$ **33.** $4,242 \div 42$ **34.** $1,350 \div 45$

Copy and complete.

★ **35.** $\blacksquare \div 30 = 9 \text{ R}15$ ★ **36.** $\blacksquare \div 46 = 2 \text{ R}1$ ★ **37.** $\blacksquare \div 84 = 5 \text{ R}51$

★ **38.** $8,160 \div \blacksquare = 96$ ★ **39.** $2,665 \div \blacksquare = 65$ ★ **40.** $336 \div \blacksquare = 8$

Solve each problem.

41. Elena puts 49 vitamin bottles on the shelves. Each shelf holds 16 bottles. How many shelves does she fill? How many bottles are left?

42. Manuel works 18 days each month. He works 6 hours a day. Manuel earns $5.25 an hour. How many hours does he work in a month?

43. There are 24 workers in the drugstore. Each worker puts on a clean jacket every morning. 144 jackets are delivered. How many days will the jackets last? Will any clean jackets be left?

★ **44.** Maria received a shipment of 600 vitamin bottles. She ordered bottles of vitamin A and vitamin C. There were 240 bottles of vitamin A. How many bottles were vitamin C? If 24 bottles were packed in each case, how many cases arrived in all?

Estimates Too Large

■ When you divide by 2-digit numbers, your first estimate may be too large.

Divide: 24)150

Find the ones.

24 rounds to 20.
Think: 20)150

$$\begin{array}{r} 7 \\ 24)\overline{1\ 5\ 0} \\ 1\ 6\ 8 \end{array}$$ ← 168 > 150
7 is too large.

Try 6.

$$\begin{array}{r} 6\ \text{R6} \\ 24)\overline{1\ 5\ 0} \\ 1\ 4\ 4 \\ \hline 6 \end{array}$$

■ Divide: 64)3,387

Find the tens.

64 rounds to 60.
Think: 60)338

$$\begin{array}{r} 5 \\ 64)\overline{3,3\ 8\ 7} \\ 3\ 2\ 0 \\ \hline 1\ 8\ 7 \end{array}$$

Find the ones.

Think: 60)187

$$\begin{array}{r} 5\ 3 \\ 64)\overline{3,3\ 8\ 7} \\ 3\ 2\ 0 \\ \hline 1\ 8\ 7 \\ 1\ 9\ 2 \end{array}$$ ← 192 > 187
3 is too large.

Try 2.

$$\begin{array}{r} 5\ 2\ \text{R59} \\ 64)\overline{3,3\ 8\ 7} \\ 3\ 2\ 0 \\ \hline 1\ 8\ 7 \\ 1\ 2\ 8 \\ \hline 5\ 9 \end{array}$$

Try These

Divide. Check each answer.

1. 52)151
2. 32)269
3. 64)387
4. 43)2,462
5. 54)2,568

6. 164 ÷ 22
7. 491 ÷ 72
8. 3,562 ÷ 74

Exercises

Divide.

1. $32\overline{)269}$ **2.** $21\overline{)106}$ **3.** $14\overline{)347}$ **4.** $43\overline{)825}$ **5.** $61\overline{)752}$

6. $23\overline{)624}$ **7.** $44\overline{)838}$ **8.** $24\overline{)1,968}$ **9.** $52\overline{)3,796}$ **10.** $44\overline{)3,036}$

11. $69\overline{)564}$ **12.** $71\overline{)619}$ **13.** $74\overline{)3,562}$ **14.** $73\overline{)2,816}$ **15.** $40\overline{)1,460}$

16. $62\overline{)5,420}$ **17.** $83\overline{)5,644}$ **18.** $73\overline{)4,246}$ **19.** $93\overline{)7,254}$ **20.** $92\overline{)6,348}$

21. $43\overline{)2,452}$ **22.** $34\overline{)7,120}$ **23.** $63\overline{)488}$ **24.** $28\overline{)166}$ **25.** $74\overline{)6,480}$

26. $151 \div 54$ **27.** $255 \div 34$ **28.** $7,140 \div 50$

29. $2,459 \div 43$ **30.** $6,806 \div 86$ **31.** $2,665 \div 41$

32. $2,154 \div 72$ **33.** $891 \div 66$ **34.** $1,272 \div 53$

Solve each problem.

35. Robert ordered milk for a large cafeteria. He ordered 50 cases of milk. There are 24 containers in a case. How many containers of milk did he order?

36. Robert expects to use about 4,000 slices of bread. There are 22 slices in a loaf. How many loaves of bread should he order?

★ **37.** The cafeteria can serve about 4,800 people in 3 hours. There are 10 serving lines. About how many people go through each serving line in an hour?

★ **38.** A steam table is out of order. Robert closes 2 of the 10 serving lines. He still must serve the 4,800 customers. How many must each of the remaining lines serve each hour?

KEEPING IN SHAPE

1. $4\overline{)36}$ **2.** $5\overline{)42}$ **3.** $8\overline{)97}$ **4.** $7\overline{)175}$ **5.** $3\overline{)121}$

6. $6\overline{)762}$ **7.** $9\overline{)927}$ **8.** $7\overline{)3,599}$ **9.** $4\overline{)\$6.72}$ **10.** $8\overline{)1,664}$

11. $500 \div 4$ **12.** $175 \div 2$ **13.** $8,916 \div 7$

14. $\$20.70 \div 9$ **15.** $1,890 \div 8$ **16.** $732 \div 5$

Estimates Too Small

■ Gary Hunter often uses a microscope in his work as a biologist. He needs 46 slides for each experiment. He has 436 slides. How many experiments can he do?

To find the number of experiments, divide 436 by 46.

Find the ones.

46 rounds to 50.
Think: $50\overline{)43}6$

Try 9.

$$
\begin{array}{r}
8 \\
46\overline{)4\,3\,6} \\
3\,6\,8 \\
\hline
6\,8
\end{array}
\quad \longleftarrow
\begin{array}{l}
68 > 46 \\
8 \text{ is too small.}
\end{array}
$$

$$
\begin{array}{r}
9\ \text{R}22 \\
46\overline{)4\,3\,6} \\
4\,1\,4 \\
\hline
2\,2
\end{array}
$$

Gary can do 9 experiments.

■ Divide: $78\overline{)3,593}$

Find the tens.

78 rounds to 80.
Think: $80\overline{)35}9$

$$
\begin{array}{r}
4 \\
78\overline{)3,5\,9\,3} \\
3\,1\,2 \\
\hline
4\,7\,3
\end{array}
$$

Find the ones.

Think: $80\overline{)47}3$

$$
\begin{array}{r}
4\,5 \\
78\overline{)3,5\,9\,3} \\
3\,1\,2 \\
\hline
4\,7\,3 \\
3\,9\,0 \\
\hline
8\,3
\end{array}
\quad \longleftarrow
\begin{array}{l}
83 > 78 \\
5 \text{ is too small.}
\end{array}
$$

Try 6.

$$
\begin{array}{r}
4\,6\ \text{R}5 \\
78\overline{)3,5\,9\,3} \\
3\,1\,2 \\
\hline
4\,7\,3 \\
4\,6\,8 \\
\hline
5
\end{array}
$$

Try These

Divide. Check each answer.

1. $28\overline{)169}$ 2. $18\overline{)164}$ 3. $26\overline{)79}$ 4. $75\overline{)4,769}$ 5. $26\overline{)1,799}$

6. $198 \div 26$ 7. $765 \div 36$ 8. $1,775 \div 25$

Exercises

Divide.

1. $67\overline{)268}$ **2.** $59\overline{)413}$ **3.** $57\overline{)400}$ **4.** $26\overline{)812}$ **5.** $47\overline{)630}$

6. $26\overline{)840}$ **7.** $23\overline{)115}$ **8.** $83\overline{)430}$ **9.** $36\overline{)149}$ **10.** $47\overline{)235}$

11. $40\overline{)680}$ **12.** $65\overline{)275}$ **13.** $45\overline{)972}$ **14.** $77\overline{)2,659}$ **15.** $34\overline{)2,174}$

16. $88\overline{)6,518}$ **17.** $76\overline{)6,992}$ **18.** $57\overline{)2,965}$ **19.** $68\overline{)7,450}$ **20.** $36\overline{)1,442}$

21. $46\overline{)2,781}$ **22.** $38\overline{)7,700}$ **23.** $68\overline{)4,795}$ **24.** $50\overline{)6,975}$ **25.** $26\overline{)5,995}$

26. $665 \div 22$ **27.** $120 \div 15$ **28.** $2,015 \div 26$

29. $1,192 \div 35$ **30.** $6,997 \div 76$ **31.** $2,899 \div 56$

Solve each problem.

32. A class collected 863 lightning bugs to sell to a lab. The students put 75 bugs in each jar. How many jars did they fill?

33. A large-winged butterfly beats its wings about 4 times per second. How many times does it beat its wings in 60 seconds?

34. Honeybees in Florida produce about 10,844,000 kilograms of honey. In Texas, honeybees produce about 4,495,000 kilograms of honey. How many kilograms of honey do both states produce?

35. In the United States, honeybees produce about 94,000,000 kilograms of honey. California produces about 7,457,000 kilograms. How many kilograms do the other states produce?

 THINK AND TRY

GUESSING AND CHECKING

You can name numbers using only 9s.

Name 1 using four 9s.

$$1 = 99 \div 99$$
or $1 = (9 - 9) + (9 \div 9)$

Name 2 using four 9s.

$$2 = (99 \div 9) - 9$$
or $2 = (9 \div 9) + (9 \div 9)$

Use addition, subtraction, multiplication, and division.
Name each number using four 9s.

1. 0 **2.** 20 **3.** 81 **4.** 98 **5.** 99 **6.** 100

Problem Solving: Applications

PROBLEM FORMULATION

The Marine Park High School Band is giving two concerts. There are 80 band members. They want to raise money for new uniforms. The uniforms will cost $16,000. There are 720 seats in the auditorium. Tickets to each concert are $5 each. All the tickets to both concerts are sold.

There are many questions you can ask using the information in this paragraph. For example, how much money does the band make from each concert?

To find how much money, multiply.

$$720 \leftarrow \text{seats in the auditorium}$$
$$\underline{\times\ \$5} \leftarrow \text{price of a ticket}$$
$$\$3,600$$

The band makes $3,600 from each concert.

Try These

Write a question. Then answer the question.

1. Use the number of band members and the number of tickets to be sold for each concert.

2. Use the number of band members and the cost of the uniforms.

3. Use the number of seats in the auditorium and the number of concerts.

4. Use the total number of tickets sold and the cost of a ticket.

5. Use the cost of the uniforms and the amount of money made on the concerts.

Exercises

The band secretary keeps a record of the number of tickets sold by each grade.

Write a question. Then answer the question.

Week	NUMBER OF TICKETS SOLD			
	9th grade	10th grade	11th grade	12th grade
1	42	36	45	31
2	69	60	84	59
3	73	71	79	67
4	84	82	83	78
5	100	97	105	95

1. Use the number of tickets sold by each grade in one week.

2. Use the numbers of tickets sold by each grade in two different weeks.

3. Use the number of tickets sold in one week and the cost of a ticket.

4. Use the number of tickets sold by one grade in five weeks.

5. Use the number of tickets sold by a grade and the number of weeks tickets were sold.

6. Use the number of tickets sold by two different grades.

7. Use the information to write another addition question.

8. Use the information to write another subtraction question.

The pictograph shows the kinds of instruments played by the band members.

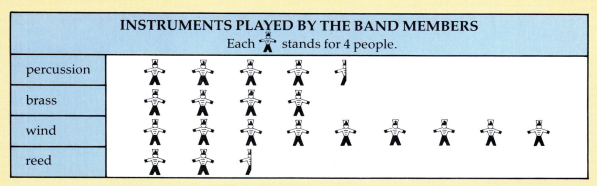

INSTRUMENTS PLAYED BY THE BAND MEMBERS
Each ⬩ stands for 4 people.

percussion
brass
wind
reed

Write a question. Then answer the question.

9. Use the number of band members who play percussion instruments and the number of band members who play wind instruments.

10. Use the number of band members who play wind instruments and the number of band members who play brass instruments.

11. Use the number of band members who play reed instruments and the cost of the uniforms.

12. Use the number of band members who play brass instruments and the cost of a ticket.

13. Use the information to write another addition question.

14. Use the information to write another subtraction question.

Problem Solving: Strategies

GENERALIZING

Sometimes **finding a pattern** and using it is a strategy that can help you solve problems.

There is a team of secret agents. Their job is to watch 7 piers for smugglers. Number-code messages tell each agent which pier to check.

Can you break the code?

Radio message: 628 beep 5 (Agent 5 goes to Pier 3.)
319 beep 2 (Agent 2 goes to Pier 1.)
458 beep 12 (Agent 12 goes to Pier 2.)

Find a relationship between the last number in the code and the agent.

Beep 5 is a message for Agent 5.
Beep 2 is a message for Agent 2.
Beep 12 is a message for Agent 12.

The last number of the message is the code for the agent number.

How does each agent know which pier to guard?

Code	Pier
628 beep 5	3
319 beep 2	1
458 beep 12	2

Replace each beep with a division sign.

$628 \div 5 = 125 \text{ R3}$ $319 \div 2 = 159 \text{ R1}$ $458 \div 12 = 38 \text{ R2}$

$$\begin{array}{r} 125 \text{ R3} \\ 5\overline{)628} \end{array} \qquad \begin{array}{r} 159 \text{ R1} \\ 2\overline{)319} \end{array} \qquad \begin{array}{r} 38 \text{ R2} \\ 12\overline{)458} \end{array}$$

Find a relationship between the remainder and the pier number.

When you find a rule, try it for these codes.

862 beep 8 (Agent 8 goes to Pier 6.)
704 beep 14 (Agent 14 goes to Pier 4.)

Using the Strategy

Use the Secret Agent code to answer each problem.
Which agent is sent to which pier with these messages?

1. 625 beep 3

2. 530 beep 15

3. 223 beep 8

4. 514 beep 34

Make up a message to send the agent to the pier.

5. Agent 3 to Pier 2

6. Agent 4 to Pier 1

7. Agent 18 to Pier 5

8. Agent 28 to Pier 3

9. Agent 7 to Pier 6

10. Agent 34 to Pier 4

11. Find a rule that sends Agent 6 to Pier 4, Agent 10 to Pier 6, Agent 12 to Pier 7, and Agent 8 to Pier 5. The rule will send Agent 2 to Pier ■, Agent 14 to Pier ■, and Agent 4 to Pier ■.

12. What does the rule in exercise 9 do to a number?

ACTIVITY

EXPLORING REMAINDERS

This is a card game for 2 to 4 players. Make a deck of cards with numbers from 10 to 40.

1. Each player gets 5 cards. The rest of the cards are placed face down in the center.

2. Use 3 as the divisor. The first player must play a card as a dividend that divided by 3 gives a remainder of 0.

3. The next player must play a card as a dividend that divided by 3 gives a remainder of 1.

4. The next person plays a card that gives a remainder of 2. The next player plays a card that gives a remainder of 0, and so on.

5. If a player cannot play a card, the player must draw from the pile in the center and lose a turn.

6. The first person who uses all the cards in his or her hand wins.

Play the game again with a different divisor.

Dividing Greater Numbers

- The Color-Your-World Paint Company makes 36,512 gallons of paint each month. It makes equal amounts of 28 colors. How many gallons of each color does the company make?

To find how many gallons, divide 36,512 by 28.

Find the thousands.	Find the hundreds.	Find the tens.	Find the ones.

```
        1 _ _ _
  28)3 6,5 1 2
    2 8
      8 5
```

```
        1 3 _ _
  28)3 6,5 1 2
    2 8
      8 5
      8 4
        1 1
```

```
        1 3 0 _
  28)3 6,5 1 2
    2 8
      8 5
      8 4
        1 1
          0
        1 1 2
```

```
        1,3 0 4
  28)3 6,5 1 2
    2 8
      8 5
      8 4
        1 1
          0
        1 1 2
        1 1 2
            0
```

The company makes 1,304 gallons of each color.

- Divide: 54)$498.42

Check.

```
  $   9.23
54)$498.42
  486
  12 4
  10 8
    1 62
    1 62
       0
```

```
     $9.23
  ×     54
    36 92
   461 50
  $498.42 ✔
```

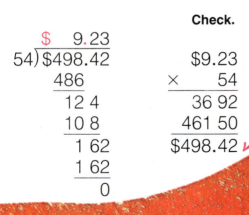

Remember: Write the $ and the . in the answer.

Try These

Divide. Check each answer.

1. $22\overline{)69,154}$ 2. $69\overline{)91,000}$ 3. $49\overline{)7,575}$ 4. $52\overline{)\$357.24}$

5. $9,525 \div 82$ 6. $98,690 \div 61$ 7. $\$249.60 \div 52$

Exercises

Divide.

1. $58\overline{)66,982}$ 2. $87\overline{)82,403}$ 3. $78\overline{)9,938}$ 4. $33\overline{)64,389}$

5. $60\overline{)256}$ 6. $42\overline{)\$96.18}$ 7. $37\overline{)91,600}$ 8. $37\overline{)240}$

9. $50\overline{)6,775}$ 10. $41\overline{)120}$ 11. $24\overline{)\$328.56}$ 12. $24\overline{)128}$

13. $88\overline{)6,518}$ 14. $18\overline{)\$814.14}$ 15. $30\overline{)4,167}$ 16. $47\overline{)69,215}$

17. $18\overline{)7,462}$ 18. $56\overline{)\$99.12}$ 19. $84\overline{)9,962}$ 20. $29\overline{)62,015}$

21. $430 \div 83$ 22. $21,912 \div 12$ 23. $\$230.47 \div 19$
24. $3,496 \div 49$ 25. $97,384 \div 45$ 26. $\$243.75 \div 25$

Solve.

27. $(97 \times 84) \div 25$ 28. $12 \times (6,886 \div 22)$ 29. $(711 \times 9) \div 3$
30. $8 \times (320 \div 16)$ 31. $(629 + 752) \div 56$ 32. $(246 \times 6) \div 2$

Find the rule. Then continue the pattern.

33. 2, 5; 5, 14; 8, 23; 9, ▧; 12, ▧
34. 1, 5; 5, 9; 9, 13; 13, ▧; ▧, 21
35. 36, 18; 30, 15; 26, 13; 24, ▧; 8, ▧
36. 1, 4, 3, 6, 5, 8, ▧, ▧, 9

 The Bay Street Barons paint the apartments of senior citizens. They paint 5,600 square feet in each apartment. A gallon of paint covers 400 square feet.

37. How many gallons of paint do the Barons need for each apartment?

38. There are 5 apartments. How many gallons of paint should they buy?

39. The store sells paint at $8.50 a gallon. How much money do they need to raise for the paint?

40. They wash cars to raise the money. At $2.50 per car, how many cars must they wash?

Division by 2-Digit Numbers   151

Estimating Quotients

■ The Great Winds Kite Company makes 45,250 kites a year. The company has kites in 7 different styles. It makes the same number of each style. About how many kites are made in each style?

To find about how many, estimate the quotient.

Find the first digit of the quotient.

$$\begin{array}{r} 6 \\ 7\overline{)45,250} \\ \underline{42} \\ 3 \end{array}$$

Write 0s for the rest of the digits.

$$\begin{array}{r} 6,000 \\ 7\overline{)45,250} \\ \underline{42} \\ 3 \end{array}$$

The company makes about 6,000 kites in each style.

■ When dividing with a 2-digit divisor, round the divisor. Then change the dividend to a number that is easy to divide by the rounded divisor.

Estimate: $83\overline{)3,491}$

Round the divisor.
83 rounds to 80.

$$80\overline{)3,491}$$

Change the dividend.

$$80\overline{)3,200}$$

Estimate the quotient.

$$\begin{array}{r} 40 \\ 80\overline{)3,200} \end{array}$$

■ Estimate: $57\overline{)46,312}$

Round the divisor.
57 rounds to 60.

$$60\overline{)46,312}$$

Change the dividend.

$$60\overline{)48,000}$$

Estimate the quotient.

$$\begin{array}{r} 800 \\ 60\overline{)48,000} \end{array}$$

Try These

Estimate each quotient.

1. $6\overline{)5,338}$ 2. $8\overline{)41,615}$ 3. $71\overline{)642}$ 4. $29\overline{)2,346}$

5. $359 \div 7$ 6. $72,904 \div 81$ 7. $41,709 \div 68$

Exercises

Estimate each quotient.

1. 3)$\overline{2,433}$
2. 7)$\overline{745}$
3. 2)$\overline{1,056}$
4. 9)$\overline{8,496}$

5. 6)$\overline{704}$
6. 5)$\overline{26,014}$
7. 39)$\overline{28,215}$
8. 41)$\overline{33,111}$

9. 87)$\overline{80,200}$
10. 18)$\overline{651}$
11. 56)$\overline{41,297}$
12. 5)$\overline{34,825}$

13. 42)$\overline{3,304}$
14. 68)$\overline{5,109}$
15. 21)$\overline{14,337}$
16. 8)$\overline{63,829}$

17. 35,274 ÷ 49
18. 6,296 ÷ 2
19. 23,483 ÷ 77
20. 2,612 ÷ 5
21. 88,944 ÷ 28
22. 64,056 ÷ 82
23. 2,974 ÷ 38
24. 554 ÷ 6
25. 27,908 ÷ 53

 Estimate. Use a calculator to find the exact answer.

26. 5)$\overline{380}$
27. 36)$\overline{1,980}$
28. 63)$\overline{26,838}$
29. 8)$\overline{5,664}$

30. 26)$\overline{1,170}$
31. 34)$\overline{1,700}$
32. 22)$\overline{12,496}$
33. 43)$\overline{18,318}$

34. 47,520 ÷ 88
35. 8,253 ÷ 9
36. 1,575 ÷ 63
37. 4,672 ÷ 64
38. 16,040 ÷ 5
39. 11,088 ÷ 48

Decide if you need an estimate or an exact answer. Then solve.

40. Steven worked on developing a new kite for a total of 128 hours in 6 weeks. About how many hours did he work on the kite each week?

41. Trisha paid a free-lance artist $1,577 for working on a kite design for 19 days. About how much was the artist paid each day?

42. An order for 2,400 butterfly kites is being packed. One carton holds 48 butterfly kites. How many cartons are needed?

43. Each rack holds 24 box kites. There are 865 box kites. How many racks will be needed to hold all the box kites?

44. A part-time employee works a total of 148 hours in 7 weeks. About how many hours is that each week?

★ 45. The company spends $19,750 on part-time help each year. About how much money is that each week?

Division by 2-Digit Numbers   153

potatoes	3 pounds for $1	5 pounds for $1.75
crackers	16 ounces for $1.79	12 ounces for $1.09
juice	6 ounces for $.79	12 ounces for $1.80

19. crackers

20. juice

Problem Solving: Applications

READ
PLAN
DO
CHECK

UNIT PRICES

■ When you are shopping, look for the **unit** price of each item. The unit price is the cost...

SKILLS CHECK

Choose the correct answer.

1. In 63,104,527,980, which number is in the millions place?

- **a.** 3
- **b.** 4
- **c.** 6
- **d.** 7

2. $7 + 7 + 8$

- **a.** 18
- **b.** 22
- **c.** 32
- **d.** 56

3. $3,076$
$+2,856$

- **a.** 1,220
- **b.** 5,822
- **c.** 5,932
- **d.** 6,934

4. $50.00
$- 19.69$

- **a.** $21.42
- **b.** $30.31
- **c.** $31.41
- **d.** $69.69

5. 0×5

- **a.** 0
- **b.** 5
- **c.** 50
- **d.** NG

6. Find the least common multiple of 6 and 8.

- **a.** 12
- **b.** 16
- **c.** 24
- **d.** 36

7. $809
$\times\ 46$

- **a.** 8,090
- **b.** 37,205
- **c.** 37,214
- **d.** NG

8. $3\overline{)39}$

- **a.** 8 R2
- **b.** 10 R1
- **c.** 12
- **d.** NG

9. $134.40 \div 35$

- **a.** $2.98
- **b.** $3.84
- **c.** $4.02
- **d.** $4.16

10. Eli baked 12 muffins. Fran baked 18 muffins. How many muffins were there in all?

- **a.** 6 muffins
- **b.** 20 muffins
- **c.** 30 muffins
- **d.** 40 muffins

11. You buy a tennis racket for $46.85. You give the clerk $60. How much change should you get?

- **a.** $12.50
- **b.** $13.15
- **c.** $14.85
- **d.** $26.35

12. Lee has three bowling scores: 186, 208, 161. What is her average?

- **a.** 184
- **b.** 192
- **c.** 185
- **d.** NG

Exercises

Estimate each quotient.

1. $3\overline{)2,433}$

2. $7\overline{)745}$

3. $2\overline{)1,056}$

4. $9\overline{)8,496}$

5. $6\overline{)704}$

6. $5\overline{)26,014}$

7. $39\overline{)28,215}$

8. $41\overline{)33,111}$

9. $87\overline{)80,200}$

10. $18\overline{)651}$

11. $56\overline{)41,297}$

12. $5\overline{)34,825}$

13. $42\overline{)3,304}$

14. $68\overline{)5,109}$

15. $21\overline{)14,337}$

16. $8\overline{)63,829}$

17. $35,274 \div 49$

18. $6,296 \div 2$

19. $23,483 \div 77$

20. $2,612 \div 5$

21. $88,944 \div 28$

22. $64,056 \div 82$

23. $2,974 \div 38$

24. $554 \div 6$

25. $27,908 \div 53$

 Estimate. Use a calculator to find the exact answer.

26. $5\overline{)380}$

27. $36\overline{)1,980}$

28. $63\overline{)26,838}$

29. $8\overline{)5,664}$

30. $26\overline{)1,170}$

31. $34\overline{)1,700}$

32. $22\overline{)12,496}$

33. $43\overline{)18,318}$

34. $47,520 \div 88$

35. $8,253 \div 9$

36. $1,575 \div 63$

37. $4,672 \div 64$

38. $16,040 \div 5$

39. $11,088 \div 48$

Decide if you need an estimate or an exact answer. Then solve.

40. Steven worked on developing a new kite for a total of 128 hours in 6 weeks. About how many hours did he work on the kite each week?

41. Trisha paid a free-lance artist $1,577 for working on a kite design for 19 days. About how much was the artist paid each day?

42. An order for 2,400 butterfly kites is being packed. One carton holds 48 butterfly kites. How many cartons are needed?

43. Each rack holds 24 box kites. There are 865 box kites. How many racks will be needed to hold all the box kites?

44. A part-time employee works a total of 148 hours in 7 weeks. About how many hours is that each week?

★ 45. The company spends $19,750 on part-time help each year. About how much money is that each week?

Problem Solving: Applications

UNIT PRICES

■ When you are shopping, look for the **unit price** of each item. The unit price is the cost of one unit of the item you want to buy. The unit may be ounces, pounds, or single items.

A store sells 8 oranges for $1.12. What is the unit price (cost of 1 orange)?

Divide to find the cost of 1 orange.

$$
\begin{array}{r}
\$\ .14 \\
8)\overline{\$1.12} \\
\underline{8} \\
32 \\
\underline{32} \\
0
\end{array}
$$

The unit price of oranges is $.14 per orange.

■ Use the unit price to find which item is a better buy.

A 15-ounce box of cereal is $1.69. A 24-ounce box of the same cereal is $2.39. Which box of cereal is a better buy?

Divide to find the cost of 1 ounce of each cereal. Then compare the unit prices to see which is a better buy.

$$
\begin{array}{r}
\$\ .11 \\
15)\overline{\$1.69} \\
\underline{1\ 5} \\
19 \\
\underline{15} \\
4
\end{array}
\qquad
\begin{array}{r}
\$\ .09 \\
24)\overline{\$2.39} \\
\underline{0} \\
2\ 39 \\
\underline{2\ 16} \\
23
\end{array}
$$

15 ounces for $1.69 is about $.11 per ounce.
24 ounces for $2.39 is about $.09 per ounce.
24 ounces for $2.39 is less per ounce than 15 ounces for $1.69.

24 ounces for $2.39 is a better buy.

Try These

Find the unit price for each.

1. 64 ounces of milk for $1.28
3. 18 ounces of bread for $.90
5. 3 melons for $3.27

2. 5 pounds of flour for $1.50
4. 6 grapefruits for $1.39
6. 32 ounces of juice for $1.35

Which is a better buy?

7. 4 cans for $1.49 or 6 cans for $2.39

8. 3 pounds of tomatoes for $1.75 or 5 pounds of tomatoes for $2.80

Exercises

Find the unit price for each.

1. 16 ounces of cottage cheese for $1.59
3. a 15-pound turkey for $11.25
5. 12 ounces of cheese for $1.80
7. 5 pounds of rice for $1.35
9. 6 bran muffins for $1.65

2. 18 ounces of peanut butter for $2.34
4. 12 eggs for $1.08
6. 6 grapefruits for $1.32
8. 10 ounces of soup for $.52
10. 3 pounds of peaches for $.89

Which is a better buy?

11. 32 ounces of milk for $.64 or 64 ounces of milk for $1.18

12. 3 pounds of apples for $.75 or 5 pounds for $1.10

13. 7 oranges for $.95 or 12 oranges for $1.40

14. bananas that are 3 pounds for $.72 or 4 pounds for $1

Which store has a better buy on each item?

15. pineapple

16. tuna

17. lemons

18. potatoes

19. crackers

20. juice

Item	Ed's Market	Quick Shop
pineapple	2 cans for $.78	4 cans for $1.39
tuna	6 ounces for $1.09	13 ounces for $2.47
lemons	6 for $1.19	4 for $.59
potatoes	3 pounds for $1	5 pounds for $1.75
crackers	16 ounces for $1.79	12 ounces for $1.09
juice	6 ounces for $.79	12 ounces for $1.80

5 CHAPTER CHECKPOINT

Divide. (pp. 138–145, 150–151)

1. $40\overline{)80}$　　2. $20\overline{)68}$　　3. $60\overline{)464}$　　4. $50\overline{)1,415}$

5. $60\overline{)6,300}$　　6. $30\overline{)4,527}$　　7. $80\overline{)986}$　　8. $70\overline{)7,438}$

9. $26\overline{)697}$　　10. $42\overline{)338}$　　11. $77\overline{)652}$　　12. $21\overline{)956}$

13. $39\overline{)8,980}$　　14. $79\overline{)5,000}$　　15. $46\overline{)1,356}$　　16. $87\overline{)6,318}$

17. $22\overline{)617}$　　18. $21\overline{)818}$　　19. $24\overline{)128}$　　20. $92\overline{)6,356}$

21. $64\overline{)3,364}$　　22. $43\overline{)2,064}$　　23. $36\overline{)1,194}$　　24. $44\overline{)838}$

25. $36\overline{)761}$　　26. $59\overline{)413}$　　27. $26\overline{)840}$　　28. $46\overline{)439}$

29. $38\overline{)3,086}$　　30. $47\overline{)2,468}$　　31. $78\overline{)3,590}$　　32. $36\overline{)1,450}$

33. $71\overline{)7,284}$　　34. $35\overline{)70,280}$　　35. $39\overline{)41,184}$　　36. $18\overline{)38,000}$

37. $78\overline{)9,984}$　　38. $26\overline{)\$119.08}$　　39. $43\overline{)\$488.48}$　　40. $28\overline{)36,519}$

41. $97 \div 40$　　　　42. $152 \div 52$　　　　43. $1,972 \div 61$

44. $8,996 \div 36$　　　45. $2,875 \div 56$　　　46. $3,561 \div 74$

47. $\$288.00 \div 48$　　48. $27,518 \div 26$　　49. $\$379.61 \div 29$

Estimate each quotient. (pp. 152–153)

50. $6\overline{)3,794}$　　51. $8\overline{)737}$　　52. $9\overline{)6,278}$　　53. $4\overline{)35,381}$

54. $71\overline{)5,000}$　　55. $58\overline{)43,016}$　　56. $63\overline{)25,111}$　　57. $26\overline{)899}$

Decide if you need an estimate or an exact answer. Then solve. (pp. 138–155)

58. Laura requests 48 cans of floor cleaner. The cans come in cartons of 12. How many cartons should she order?

59. The company uses 76,000 paper towels and 1,000 paper cups in 25 days. What is the average number of paper towels used each day?

60. Laura ordered 108 sponges. There were 12 sponges in each package. How many packages did she order?

61. A part-time employee works a total of 128 hours in 6 weeks. About how many hours is that each week?

62. A custodian has 6 boxes of paper cups. Each box contains 200 cups. Each dispenser holds 80 paper cups. How many dispensers are needed for the paper cups?

63. This year 440 packages of paper towels were used. The packages come in cases of 48. How many cases were used? How many additional packages were used?

64. The company spends $2,220 on supplies each year. About how much money is that for each of the 12 months?

65. 1,110 bottles are put in cases. A case holds 48 bottles. How many cases are filled? How many bottles are left?

66. Which is a better buy: 10 ounces of cheese for $1.79 or 16 ounces of cheese for $2.69?

67. Which is a better buy: 3 pounds of apples for $.65 or 5 pounds of apples for $1.15?

Find the rule. Then continue the pattern. (pp. 148–149)

68. 1, 4; 2, 6; 3, 8; 4, ■; 5, ■

69. 36, 12; 42, 14; 48, 16; 51, ■; ■, 19

Write a question. Then answer the question. (pp. 146–147)

70. Use the number of calories in a piece of fruit and the number of days in a week.

71. Use the number of calories in two pieces of fruit to write an addition question.

72. Use the number of calories in two different pieces of fruit to write a subtraction question.

CALORIE CHART	
Food	Number of Calories
apple	86
banana	101
orange	71
peach	38
pear	100

COMPUTERS AND PROBLEM SOLVING

■ A loop is part of a program that repeats. You have already made loops in programs with the GOTO statement. You can also make loops by using the IF. . .THEN statement.

Look at the flow chart at right. It will print even numbers from 2 to 10. The IF. . .THEN box is diamond shaped. It has two paths coming out of it. One path ends the program. The other loops back to repeat steps.

The program would look like this.

```
NEW
10   LET A=0
20   LET A=A+2
30   PRINT A
40   IF A<10 THEN GOTO 20
50   END
```

The number of times the program loops depends on the test at line 40. As long as A is less than 10, the computer loops back to run through the program again. When A is equal to or greater than 10, you fall through the loop and the program ends.

Solve each problem.

1. In the program below, what will be the output?

```
NEW
10   LET B = 0
20   LET B = B + 3
30   IF B > 30 THEN GOTO 50
40     GOTO 20
50   PRINT B
60   END
```

2. Change line 20 to read:

LET B = B + 4

What will be the output?

3. Remove line 40. What will the program do?

4. Reinsert line 40. Add a statement to print out all the numbers being tested.

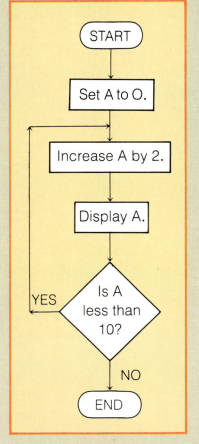

START

Set A to O.

Increase A by 2.

Display A.

Is A less than 10?

YES

NO

END

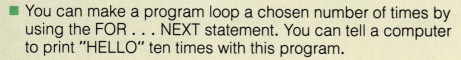

You can make a program loop a chosen number of times by using the FOR . . . NEXT statement. You can tell a computer to print "HELLO" ten times with this program.

```
NEW
10   FOR T=1 TO 10
20   PRINT "HELLO"
30   NEXT T
40   END
```

Look at this program. It uses the FOR . . . NEXT statement to control the number of loops.

```
NEW
10   FOR T=1 TO 5
20   INPUT A
30   INPUT B
40   PRINT A; "/"; B; "=";
50   PRINT A / B
60   NEXT T
70   END
```

This program will loop until five problems have been solved. What would happen if you changed line 10 to FOR T=0 TO 4? What would happen if you changed line 10 to FOR T=1 TO 7?

Solve each problem.

1. Look at the program below. What will the output be using the following inputs: 13, 5, 22, 8, 9, 16?

```
NEW
10   FOR T=1 TO 2
20   INPUT A
30   INPUT B
40   INPUT C
50   PRINT A; "*"; B; "*"; C; "=";
60   PRINT A * B * C
70   NEXT T
80   END
```

2. How would you change the above program to solve three problems?

ENRICHMENT

PRIME AND COMPOSITE NUMBERS

A **prime number** is a whole number with exactly two factors, itself and 1.

$5 = 1 \times 5$ The factors of 5 are 1 and 5.
5 is a prime number.

A **composite number** is a whole number with more than two factors.

$6 = 1 \times 6$ The factors of 6 are 1, 2, 3, and 6.
$6 = 2 \times 3$ 6 is a composite number.

1 has only one factor, itself.
1 is not prime. 1 is not composite.

The Sieve of Eratosthenes is a way to find prime numbers.

Copy the table of numbers from 1 to 50.

1	2	3	4	5	6	7	8	9	10
11	12	13	14	15	16	17	18	19	20
21	22	23	24	25	26	27	28	29	30
31	32	33	34	35	36	37	38	39	40
41	42	43	44	45	46	47	48	49	50

1. Cross out 1. (1 is not prime.)

2. Circle 2. (2 is prime.)

3. Cross out other multiples of 2. Why are they not prime?

4. Circle 3. (3 is prime.)

5. Cross out other multiples of 3. Why?

6. Circle 5. Circle 7. Cross out their other multiples.

7. The numbers left are prime, or "caught in the sieve." List them.

8. Continue the table of numbers to 100. Repeat steps 3, 5, and 6.

9. List the prime numbers between 50 and 100.

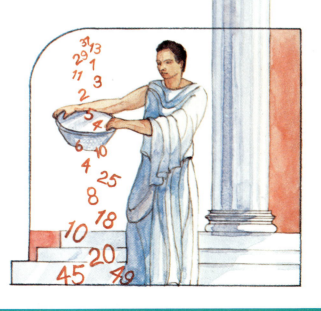

BUILDING A DOGHOUSE

You just bought a puppy. Now you will need a doghouse for it.
You can buy one for $100. Can you build one for less money?

Some Questions to Explore

- What do you need to know about building a doghouse?
- What materials will you need to build it?
- How much will materials cost?

Some Strategies to Explore

Consider the first question. You can find information in books
and magazines to help answer the question.

- Find out what materials are recommended.
- Find information about size requirements. Take into
  consideration the size your puppy will be when it is
  full grown.

Decide what strategies you will use to answer the other
questions above. What other questions and strategies do you
need to explore? List them. Then use them to solve the
problem.

SKILLS CHECK

Choose the correct answer.

1. In 63,104,527,980, which number is in the millions place?

   a. 3
   b. 4
   c. 6
   d. 7

2. 7 + 7 + 8

   a. 18
   b. 22
   c. 32
   d. 56

3.
$$\begin{array}{r} 3,076 \\ +2,856 \\ \hline \end{array}$$

   a. 1,220
   b. 5,822
   c. 5,932
   d. 6,934

4.
$$\begin{array}{r} \$50.00 \\ -\ 19.69 \\ \hline \end{array}$$

   a. $21.42
   b. $30.31
   c. $31.41
   d. $69.69

5. 0 × 5

   a. 0
   b. 5
   c. 50
   d. NG

6. Find the least common multiple of 6 and 8.

   a. 12
   b. 16
   c. 24
   d. 36

7.
$$\begin{array}{r} 809 \\ \times\ 46 \\ \hline \end{array}$$

   a. 8,090
   b. 37,205
   c. 37,214
   d. NG

8. 3)$\overline{39}$

   a. 8 R2
   b. 10 R1
   c. 12
   d. NG

9. $134.40 ÷ 35

   a. $2.98
   b. $3.84
   c. $4.02
   d. $4.16

10. Eli baked 12 muffins. Fran baked 18 muffins. How many muffins were there in all?

   a. 6 muffins
   b. 20 muffins
   c. 30 muffins
   d. 40 muffins

11. You buy a tennis racket for $46.85. You give the clerk $60. How much change should you get?

   a. $12.50
   b. $13.15
   c. $14.85
   d. $26.35

12. Lee has three bowling scores: 186, 208, 161. What is her average?

   a. 184
   b. 192
   c. 185
   d. NG

MEASUREMENT

6

Time

■ You can read time in more than one way.

Read: one twenty *or*
          twenty minutes past one

Write: 1:20

Read: three forty-one *or*
          forty-one minutes past three *or*
          nineteen minutes to four

Write: 3:41

■ Use A.M. for the hours from 12 midnight to 12 noon.

Use P.M. for the hours from 12 noon to 12 midnight.

4 A.M.

4 P.M.

■ Find the time 3 hours 16 minutes after 9:15 A.M.

Think: Start at 9:15 A.M.
          3 hours later is 12:15 P.M.
          16 minutes later is 12:31 P.M.

3 hours 16 minutes after 9:15 A.M. is 12:31 P.M.

■ Find the amount of time between 2:54 P.M. and 4:08 P.M.

Think: Start at 2:54 P.M.
          1 hour later is 3:54 P.M.
          14 minutes later is 4:08 P.M.

The amount of time between 2:54 P.M. and 4:08 P.M. is
1 hour 14 minutes.

Try These

Write each time.

1.

2.

3.

What time is it?

4. 1 hour 15 minutes after 6:30 A.M.

5. 4 hours 19 minutes after 10:05 P.M.

How much time is between these times?

6. 11:05 A.M. and 1:15 P.M.

7. 5:45 P.M. and 9:31 P.M.

Exercises

Write each time.

1.

2.

3.

What time is it?

4. 1 hour 30 minutes after 3:20 P.M.

5. 4 hours 12 minutes after 10:39 A.M.

6. 5 hours 33 minutes after 7:11 P.M.

7. 1 hour 40 minutes after 11:25 A.M.

8. 30 minutes before 2:30 P.M.

9. 2 hours 15 minutes before 6:00 P.M.

How much time is between these times?

10. 5:30 P.M. and 7:20 P.M.

11. 6:05 A.M. and 8:30 A.M.

12. 4:35 P.M. and 6:19 P.M.

13. 10:15 A.M. and 3:45 P.M.

Solve each problem.

14. The Harts left home at 8:15 A.M. They arrived at the park at 10:40 A.M. How long did it take the Harts to get to the park?

★ **15.** Lindsay started hiking at 1:45 P.M. She stopped at 3:10 P.M. Then she hiked from 3:38 P.M. to 5:50 P.M. For how long did Lindsay hike?

Units of Time

- The **second (s)**, the **minute (min)**, the **hour (h)**, the **day**, the **week**, the **month**, and the **year** are used to measure time.

> 1 minute = 60 seconds
> 1 hour = 60 minutes
> 1 day = 24 hours
> 1 week = 7 days
> 1 year = 365 days
> 1 year = 12 months

⟵ **Leap years have 366 days.**

- Use the chart to find the number of days in 3 weeks 5 days.

  3 weeks 5 days = ▪ days
  1 week = 7 days
  3 weeks = 3 × 7 days
  3 weeks = 21 days
  3 weeks 5 days = 21 days + 5 days
  3 weeks 5 days = 26 days

- Use the chart to find the number of hours and minutes in 158 minutes.

  158 minutes = ▪ hours ▪ minutes
  60 minutes = 1 hour

  158 minutes = 2 hours 38 minutes

$$\begin{array}{r} 2\ \text{R}38 \\ 60\overline{)158} \\ 120 \\ \hline 38 \end{array}$$

- You can add and subtract units of time.

  Add: 1 h 25 min + 2 h 30 min

  Subtract: 3 h 40 min − 1 h 25 min

  $$\begin{array}{r} 1\ \text{h}\ 25\ \text{min} \\ +2\ \text{h}\ 30\ \text{min} \\ \hline 3\ \text{h}\ 55\ \text{min} \end{array}$$

  $$\begin{array}{r} \overset{3\ 10}{3\ \text{h}\ \cancel{4}\ \cancel{0}\ \text{min}} \\ -1\ \text{h}\ 2\ 5\ \text{min} \\ \hline 2\ \text{h}\ 1\ 5\ \text{min} \end{array}$$

Try These

Copy and complete.

1. 4 weeks = ▨ days
2. 30 months = ▨ years ▨ months
3. 246 seconds = ▨ minutes ▨ seconds
4. 3 hours 20 minutes = ▨ minutes

Add or subtract.

5. 2 h 18 min
   +1 h 21 min
   _____

6. 4 h 36 min
   −3 h 15 min
   _____

7. 6 h 52 min
   −2 h 27 min
   _____

8. 5 h 40 min
   +2 h
   _____

Exercises

Copy and complete.

1. 3 weeks = ▨ days
2. 2 days = ▨ hours
3. 51 hours = ▨ days ▨ hours
4. 2 years 5 months = ▨ months
5. 1 minute 47 seconds = ▨ seconds
6. 6 hours = ▨ minutes
7. 2 days 11 hours = ▨ hours
8. 77 hours = ▨ days ▨ hours
9. 31 days = ▨ weeks ▨ days
10. 1 hour 34 minutes = ▨ minutes
11. 44 months = ▨ years ▨ months
12. 145 minutes = ▨ hours ▨ minutes
13. 199 seconds = ▨ minutes ▨ seconds
14. 5 weeks 6 days = ▨ days

Add or subtract.

15. 3 h 20 min
    +2 h 15 min
    _____

16. 6 h 52 min
    −6 h 24 min
    _____

17. 4 h 9 min
    +1 h 33 min
    _____

★ 18. 3 h 12 min
      −2 h 45 min
      _____

Solve each problem.

19. Anna started her homework at 3:30 P.M. She worked for 2 hours and 20 minutes. What time did Anna finish her homework?

20. Gene worked in the library from 4:15 P.M. to 7:30 P.M. How long did Gene work in the library?

21. Larry worked on his science project for 2 h 30 min on Monday. He worked 3 h 25 min on Tuesday. How long did Larry work on his science project?

★ 22. Marcia spent 40 min on her math homework, 50 min on science homework, and 30 min on English homework. How many hours did Marcia spend on her homework?

Problem Solving: Applications

TIME ZONES

■ This map shows the five **time zones** in the United States.

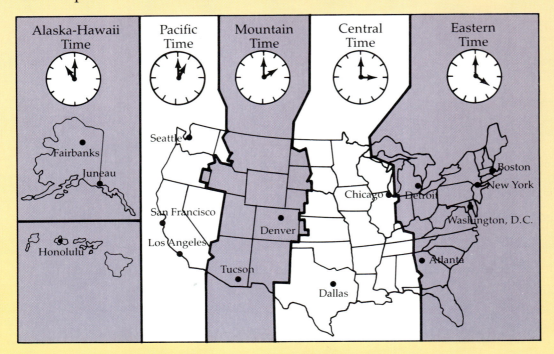

The clocks show that when it is 1 P.M. in the Pacific Time Zone, it is:

> 11 A.M. in the Alaska-Hawaii Time Zone.
> 2 P.M. in the Mountain Time Zone.
> 3 P.M. in the Central Time Zone.
> 4 P.M. in the Eastern Time Zone.

■ Flight 124 lands in Los Angeles at 11 A.M. Joseph Andrew receives a message to call his office in Boston. What time is it in Boston?

Los Angeles is in the Pacific Time Zone.
Boston is in the Eastern Time Zone.
Pacific Time is 3 hours earlier than Eastern Time.

It is 2 P.M. in Boston.

Try These

Complete.

1. At 10 P.M. Mountain Time, it is ▦ Central Time.

2. At 6 P.M. Central Time, it is ▦ Pacific Time.

3. At 12 noon Eastern Time, it is ▦ Pacific Time.

4. At 7 P.M. Alaska-Hawaii Time, it is ▦ Mountain Time.

Solve each problem.

5. Helena is in Washington, D.C. She calls Bob in Denver. Bob's clock reads 7 A.M. What time is it in Washington, D.C.?

6. Anthony is in Denver. It is 4 P.M. He calls his sister in Honolulu. What time is it in Honolulu?

Exercises

Copy and complete the table. Give the times in other cities when it is 9 A.M. in Denver. Give the times in other cities when it is 1 P.M. in Dallas.

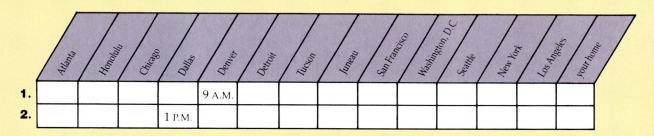

	Atlanta	Honolulu	Chicago	Dallas	Denver	Detroit	Tucson	Juneau	San Francisco	Washington, D.C.	Seattle	New York	Los Angeles	your home
1.					9 A.M.									
2.				1 P.M.										

Solve each problem.

3. Brian is in Dallas. It is 12 noon. He calls his sister in Seattle. What time is it in Seattle?

4. Louis is in Juneau. It is 1 P.M. He calls his mother in Atlanta. What time is it in Atlanta?

5. Isabel is in Detroit. She calls her husband in San Francisco. His clock reads 11 P.M. What time is it in Detroit?

6. A flight leaves Boston at 5 P.M. for Chicago. The flight time is 2 h 50 min. What time will it be in Chicago when the flight arrives?

7. A flight leaves New York at 9 A.M. for Los Angeles. The flight time is 6 h. What time will it be in Los Angeles when the flight lands?

★ 8. A flight leaves Seattle at 12 noon. The flight to Boston is 6 h 20 min. What time will it be in Boston when the flight arrives?

Centimeter and Millimeter

■ The **centimeter (cm)** is a unit used to measure length in the metric system.

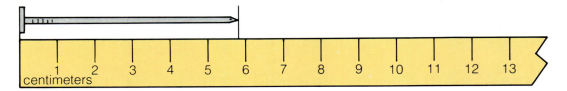

This nail is between 5 and 6 centimeters long. The length is nearer to 6 centimeters than to 5 centimeters. It is 6 centimeters long to the nearest centimeter.

■ The **millimeter (mm)** is a unit used to measure small lengths in the metric system.

1 centimeter = 10 millimeters

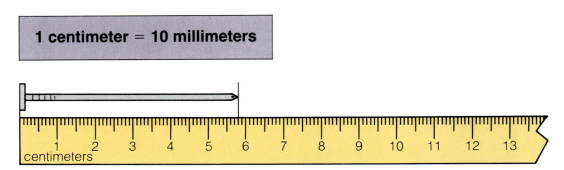

The nail is about 58 millimeters long.

Try These

Measure to the nearest centimeter and to the nearest millimeter.

1.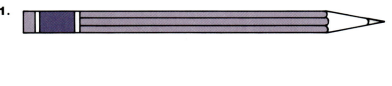

2.

Exercises

Measure to the nearest centimeter and to the nearest millimeter.

1.

2.

3. ▱▱▱▱▱▱▱▱▱▱

4.    **5.** 🦴

6. the width of this book   **7.** the length of this book

Write *mm* or *cm*.

8. The head of a pin is about 1 ▥ wide.   **9.** A paper clip is about 1 ▥ wide.

10. A toothbrush is about 16 ▥ long.   **11.** A bee is about 9 ▥ long.

Choose the sensible measurement.

12. A postage stamp is ▥ wide.   **a.** 2 cm   **b.** 2 mm   **c.** 20 cm
13. A pen is ▥ long.   **a.** 6 mm   **b.** 15 mm   **c.** 15 cm
14. A button is ▥ wide.   **a.** 18 cm   **b.** 18 mm   **c.** 2 mm
15. Carlos is ▥ tall.   **a.** 172 mm   **b.** 10 cm   **c.** 172 cm

THINK AND TRY

USING ESTIMATION

Find five objects in the classroom that can be measured in centimeters. Make a table of your data.

Object	Estimate	Measurement	Difference

1. Estimate the length of each object.

2. Measure each object to the nearest centimeter.

3. Compare your estimate with the measurement.

Meter and Kilometer

■ The **meter (m)** and the **kilometer (km)** are units used to measure long distances in the metric system.

1 meter = 100 centimeters

The distance from a doorknob to the floor is about 1 meter. The length of a baseball bat is about 1 meter.

1 kilometer = 1,000 meters

It takes about 10 minutes to walk a distance of 1 kilometer. A good athlete can run a kilometer in about 2 minutes.

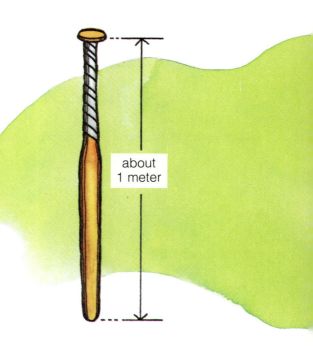

about 1 meter

■ Measurements can be changed from one unit to another.

$$5 \text{ m} = \blacksquare \text{ cm} \qquad\qquad 8{,}000 \text{ m} = \blacksquare \text{ km}$$
$$1 \text{ m} = 100 \text{ cm} \qquad\qquad 1{,}000 \text{ m} = 1 \text{ km}$$
$$\text{so} \quad 5 \text{ m} = 500 \text{ cm} \qquad\qquad \text{so} \quad 8{,}000 \text{ m} = 8 \text{ km}$$

Try These

Write _m_ or _km_.

1. The length of a car is about 5 ▉.

2. The distance from San Francisco to Los Angeles is about 650 ▉.

3. The height of a flagpole is about 20 ▉.

4. The height of a mountain is about 4 ▉.

Copy and complete.

5. 3 km = ▉ m

6. 5,000 m = ▉ km

7. 7,000 m = ▉ km

8. 6 km = ▉ m

9. 13,000 m = ▉ km

10. 15 km = ▉ m

Exercises

Write *mm, cm, m,* or *km*.

1. The width of this page is about 20 ■.

2. The thickness of a quarter is about 2 ■.

3. The distance from St. Paul to Chicago is 483 ■.

4. The length of a golf club is about 1 ■.

5. The length of a classroom is about 7 ■.

6. The width of a dollar bill is about 7 ■.

7. The Grand Canyon is about 1 ■ deep.

8. The length of a safety pin is about 26 ■.

Choose the sensible measurement.

	a.	**b.**	**c.**
9. A tennis court is ■ long.	23 mm	23 cm	23 m
10. The World Trade Towers are ■ high.	405 m	405 mm	405 km
11. A piece of chalk is ■ long.	6 m	6 cm	6 km
12. The Mississippi River is ■ long.	3,800 km	3,800 cm	3,800 mm
13. A pencil point is ■ wide.	1 m	1 km	1 mm
14. Distance from Dallas to Denver is ■.	1,255 mm	1,255 km	1,255 cm
15. A carrot is ■ long.	15 cm	15 km	15 m
16. A dime is ■ thick.	1 m	1 cm	1 mm

Copy and complete.

17. 2 km = ■ m

18. 5 cm = ■ mm

19. 4 m = ■ cm

20. 30 mm = ■ cm

21. 2 m = ■ cm

22. 9,000 m = ■ km

23. 600 cm = ■ m

24. 18,000 m = ■ km

25. 12 km = ■ m

Solve each problem.

This sign shows the speed limit in kilometers per hour.

26. Sara drove for 2 h at the speed limit. How far did she go?

27. John had 310 km to drive. He drove for 3 h at the speed limit. How far did John drive? How much farther did he have to go?

★ 28. Felipe drove for 4 h at the speed limit. Then he was 65 km from his destination. How far did Felipe travel in all to arrive at his destination?

Milliliter and Liter

■ The **liter (L)** and the **milliliter (mL)** are used to measure **capacity** in the metric system. Capacity is the amount of a substance that a container can hold.

The small cube holds 1 milliliter of water. The large cube holds 1 liter of water.

1 liter = 1,000 milliliters

16 drops of water is about 1 milliliter.
1 cup holds about 250 milliliters of water.
Orange juice is sometimes sold by the liter.

■ You can change measurements from one unit to another.

$3 L = \blacksquare mL$ $2,000 mL = \blacksquare L$
$1 L = 1,000 mL$ $1,000 mL = 1 L$
so $3 L = 3,000 mL$ so $2,000 mL = 2 L$

Try These

Write *L* or *mL*.

1. An eyedropper holds 1 ▧ of water.

2. A sink holds about 50 ▧ of water.

3. A pitcher holds about 1 ▧ of water.

4. A can holds 300 ▧ of soup.

Copy and complete.

5. $5 L = \blacksquare mL$

6. $4,000 mL = \blacksquare L$

7. $15 L = \blacksquare mL$

Exercises

Write *L* or *mL*.

1. A drinking glass holds about 250 ▧ of liquid.

2. A pitcher holds about 1 ▧ of liquid.

3. A teaspoon holds 5 ▧ of liquid.

4. A fish tank holds 25 ▧ of water.

Choose the sensible measurement.

5. The gas tank of a car holds ▦. **a.** 60 mL   **b.** 20 L   **c.** 55 L

6. A bathtub holds ▦ of water. **a.** 150 mL   **b.** 250 L   **c.** 10 L

7. A tablespoon holds ▦ of liquid. **a.** 15 mL   **b.** 15 L   **c.** 2 L

8. The height of a building is ▦. **a.** 60 mm   **b.** 60 km   **c.** 60 m

9. A barrel of oil holds ▦. **a.** 200 mL   **b.** 200 L   **c.** 2 mL

10. A punch bowl holds ▦ of punch. **a.** 2 L   **b.** 2 mL   **c.** 20 mL

11. A pencil is about ▦ long. **a.** 5 mm   **b.** 15 cm   **c.** 15 m

12. A bottle of shampoo holds ▦. **a.** 3 mL   **b.** 31 L   **c.** 310 mL

13. A quarter is ▦ wide. **a.** 23 mm   **b.** 23 cm   **c.** 23 km

Copy and complete.

14. 2,000 mL = ▦ L   15. 6 L = ▦ mL   16. 9,000 mL = ▦ L
17. 4 cm = ▦ mm   18. 12 L = ▦ mL   19. 5 m = ▦ cm
20. 10,000 mL = ▦ L   21. 3 km = ▦ m   22. 8 L = ▦ mL
23. 600 cm = ▦ m   24. 90 mm = ▦ cm   25. 21,000 mL = ▦ L

About how many milliliters are there in the following?

26. 2 cups   27. 4 cups   28. 10 cups   29. 100 cups

About how many drops of water are there in the following?

30. 1 cup   ★ 31. 1 liter   ★ 32. 10 liters   ★ 33. 100 liters

Solve each problem.

34. Maria used 3 L of juice to make a fruit punch. How many milliliters of juice did she use to make the punch?

35. A bottle contains 59 mL of vanilla. Leah uses 12 mL of vanilla for baking. How much vanilla is left in the bottle?

36. A can holds 500 mL of frozen orange juice. You add 3 cans of water to mix the juice. How many liters of juice will you make in all?

★ 37. John had a liter container of milk. He used 3 cups of milk for baking. How much milk is left in the container?

Gram and Kilogram

■ The **gram (g)** and the **kilogram (kg)** are used to measure weight in the metric system.

1 milliliter of water weighs 1 gram.
1 liter of water weighs 1 kilogram.

> **1 kilogram = 1,000 grams**

A peanut weighs about 1 gram.
A cup weighs about 250 grams.
An iron weighs about 1 kilogram.
A horse weighs about 500 kilograms.

■ You can change measurements from one unit to another.

$$4 \text{ kg} = \blacksquare \text{ g} \qquad\qquad 9{,}000 \text{ g} = \blacksquare \text{ kg}$$
$$1 \text{ kg} = 1{,}000 \text{ g} \qquad\qquad 1{,}000 \text{ g} = 1 \text{ kg}$$
$$\text{so} \quad 4 \text{ kg} = 4{,}000 \text{ g} \qquad \text{so} \quad 9{,}000 \text{ g} = 9 \text{ kg}$$

Try These

Write g or kg.

1. A nickel weighs about 5 ■.

2. A bag of potatoes weighs about 2 ■.

3. A bar of soap weighs about 120 ■.

4. A basketball weighs about 1 ■.

Copy and complete.

5. 3 kg = ■ g

6. 2,000 g = ■ kg

7. 16,000 g = ■ kg

Exercises

Write *g* or *kg*.

1. Your math book weighs about 1 ▓.

2. A paper clip weighs about 1 ▓.

3. A box of detergent weighs about 2 ▓.

4. An egg weighs about 40 ▓.

5. A slice of bread weighs about 28 ▓.

6. A bowling ball weighs about 6 ▓.

Choose the sensible measurement.

7. A dollar bill weighs about ▓. **a.** 1 kg **b.** 1 g **c.** 300 g

8. A cat weighs about ▓. **a.** 6 kg **b.** 6 g **c.** 600 kg

9. A bed is about ▓ long. **a.** 2 cm **b.** 2 m **c.** 2 km

10. A watermelon weighs about ▓. **a.** 3 g **b.** 30 g **c.** 3 kg

11. A bottle of perfume holds about ▓. **a.** 120 mL **b.** 12 L **c.** 120 L

12. An apple weighs about ▓. **a.** 15 g **b.** 150 g **c.** 15 kg

13. A tennis racket is about ▓ long. **a.** 65 mm **b.** 65 m **c.** 65 cm

14. A pail holds about ▓ of water. **a.** 4 L **b.** 4 mL **c.** 40 mL

15. A toothbrush weighs about ▓. **a.** 30 kg **b.** 30 g **c.** 3 kg

16. A bunch of carrots weighs about ▓. **a.** 1 g **b.** 10 g **c.** 1 kg

Copy and complete.

17. 5 kg = ▓ g

18. 6,000 g = ▓ kg

19. 8 kg = ▓ g

20. 3 L = ▓ mL

21. 70 mm = ▓ cm

22. 4,000 g = ▓ kg

23. 2 m = ▓ cm

24. 2,000 mL = ▓ L

25. 12 kg = ▓ g

26. 9 km = ▓ m

27. 400 cm = ▓ m

28. 20,000 g = ▓ kg

 You need about 1,000 milligrams of calcium each day. Each cup of milk has about 290 milligrams of calcium.

> *1 gram = 1,000 milligrams*

29. How many glasses of milk must you drink to be sure you get enough calcium? Give the answer in a whole number of glasses.

30. Did you round your answer up or down? Why?

Problem Solving: Applications

READ
PLAN
DO
CHECK

METRIC MEASURES

Jon Brighton is a carpenter. He builds bookshelves for the science lab. A shelf is 1 m long. Each science book is 3 cm thick. How many books will fit on each shelf?

3cm

1m

The shelf is 1 m long. The book is 3 cm thick.

Change the measurements to the same unit. Then divide to find how many books will fit.

1 m = 100 cm

100 cm ÷ 3 cm = 33 R1

$$\begin{array}{r} 33 \text{ R1} \\ 3\overline{)100} \\ \underline{9} \\ 10 \\ \underline{9} \\ 1 \end{array}$$

33 books will fit on each shelf.

Try These

Solve each problem.

1. Joe wants to fill a 1-L beaker using a 100-mL cup. How many full 100-mL cups must he use to fill the beaker?

2. A box contains 1 kg of salt. Paula uses 350 g of salt in an experiment. How much salt is left in the box?

3. Mrs. Stein has a piece of string 3 m long. She needs pieces of string 25 cm long. How many 25-cm pieces can Mrs. Stein cut from her piece of string?

4. Jane has 2 L of a solution. She pours out 650 mL. How much does she have left?

Exercises

Solve each problem.

1. Mr. Rice used plastic tubing 1 m 32 cm long in an experiment. How many centimeters long was the tubing?

2. 1 tablespoon holds 15 mL. How many tablespoons of water can be poured from a beaker containing 210 mL of water?

3. Gene has a 1-kg bag of sand. He uses 475 g in an experiment. How much sand is left in the bag?

4. Ellen mixes 35 mL of acid with 965 mL of water to make a solution. How many liters of solution does Ellen make?

5. Bob is making additional shelves for the lab. He has a board 3 m long. He wants to make 3 shelves that are each 110 cm long. Is the board long enough?

6. Denise is mixing some dry chemicals. She uses 75 g of one. She uses 45 g of each of two other chemicals. How much does her total mixture weigh?

7. There is a 5-m roll of wire on the science lab shelf. Jay uses 75 cm of wire for one experiment and 125 cm for another experiment. How much wire is left on the roll?

8. Sam uses a balance scale to weigh an object. He places a 1-kg, a 100-g, and a 25-g weight on the scale to balance the object. How many grams does the object weigh?

★ 9. Peggy has 2 L of water for an experiment. A liter of water weighs 1 kg. How many grams of water does Peggy have?

★ 10. Ronald Chin is a carpenter. He is remodeling the science lab. He buys 10d (tenpenny) nails by weight. He needs about 1,000 nails. He knows that each nail weighs about 7 g. How many kilograms of nails should he buy?

Problem Solving: Strategies

LOGICAL REASONING

■ Julio and Donna want pumpkins by October 31. The package of seeds says that pumpkins take 110 days to grow and ripen. Julio plants seeds on May 27. Donna plants seeds on June 17. Will either person have pumpkins by October 31?

One way to solve this problem is to **work backward.** Add the days back from October 31.

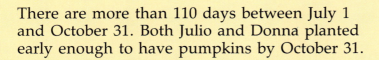

	Days
October	31
September	30
August	31
July	+31
	123

There are more than 110 days between July 1 and October 31. Both Julio and Donna planted early enough to have pumpkins by October 31.

■ When is the last possible date to plant pumpkin seeds to have pumpkins by October 31?

Count back the months.

October	31
September	30
August	+31
	92

Between August 1 and October 31, there are 92 days. Count back further.

    110 days needed to grow pumpkins
− 92 days between August 1 and October 31
     18

Count back 18 more days.

    31 days in July
−18
 13

The last date to plant pumpkin seeds is July 13.

Using the Strategy

Solve each problem.

1. Jerry wants carrots by July 10. The seed package says that carrots take 70 days to grow. When is the last day Jerry can plant carrot seeds?

2. Josephine wants beans by September 15. The seed package says that beans take 59 days to grow. When is the last day Josephine can plant beans?

3. Debbie has $327 in her bank account. Last week she deposited $100. Two weeks ago she withdrew $45. How much was in her account before she withdrew the money?

4. Gary has 67 baseball cards. Linda has 71 baseball cards. Last week Gary traded 4 cards to Linda for 2 of her cards. How many cards did each of them have before the trade?

5. Divide the number by 4. Add 11. The sum is 19. What is the number?

6. Multiply the number by 5. Divide by 2. The quotient is 10. What is the number?

7. Multiply the number by 7. Divide by 3. The quotient is 14. What is the number?

8. Subtract 5 from the number. Divide by 2. The quotient is 3. What is the number?

9. Divide the number by 7. Add 5. The sum is 15. What is the number?

10. Multiply the number by 6. Subtract 18. The difference is 24. What is the number?

ACTIVITY

ESTIMATING TIME

How well can you estimate time? Try these activities.

1. Stand back-to-back with a partner. At the word *go*, try to estimate 60 seconds. Hold up your hand when you think 60 seconds have passed.

2. Put your head down and close your eyes. Estimate 3 minutes. Raise your head when you think 3 minutes have passed.

3. Write a television commercial that you think will take 30 seconds. Try it and time it.

Using an Inch Ruler

The **inch (in.)** is a unit used to measure length in the customary system.

This ruler is marked in inches and parts of an inch.

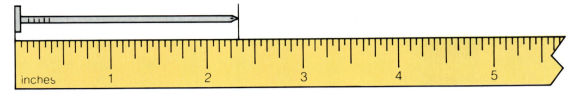

The nail is 2 inches long to the nearest inch.

It is $2\frac{1}{2}$ inches long to the nearest half-inch.

It is $2\frac{1}{4}$ inches long to the nearest quarter-inch.

It is $2\frac{3}{8}$ inches long to the nearest eighth-inch.

It is $2\frac{5}{16}$ inches long to the nearest sixteenth-inch.

Try These

Read the ruler at the place marked.

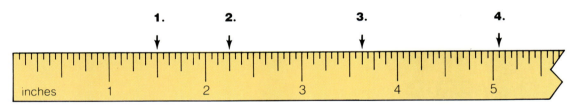

Measure the chain to the nearest inch, half-inch, quarter-inch, and eighth-inch.

5.

Exercises

Read the ruler at the place marked.

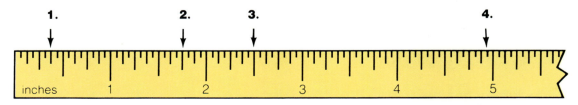

Measure to the nearest inch, half-inch, quarter-inch, and eighth-inch.

5.

6.

7.

Measure to the nearest inch and half-inch.

8. the width of this book

9. the length of this book

10. the width of your thumb

11. the length of your index finger

Draw a nail to show each length.

12. 1 inch

13. $2\frac{1}{2}$ inches

14. $\frac{3}{4}$ inch

15. $3\frac{1}{4}$ inches

16. $1\frac{3}{8}$ inches

17. $2\frac{13}{16}$ inches

KEEPING IN SHAPE

1. $\begin{array}{r} 371 \\ +256 \\ \hline \end{array}$

2. $\begin{array}{r} 780 \\ -634 \\ \hline \end{array}$

3. $\begin{array}{r} 25 \\ \times 18 \\ \hline \end{array}$

4. $\begin{array}{r} 406 \\ \times 32 \\ \hline \end{array}$

5. $\begin{array}{r} 678 \\ + 49 \\ \hline \end{array}$

6. $\begin{array}{r} 2,603 \\ - 587 \\ \hline \end{array}$

7. $\begin{array}{r} 145 \\ \times 226 \\ \hline \end{array}$

8. $\begin{array}{r} 6,334 \\ +3,826 \\ \hline \end{array}$

9. $\begin{array}{r} 7,145 \\ -6,328 \\ \hline \end{array}$

10. $\begin{array}{r} 2,134 \\ \times 705 \\ \hline \end{array}$

11. $826 + 234$

12. $79 \div 4$

13. $518 - 79$

14. 355×46

15. $871 \div 27$

16. $1,204 \div 53$

Customary Units of Length

■ The **foot (ft)**, the **yard (yd)**, and the **mile (mi)** are units used to measure length.

1 foot = 12 inches **1 yard = 3 feet** **1 yard = 36 inches**

1 mile = 5,280 feet **1 mile = 1,760 yards**

A postage stamp is about 1 inch wide.
The height of a room is about 8 feet.
A door is about 1 yard wide.
The distance between Dallas and
    New York is about 1,374 miles.

■ Use the chart to find the number of feet in 4 yards 2 feet.

$$4 \text{ yd } 2 \text{ ft} = \blacksquare \text{ ft}$$
$$1 \text{ yd} = 3 \text{ ft}$$
$$4 \text{ yd} = 4 \times 3 \text{ ft}$$
$$4 \text{ yd} = 12 \text{ ft}$$
$$4 \text{ yd } 2 \text{ ft} = 12 \text{ ft} + 2 \text{ ft}$$
$$4 \text{ yd } 2 \text{ ft} = 14 \text{ ft}$$

■ Use the chart to find the number of feet and inches in 50 inches.

$$50 \text{ in.} = \blacksquare \text{ ft } \blacksquare \text{ in.}$$
$$12 \text{ in.} = 1 \text{ ft}$$

$$50 \text{ in.} = 4 \text{ ft } 2 \text{ in.}$$

$$\begin{array}{r} 4 \text{ R2} \\ 12\overline{)50} \\ \underline{48} \\ 2 \end{array}$$

Try These

Write *in., ft, yd,* or *mi*.

1. A football field is 100 ▦ long.

2. An airplane can fly 600 ▦ per hour.

3. A paper clip is about 1 ▦ long.

4. Jana is about 4 ▦ tall.

Copy and complete.

5. 24 in. = ▦ ft

6. 1 yd 1 ft = ▦ ft

7. 72 in. = ▦ yd

Exercises

Write *in., ft, yd,* or *mi.*

1. It takes about 28 min to walk 1 ▪.

2. The width of this book is about 8 ▪.

3. A car is about 16 ▪ long.

4. A desk is about 1 ▪ high.

5. The distance between New York and California is about 3,000 ▪.

6. A crayon is about 4 ▪ long.

Choose the sensible measurement.

7. A radio is about ▪ long.   **a.** 8 in.   **b.** 8 ft   **c.** 8 yd

8. Kim's cat is about ▪ high.   **a.** 1 yd   **b.** 1 mi   **c.** 1 ft

9. A car can travel ▪ per hour.   **a.** 55 ft   **b.** 55 mi   **c.** 55 in.

10. A refrigerator is about ▪ high.   **a.** 2 ft   **b.** 2 yd   **c.** 2 mi

11. A worm is about ▪ long.   **a.** 3 in.   **b.** 3 yd   **c.** 3 mi

12. The distance from Miami to Atlanta is about ▪.   **a.** 665 mi   **b.** 665 yd   **c.** 665 ft

13. A washing machine is about ▪ high.   **a.** 1 ft   **b.** 1 yd   **c.** 1 in.

14. The policeman is about ▪ tall.   **a.** 6 yd   **b.** 6 in.   **c.** 6 ft

Copy and complete.

15. 5 yd = ▪ ft

16. 1 ft 2 in. = ▪ in.

17. 8 ft = ▪ yd ▪ ft

18. 3 yd 2 ft = ▪ ft

19. 2 mi = ▪ yd

20. 32 in. = ▪ ft ▪ in.

21. 4 yd = ▪ in.

22. 300 ft = ▪ yd

23. 2 mi = ▪ ft

24. 180 in. = ▪ yd

25. 1 mi 350 yd = ▪ yd

★ **26.** 420 in. = ▪ yd ▪ ft

Solve each problem.

27. Paige has 8 ft 9 in. of ribbon. How many inches of ribbon does she have?

28. A tailor has 3 yd 2 ft of fabric. How many feet of fabric does she have?

29. Lisa needs 7 ft of fabric to make curtains. She has a piece of fabric 2 yd 20 in. long. Does she have enough fabric to make the curtains?

30. A weaver has 6,370 yards of yarn. He wants to weave 13 rugs of equal size. How much yarn will he use for each rug?

Customary Units of Capacity

■ The **fluid ounce (fl oz)**, the **cup (c)**, the **pint (pt)**, the **quart (qt)**, and the **gallon (gal)** are units used to measure liquid capacity.

1 cup	**= 8 fluid ounces**
1 pint	**= 2 cups**
1 quart	**= 2 pints**
1 gallon	**= 4 quarts**

A bottle of food flavoring is about 1 fluid ounce.

A drinking glass holds about 1 cup of water.

A bottle of lemon juice is about 1 pint.

Milk is often sold in 1-quart containers.

A can of paint holds 1 gallon.

■ Use the chart to find the number of pints in 4 qt 3 pt.

$$4 \text{ qt } 3 \text{ pt} = \blacksquare \text{ pt}$$
$$1 \text{ qt} = 2 \text{ pt}$$
$$4 \text{ qt} = 4 \times 2 \text{ pt}$$
$$4 \text{ qt} = 8 \text{ pt}$$
$$4 \text{ qt } 3 \text{ pt} = 8 \text{ pt} + 3 \text{ pt}$$
$$4 \text{ qt } 3 \text{ pt} = 11 \text{ pt}$$

■ Use the chart to find the number of cups and fluid ounces in 46 fl oz.

$$46 \text{ fl oz} = \blacksquare \text{ c } \blacksquare \text{ fl oz}$$
$$8 \text{ fl oz} = 1 \text{ c}$$

$$46 \text{ fl oz} = 5 \text{ c } 6 \text{ fl oz}$$

$$\begin{array}{r} 5 \text{ R6} \\ 8)\overline{46} \\ \underline{40} \\ 6 \end{array}$$

Try These

Write *fl oz, c, pt, qt,* or *gal*.

1. The tank of a car holds about 15 ▦ of gas.

2. A soup recipe calls for 8 ▦ of water.

3. A bowl holds about 1 ▦ of gravy.

4. A can contains 1 ▦ of oil.

5. A bottle holds 4 ▦ of perfume.

6. A glass contains 1 ▦ of milk.

Copy and complete.

7. 3 gal = ▦ qt

8. 16 fl oz = ▦ c

9. 2 pt 1 c = ▦ c

Exercises

Write *fl oz, c, pt, qt,* or *gal*.

1. A fish tank holds 5 ▦ of water.

2. A jar contains 2 ▦ of paint.

3. A jar of salad dressing contains 8 ▦.

4. A baby bottle holds 1 ▦.

5. A pitcher holds 1 ▦ of juice.

6. A bird bath holds 5 ▦ of water.

Choose the sensible measurement.

7. A bottle contains ▦ of vanilla. **a.** 2 fl oz **b.** 2 qt **c.** 2 gal

8. A large pot holds ▦. **a.** 6 fl oz **b.** 6 qt **c.** 6 c

9. Jerry used ▦ of milk on his cereal. **a.** 1 qt **b.** 1 gal **c.** 1 c

10. A pencil is about ▦ long. **a.** 7 ft **b.** 7 in. **c.** 7 yd

11. Robin walks about ▦ to school. **a.** 1 mi **b.** 1 yd **c.** 1 ft

Copy and complete.

12. 5 qt = ▦ pt

13. 8 qt = ▦ gal

14. 2 gal 3 qt = ▦ qt

15. 4 c = ▦ fl oz

16. 2 ft 4 in. = ▦ in.

17. 3 pt 1 c = ▦ c

18. 13 ft = ▦ yd ▦ ft

19. 29 fl oz = ▦ c ▦ fl oz

20. 15 qt = ▦ gal ▦ qt

Solve each problem.

21. Dawn uses about 30 gal of water to take a bath. Jody uses about 80 qt to take a shower. Who uses more water?

★ **22.** A bottle contains 16 fl oz of shampoo. How many pints of shampoo does the bottle contain?

Customary Units of Weight

- The **ounce (oz)**, the **pound (lb)**, and the **ton** are used to measure weight.

> **1 pound = 16 ounces**
> **1 ton   = 2,000 pounds**

A letter weighs about 1 ounce.
A loaf of bread weighs about 1 pound.
A small car weighs about 1 ton.

- Use the chart to find the number of pounds in 2 tons 1,500 lb.

$$2 \text{ tons } 1{,}500 \text{ lb} = \blacksquare \text{ lb}$$
$$1 \text{ ton} = 2{,}000 \text{ lb}$$
$$2 \text{ tons} = 2 \times 2{,}000 \text{ lb}$$
$$2 \text{ tons} = 4{,}000 \text{ lb}$$
$$2 \text{ tons } 1{,}500 \text{ lb} = 4{,}000 \text{ lb} + 1{,}500 \text{ lb}$$
$$2 \text{ tons } 1{,}500 \text{ lb} = 5{,}500 \text{ lb}$$

- Use the chart to find the number of pounds and ounces in 60 oz.

$$60 \text{ oz} = \blacksquare \text{ lb} \blacksquare \text{ oz}$$
$$16 \text{ oz} = 1 \text{ lb}$$

$$60 \text{ oz} = 3 \text{ lb } 12 \text{ oz}$$

$$\begin{array}{r} 3 \text{ R}12 \\ 16\overline{)60} \\ 48 \\ \hline 12 \end{array}$$

Try These

Write *oz*, *lb*, or *ton*.

1. A bag of potatoes weighs 5 ■.

2. An apple weighs about 5 ■.

3. A large truck can carry 2 ■ of cement.

4. A man weighs about 175 ■.

Copy and complete.

5. 4 lb = ■ oz

6. 41 oz = ■ lb ■ oz

7. 3 tons = ■ lb

Exercises

Write *oz, lb,* or *ton.*

1. Jason weighs about 55 ▦.

2. A crane lifted a 5-▦ truck.

3. A slice of cheese weighs about 1 ▦.

4. A package of butter weighs about 1 ▦.

5. A box of cereal weighs about 13 ▦.

6. An elephant weighs about 2 ▦.

Choose the sensible measurement.

7. An elephant weighs about ▦ .   **a.** 1 lb   **b.** 1 ton   **c.** 10 oz

8. Sue's car holds about ▦ of oil.   **a.** 5 qt   **b.** 5 fl oz   **c.** 5 c

9. Mr. Lee cooked a ▦ turkey.   **a.** 10-oz   **b.** 10-ton   **c.** 10-lb

10. A bottle contains ▦ of vinegar.   **a.** 1 fl oz   **b.** 1 pt   **c.** 1 gal

11. A can of tuna fish weighs about ▦.   **a.** 6 oz   **b.** 6 lb   **c.** 6 tons

12. Sandra is about ▦ tall.   **a.** 5 yd   **b.** 5 ft   **c.** 5 in.

Copy and complete.

13. 3 lb = ▦ oz

14. 1 lb 4 oz = ▦ oz

15. 5 tons = ▦ lb

16. 50 oz = ▦ lb ▦ oz

17. 3 tons 400 lb = ▦ lb

18. 3 qt = ▦ pt

19. 20 ft = ▦ yd ▦ ft

20. 4,000 lb = ▦ tons

21. 1 mi = ▦ yd

22. 2 lb 14 oz = ▦ oz

23. 23 qt = ▦ gal ▦ qt

24. 1,920 oz = ▦ lb

Solve each problem.

25. A customer buys 2 lb 11 oz of meat. How many ounces of meat does the customer buy?

26. Brand X cereal weighs 1 lb 2 oz. Brand Y cereal weighs 20 oz. Which cereal weighs more?

27. A roll of Brand A paper toweling is 28 yd 1 ft long. A roll of Brand B toweling is 88 ft long. Which roll of toweling is longer?

28. Mr. King buys 32 oz of meat. The meat costs $2.39 per pound. How much does Mr. King pay for the meat?

29. Mrs. Haber buys a 48-fl oz bottle of apple juice. How many cups of juice can she pour from the bottle?

★ 30. A customer buys 4 lb 8 oz of meat. Can she serve 10 people 8 oz of meat each?

Working with Measurements

■ Steve is making a fishing pole. He has two pieces of fishing line. One is 8 ft 6 in. long. The other is 7 ft 8 in. long. Steve ties the fishing lines together. How long is his fishing line?

To find the length of the fishing line, add.

Add the inches.

$$\begin{array}{r} 8 \text{ ft } 6 \text{ in.} \\ +7 \text{ ft } 8 \text{ in.} \\ \hline 14 \text{ in.} \end{array}$$

Add the feet.

$$\begin{array}{r} 8 \text{ ft } 6 \text{ in.} \\ +7 \text{ ft } 8 \text{ in.} \\ \hline 15 \text{ ft } 14 \text{ in.} \end{array}$$

Rename the answer.

14 in. = 1 ft 2 in.
15 ft 14 in. = 16 ft 2 in.

The fishing line is 16 ft 2 in. long.

■ How much longer is one fishing line than the other fishing line?

Subtract to find the difference in the lengths.

$$\begin{array}{r} 8 \text{ ft } 6 \text{ in.} \\ -7 \text{ ft } 8 \text{ in.} \\ \hline \end{array}$$

6 in. < 8 in.
Rename 1 ft as 12 in.
12 in. + 6 in. = 18 in.

$$\begin{array}{r} {}^{7}{}^{18} \\ \cancel{8} \text{ ft } \cancel{6} \text{ in.} \\ -7 \text{ ft } 8 \text{ in.} \\ \hline 10 \text{ in.} \end{array}$$

One fishing line is 10 in. longer than the other fishing line.

Try These

Add. Rename when necessary.

1. $\begin{array}{r} 2 \text{ ft } 4 \text{ in.} \\ +1 \text{ ft } 6 \text{ in.} \\ \hline \end{array}$

2. $\begin{array}{r} 3 \text{ ft } 6 \text{ in.} \\ +4 \text{ ft } 9 \text{ in.} \\ \hline \end{array}$

3. $\begin{array}{r} 2 \text{ lb } 9 \text{ oz} \\ +4 \text{ lb } 11 \text{ oz} \\ \hline \end{array}$

4. $\begin{array}{r} 5 \text{ gal } 2 \text{ qt} \\ +2 \text{ gal } 1 \text{ qt} \\ \hline \end{array}$

Subtract. Rename when necessary.

5. $\begin{array}{r} 6 \text{ ft } 8 \text{ in.} \\ -2 \text{ ft } 5 \text{ in.} \\ \hline \end{array}$

6. $\begin{array}{r} 5 \text{ yd } 1 \text{ ft} \\ -3 \text{ yd } 2 \text{ ft} \\ \hline \end{array}$

7. $\begin{array}{r} 3 \text{ c } 7 \text{ fl oz} \\ -2 \text{ c } 3 \text{ fl oz} \\ \hline \end{array}$

8. $\begin{array}{r} 4 \text{ lb } 6 \text{ oz} \\ -3 \text{ lb } 13 \text{ oz} \\ \hline \end{array}$

Exercises

Add. Rename when necessary.

1. 2 lb 8 oz
+ 1 lb 4 oz

2. 8 ft 10 in.
+ 1 ft 10 in.

3. 3 gal 2 qt
+ 2 gal 3 qt

4. 4 yd 2 ft
+ 2 yd 1 ft

5. 3 lb 12 oz
+ 4 lb 11 oz

6. 1 qt 1 pt
+ 5 qt 1 pt

7. 6 ft 1 in.
+ 1 ft 9 in.

8. 3 yd 2 ft
+ 7 yd 2 ft

Subtract. Rename when necessary.

9. 8 ft 11 in.
− 5 ft 4 in.

10. 8 lb 2 oz
− 6 lb 12 oz

11. 4 gal 1 qt
− 2 gal 3 qt

12. 5 yd 1 ft
− 4 yd 2 ft

13. 2 ft 6 in.
−   9 in.

14. 6 qt
− 3 qt 1 pt

15. 1 lb 5 oz
−   9 oz

16. 8 lb
− 2 lb 7 oz

Add or subtract. Rename when necessary.

17. 7 lb 10 oz
+ 8 lb

18. 12 ft 8 in.
− 6 ft 10 in.

19. 5 c 4 fl oz
+ 3 c 6 fl oz

20. 7 yd
− 2 yd 2 ft

21. 3 lb 14 oz
+ 2 lb 10 oz

22. 4 gal
− 3 gal 2 qt

★ **23.** 1 h 45 min
+ 1 h 30 min

★ **24.** 6 h 5 min
− 2 h 38 min

Solve each problem.

25. Beth catches two fish. One fish weighs 2 lb 6 oz, and the other weighs 1 lb 13 oz. How much do the fish weigh in all?

26. Bernie has 5 yd of rope. He uses 1 yd 2 ft of rope to put up his tent. How much rope does Bernie have left?

27. The campers used 2 gal 2 qt of water for drinking and 1 gal 3 qt of water for cooking. How much water did they use in all?

28. Tim's backpack weighs 1 lb 2 oz. He puts 7 lb 13 oz of equipment in the backpack. How much does it weigh in all?

29. Mike's boat is 6 yd 2 ft long. Karen's boat is 7 yd 1 ft long. How much longer is Karen's boat?

★ **30.** Cindy hiked 4 mi 180 yd. Dan hiked 5 mi 45 yd. How much farther did Dan hike?

Measurement   191

Problem Solving: Applications

READ
PLAN
DO
CHECK

MEAN AND RANGE

The table shows the length and wingspan of some birds of prey that live in North America.

SOME BIRDS OF PREY OF NORTH AMERICA		
Bird	Length (in inches)	Wingspan (in inches)
osprey	22	54
bald eagle	30	80
peregrine falcon	18	40
red-tailed hawk	21	48
golden eagle	34	78

■ Find the **mean** length of these birds. Mean is another name for average.

Add the lengths of each bird.

$$
\begin{array}{r}
22 \\
30 \\
18 \\
21 \\
+34 \\
\hline
125
\end{array}
$$

Divide by the number of birds, 5.

$$
\begin{array}{r}
25 \\
5)\overline{125} \\
\underline{10} \\
25 \\
\underline{25} \\
0
\end{array}
$$

The mean length of these birds is 25 inches.

■ Find the **range** of the lengths. Range is the difference between the least and the greatest length.

The golden eagle has the greatest length, 34 in. The peregrine falcon has the least length, 18 in.

$$
\begin{array}{r}
34 \\
-18 \\
\hline
16
\end{array}
$$

The range of the lengths is 16 in.

Try These

Solve each problem.

1. What is the mean wingspan of these birds?

2. What is the range of the wingspans of these birds?

3. What is the range of the wingspans of the two kinds of eagles?

4. What is the mean length of the two kinds of eagles?

Exercises

Solve each problem.

This table shows the lengths and wingspans of some shorebirds that live in North America.

SOME SHOREBIRDS OF NORTH AMERICA		
Bird	Length (in inches)	Wingspan (in inches)
snowy egret	22	38
great egret	34	55
great blue heron	40	70
whooping crane	46	90
sandhill crane	37	80
American bittern	25	45

1. What is the mean length of the birds in this table?

2. What is the mean length of the egrets?

3. What is the range of the lengths of these birds?

4. What is the range of the lengths of the cranes?

5. What is the mean wingspan of these birds?

6. What is the mean wingspan of the cranes?

7. What is the range of the wingspans of these birds?

8. What is the range of the wingspans of the egrets?

The nature club took a survey of the birds in a city park. They made this graph based on the data they collected.

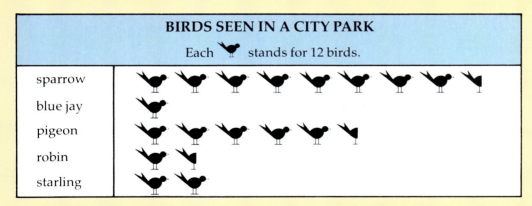

BIRDS SEEN IN A CITY PARK

Each 🐦 stands for 12 birds.

sparrow	🐦🐦🐦🐦🐦🐦🐦🐦🐦
blue jay	🐦
pigeon	🐦🐦🐦🐦🐦
robin	🐦
starling	🐦

9. How many starlings did the members of the nature club count?

10. How many sparrows did the members of the nature club count?

11. Did they see more robins or blue jays? How many more?

12. Did they see more robins or starlings? How many more?

13. How many birds did the members of the nature club count altogether?

14. There are three city parks about the same size. How many pigeons live in the city parks in all?

6 CHAPTER CHECKPOINT

What time will it be? (pp. 164–165)

1. 3 hours after 7:00 A.M.

2. 1 hour 15 minutes before 8:10 P.M.

3. 4 hours 20 minutes after 10:23 A.M.

4. 2 hours 19 minutes after 11:34 P.M.

Copy and complete. (pp. 166–167)

5. 4 weeks = ▦ days

6. 58 h = ▦ days ▦ h

7. 2 min 36 s = ▦ s

8. 3 h = ▦ min

9. Measure this string to the nearest centimeter and millimeter. (pp. 170–171)

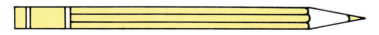

Choose the sensible measurement. (pp. 170–177)

10. The width of a penny is about ▦. **a.** 20 m **b.** 20 cm **c.** 20 mm

11. A large pitcher holds about ▦ of water. **a.** 1 L **b.** 1 mL **c.** 10 mL

12. A pen weighs ▦. **a.** 8 kg **b.** 8 g **c.** 800 g

13. An airplane flew ▦. **a.** 500 km **b.** 500 cm **c.** 500 mm

14. A drinking cup holds about ▦ of water. **a.** 2 L **b.** 250 L **c.** 250 mL

Copy and complete. (pp. 170–177)

15. 3 km = ▦ m

16. 4,000 mL = ▦ L

17. 800 cm = ▦

18. 5 kg = ▦ g

19. 13,000 g = ▦ kg

20. 9 cm = ▦

21. 10 L = ▦ mL

22. 60 mm = ▦ cm

23. 12 m = ▦

24. Measure the pencil to the nearest inch, half-inch, quarter-inch, and eighth-inch. (pp. 182–183)

Choose the sensible measurement. (pp. 184–189)

25. A pear weighs about ▦. **a.** 4 lb **b.** 4 oz **c.** 4 tons

26. The length of a room is about ▦. **a.** 5 mi **b.** 5 in. **c.** 5 yd

27. A jug contains ▦ of juice. **a.** 1 gal **b.** 1 c **c.** 1 fl oz

28. A pickup truck weighs about ▦. **a.** 2 oz **b.** 2 tons **c.** 2 lb

Copy and complete. (pp. 184–189)

29. 4 lb = ■ oz   **30.** 3 gal = ■ qt   **31.** 12 ft = ■ yd

32. 2 ft 11 in. = ■ in.   **33.** 3 lb 8 oz = ■ oz   **34.** 5 qt 1 pt = ■ pt

35. 20 ft = ■ yd ■ ft   **36.** 2 tons = ■ lb   **37.** 2 mi = ■ ft

38. 70 oz = ■ lb ■ oz   **39.** 17 c = ■ pt ■ c   **40.** 10,000 lb = ■ tons

Add or subtract. Rename when necessary. (pp. 190–191)

41.   3 ft 4 in.
    + 1 ft 7 in.

42.   8 lb 14 oz
    − 5 lb 9 oz

43.   4 yd 1 ft
    − 2 yd 2 ft

44.   7 gal 1 qt
    + 8 gal 3 qt

45.   3 ft 1 in.
    − 2 ft 9 in.

46.   6 lb 11 oz
    +   13 oz

47.   7 ft 8 in.
    + 5 ft 10 in.

48.   12 qt
    − 9 qt 1 pt

Solve each problem. (pp. 164–193)

49. Marge worked from 3:30 P.M. to 6:45 P.M. How long did Marge work?

50. Pearl is in Boston. It is 2 P.M. She calls her friend in Los Angeles. What time is it in Los Angeles?

51. You have 2 L of water in a bottle. You pour out 450 mL of water. How many milliliters of water are left?

52. A box contains 1 kg of detergent. Walter uses 250 g of detergent in a wash. How much detergent is left in the box?

53. You buy 48 oz of meat. The meat costs $3.19 per pound. How much do you pay for the meat?

54. A bottle contains 40 fl oz of juice. How many cups of juice can you pour from the bottle?

Sam recorded the amount of snow that fell in his town for the last 5 weeks.

55. What is the mean weekly snowfall for the 5 weeks?

56. What is the snowfall range for the 5 weeks?

Snowfall	
week 1	15 cm
week 2	2 cm
week 3	3 cm
week 4	0 cm
week 5	10 cm

COMPUTERS AND
PROBLEM SOLVING

■ Computers sometimes do things too quickly. You can slow a program down by building a delay into it. A time-delay loop tells the computer to count to a certain number without printing what it is counting.

Here is a time-delay loop.

```
NEW
10   FOR N=1 TO 1000
20   NEXT N
30   END
```

Line 10 sets up a loop. It assigns N the starting value of 1.

Line 20 sends the computer back to line 10. There, it increases N by 1. N is now 2.

The looping continues until N reaches a value of 1,000.

The computer then skips line 20 and continues on to other lines in the program. This takes about 1 second.

Solve each problem.

1. Write a time-delay loop that will take about 5 seconds to run.

2. Write a time-delay loop that will take about $\frac{1}{2}$ second to run.

3. Decide what this program would do.

```
NEW
10    LET A$="ROW"
20    FOR N=1 TO 3
30    PRINT A$
40    NEXT N
50    PRINT "YOUR BOAT"
60    PRINT "GENTLY DOWN THE STREAM "
70    END
```

4. Remove END from line 70. Write lines 70 to 120 using B$ and a FOR . . . NEXT loop to print out the rest of the song.

5. Add a 10-second time delay between lines 60 and 70 to make the computer pause after printing the first half of the song.

ENRICHMENT

FAHRENHEIT SCALE

Temperature can be measured in degrees Fahrenheit (°F).

Water boils at 212°F.
Water freezes at 32°F.
The normal body temperature is about 98°F.

The highest temperature recorded in the United States is
134°F in Death Valley, California, on July 10, 1913.
The lowest temperature recorded in the United States is
−80°F (the − means below 0°) in Prospect Creek, Alaska,
on January 23, 1971.

Write *true* or *false*.

1. Lucy's body temperature is 101°F. She is sick.

2. Jerry measured the temperature of a
   glass of water. It was 18°F.

3. The temperature outside is 40°F.
   You need to wear a coat outside.

4. The temperature outside is 50°F.
   Tommy went ice skating on the pond.

 The National Weather Service keeps a record of the
high and low temperatures each day.

5. Find the average high temperature
   for the week.

6. Find the average low temperature
   for the week.

7. What is the temperature range for
   each day?

8. What is the mean temperature for
   each day?

9. What is the mean temperature for
   the week?

Temperature Readings		
Day	High	Low
Monday	86°F	68°F
Tuesday	85°F	65°F
Wednesday	82°F	64°F
Thursday	81°F	65°F
Friday	82°F	66°F
Saturday	85°F	65°F
Sunday	87°F	69°F

CUMULATIVE REVIEW

Write each number.

1. 15 million 24 thousand 11
2. four hundred thousand, two hundred three
3. three billion, one hundred seventeen million, fifty thousand, six

Round each number.

4. 348 to the nearest ten
5. 1,652 to the nearest hundred
6. 8,493 to the nearest thousand
7. 52,740,136 to the nearest million

Add or subtract.

8.	9.	10.	11.	12.
39 + 57	473 − 165	215 + 487	644 − 85	3,041 − 729

13.	14.	15.	16.	17.
$11.35 + 29.83	32,081 + 19,426	$46.50 − 28.75	72,304 − 9,586	18,440 − 7,962

Multiply.

18.	19.	20.	21.	22.
23 × 3	175 × 4	$36.22 × 6	14,832 × 8	526 × 70

23.	24.	25.	26.	27.
847 × 39	$17.95 × 24	2,783 × 600	509 × 157	3,481 × 698

Divide.

28. $9\overline{)72}$
29. $8\overline{)68}$
30. $2\overline{)59}$
31. $3\overline{)963}$
32. $6\overline{)218}$

33. $7\overline{)4,906}$
34. $8\overline{)2,436}$
35. $40\overline{)253}$
36. $36\overline{)648}$
37. $57\overline{)1,670}$

38. $61\overline{)2,028}$
39. $19\overline{)485}$
40. $67\overline{)8,583}$
41. $38\overline{)39,126}$
42. $25\overline{)\$356.50}$

Add, subtract, multiply, or divide.

43. 375 + 68 + 719
44. 32,164 − 9,857
45. 458 × 17
46. 564 ÷ 18
47. 2,389 × 407
48. 8,052 ÷ 77

(Continued)

Estimate each answer.

49. 384 + 529

50. 8,241 − 2,516

51. 475 × 32

52. 18,267 − 6,039

53. 6,731 + 4,225

54. 74 × 4,129

Choose the sensible measurement.

55. The height of a dining table is about ▦.   **a.** 75 mm   **b.** 75 cm   **c.** 75 m

56. A can of paint holds about ▦ of paint.   **a.** 4 mL   **b.** 40 mL   **c.** 4 L

57. A brick weighs about ▦.   **a.** 2 kg   **b.** 2 g   **c.** 20 g

58. A sink holds about ▦ of water.   **a.** 5 c   **b.** 5 pt   **c.** 5 gal

59. A sailboat is about ▦ long.   **a.** 22 ft   **b.** 22 in.   **c.** 22 mi

60. A tube of toothpaste weighs about ▦.   **a.** 7 lb   **b.** 7 tons   **c.** 7 oz

Copy and complete.

61. 2 km = ▦ m

62. 8,000 g = ▦ kg

63. 60 mm = ▦ cm

64. 7 L = ▦ mL

65. 400 cm = ▦ m

66. 11 kg = ▦ g

67. 5 lb = ▦ oz

68. 39 ft = ▦ yd

69. 2 ft 7 in. = ▦ in.

70. 3 gal 2 qt = ▦ qt

71. 42 oz = ▦ lb ▦ oz

72. 13 c = ▦ pt ▦ c

Solve each problem.

73. Marie buys a book for $24.95. She gives the clerk $40. How much change should Marie get?

74. Robert types 95 words per minute. How many words can he type in 15 minutes?

75. There are 432 sweaters and 93 hats to display. 18 sweaters fit on each shelf. How many shelves can be filled with sweaters?

76. Carol started baby-sitting at 7:20 P.M. She finished baby-sitting at 12:45 A.M. For how long did Carol baby-sit?

77. Ray started painting at 10:15 A.M. He painted for 4 h 30 min. What time did Ray stop painting?

78. The speed limit is 85 kilometers per hour. How long will it take to drive 340 km at the speed limit?

79. The contents of a can weigh 250 g. How many kilograms will 4 cans weigh?

80. Mrs. Fine buys 6 lb of meat. She uses 2 lb 10 oz of the meat for stew. How much meat is left?

7

FRACTIONS:
ADDITION AND SUBTRACTION

Fractions

■ A **fraction** may name part of a region.

1 part is planted.
There are 4 equal parts.
One-fourth of the lot is planted.

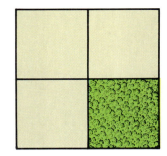

$\dfrac{1}{4}$ ←—— parts planted
←—— equal parts in all

■ A fraction may name part of a set.

There are 3 tulips.
There are 5 flowers in all.
Three-fifths of the flowers are tulips.

$\dfrac{3}{5}$ ←—— tulips
←—— flowers

■ This number line is marked in four equal segments. It shows fourths.

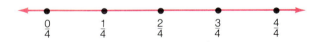

$\dfrac{0}{4}$ $\dfrac{1}{4}$ $\dfrac{2}{4}$ $\dfrac{3}{4}$ $\dfrac{4}{4}$

■ A fraction is written with two numbers.

$\dfrac{1}{4}$ ←—— **numerator**
←—— **denominator**

The numerator and the denominator are called the **terms** of a fraction.

Try These

Write a fraction for the shaded part.

1.

2.

3.

Write the missing fractions.

4.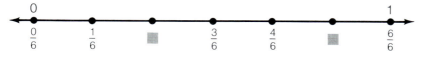

Exercises

Write a fraction for the shaded part.

1.

2.

3.

4.

5.

6.

7.

8.

9.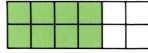

Count the equal segments.
Then name each point with a fraction.

10.

11.

Solve each problem.
Write a fraction to answer each question.

12. 5 bushes are shipped. 2 of them are rosebushes. What part of the shipment of bushes is roses?

13. There are 12 roses. 7 of them are yellow. What part of the roses are yellow?

14. 7 people buy seeds. 4 of them buy vegetable seeds. What part of the people buy vegetable seeds?

15. 16 tulip bulbs are in a package. 5 are for red tulips. What part of the bulbs are for red tulips?

Fractions: Addition and Subtraction   203

Equivalent Fractions

$\frac{1}{2}$ of the circle is shaded.

$\frac{2}{4}$ of the circle is shaded.

$\frac{3}{6}$ of the circle is shaded.

The same part of each circle is shaded.
$\frac{1}{2}$, $\frac{2}{4}$, and $\frac{3}{6}$ are **equivalent fractions**.
They are names for the same number.

■ Equivalent fractions can be shown on a number line.

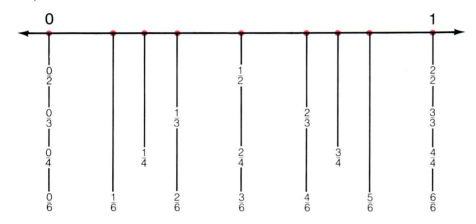

■ You can multiply to find equivalent fractions.

> *To find an equivalent fraction, multiply the numerator and the denominator by the same number.*

$$\frac{1}{2} = \frac{1 \times 2}{2 \times 2} = \frac{2}{4} \qquad \frac{1}{2} = \frac{1 \times 3}{2 \times 3} = \frac{3}{6}$$

$\frac{1}{2}$, $\frac{2}{4}$, and $\frac{3}{6}$ are equivalent fractions.

■ Find the missing numerator.

Think: The denominator is multiplied by 3. So multiply the numerator by 3.

$$\frac{2}{3} = \frac{\blacksquare}{9}$$

$$\frac{2}{3} = \frac{}{3 \times 3} = \frac{}{9}$$

$$\frac{2}{3} = \frac{2 \times 3}{3 \times 3} = \frac{6}{9}$$

Try These

Write two equivalent fractions for the shaded part.

1.   2.   3.

Copy and complete.

4. $\dfrac{2}{7} = \dfrac{2 \times 3}{7 \times 3} = \dfrac{\blacksquare}{\blacksquare}$

5. $\dfrac{3}{4} = \dfrac{3 \times \blacksquare}{4 \times \blacksquare} = \dfrac{\blacksquare}{8}$

6. $\dfrac{3}{8} = \dfrac{3 \times \blacksquare}{8 \times \blacksquare} = \dfrac{6}{\blacksquare}$

Write the missing fractions.

7.
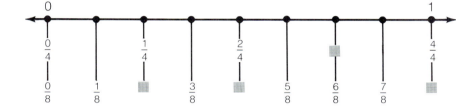

Exercises

Write two equivalent fractions for the shaded part.

1.   2.   3.

Copy and complete. Do as many as you can mentally.

4. $\dfrac{2}{5} = \dfrac{2 \times 3}{5 \times 3} = \dfrac{\blacksquare}{\blacksquare}$

5. $\dfrac{1}{10} = \dfrac{1 \times \blacksquare}{10 \times 3} = \dfrac{\blacksquare}{\blacksquare}$

6. $\dfrac{7}{8} = \dfrac{7 \times \blacksquare}{8 \times \blacksquare} = \dfrac{\blacksquare}{24}$

7. $\dfrac{1}{3} = \dfrac{\blacksquare}{6}$

8. $\dfrac{3}{6} = \dfrac{\blacksquare}{18}$

9. $\dfrac{1}{2} = \dfrac{\blacksquare}{12}$

10. $\dfrac{5}{6} = \dfrac{\blacksquare}{24}$

11. $\dfrac{2}{3} = \dfrac{\blacksquare}{24}$

12. $\dfrac{3}{10} = \dfrac{\blacksquare}{100}$

13. $\dfrac{2}{3} = \dfrac{8}{\blacksquare}$

14. $\dfrac{1}{2} = \dfrac{5}{\blacksquare}$

15. $\dfrac{3}{5} = \dfrac{6}{\blacksquare}$

16. $\dfrac{7}{10} = \dfrac{\blacksquare}{100}$

17. $\dfrac{4}{5} = \dfrac{\blacksquare}{100}$

18. $\dfrac{1}{2} = \dfrac{\blacksquare}{100}$

19. $\dfrac{1}{3} = \dfrac{4}{\blacksquare}$

20. $\dfrac{2}{5} = \dfrac{\blacksquare}{10}$

21. $\dfrac{4}{4} = \dfrac{\blacksquare}{12}$

22. $\dfrac{5}{9} = \dfrac{10}{\blacksquare}$

Fractions in Lowest Terms

■ Another way to find equivalent fractions is to divide both terms by a common factor.

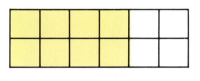

2 is a common factor of 8 and 12.
$$\frac{8}{12} = \frac{8 \div 2}{12 \div 2} = \frac{4}{6} \qquad \frac{8}{12} = \frac{4}{6}$$

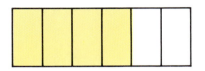

4 is a common factor of 8 and 12.
$$\frac{8}{12} = \frac{8 \div 4}{12 \div 4} = \frac{2}{3} \qquad \frac{8}{12} = \frac{2}{3}$$

$\frac{8}{12}$, $\frac{4}{6}$, and $\frac{2}{3}$ are equivalent fractions.

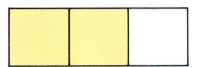

When both terms have no common factors greater than 1, the fraction is in **lowest terms**.

$\frac{8}{12}$ in lowest terms is $\frac{2}{3}$.

■ Write $\frac{6}{18}$ in lowest terms.

> *To write a fraction in lowest terms, divide the numerator and the denominator by the greatest common factor.*

Factors of 6:   1, 2, 3, 6

Factors of 18:   1, 2, 3, 6, 9

Common factors of 6 and 18:   1, 2, 3, 6

Greatest common factor of 6 and 18:   6

Divide both terms by 6.

$$\frac{6}{18} = \frac{6 \div 6}{18 \div 6} = \frac{1}{3}$$

$\frac{6}{18}$ in lowest terms is $\frac{1}{3}$.

Try These

Find the greatest common factor.

1. 4 and 6

2. 12 and 6

3. 9 and 18

4. 8 and 24

Copy and complete.

5. $\dfrac{6}{9} = \dfrac{6 \div 3}{9 \div 3} = \dfrac{\blacksquare}{\blacksquare}$

6. $\dfrac{10}{15} = \dfrac{10 \div 5}{15 \div \blacksquare} = \dfrac{\blacksquare}{\blacksquare}$

7. $\dfrac{8}{10} = \dfrac{8 \div \blacksquare}{10 \div 2} = \dfrac{\blacksquare}{\blacksquare}$

Exercises

Find the greatest common factor.

1. 18 and 24

2. 15 and 20

3. 27 and 45

4. 9 and 12

5. 20 and 30

6. 35 and 50

7. 16 and 30

8. 28 and 21

Copy and complete.

9. $\dfrac{6}{15} = \dfrac{6 \div 3}{15 \div 3} = \dfrac{\blacksquare}{\blacksquare}$

10. $\dfrac{16}{20} = \dfrac{16 \div 4}{20 \div \blacksquare} = \dfrac{\blacksquare}{\blacksquare}$

11. $\dfrac{25}{40} = \dfrac{25 \div \blacksquare}{40 \div 5} = \dfrac{\blacksquare}{\blacksquare}$

Write each fraction in lowest terms. Do as many as you can mentally.

12. $\dfrac{3}{6}$

13. $\dfrac{6}{8}$

14. $\dfrac{9}{12}$

15. $\dfrac{9}{18}$

16. $\dfrac{7}{21}$

17. $\dfrac{4}{16}$

18. $\dfrac{5}{10}$

19. $\dfrac{15}{20}$

20. $\dfrac{6}{15}$

21. $\dfrac{10}{30}$

22. $\dfrac{15}{25}$

23. $\dfrac{20}{60}$

24. $\dfrac{8}{14}$

25. $\dfrac{12}{24}$

26. $\dfrac{27}{45}$

27. $\dfrac{9}{15}$

28. $\dfrac{25}{75}$

29. $\dfrac{50}{100}$

30. $\dfrac{10}{20}$

31. $\dfrac{20}{30}$

32. $\dfrac{3}{27}$

33. $\dfrac{5}{30}$

34. $\dfrac{20}{40}$

35. $\dfrac{300}{900}$

Solve each problem.
Write each answer in lowest terms.

36. You know that 1 hour is equal to 60 minutes. What part of an hour is 20 minutes? 30 minutes? 45 minutes?

37. Brian practices the piano for 40 min. What part of an hour does he practice?

38. Mrs. Burke gives Brian a 50-min piano lesson each week. What part of an hour is each lesson?

39. Brian practices a new piece for 24 min. What part of an hour does he practice the new piece?

Fractions: Addition and Subtraction   207

Mixed Numbers

■ Fractions can name numbers greater than 1.

You can write a fraction or a
mixed number to tell how
much of the circles is shaded.

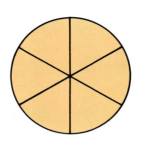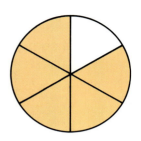

$$\frac{6}{6} + \frac{5}{6} = \frac{11}{6} \longleftarrow \text{fraction}$$

$$1 + \frac{5}{6} = 1\frac{5}{6} \longleftarrow \text{mixed number}$$

■ You can use division to write a fraction as a mixed number.

Write $\frac{18}{8}$ as a mixed number.
$\frac{18}{8}$ means $18 \div 8$.

Think:

$$\begin{array}{r} 2 \text{ R2 or } 2\frac{2}{8} \\ 8\overline{)18} \\ \underline{16} \\ 2 \end{array}$$

$\longleftarrow$ remainder
$\longleftarrow$ divisor

Write $2\frac{2}{8}$ in lowest terms.

$$\frac{2}{8} = \frac{2 \div 2}{8 \div 2} = \frac{1}{4}$$

$$2\frac{2}{8} = 2\frac{1}{4}$$

$$\frac{18}{8} = 2\frac{1}{4}$$

■ Sometimes a fraction names a whole number.

Write $\frac{8}{2}$ as a whole number.
$\frac{8}{2}$ means $8 \div 2$.

$$\frac{8}{2} = 4 \qquad \begin{array}{r} 4 \\ 2\overline{)8} \end{array}$$

Try These

Write the fraction as a whole number or as a mixed number in lowest terms. Do as many as you can mentally.

1. $\frac{5}{5}$
2. $\frac{8}{5}$
3. $\frac{12}{6}$
4. $\frac{12}{7}$
5. $\frac{14}{4}$
6. $\frac{12}{3}$

Exercises

Write the fraction as a whole number or as a mixed number in lowest terms. Do as many as you can mentally.

1. $\frac{12}{4}$
2. $\frac{20}{6}$
3. $\frac{35}{6}$
4. $\frac{20}{4}$
5. $\frac{8}{8}$
6. $\frac{54}{6}$

7. $\frac{27}{5}$
8. $\frac{35}{5}$
9. $\frac{16}{10}$
10. $\frac{15}{3}$
11. $\frac{20}{10}$
12. $\frac{45}{7}$

13. $\frac{17}{5}$
14. $\frac{27}{10}$
15. $\frac{40}{8}$
16. $\frac{63}{9}$
17. $\frac{88}{10}$
18. $\frac{27}{4}$

19. $\frac{30}{5}$
20. $\frac{58}{7}$
21. $\frac{80}{10}$
22. $\frac{36}{6}$
23. $\frac{48}{9}$
24. $\frac{32}{8}$

25. $\frac{31}{7}$
26. $\frac{46}{6}$
27. $\frac{45}{7}$
28. $\frac{81}{9}$
29. $\frac{500}{100}$
30. $\frac{28}{8}$

Divide. Write the quotient as a mixed number in lowest terms.

31. $7\overline{)32}$
32. $6\overline{)47}$
33. $9\overline{)97}$
34. $4\overline{)106}$
35. $5\overline{)113}$

36. $8\overline{)212}$
37. $10\overline{)98}$
38. $30\overline{)69}$
39. $12\overline{)145}$
40. $40\overline{)195}$

Solve each problem.
Write each answer in lowest terms.

41. You know that 1 lb is equal to 16 oz. Tom used 8 oz of cheese on a pizza. What part of a pound did he use?

42. Tom used 40 oz of cheese on special party pizzas. How many pounds of cheese did he use?

43. Tom cut a pizza into 8 equal pieces. He put mushrooms on 3 of the pieces. What part of the pizza has mushrooms?

★ 44. Tom baked 2 pizzas. He cut each one into 4 equal pieces. He and a friend ate 6 of the pieces. What part of a pizza was left?

Adding Fractions

■ Bob Kaminski drives a delivery truck. One day he delivered $\frac{2}{12}$ of his packages to a school. He delivered $\frac{3}{12}$ of his packages to an office building. What part of the packages did he deliver to these two buildings?

To find the part Bob delivered, add $\frac{2}{12}$ and $\frac{3}{12}$.

To add fractions with common denominators:

1. Add the numerators.

$$\frac{2}{12} + \frac{3}{12} = \frac{5}{}$$

> $\frac{2}{12}$ and $\frac{3}{12}$ have a **common denominator**, 12.

2. Use the common denominator.

$$\frac{2}{12} + \frac{3}{12} = \frac{5}{12}$$

Bob delivered $\frac{5}{12}$ of the packages to the two buildings.

■ Sometimes the answer is not in lowest terms.

Add: $\frac{4}{9} + \frac{2}{9}$

$$\frac{4}{9} + \frac{2}{9} = \frac{6}{9}$$
$$= \frac{2}{3}$$

$$\begin{array}{r} \frac{4}{9} \\ + \frac{2}{9} \\ \hline \frac{6}{9} = \frac{2}{3} \end{array}$$

■ Sometimes the answer is a mixed number.

Add: $\frac{2}{4} + \frac{3}{4}$

$$\frac{2}{4} + \frac{3}{4} = \frac{5}{4}$$
$$= 1\frac{1}{4}$$

Try These

Add. Write each sum in lowest terms.

1. $\frac{1}{5} + \frac{2}{5}$ **2.** $\frac{1}{8} + \frac{1}{8}$ **3.** $\frac{1}{6} + \frac{2}{6}$ **4.** $\frac{7}{8} + \frac{2}{8}$

Exercises

Add. Write each sum in lowest terms.

1. $\frac{1}{3} + \frac{1}{3}$ **2.** $\frac{1}{5} + \frac{1}{5}$ **3.** $\frac{3}{7} + \frac{2}{7}$ **4.** $\frac{1}{8} + \frac{3}{8}$

5. $\frac{2}{5} + \frac{2}{5}$ **6.** $\frac{1}{4} + \frac{1}{4}$ **7.** $\frac{1}{6} + \frac{1}{6}$ **8.** $\frac{3}{10} + \frac{3}{10}$

9. $\frac{3}{4} + \frac{1}{4}$ **10.** $\frac{4}{5} + \frac{3}{5}$ **11.** $\frac{7}{10} + \frac{3}{10}$ **12.** $\frac{5}{7} + \frac{6}{7}$

13. $\frac{5}{6} + \frac{5}{6}$ **14.** $\frac{7}{8} + \frac{5}{8}$ **15.** $\frac{7}{12} + \frac{5}{12}$ **16.** $\frac{31}{100} + \frac{87}{100}$

17. $\begin{array}{r} \frac{1}{12} \\ + \frac{2}{12} \\ \hline \end{array}$ **18.** $\begin{array}{r} \frac{2}{6} \\ + \frac{2}{6} \\ \hline \end{array}$ **19.** $\begin{array}{r} \frac{2}{9} \\ + \frac{7}{9} \\ \hline \end{array}$ **20.** $\begin{array}{r} \frac{1}{5} \\ + \frac{4}{5} \\ \hline \end{array}$ **21.** $\begin{array}{r} \frac{1}{4} \\ + \frac{1}{4} \\ \hline \end{array}$ **22.** $\begin{array}{r} \frac{9}{10} \\ + \frac{9}{10} \\ \hline \end{array}$

23. $\begin{array}{r} \frac{1}{7} \\ + \frac{5}{7} \\ \hline \end{array}$ **24.** $\begin{array}{r} \frac{3}{4} \\ + \frac{3}{4} \\ \hline \end{array}$ **25.** $\begin{array}{r} \frac{3}{6} \\ + \frac{5}{6} \\ \hline \end{array}$ **26.** $\begin{array}{r} \frac{8}{10} \\ + \frac{4}{10} \\ \hline \end{array}$ **27.** $\begin{array}{r} \frac{3}{7} \\ + \frac{4}{7} \\ \hline \end{array}$ **28.** $\begin{array}{r} \frac{45}{100} \\ + \frac{59}{100} \\ \hline \end{array}$

Solve each problem.
Write each answer in lowest terms.

29. Bob has 18 boxes to deliver in Area E. 6 of them are for Ed's Hardware. What part of the boxes are for Ed's Hardware?

30. From the store, Bob drives $\frac{3}{10}$ km south for delivery A. Then he drives $\frac{7}{10}$ km north for delivery B. How far does he drive altogether?

31. Bob delivers about $\frac{2}{6}$ of the packages by 10 A.M. He delivers another $\frac{2}{6}$ by noon. What part of the group of packages is delivered by noon?

★ **32.** Bob drives $\frac{3}{10}$ km east for delivery A. Then he drives $\frac{7}{10}$ km north for delivery B. Then he drives $\frac{9}{10}$ km west for delivery C. How far does he drive altogether?

Fractions: Addition and Subtraction   211

Subtracting Fractions

■ Jeff used $\frac{3}{4}$ cup of whole wheat flour in a recipe. He also used $\frac{2}{4}$ cup of white flour. How much more whole wheat flour than white flour did Jeff use?

Subtract $\frac{2}{4}$ from $\frac{3}{4}$ to find how much more.

To subtract fractions with common denominators:

1. Subtract the numerators.

$$\frac{3}{4} - \frac{2}{4} = \frac{1}{}$$

> $\frac{3}{4}$ and $\frac{2}{4}$ have a common denominator, 4.

2. Use the common denominator.

$$\frac{3}{4} - \frac{2}{4} = \frac{1}{4}$$

Jeff used $\frac{1}{4}$ cup more whole wheat flour.

■ Sometimes the answer is not in lowest terms.

Subtract: $\frac{5}{6} - \frac{3}{6}$

$$\frac{5}{6} - \frac{3}{6} = \frac{2}{6}$$
$$= \frac{1}{3}$$

$$\begin{array}{r} \frac{5}{6} \\ -\frac{3}{6} \\ \hline \frac{2}{6} = \frac{1}{3} \end{array}$$

Try These

Subtract. Write each difference in lowest terms.

1. $\frac{3}{5} - \frac{1}{5}$

2. $\frac{5}{10} - \frac{2}{10}$

3. $\frac{6}{8} - \frac{4}{8}$

4. $\frac{5}{6} - \frac{2}{6}$

Exercises

Subtract. Write each difference in lowest terms.

1. $\dfrac{2}{3} - \dfrac{1}{3}$ **2.** $\dfrac{3}{5} - \dfrac{2}{5}$ **3.** $\dfrac{5}{7} - \dfrac{3}{7}$ **4.** $\dfrac{5}{6} - \dfrac{1}{6}$

5. $\dfrac{3}{8} - \dfrac{1}{8}$ **6.** $\dfrac{7}{10} - \dfrac{3}{10}$ **7.** $\dfrac{7}{12} - \dfrac{1}{12}$ **8.** $\dfrac{3}{4} - \dfrac{2}{4}$

9. $\dfrac{5}{8} - \dfrac{3}{8}$ **10.** $\dfrac{5}{12} - \dfrac{1}{12}$ **11.** $\dfrac{8}{10} - \dfrac{4}{10}$ **12.** $\dfrac{61}{100} - \dfrac{11}{100}$

13. $\dfrac{5}{10} - \dfrac{3}{10}$ **14.** $\dfrac{6}{12} - \dfrac{3}{12}$ **15.** $\dfrac{3}{8} - \dfrac{2}{8}$ **16.** $\dfrac{4}{4} - \dfrac{2}{4}$ **17.** $\dfrac{9}{10} - \dfrac{3}{10}$ **18.** $\dfrac{7}{8} - \dfrac{3}{8}$

19. $\dfrac{4}{9} - \dfrac{1}{9}$ **20.** $\dfrac{4}{7} - \dfrac{3}{7}$ **21.** $\dfrac{9}{12} - \dfrac{3}{12}$ **22.** $\dfrac{7}{8} - \dfrac{3}{8}$ **23.** $\dfrac{11}{12} - \dfrac{7}{12}$ **24.** $\dfrac{75}{100} - \dfrac{25}{100}$

Solve each problem.
Write each answer in lowest terms.

25. Jeff had $\dfrac{3}{4}$ c of milk. He used $\dfrac{1}{4}$ c to make cornbread batter. How much milk does he have left?

26. A recipe calls for $\dfrac{3}{8}$ c lemon juice. Jeff has $\dfrac{2}{8}$ c juice. How much more juice does he need?

27. Jeff makes a salad that has two layers. He uses $\dfrac{3}{4}$ c pineapple in each of the two layers. How much pineapple does he use?

★ **28.** Jeff has one dozen eggs. He uses 3 eggs to make one omelette. If Jeff makes 3 omelettes, what part of a dozen eggs will be left?

KEEPING IN SHAPE

1. 4 cm = ▨ mm   **2.** 100 cm = ▨ mm   **3.** 280 mm = ▨ cm

4. 5 m = ▨ cm   **5.** 60 m = ▨ cm   **6.** 300 cm = ▨ m

7. 3 km = ▨ m   **8.** 4,000 m = ▨ km   **9.** 5 L = ▨ mL

10. 9,000 mL = ▨ L   **11.** 7 kg = ▨ g   **12.** 8,000 g = ▨ kg

Problem Solving: Strategies

ORGANIZING INFORMATION

Organizing information can help you solve problems. One way to organize information is to **make a model**.

Bill Malone is making wooden blocks. He has a piece of wood that is already painted on the top and sides. He plans to cut the wood into 12 blocks.

How many blocks are already painted on 3 faces?

Make a model. Use grid paper. Fold the grid paper to resemble the piece of wood.

> Each corner block has 3 faces already painted. There are 4 corner blocks.

4 blocks are already painted on 3 faces.

What fraction of the blocks are painted on 3 faces?

> 4 blocks are painted on 3 faces. There are 12 blocks in all.

$$\frac{4}{12} = \frac{4 \div 4}{12 \div 4} = \frac{1}{3}$$

$\frac{1}{3}$ of the blocks are painted on 3 faces.

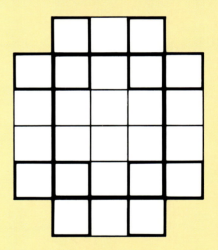

Using the Strategy

Use the model to solve each problem.

1. How many blocks are already painted on only 2 faces?

2. What fraction of the blocks are painted on only 2 faces?

3. How many blocks are painted on only 1 face?

4. What fraction of the blocks are painted on only 1 face?

Bill cuts the piece of wood into 12 blocks. This is a model of a corner block.

5. How many faces does each block have?

6. What fraction of each corner block is already painted?

Make a model of each block to solve each problem.

7. What fraction of each edge block is already painted?

8. What fraction of each middle block is already painted?

9. What is the total number of faces that are already painted?

10. What is the total number of faces for all the blocks?

11. Bill wants to paint all the faces of each block. How many faces must still be painted?

12. What fraction of the faces must still be painted?

 ## ACTIVITY

USING A MODEL

This large cube is made of 27 small cubes.

Find or make a model of the cube to help you answer each question.

1. What fraction of the small cubes have only 1 outside face?

2. What fraction of the small cubes have exactly 2 outside faces?

3. What fraction of the small cubes have exactly 3 outside faces?

4. What fraction of the small cubes have no outside faces?

Least Common Denominator

■ Compare $\frac{2}{5}$ and $\frac{3}{5}$.

The fractions have a common denominator, so compare the numerators.

$$2 < 3$$

$$\text{so}\quad \frac{2}{5} < \frac{3}{5} \quad \text{or} \quad \frac{3}{5} > \frac{2}{5}$$

■ Compare $\frac{1}{2}$ and $\frac{1}{3}$.

The fractions have different denominators. First find equivalent fractions with a common denominator. Think of multiples of the denominators.

Common multiples of 2 and 3:   6, 12
Least common multiple of 2 and 3:   6

Write equivalent fractions for $\frac{1}{2}$ and $\frac{1}{3}$. Use 6 as the **least common denominator**.

$$\frac{1}{2} = \frac{\blacksquare}{6} \qquad\qquad \frac{1}{3} = \frac{\blacksquare}{6}$$

$$\frac{1}{2} = \frac{1 \times 3}{2 \times 3} = \frac{3}{6} \qquad \frac{1}{3} = \frac{1 \times 2}{3 \times 2} = \frac{2}{6}$$

Compare.

$$\frac{3}{6} > \frac{2}{6} \quad \text{so} \quad \frac{1}{2} > \frac{1}{3}$$

Try These

Find the least common denominator.
Then write equivalent fractions with that denominator.

1. $\frac{1}{4}, \frac{2}{3}$

2. $\frac{1}{3}, \frac{2}{5}$

3. $\frac{3}{7}, \frac{4}{9}$

4. $\frac{3}{8}, \frac{5}{6}$

Write >, <, or =.

5. $\frac{4}{5} \blacksquare \frac{3}{5}$

6. $\frac{3}{4} \blacksquare \frac{3}{5}$

7. $\frac{5}{6} \blacksquare \frac{10}{12}$

8. $\frac{4}{9} \blacksquare \frac{2}{3}$

Exercises

Find the least common denominator.
Then write equivalent fractions with that denominator.

1. $\frac{5}{6}, \frac{7}{9}$

2. $\frac{3}{4}, \frac{5}{6}$

3. $\frac{3}{5}, \frac{1}{10}$

4. $\frac{2}{3}, \frac{5}{7}$

5. $\frac{7}{8}, \frac{5}{6}$

6. $\frac{5}{12}, \frac{3}{8}$

7. $\frac{1}{7}, \frac{1}{11}$

8. $\frac{1}{2}, \frac{3}{5}$

Write >, <, or =.

9. $\frac{1}{5}$ ▨ $\frac{3}{5}$

10. $\frac{7}{8}$ ▨ $\frac{3}{8}$

11. $\frac{1}{3}$ ▨ $\frac{2}{3}$

12. $\frac{5}{6}$ ▨ $\frac{1}{4}$

13. $\frac{1}{4}$ ▨ $\frac{2}{8}$

14. $\frac{1}{3}$ ▨ $\frac{2}{5}$

15. $\frac{3}{7}$ ▨ $\frac{4}{9}$

16. $\frac{3}{8}$ ▨ $\frac{5}{6}$

17. $\frac{5}{6}$ ▨ $\frac{7}{9}$

18. $\frac{3}{4}$ ▨ $\frac{9}{12}$

19. $\frac{2}{3}$ ▨ $\frac{6}{9}$

20. $\frac{4}{7}$ ▨ $\frac{3}{4}$

Solve each problem. Write each answer in lowest terms.

21. Joan played the tuba for $\frac{1}{3}$ h. Andrew played the flute for $\frac{1}{2}$ h. Who played longer?

22. Andrew practices his solo for $\frac{2}{3}$ h in the morning. He practices again in the afternoon for $\frac{2}{3}$ h. How long does he practice in all?

23. In Mr. Barrett's class, $\frac{1}{4}$ of the students own clarinets. $\frac{3}{5}$ of the students own flutes. Do more students own clarinets or flutes?

★ **24.** Andrew travels $\frac{9}{10}$ km to get to Mr. Barrett's for his lesson. Joan travels 2 km. Who travels farther? How much farther?

THINK AND TRY

ORDERING FRACTIONS

Write the fractions in order from least to greatest.

1. $\frac{3}{8}$ $\frac{5}{8}$ $\frac{3}{4}$ $\frac{1}{4}$

2. $\frac{5}{6}$ $\frac{3}{4}$ $\frac{1}{4}$ $\frac{1}{3}$

3. $\frac{5}{6}$ $\frac{1}{2}$ $\frac{2}{3}$ $\frac{7}{8}$

4. $\frac{3}{4}$ $\frac{4}{5}$ $\frac{1}{2}$ $\frac{3}{10}$ $\frac{3}{8}$

Adding with Different Denominators

■ Anna and her friends are having a picnic. Anna brought $\frac{1}{4}$ of a watermelon. Dan brought $\frac{4}{8}$ of a watermelon. How much watermelon did they have at the picnic altogether?

Add $\frac{1}{4}$ and $\frac{4}{8}$ to find how much altogether.

To add fractions with different denominators:
1. Find the least common denominator.

    8 is a multiple of 4. Use 8 as the least common denominator.

2. Write equivalent fractions. $\frac{1}{4} = \frac{2}{8}$

3. Add.

$$\frac{1}{4} + \frac{4}{8}$$

$$\downarrow$$

$$\frac{2}{8} + \frac{4}{8} = \frac{6}{8}$$

$$= \frac{3}{4}$$

They had $\frac{3}{4}$ of a watermelon at the picnic.

■ Add: $\frac{7}{8} + \frac{1}{6}$

Find the least common denominator.

Multiples of 8:   8, 16, 24, 32, 40, . . .
Multiples of 6:   6, 12, 18, 24, 30, . . .

The least common denominator is 24.

Write equivalent fractions. $\frac{7}{8} = \frac{21}{24}$ $\frac{1}{6} = \frac{4}{24}$

Add.

$$\frac{7}{8} + \frac{1}{6}$$

$$\downarrow \qquad \downarrow$$

$$\frac{21}{24} + \frac{4}{24} = \frac{25}{24}$$

$$= 1\frac{1}{24}$$

Try These

Add. Write each sum in lowest terms.

1. $\frac{4}{5} + \frac{1}{2}$ **2.** $\frac{4}{6} + \frac{2}{3}$ **3.** $\frac{2}{6} + \frac{1}{4}$ **4.** $\frac{2}{3} + \frac{2}{9}$

Exercises

Add. Write each sum in lowest terms.

1. $\frac{5}{12} + \frac{1}{4}$ **2.** $\frac{3}{8} + \frac{1}{6}$ **3.** $\frac{1}{5} + \frac{3}{10}$ **4.** $\frac{3}{10} + \frac{7}{100}$

5. $\frac{3}{4} + \frac{3}{5}$ **6.** $\frac{2}{5} + \frac{9}{100}$ **7.** $\frac{2}{3} + \frac{5}{6}$ **8.** $\frac{4}{5} + \frac{2}{8}$

9. $\frac{3}{5} + \frac{7}{10}$ **10.** $\frac{2}{3} + \frac{3}{9}$ **11.** $\frac{3}{4} + \frac{1}{6}$ **12.** $\frac{4}{9} + \frac{1}{9}$

13. $\frac{3}{7} + \frac{1}{4}$ **14.** $\frac{1}{4} + \frac{1}{10}$ **15.** $\frac{4}{9} + \frac{2}{27}$ **16.** $\frac{7}{8} + \frac{3}{4}$

17. $\begin{array}{r} \frac{1}{8} \\ + \frac{1}{4} \\ \hline \end{array}$
18. $\begin{array}{r} \frac{3}{5} \\ + \frac{2}{7} \\ \hline \end{array}$
19. $\begin{array}{r} \frac{1}{2} \\ + \frac{3}{10} \\ \hline \end{array}$
20. $\begin{array}{r} \frac{1}{6} \\ + \frac{1}{2} \\ \hline \end{array}$
21. $\begin{array}{r} \frac{1}{8} \\ + \frac{3}{8} \\ \hline \end{array}$
22. $\begin{array}{r} \frac{1}{3} \\ + \frac{3}{5} \\ \hline \end{array}$

23. $\begin{array}{r} \frac{1}{2} \\ + \frac{1}{5} \\ \hline \end{array}$
24. $\begin{array}{r} \frac{2}{6} \\ + \frac{9}{12} \\ \hline \end{array}$
25. $\begin{array}{r} \frac{3}{7} \\ + \frac{1}{3} \\ \hline \end{array}$
26. $\begin{array}{r} \frac{3}{4} \\ + \frac{1}{12} \\ \hline \end{array}$
27. $\begin{array}{r} \frac{5}{9} \\ + \frac{3}{5} \\ \hline \end{array}$
28. $\begin{array}{r} \frac{7}{8} \\ + \frac{1}{6} \\ \hline \end{array}$

Solve each problem.
Write each answer in lowest terms.

29. Anna and some of her friends take a hike after eating. Luis and Tim hike $\frac{5}{8}$ mi. Anna hikes $\frac{1}{4}$ mi farther than Luis and Tim. How many miles does Anna hike?

30. Luis and John make sandwiches for the picnic. They use $\frac{6}{10}$ lb of American cheese. They use $\frac{2}{5}$ lb of Swiss cheese. How much cheese did they use in all?

31. Dan and some of his friends spend $\frac{2}{3}$ h playing ball. Then they spend $\frac{1}{3}$ h running relay races. How much longer do they spend playing ball?

★ **32.** Kim brings $\frac{1}{4}$ of the forks and knives to the picnic. John brings the rest. What part does John bring?

Subtracting with Different Denominators

■ Diane Heiser designs clothes. One outfit uses $\frac{5}{6}$ yd of lace. Diane changes the design to use only $\frac{1}{2}$ yd. How much lace is saved on each outfit?

Subtract $\frac{1}{2}$ from $\frac{5}{6}$ to find how much is saved.

To subtract fractions with different denominators:
1. Find the least common denominator.

> 6 is a multiple of 2. Use 6 as the least common denominator.

2. Write equivalent fractions. $\qquad \frac{1}{2} = \frac{3}{6}$

3. Subtract.

$$\frac{5}{6} - \frac{1}{2}$$
$$\downarrow$$
$$\frac{5}{6} - \frac{3}{6} = \frac{2}{6}$$
$$= \frac{1}{3}$$

$\frac{1}{3}$ yd of lace is saved on each outfit.

■ Subtract: $\frac{4}{5} - \frac{1}{2}$

Find the least common denominator.

Multiples of 5: 5, 10, 15, 20, . . .
Multiples of 2: 2, 4, 6, 8, 10, 12, . . .

The least common denominator is 10.

Write equivalent fractions.

$$\frac{4}{5} = \frac{8}{10} \qquad \frac{1}{2} = \frac{5}{10}$$

Subtract.

$$\frac{4}{5} - \frac{1}{2}$$
$$\downarrow \qquad \downarrow$$
$$\frac{8}{10} - \frac{5}{10} = \frac{3}{10}$$

Try These

Subtract. Write each difference in lowest terms.

1. $\frac{7}{10} - \frac{2}{5}$

2. $\frac{3}{4} - \frac{1}{6}$

3. $\frac{2}{3} - \frac{1}{6}$

4. $\frac{6}{7} - \frac{1}{2}$

Exercises

Subtract. Write each difference in lowest terms.

1. $\frac{5}{6} - \frac{1}{2}$

2. $\frac{2}{3} - \frac{3}{8}$

3. $\frac{2}{3} - \frac{3}{10}$

4. $\frac{3}{8} - \frac{1}{4}$

5. $\frac{1}{3} - \frac{1}{5}$

6. $\frac{3}{4} - \frac{1}{2}$

7. $\frac{1}{2} - \frac{1}{8}$

8. $\frac{5}{6} - \frac{3}{4}$

9. $\frac{5}{7} - \frac{2}{14}$

10. $\frac{5}{6} - \frac{2}{4}$

11. $\frac{6}{12} - \frac{1}{12}$

12. $\frac{3}{4} - \frac{3}{5}$

13. $\frac{3}{10} - \frac{1}{5}$

14. $\frac{4}{9} - \frac{1}{3}$

15. $\frac{9}{10} - \frac{5}{6}$

16. $\frac{93}{100} - \frac{7}{10}$

17. $\begin{array}{r} \frac{2}{5} \\ -\frac{1}{10} \\ \hline \end{array}$

18. $\begin{array}{r} \frac{3}{5} \\ -\frac{1}{2} \\ \hline \end{array}$

19. $\begin{array}{r} \frac{8}{9} \\ -\frac{1}{3} \\ \hline \end{array}$

20. $\begin{array}{r} \frac{7}{8} \\ -\frac{3}{4} \\ \hline \end{array}$

21. $\begin{array}{r} \frac{9}{10} \\ -\frac{1}{2} \\ \hline \end{array}$

22. $\begin{array}{r} \frac{2}{3} \\ -\frac{1}{2} \\ \hline \end{array}$

23. $\begin{array}{r} \frac{5}{7} \\ -\frac{2}{3} \\ \hline \end{array}$

24. $\begin{array}{r} \frac{6}{8} \\ -\frac{3}{8} \\ \hline \end{array}$

25. $\begin{array}{r} \frac{3}{4} \\ -\frac{1}{3} \\ \hline \end{array}$

26. $\begin{array}{r} \frac{3}{8} \\ -\frac{1}{16} \\ \hline \end{array}$

27. $\begin{array}{r} \frac{4}{5} \\ -\frac{3}{4} \\ \hline \end{array}$

28. $\begin{array}{r} \frac{1}{2} \\ -\frac{1}{5} \\ \hline \end{array}$

Solve each problem. Write each answer in lowest terms.

29. Diane used $\frac{2}{3}$ yd of silk for a scarf. She used $\frac{5}{6}$ yd of silk for a blouse. Which item required more silk to make? How much more?

30. Diane had $\frac{7}{8}$ yd of ribbon. She bought $\frac{1}{2}$ yd more. How much ribbon did she have then?

★ **31.** Diane is making a dress. She needs $\frac{1}{4}$ yd of lace for each sleeve. She needs $\frac{1}{2}$ yd for the neck. How much lace does Diane need altogether?

★ **32.** Diane had $\frac{7}{8}$ yd of fabric. She made a scarf using $\frac{1}{3}$ yd and a tie using $\frac{1}{4}$ yd of the fabric. How much fabric was left?

Problem Solving: Applications

USING FRACTIONS

■ The ranch hands at the Cross River Ranch are building a new fence around the corral. They built $\frac{1}{5}$ of the fence on Monday. They built $\frac{2}{6}$ of the fence on Tuesday. How much of the corral fence have the ranch hands built altogether?

Add to find how much altogether.

$$\frac{1}{5} \; + \; \frac{2}{6}$$
$$\downarrow \qquad \downarrow$$
$$\frac{6}{30} + \frac{10}{30} = \frac{16}{30}$$
$$= \frac{8}{15}$$

The ranch hands have built $\frac{8}{15}$ of the corral fence.

■ How much of the corral fence is left to build?

Subtract to find how much is left.

The whole fence is $\frac{15}{15}$. $\qquad \frac{15}{15} - \frac{8}{15} = \frac{7}{15}$

There is $\frac{7}{15}$ of the corral fence left to build.

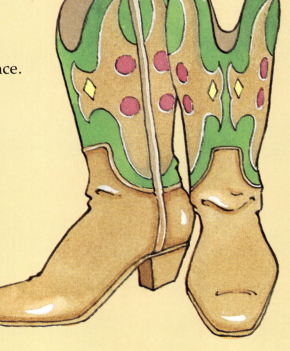

Try These

Solve each problem. Write each answer in lowest terms.

1. Ben paints $\frac{1}{5}$ of the bunkhouse in the morning. He paints $\frac{1}{4}$ of the bunkhouse in the afternoon. What part of the bunkhouse has been painted so far? What part of the bunkhouse is left to paint?

2. Ben rides $\frac{3}{10}$ km to the south property line to check the fence. Then he rides $\frac{9}{10}$ km to check the main gate. How far does he ride altogether?

Exercises

**Solve each problem.
Write each answer in lowest terms.**

1. Amy roped off the paddock area into 3 equal sections. She put the ponies in 2 of the sections. What part of the paddock area contains ponies?

2. $\frac{1}{3}$ of Ben's ranch hands come from New Mexico. $\frac{2}{5}$ of his ranch hands come from Texas. Do more ranch hands come from New Mexico or Texas?

3. Ted needs $\frac{3}{4}$ of a bucket of oats to feed the horses in the stable. He has $\frac{1}{4}$ of a bucket. How much more does he need?

4. Ann needed $\frac{3}{4}$ yd of rope to make a halter for her pony. She needed $\frac{1}{2}$ yd more as a lead rope. How much rope did she need in all?

5. Ben needed to split $\frac{1}{2}$ cord of wood for the bunkhouse fireplace. He split $\frac{1}{4}$ cord. How much more wood did Ben need to split?

6. Ted spends 20 min grooming each horse. He spends 50 min cleaning the stable. What part of an hour does he spend grooming each horse?

7. One load of hay was delivered to Cross River Ranch $\frac{1}{4}$ of the load was placed in the north field. $\frac{1}{3}$ of the load was placed by the pond. The rest was placed in the barn. What part was placed in the barn?

8. Ann spends $\frac{2}{3}$ h with her beginner riding students. Then she spends $\frac{1}{2}$ h with her advanced students. How much longer does she spend with the beginners?

★ 9. Ted has a garden on the ranch. He planted $\frac{1}{3}$ of his garden in tomatoes. He planted $\frac{1}{6}$ in peas and $\frac{1}{4}$ in carrots. What part of his garden has he planted? How much more of his garden is tomatoes than is carrots?

★ 10. Ted said to Ben, "I have more rope than you." Ted had two pieces of rope that were $\frac{1}{2}$ yd and $\frac{1}{3}$ yd. Ben had two pieces that were $\frac{2}{3}$ yd and $\frac{2}{6}$ yd. Ben said, "No, you don't." Who was right, Ted or Ben?

Probability

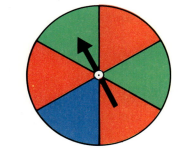

■ A **probability** tells the chance that a certain event will happen. A fraction can be used to show a probability.

This spinner has 6 sections. It has 3 red sections, 2 green sections, and 1 blue section. The pointer is equally likely to land on any one of the sections. If you spin the pointer, there are 6 possible **outcomes**.

A list of all possible outcomes is called the sample space. The sample space for this spinner is red, red, red, green, green, blue.

Find the probability that the pointer will land on green.

2 of the possible outcomes are that the spinner will land on green.

$\dfrac{2}{6}$ ←—— number of greens
　　←—— number of possible outcomes

$\dfrac{2}{6} = \dfrac{1}{3}$

The probability of spinning green is $\dfrac{1}{3}$.

■ Find the probability of spinning orange.

$\dfrac{0}{6}$ ←—— number of oranges
　　←—— number of possible outcomes

The probability of spinning orange is $\dfrac{0}{6}$, or 0.

■ Find the probability of spinning red or blue.

$\dfrac{3}{6}$ ←—— number of reds
　　←—— number of possible outcomes

$\dfrac{1}{6}$ ←—— number of blues
　　←—— number of possible outcomes

$\dfrac{3}{6} + \dfrac{1}{6} = \dfrac{4}{6}$ ←—— number of reds or blues
　　　　　　　←—— number of possible outcomes
　　　　$= \dfrac{2}{3}$

The probability of spinning red or blue is $\dfrac{2}{3}$.

Try These

Pick a marble with your eyes closed. Find the probability of picking the following.

1. a blue marble

2. a red marble

3. a green marble

4. a red or yellow marble

Exercises

Find the probability of spinning the following.

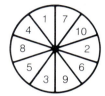

1. 3

2. 4

3. 5 or 6

4. an even number

★ **5.** an odd number less than 4

Here are two views of the same cube. The views show all six faces.

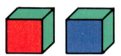

Find the probability of rolling the following.

6. green

7. red

8. blue or red

Here are views of three different cubes.

Cube I

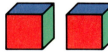

Cube II

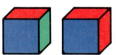

Cube III

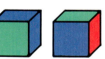

Which cube would you choose for a game with these rules?

9. You win 10 points if you roll blue.

10. You lose 5 points if you roll green.

11. You want an equal probability of rolling red or green.

12. You win 5 points if you roll green or blue and lose 5 points if you roll red.

Tell how many red, green, and blue faces the cube would have.

★ **13.** The probability of rolling green is $\frac{1}{6}$, the probability of rolling red is $\frac{5}{6}$, and the probability of rolling blue is 0.

★ **14.** The probability of rolling green is $\frac{1}{6}$, the probability of rolling red is $\frac{1}{3}$, and the probability of rolling blue is $\frac{1}{2}$.

Finding Outcomes

■ Karen bought blue pants and black pants. She bought a
white blouse and a yellow blouse. How many different
outfits can Karen make with her new clothes?

Use a **tree diagram** to find out.

pants

blouse

For each pair of
pants, there are 2
choices for the
blouse.

Each branch of the tree gives a different outfit.

Karen can make 4 different outfits.

■ Karen is making lunch. She can have a
turkey sandwich or a cheese sandwich.
She can have wheat bread or rye bread.
Karen can have her sandwich with
lettuce or without lettuce. How many
different choices does Karen have?

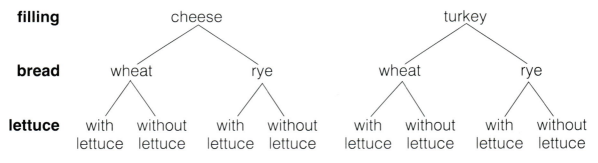

filling	cheese				turkey		
bread	wheat		rye		wheat		rye
lettuce	with lettuce	without lettuce	with lettuce	without lettuce	with lettuce	without lettuce	with lettuce	without lettuce

Karen has 8 possible choices.

Try These

Solve each problem.

You flip a nickel and a dime.

1. Complete the tree diagram.
2. How many combinations are there?

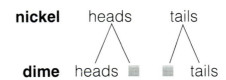

nickel   heads   tails

dime   heads   ▨   ▨   tails

Exercises

Complete each tree diagram to solve each problem.

1. You have a brown skirt, a blue skirt, and a green skirt. You buy a yellow sweater and a white sweater. How many different outfits can you make?

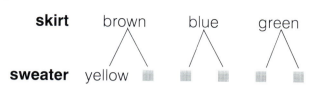

2. You are planning a meal. You have a choice of beef, fish, or turkey. You can have a tossed salad or a tomato salad. You can have peas or beans. How many different meals can you make?

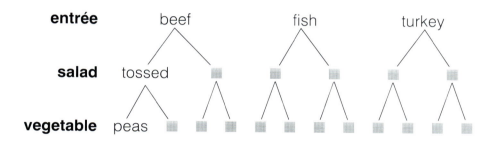

Solve each problem.

3. John has blue pants and brown pants. He bought a white shirt, a yellow shirt, and a blue shirt. How many different outfits can he make?

4. You have a penny, a nickel, and a dime. How many possible combinations of heads and tails are there?

5. Amy is buying a car. She has a choice of a two-door or a four-door car. She has a choice of these colors: red, blue, green, or brown. How many choices does Amy have for a car?

6. Connie Chan is buying a bicycle. She has a choice of a 3-speed, a 5-speed, or a 10-speed. She has a choice of red, blue, yellow, white, or green. How many choices does Connie have for a bicycle?

★ **7.** You are given these four cards with the letters W, X, Y, and Z. You can arrange them in any order. No letter may be used more than once. How many different arrangements can you make?

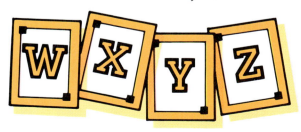

Predicting from a Sample

Ruth is running for school president. Jim took a poll of 10 sixth graders. 8 of the 10 students said they planned to vote for Ruth. Jim decided that Ruth would get $\frac{8}{10}$ of all the votes for president.

Jim took a **sample**. He polled a small number of the students who would vote for school president. He used the results of the sample to make a **prediction**. He predicted how the whole school would vote.

Nancy said that Jim's sample was no good. This is why.

1. He asked only sixth graders.
2. Ruth is a sixth grader.
3. Jim asked only 10 students.
4. There are more than 500 students in the school.

What makes a good sample?

Every student in the school should have the same chance to be included in a sample. The larger a sample is, the more it will be like the whole school population.

For his next poll, Jim asked 5 students in each class. The results are shown in the table.

WILL YOU VOTE FOR RUTH?			
Grade	Yes	No	Undecided
1st	3	2	
2nd	2	2	1
3rd	4	1	
4th	2	1	2
5th	4	0	1
6th	5	0	
Totals	▦	▦	▦

Try These

Use the table to solve each problem.

1. Find the totals for *Yes*, *No*, and *Undecided*.

2. What fraction of the sample said *Yes*?

3. Predict whether Ruth is likely to win.

Exercises

Solve each problem.

Vincent is running for school secretary. Ellen took a sample so she could predict the number of votes Vincent would receive.

She polled 8 students in each class. The results are shown in the table.

1. Find the totals for *Yes*, *No*, and *Undecided*.

2. What fraction of the sample said *Yes*?

3. Predict whether Vincent is likely to win.

WILL YOU VOTE FOR VINCENT?			
Grade	Yes	No	Undecided
1st	1	6	1
2nd	2	5	1
3rd	6	2	
4th	4	1	3
5th	2	6	
6th	1	7	
Totals	▦	▦	▦

Marcia asked 50 students in her school to name their favorite subject. The results are shown in the table.

4. Find the fractions to complete the table.

5. What fraction of the sample named math as their favorite subject?

Favorite Subject	Number	Fraction
language	11	$\frac{11}{50}$
math	20	▦
science	9	▦
social studies	10	▦

Suppose Marcia's school had a population of 300 students.

6. How many times larger than Marcia's sample is the school population?

7. Use the results of Marcia's sample to predict the number of students who would choose each subject.

8. What fraction of the school population chose social studies? Is it the same as the fraction of the sample that chose social studies?

9. Suppose Marcia's school had 400 students. Predict how many students would choose each subject.

Favorite Subject	Number in Sample	Prediction for School
language	11	66
math	20	▦
science	9	▦
social studies	10	▦

CHAPTER CHECKPOINT

Write a fraction for the shaded part. (pp. 202–203)

1.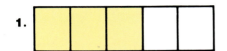

2.

Copy and complete. (pp. 204–205)

3. $\frac{4}{5} = \frac{\blacksquare}{10}$

4. $\frac{2}{3} = \frac{\blacksquare}{6}$

5. $\frac{3}{4} = \frac{\blacksquare}{8}$

6. $\frac{1}{2} = \frac{\blacksquare}{6}$

Write each fraction in lowest terms. (pp. 206–207)

7. $\frac{6}{9}$

8. $\frac{4}{16}$

9. $\frac{5}{20}$

10. $\frac{14}{16}$

11. $\frac{6}{21}$

12. $\frac{6}{8}$

13. $\frac{3}{12}$

14. $\frac{12}{15}$

15. $\frac{3}{9}$

16. $\frac{12}{24}$

Write the fraction as a whole number or as a mixed number in lowest terms. (pp. 208–209)

17. $\frac{7}{5}$

18. $\frac{18}{4}$

19. $\frac{16}{5}$

20. $\frac{25}{5}$

21. $\frac{26}{4}$

22. $\frac{5}{3}$

23. $\frac{12}{4}$

24. $\frac{14}{5}$

25. $\frac{18}{3}$

26. $\frac{34}{8}$

Write >, <, or =. (pp. 216–217)

27. $\frac{2}{3} \ \blacksquare \ \frac{4}{5}$

28. $\frac{1}{3} \ \blacksquare \ \frac{1}{5}$

29. $\frac{3}{4} \ \blacksquare \ \frac{9}{12}$

30. $\frac{3}{8} \ \blacksquare \ \frac{5}{8}$

31. $\frac{1}{2} \ \blacksquare \ \frac{1}{3}$

32. $\frac{3}{4} \ \blacksquare \ \frac{6}{8}$

33. $\frac{1}{4} \ \blacksquare \ \frac{1}{5}$

34. $\frac{2}{5} \ \blacksquare \ \frac{5}{7}$

Add. Write each sum in lowest terms. (pp. 210–211, 218–219)

35. $\frac{3}{7} + \frac{2}{7}$

36. $\frac{5}{6} + \frac{1}{3}$

37. $\frac{2}{5} + \frac{2}{5}$

38. $\frac{2}{3} + \frac{1}{2}$

39. $\begin{array}{r} \frac{3}{4} \\ + \frac{1}{8} \\ \hline \end{array}$

40. $\begin{array}{r} \frac{3}{5} \\ + \frac{1}{3} \\ \hline \end{array}$

41. $\begin{array}{r} \frac{2}{3} \\ + \frac{3}{9} \\ \hline \end{array}$

42. $\begin{array}{r} \frac{5}{6} \\ + \frac{1}{9} \\ \hline \end{array}$

43. $\begin{array}{r} \frac{2}{5} \\ + \frac{4}{15} \\ \hline \end{array}$

Subtract. Write each difference in lowest terms. (pp. 212–213, 220–221)

44. $\frac{7}{8} - \frac{3}{8}$

45. $\frac{3}{4} - \frac{1}{6}$

46. $\frac{1}{2} - \frac{1}{3}$

47. $\frac{5}{7} - \frac{2}{7}$

48. $\begin{array}{r} \frac{3}{4} \\ -\frac{1}{2} \\ \hline \end{array}$

49. $\begin{array}{r} \frac{3}{5} \\ -\frac{1}{3} \\ \hline \end{array}$

50. $\begin{array}{r} \frac{5}{8} \\ -\frac{1}{16} \\ \hline \end{array}$

51. $\begin{array}{r} \frac{5}{12} \\ -\frac{1}{4} \\ \hline \end{array}$

52. $\begin{array}{r} \frac{3}{5} \\ -\frac{2}{6} \\ \hline \end{array}$

Find the probability of spinning the following. (pp. 224–225)

53. red

54. blue

55. orange

56. green or red

Complete the tree diagram. (pp. 226–227)

Frank is buying a car. He has a choice of two-door, four-door, or hatchback. He has a choice of green, white, blue, or red.

type	2-door	4-door	hatchback
color			

57. How many choices are there?

Use the table to solve each problem. (pp. 228–229)

Ray is running for school treasurer. Jane polled 10 students in each class. The results are shown in the table.

58. Find the totals for *Yes*, *No*, and *Undecided*.

59. Predict whether Ray is likely to win.

WILL YOU VOTE FOR RAY?			
Grade	Yes	No	Undecided
3rd	8	2	
4th	5	3	2
5th	4	1	5
6th	10		
Totals	▦	▦	▦

Solve each problem. Write each answer in lowest terms. (pp. 202–223)

60. Kim had $\frac{3}{4}$ yd of ribbon. She used $\frac{1}{3}$ yd. How much was left?

61. Ruth had $\frac{2}{3}$ yd of ribbon. She bought $\frac{1}{2}$ yd more. How much ribbon did she have in all?

COMPUTERS AND PROBLEM SOLVING

■ Logo commands, symbols, and terms allow you to work with numbers, display messages, and create turtle graphics.

See how many you remember. Complete each sentence with a word from the box. Then complete the turtle's message.

WORD BOX			
HOME	ERASE	ASTERISK	TRIANGLE
REPEAT	EXIT	PENUP	DEGREES	VARIABLE

1. The Logo turtle appears as a small
■ ■ ■ ■ ■ ■ ■ ■ on the screen.
1 2 3 4 5 6 7 8

2. The Logo symbol for multiplication is an
■ ■ ■ ■ ■ ■ ■ ■.
9 10 11 12 13 14 15 16

3. You must type CTRL-G to ■ ■ ■ ■
a procedure.   17 18 19 20

4. The turtle will return to its place at the center of the screen when you type ■ ■ ■ ■.
21 22 23 24

5. The term :SIDE is a ■ ■ ■ ■ ■ ■ ■ ■
name.   25 26 27 28 29 30 31 32

6. PU is the abbreviation for ■ ■ ■ ■ ■.
33 34 35 36 37

7. The command RIGHT 90 tells the turtle to turn 90
■ ■ ■ ■ ■ ■ ■ to the right.
38 39 40 41 42 43 44

8. You can display a triangle by typing
■ ■ ■ ■ ■ ■ 3 [FD 50 LT 120].
45 46 47 48 49 50

9. The left arrow key allows you to ■ ■ ■ ■ ■
a character from the screen.   51 52 53 54 55

■	■	K		A
11	4		17	

■	■	■	■	■	E
50	36	2	1	31	

T	■	■	■	■	C	■ !
	22	7	36	35		21

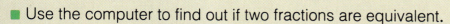

■ Use the computer to find out if two fractions are equivalent.

You type: PRINT 6/8 = 3/4

Then, the computer finds:

the value of $\frac{6}{8}$	$6 \div 8 = .75$
the value of $\frac{3}{4}$	$3 \div 4 = .75$
and compares them	$.75 = .75$

Since they are equal, the computer displays TRUE.

```
?PRINT 6/8=3/4
TRUE
?▒
```

Here is a procedure that will test several sets of fractions

```
TO EQUIVALENT
PRINT RUN READLIST
PRINT [ ]
EQUIVALENT
END
```

EQUIVALENT is the name of the procedure.
PRINT RUN READLIST tells the computer to display its response to a problem you type in.
PRINT [ ] tells the computer to print a blank line.
The second EQUIVALENT tells the computer to repeat the procedure.

Type EQUIVALENT to run this procedure. The computer waits for you to type your input, tests it for true or false, then repeats the procedure.

Input:
```
?EQUIVALENT
3/4 = 6/8
TRUE

▒
```

Input:
```
?EQUIVALENT
3/4 = 1/2
FALSE

▒
```

What word will the computer display after each of these:

1. $\frac{4}{5} = \frac{3}{8}$ **2.** $\frac{2}{3} = \frac{6}{9}$ **3.** $\frac{4}{5} = \frac{12}{15}$

Write fractions that will make the computer display TRUE.

4. $\frac{3}{12} =$ ▒ **5.** $\frac{1}{4} =$ ▒ **6.** ▒ $= \frac{7}{8}$

ENRICHMENT

UNIT FRACTIONS

An ancient Egyptian papyrus written by Ahmes the Scribe shows only **unit fractions**. A unit fraction has 1 as a numerator. These are unit fractions:

$$\frac{1}{2}, \frac{1}{3}, \frac{1}{4}, \frac{1}{5}$$

This is the way Egyptians wrote unit fractions:

Fraction $\frac{1}{3}$ $\frac{1}{10}$ $\frac{1}{13}$

Egyptian

Write the fraction for each of these.

1.   2.   3.   4.

Write the Egyptian unit fraction for each of these.

5. $\frac{1}{4}$ 6. $\frac{1}{5}$ 7. $\frac{1}{12}$ 8. $\frac{1}{21}$

The Egyptians wrote other fractions as the sum of unit fractions.

$$\frac{2}{3} = \frac{1}{3} + \frac{1}{3} \qquad \begin{aligned} \frac{8}{15} &= \frac{\blacksquare}{15} + \frac{\blacksquare}{15} \\ &= \frac{5}{15} + \frac{3}{15} \\ &= \frac{1}{3} + \frac{1}{5} \end{aligned}$$

Write each of these as the sum of two unit fractions.

9. $\frac{2}{5}$ 10. $\frac{3}{4}$ 11. $\frac{5}{6}$ 12. $\frac{7}{10}$

13. $\frac{7}{12}$ 14. $\frac{5}{8}$ 15. $\frac{7}{24}$ 16. $\frac{5}{24}$

What does the digit 6 mean in each number?

1. 346,075

2. 1,758,962

3. 35,762,079,004

4. 16,098,523

Write >, <, or =.

5. 404 ▩ 440

6. 7,164 ▩ 7,164

7. 263,048 ▩ 236,804

8. 7,935 ▩ 7,935

9. 8,027,913 ▩ 8,072,913

10. 916,008,012 ▩ 916,080,120

Add, subtract, or multiply.

11. 69 +58

12. 48 ×16

13. $15.29 + 85.56

14. 9,361 −6,815

15. 804 −359

16. 356 + 74

17. 904 × 33

18. $18.59 × 49

19. 400 − 267

20. 37 × $5.65

21. 68,175 + 84,597

22. (6 × 1) × 8

23. 86,015 − 19,219

24. 320 × 8,487

Divide.

25. 7)45

26. 3)$6.75

27. 40)537

28. 76)3,417

29. 99 ÷ 8

30. 409 ÷ 23

31. 36,841 ÷ 48

Copy and complete.

32. 4 cm = ▩ mm

33. 5 m = ▩ cm

34. 3 kg = ▩ g

35. 5 L = ▩ mL

36. 4 ft = ▩ in.

37. 8 pt = ▩ gal

38. 4 lb = ▩ oz

39. 3 tons = ▩ lb

40. 8 ft = ▩ yd ▩ ft

Solve each problem.

41. Mr. Brooks spent $8.79 for meat, $2.65 for bread, and $1.79 for vegetables. How much did he spend altogether?

42. Tim had $\frac{1}{2}$ gal of dark blue paint. He mixed in $\frac{1}{8}$ gal of white paint to make it lighter. How much paint did he have?

SKILLS CHECK

Choose the correct answer.

1. Which is the number for two thousand, four hundred three?

a. 243
b. 2,043
c. 2,403
d. 4,032

2. 256
    + 194

a. 340
b. 350
c. 440
d. 450

3. 837
    − 274

a. 563
b. 643
c. 663
d. NG

4. $4 \times 6{,}318$

a. 24,242
b. 25,272
c. 25,372
d. 26,162

5. $18 \div 3$

a. 6
b. 21
c. 34
d. 54

6. $8\overline{)3{,}391}$

a. 311 R3
b. 420 R1
c. 423 R7
d. 4,010 R1

7. Find the greatest common factor of 16 and 40.

a. 4
b. 8
c. 10
d. 12

8. $7{,}000 \text{ g} = \blacksquare \text{ kg}$

a. 10
b. 100
c. 1,000
d. NG

9. $\frac{2}{3} - \frac{1}{4}$

a. $\frac{1}{3}$
b. $\frac{5}{12}$
c. $\frac{11}{12}$
d. NG

10. Geraldo buys a shirt for $13.45. He gives the sales clerk $20. How much change should Geraldo receive?

a. $6.55
b. $6.60
c. $7.50
d. $7.55

11. One bedspread costs $35. How much would 4 bedspreads cost?

a. $105
b. $120
c. $140
d. $150

12. 45 club members share the cost of a wristwatch. The watch costs $228.60. What is each member's share of the cost?

a. $4.76
b. $5.08
c. $5.24
d. $6.16

8

DECIMALS:
ADDITION AND SUBTRACTION

Tenths

■ A fraction or a **decimal** may be used to tell what part of the region is shaded.

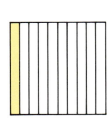

This is a **decimal point**.

Write: $\frac{1}{10}$ or 0.1

Read: one tenth or
zero point one

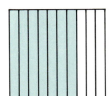

Write: $\frac{7}{10}$ or 0.7

Read: seven tenths or
zero point seven

■ A mixed number or a decimal may be used to tell how much is shaded.

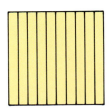 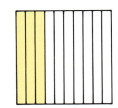

Write: $1\frac{3}{10}$ or 1.3

Read: one and three tenths

The decimal point separates the ones and the tenths.

■ Decimals can be shown in a place value chart.

Ones		Tenths
2	.	6

The digit 2 means 2 ones, or 2.
The digit 6 means 6 tenths, or 0.6.

Write: 2.6
Read: 2 and 6 tenths

Try These

Write a decimal to tell how much is shaded.

1.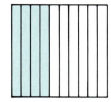

2.

3.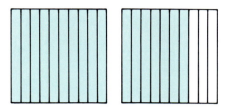

Write as a decimal.

4. $\frac{2}{10}$ **5.** $\frac{6}{10}$ **6.** $\frac{1}{10}$ **7.** $\frac{4}{10}$ **8.** $2\frac{1}{10}$ **9.** $8\frac{3}{10}$

10. 8 tenths   **11.** 3 and 5 tenths   **12.** 42 and 7 tenths

Exercises

Write a decimal to tell how much is shaded.

1.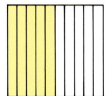

2.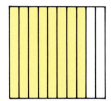

3.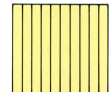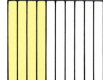

Write as a decimal.

4. $\frac{1}{10}$ **5.** $\frac{10}{10}$ **6.** $\frac{7}{10}$ **7.** $4\frac{9}{10}$ **8.** $7\frac{3}{10}$ **9.** $16\frac{2}{10}$

10. 3 tenths   **11.** 6 tenths   **12.** 7 and 2 tenths

13. 5 and 4 tenths   **14.** 9 and 1 tenth   **15.** 18 and 7 tenths

16. nine tenths   **17.** four and three tenths   **18.** two tenths

19. eight tenths   **20.** twelve and six tenths   **21.** one and one tenth

Write the underlined words as a decimal.

22. The museum exhibit room is <u>thirty and six tenths</u> m long.

23. A mummy case is <u>eight tenths</u> m wide.

24. An Egyptian statue weighs <u>four and five tenths</u> kg.

25. The pharaoh's throne stands <u>one and seven tenths</u> m high.

26. A statue of a bird has a wingspread of <u>three tenths</u> m.

27. A carved scarab stone is <u>nine and six tenths</u> cm long.

Hundredths

- These regions are divided into 100 equal parts. A fraction or a decimal may be used to tell how much is shaded.

   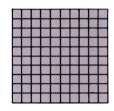   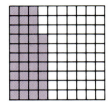

Write: $\frac{1}{100}$ or 0.01

Read: one hundredth

Write: $1\frac{37}{100}$ or 1.37

Read: one and thirty-seven hundredths

Ones		Tenths	Hundredths
7	.	4	8

The digit 8 means 8 hundredths, or 0.08.

Write: 7.48

Read: 7 and 48 hundredths

- You can think of hundredths as tenths and hundredths.

2 tenths

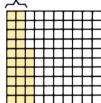

0.26 = 26 hundredths
= 2 tenths 6 hundredths

- Decimals that name the same number are **equivalent decimals**.

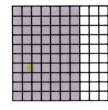

0.7 and 0.70 name the same number. They are equivalent decimals.

0.7

0.70

Try These

Write a decimal to tell how much is shaded.

1. 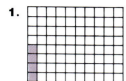 **2.** 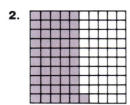 **3.**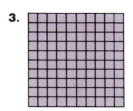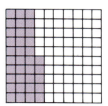

Write as a decimal.

4. $\frac{7}{100}$ **5.** $\frac{39}{100}$ **6.** $\frac{13}{100}$ **7.** $\frac{2}{100}$ **8.** $1\frac{18}{100}$ **9.** $2\frac{4}{100}$

10. 4 hundredths   **11.** 19 hundredths   **12.** 3 and 50 hundredths

Write an equivalent decimal.

13. 0.6   **14.** 0.10   **15.** 6.50   **16.** 0.7   **17.** 9.9   **18.** 5.80

Exercises

Write a decimal to tell how much is shaded.

1. 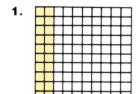 **2.** 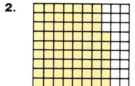 **3.**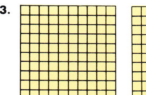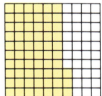

Write as a decimal.

4. $\frac{55}{100}$ **5.** $\frac{9}{100}$ **6.** $5\frac{70}{100}$ **7.** $13\frac{8}{100}$ **8.** $63\frac{47}{100}$ **9.** $115\frac{6}{100}$

10. 5 hundredths   **11.** 16 hundredths   **12.** 27 hundredths

13. 8 and 15 hundredths   **14.** 75 and 96 hundredths   **15.** 120 and 2 hundredths

16. three and seventy-eight hundredths   **17.** two and ninety hundredths

18. sixteen and forty-two hundredths   **19.** five hundred and fourteen hundredths

Write an equivalent decimal.

20. 0.1   **21.** 0.40   **22.** 0.9   **23.** 0.50   **24.** 0.8   **25.** 7.9

26. 3.7   **27.** 0.60   **28.** 8.3   **29.** 12.1   **30.** 0.20   **31.** 1.70

32. 9.50   **33.** 1.4   **34.** 6.10   **35.** 32.5   **36.** 17.90   **37.** 40.40

Thousandths

■ This region is divided into hundredths. Each hundredth can be divided into 10 equal parts. Then the region is divided into thousandths.

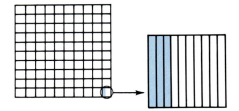

Write: 0.003

Read: three thousandths

Tens	Ones		Tenths	Hundredths	Thousandths
2	8	.	1	5	4

The digit 4 means 4 thousandths, or 0.004.

Write: 28.154

Read: 28 and 154 thousandths

Try These

What does the digit 3 mean in each number?

1. 3.465   **2.** 26.304   **3.** 15.239   **4.** 94.123   **5.** 36.192

Use 321.807. Write the digit that is in each place.

6. thousandths place   **7.** tens place   **8.** hundredths place

Write each decimal.

9. 5 and 36 thousandths   **10.** 19 and 267 thousandths   **11.** 58 and 900 thousandths

Exercises

What does the digit 5 mean in each number?

1. 156.824   **2.** 97.853   **3.** 520.967   **4.** 2,471.345   **5.** 5,683.049

Use 6,754.089. Write the digit that is in each place.

6. tenths place   **7.** thousands place   **8.** hundredths place
9. thousandths place   **10.** hundreds place   **11.** tens place

Write each decimal.

12. 683 thousandths   **13.** 7 and 25 thousandths   **14.** 8 and 200 thousandths

15. 15 and 18 thousandths   **16.** 96 and 137 thousandths   **17.** 82 and 629 thousandths

18. 61 and 10 thousandths   **19.** 809 and 4 thousandths   **20.** 376 and 50 thousandths

21. three and four hundred seventy-two thousandths
22. fifty-four and seven hundred eighteen thousandths
23. one hundred sixty and twenty-four thousandths
24. ninety-three thousandths
25. one hundred and five thousandths

Build your own decimal.

26. 4 in the tenths place
8 in the ones place
6 in the thousandths place
2 in the tens place
9 in the hundredths place

27. 9 in the hundredths place
6 in the ones place
3 in the tenths place
7 in the thousandths place
8 in the hundreds place
4 in the thousands place
2 in the tens place

Choose the decimal that makes sense.

28. The length of an adult's foot is ▓ cm.   **a.** 18.8   **b.** 188   **c.** 0.188
29. The length of an adult's arm is ▓ cm.   **a.** 60   **b.** 0.6   **c.** 0.006
30. The length of an adult's index finger is ▓ mm.   **a.** 0.76   **b.** 760   **c.** 76
31. The length of an adult's thigh bone is ▓ cm.   **a.** 0.498   **b.** 49.8   **c.** 4.98
32. The length of an adult's eye is ▓ mm.   **a.** 2.1   **b.** 0.21   **c.** 21

Comparing and Ordering Decimals

■ You can compare decimals by starting at the left and comparing the digits in each place.

Compare 3.436 and 3.475.

Line up the decimal points.

Compare the ones.	Compare the tenths.	Compare the hundredths.
3 . 4 3 6	3 . 4 3 6	3 . 4 3 6
3 . 4 7 5	3 . 4 7 5	3 . 4 7 5
same	same	3 < 7

so

3.436 < 3.475

■ Compare 12.6 and 12.

Write 12.0 for 12.

1 2 . 6   6 > 0 so
1 2 . 0   12.6 > 12

■ Write 9.87, 8.573, and 9 in order from least to greatest.

Compare the 3 numbers.   Compare 9.87 and 9.

9 . 8 7   9 . 8 7
8 . 5 7 3   8.573 is the least.   9 . 0   9.87 > 9
9 . 0

The order from least to greatest is 8.573, 9, 9.87.

Try These

Write >, <, or =.

1. 0.3 ▨ 0.4
2. 6.2 ▨ 8.2
3. 2.43 ▨ 1.43
4. 8.37 ▨ 87.3
5. 0.26 ▨ 0.2
6. 0.500 ▨ 0.005
7. 2.110 ▨ 2.11
8. 46.35 ▨ 4.624
9. 356.728 ▨ 356.27

Write in order from least to greatest.

10. 7.58   7.62   7.59
11. 43.421   43.419   43.412

Exercises

Write >, <, or =.

1. 0.7 ▨ 0.6
2. 3.79 ▨ 2.97
3. 4.7 ▨ 7.4
4. 6.66 ▨ 0.666
5. 5.2 ▨ 0.502
6. 4.370 ▨ 4.36
7. 51.49 ▨ 5.141
8. 0.34 ▨ 0.340
9. 53.106 ▨ 53.016
10. 0.80 ▨ 0.8
11. 8.26 ▨ 0.811
12. 40.6 ▨ 4.60
13. 100.7 ▨ 100.07
14. 37.800 ▨ 37.80
15. 50.32 ▨ 5.032

Write in order from least to greatest.

16. 14.003   14.013   17.310   14.001
17. 50.42   52.825   50.427   52.83
18. 116.28   116.28   116.278   116.27
★ **19.** 4.004   4.404   4.04   4.440   4.044

Use the digits 0, 1, 2, 3, 4. Use each digit only once.

★ **20.** Write the largest number possible. __ __ . __ __ __

★ **21.** Write the smallest number possible. __ . __ __ __ __

★ **22.** Write the number closest to 3. __ . __ __ __ __

Solve each problem.

These girls were the first four to finish a 200-m race. Etta
finished in 44.02 s. Gretel finished in 44.51 s. Diana finished
in 43.33 s. Anne finished in 42.69 s.

23. Who finished first?

24. Who finished second?

25. Who finished third?

26. Who finished fourth?

Decimals: Addition and Subtraction   245

Rounding Decimals

■ You can use a number line to round decimals.

Round 15.6 to the nearest whole number.

15.0   15.6   16.0

15.6 is between 15 and 16.
15.6 is nearer to 16.
15.6 rounds up to 16.

■ You can use this rule for rounding decimals.

> *To round a decimal, find the place you are rounding to. Look at the digit to the right. If the digit is less than 5, round down. If the digit is 5 or greater, round up.*

Round 9.431 to the nearest tenth.

9.4③1   Look at the digit in the hundredths place.
3 < 5   Compare this digit with 5.
             Round down.

9.431 to the nearest tenth is 9.4.

■ Round 63.815 to the nearest hundredth.

6 3.8 1⑤   Look at the digit in the thousandths place.
5 = 5   Compare this digit with 5.
             Round up.

63.815 to the nearest hundredth is 63.82.

Try These

Round to the nearest whole number.

1. 6.2   **2.** 8.5   **3.** 19.64   **4.** 34.89   **5.** 87.196

Round to the nearest tenth.

6. 4.16   **7.** 9.25   **8.** 15.067   **9.** 82.123   **10.** 64.444

Exercises

Round to the nearest whole number.

1. 5.8	**2.** 15.14	**3.** 49.365	**4.** 12.9	**5.** 6.5
6. 24.52	**7.** 48.07	**8.** 124.3	**9.** 86.37	**10.** 75.094
11. 9.505	**12.** 38.16	**13.** 29.734	**14.** 325.1	**15.** 409.91

Round to the nearest tenth.

16. 4.46	**17.** 15.31	**18.** 49.08	**19.** 224.55	**20.** 96.324
21. 63.72	**22.** 9.405	**23.** 165.91	**24.** 407.218	**25.** 74.885

Round to the nearest hundredth.

26. 4.264	**27.** 9.137	**28.** 14.036	**29.** 68.345	**30.** 156.051
31. 6.555	**32.** 32.464	**33.** 251.811	**34.** 73.375	**35.** 11.002

Solve each problem.

36. Which fort is the largest?

37. Which fort is the smallest?

38. Round the total acreage of each fort to the nearest whole number.

39. Write the names of the forts in order from the smallest fort to the largest fort.

SOME NATIONAL MONUMENTS	
Name	Total Acreage
Fort Frederica, Georgia	213.72
Fort Matanzas, Florida	298.51
Fort McHenry, Maryland	43.26
Fort Stanwix, New York	15.52
Fort Sumter, South Carolina	66.77
Fort Union, New Mexico	720.60

 KEEPING IN SHAPE

Add or subtract. Write the answer in lowest terms.

1. $\frac{1}{8} + \frac{3}{8}$ **2.** $\frac{5}{6} - \frac{1}{6}$ **3.** $\frac{5}{8} + \frac{5}{8}$ **4.** $\frac{1}{2} - \frac{1}{6}$

5. $\frac{2}{3}$ $-\frac{1}{4}$ **6.** $\frac{1}{3}$ $+\frac{1}{5}$ **7.** $\frac{1}{4}$ $+\frac{1}{10}$ **8.** $\frac{2}{3}$ $+\frac{1}{2}$ **9.** $\frac{1}{2}$ $-\frac{1}{5}$ **10.** $\frac{3}{8}$ $-\frac{1}{6}$

Adding Decimals

■ Add decimals as you would whole numbers.

Mike made a rope ladder for his tree house. He used 2.75 m of rope for the sides. He used 1.48 m of rope for the rungs. How much rope did he use in all?

Add 2.75 and 1.48 to find how much in all.

Line up the decimal points. Add the hundredths. Regroup.

$$\begin{array}{r} \overset{1}{} \\ 2.75 \\ +1.48 \\ \hline 3 \end{array}$$

13 hundredths is 1 tenth 3 hundredths.

Add the tenths. Regroup.

$$\begin{array}{r} \overset{1\ 1}{} \\ 2.75 \\ +1.48 \\ \hline 23 \end{array}$$

12 tenths is 1 one 2 tenths.

Add the ones. Write the decimal point in the sum.

$$\begin{array}{r} \overset{1\ 1}{} \\ 2.75 \\ +1.48 \\ \hline 4.23 \end{array}$$

Mike used 4.23 m of rope.

■ Sometimes you add decimals with different numbers of decimal places.

Add: 0.78 + 0.253 + 3

Write equivalent decimals for 0.78 and 3.

$$\begin{array}{r} 0.780 \\ 0.253 \\ +3.000 \\ \hline \end{array}$$

Add. Write the decimal point in the sum.

$$\begin{array}{r} \overset{1}{} \\ 0.780 \\ 0.253 \\ +3.000 \\ \hline 4.033 \end{array}$$

Try These

Add.

1. $\begin{array}{r} 0.71 \\ +2.67 \\ \hline \end{array}$

2. $\begin{array}{r} 14.91 \\ +\ 8.7 \\ \hline \end{array}$

3. $\begin{array}{r} 6.573 \\ +1.14 \\ \hline \end{array}$

4. $\begin{array}{r} 12.85 \\ +\ 4.672 \\ \hline \end{array}$

5. $\begin{array}{r} 48.576 \\ +\ 9.03 \\ \hline \end{array}$

6. 0.948 + 2.13 + 3.56

7. 86.2 + 11.927

8. 14.93 + 82.009 + 98

Exercises

Add.

1. $\begin{array}{r} 1.2 \\ +3.5 \\ \hline \end{array}$	**2.** $\begin{array}{r} 0.8 \\ +0.7 \\ \hline \end{array}$	**3.** $\begin{array}{r} 2.4 \\ +1.9 \\ \hline \end{array}$	**4.** $\begin{array}{r} 13.0 \\ +18.9 \\ \hline \end{array}$	**5.** $\begin{array}{r} 23.6 \\ +77.8 \\ \hline \end{array}$
6. $\begin{array}{r} 0.37 \\ +0.61 \\ \hline \end{array}$	**7.** $\begin{array}{r} 2.72 \\ +3.16 \\ \hline \end{array}$	**8.** $\begin{array}{r} 6.02 \\ +5.13 \\ \hline \end{array}$	**9.** $\begin{array}{r} 22.56 \\ +58.85 \\ \hline \end{array}$	**10.** $\begin{array}{r} 40.09 \\ +17.95 \\ \hline \end{array}$
11. $\begin{array}{r} 0.431 \\ +0.207 \\ \hline \end{array}$	**12.** $\begin{array}{r} 6.072 \\ +1.156 \\ \hline \end{array}$	**13.** $\begin{array}{r} 0.789 \\ +0.136 \\ \hline \end{array}$	**14.** $\begin{array}{r} 3.256 \\ +1.784 \\ \hline \end{array}$	**15.** $\begin{array}{r} 7.903 \\ +7.199 \\ \hline \end{array}$
16. $\begin{array}{r} 0.78 \\ +12.29 \\ \hline \end{array}$	**17.** $\begin{array}{r} 6.4 \\ +5.72 \\ \hline \end{array}$	**18.** $\begin{array}{r} 18.03 \\ +\ \ 4.1 \\ \hline \end{array}$	**19.** $\begin{array}{r} 35.5 \\ +12.342 \\ \hline \end{array}$	**20.** $\begin{array}{r} 8.107 \\ +13.7 \\ \hline \end{array}$
21. $\begin{array}{r} 3.744 \\ 1.25 \\ +54 \\ \hline \end{array}$	**22.** $\begin{array}{r} 9.925 \\ 9.2 \\ +16.49 \\ \hline \end{array}$	**23.** $\begin{array}{r} 6.145 \\ 8.26 \\ +9.009 \\ \hline \end{array}$	**24.** $\begin{array}{r} 4.38 \\ 7.135 \\ +25.3 \\ \hline \end{array}$	**25.** $\begin{array}{r} 25.05 \\ 416.008 \\ +\ \ 89.6 \\ \hline \end{array}$

26. $0.3 + 0.79$

27. $56.3 + 4.976$

28. $8.63 + 47.5 + 9.764$

29. $34.73 + 5.08$

30. $76.1 + 18.62$

31. $58.6 + 0.973 + 8.28$

★ **32.** $4.87 + 17.667 + 20 + 6.5$

★ **33.** $506.19 + 16 + 84.502 + 914.002$

★ **34.** $3.4 + 19.562 + 35 + 17.26$

★ **35.** $207.9 + 54 + 19.506 + 8.17$

Solve each problem.

36. Mike used 3.5 m of wire to help secure the north side of his tree house. He used 4.8 m of wire to secure the south side. How much wire did Mike use in all?

37. Brian bought 0.6 kg of nails to use when building the tree house. Mike bought 0.45 kg of nails to use for the tree house. Who bought more nails?

38. Mike spent $5.46 on lumber for a bench and $13.89 on lumber for shelves. How much money did Mike spend in all?

39. Mike's tree house is 2.4 m wide. How wide is Mike's tree house to the nearest whole number?

40. Brian rode his bicycle 1.8 km from home to the tree house. He left the tree house and rode 2.3 km to the hardware store. Then he returned to the tree house using a route that was 2 km long. How far did Brian ride his bicycle in all?

★ **41.** In Mike's tree house, there are two shelves on one wall. The first shelf is 0.4 m off the floor. The second shelf is 0.6 m above the first shelf. The second shelf is 0.6 m from the ceiling. How high is the tree house?

Subtracting Decimals

■ Subtract decimals as you would whole numbers.

Marie Wilson is designing a display for a museum showcase. The showcase holds a limited amount of weight. One mask weighs 0.834 kg. A second mask weighs 0.575 kg. How much weight can Marie save by using the second mask?

To find the answer, subtract.

Line up the decimal points. Regroup. Subtract the thousandths.

$$
\begin{array}{r}
\overset{2\ 14}{0.8\ \cancel{3}\ \cancel{4}} \\
-0.5\ 7\ 5 \\
\hline
9
\end{array}
$$

3 hundredths 4 thousandths is 2 hundredths 14 thousandths.

Regroup. Subtract the hundredths.

$$
\begin{array}{r}
\overset{12}{}\ \overset{7\ \cancel{2}\ 14}{} \\
0.\cancel{8}\ \cancel{3}\ \cancel{4} \\
-0.5\ 7\ 5 \\
\hline
5\ 9
\end{array}
$$

8 tenths 2 hundredths is 7 tenths 12 hundredths.

Subtract the tenths. Write the decimal point in the difference.

$$
\begin{array}{r}
\overset{12}{}\ \overset{7\ \cancel{2}\ 14}{} \\
0.\cancel{8}\ \cancel{3}\ \cancel{4} \\
-0.5\ 7\ 5 \\
\hline
0.2\ 5\ 9
\end{array}
$$

Marie can save 0.259 kg by using the second mask.

■ Sometimes you subtract decimals with different numbers of decimal places.

Subtract: 6.4 − 1.25

Write an equivalent decimal for 6.4.

$$
\begin{array}{r}
6.40 \\
-1.25 \\
\hline
\end{array}
$$

Subtract.

$$
\begin{array}{r}
\overset{3\ 10}{6.\cancel{4}\ \cancel{0}} \\
-1.2\ 5 \\
\hline
5.1\ 5
\end{array}
$$

Check.

$$
\begin{array}{r}
5.15 \\
+1.25 \\
\hline
6.40\ ✔
\end{array}
$$

Try These

Subtract. Check each answer.

1. $\begin{array}{r} 0.7 \\ -0.4 \\ \hline \end{array}$

2. $\begin{array}{r} 47.48 \\ -26.92 \\ \hline \end{array}$

3. $\begin{array}{r} 5.531 \\ -3.219 \\ \hline \end{array}$

4. $\begin{array}{r} 6.54 \\ -1.8 \\ \hline \end{array}$

5. $\begin{array}{r} 19.6 \\ -\ 6.18 \\ \hline \end{array}$

6. 0.462 − 0.388

7. 18.2 − 11.46

8. 64.5 − 17.89

Exercises

Subtract.

1. 0.8 −0.3	**2.** 14.35 −11.16	**3.** 4.123 −0.845	**4.** 0.53 −0.417	**5.** 42.6 −35.8
6. 19.027 − 9.066	**7.** 4.38 −0.162	**8.** 1.82 −0.017	**9.** 3.269 −1.19	**10.** 0.54 −0.498
11. 7.053 −1.956	**12.** 55.36 −12.618	**13.** 11.9 − 0.684	**14.** 37.36 −19.2	**15.** 1.786 −0.979
16. 0.609 −0.596	**17.** 3.42 −1.975	**18.** 16.8 − 2.437	**19.** 25.09 −18.7	**20.** 245.9 −176.041

21. 0.5 − 0.1 **22.** 0.924 − 0.89 **23.** 19.006 − 16.83

24. 56.072 − 9.128 **25.** 23.684 − 17.8 **26.** 76.34 − 8.045

★ **27.** 172.6 − ▦ = 34.18 ★ **28.** 37.248 − ▦ = 7.748

★ **29.** 6 − ▦ = 1.613 ★ **30.** 300.003 − ▦ = 23.988

Solve each problem.

31. A display case is 1.4 m high. Marie places a statue in the case. It is 0.985 m high. How much space is left above the statue?

32. Marie has $20.00 to spend on a showcase. She spends $8.75 on a shelf and $4.68 on a piece of velvet cloth. How much money is left?

 THINK AND TRY

USING MAGIC SQUARES

Find the magic sum. Then complete each magic square.

1.

4.13		2.11
	5.14	
8.17		

2.

3	5.5	
	3.5	
5	1.5	

3.

6.25		11.25
	7.5	
3.75		

Decimals: Addition and Subtraction   251

Problem Solving: Strategies

FINDING INFORMATION

This is a map
of Colonial
Williamsburg
in Virginia.

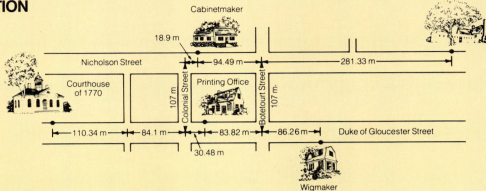

Find the distance from the Cabinetmaker to the Wigmaker.
Plan a route that goes down Botetourt Street.

Locate the Cabinetmaker and the Wigmaker. The Cabinetmaker
is on Nicholson Street. The Wigmaker is on Duke of
Gloucester Street.

Find the distances.
    from the Cabinetmaker to Botetourt Street: 94.49 m
    along Botetourt Street to Duke of Gloucester Street: 107 m
    along Duke of Gloucester Street to the Wigmaker: 86.26 m

Add to find the total distance.

$$
\begin{array}{r}
94.49 \\
107.00 \\
+\ 86.26 \\
\hline
287.75
\end{array}
$$

The distance from the Cabinetmaker to the Wigmaker is
287.75 m.

Using the Strategy

Solve each problem.

1. How far is it from the Printing
   Office to the Wigmaker?

2. What is the shortest distance from
   the Printing Office to the
   Cabinetmaker?

3. Which is farther from the
   Wigmaker, the Public Jail or the
   Courthouse? How much farther?

4. Which is closer to the Printing
   Office, the Courthouse or the
   Wigmaker? How much closer?

These are weather maps. The lines are called **isotherms**.
They connect areas that have the same temperature.
The temperatures are in degrees Celsius.

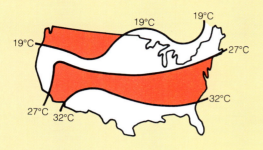

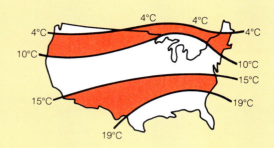

5. Which map, A or B, shows summertime?

6. What is the mean temperature on map A?

7. What is the range of temperatures on map A?

8. What is the mean temperature on map B?

9. What is the range of temperatures on map B?

10. On map A, about what is Florida's temperature?

ACTIVITY

USING A MAP

This is a map of Virginia.

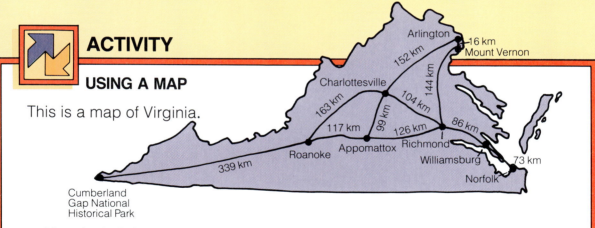

1. How far is it from Williamsburg to Mount Vernon?

2. How far is it from Arlington to Appomattox?

3. Which trip is longer, Arlington to Mount Vernon to Richmond or Richmond to Williamsburg to Norfolk? How much longer?

4. Which trip is shorter, Richmond to Charlottesville to Roanoke or Richmond to Appomattox to Roanoke? How much shorter?

Plan a trip to Virginia. Research the places to visit.
Use the map to help plan how far you will travel each day.

Estimating Sums and Differences

■ Lisa Bristol works for the Spring Valley Arboretum. She ordered 28.75 kg of soil for the rose garden. Lisa ordered 16.5 kg of soil for the morning glory display. About how many kilograms of soil did Lisa order?

To find about how many, estimate the sum.

Circle the first digit in each addend. Round each addend to the circled place.
Add to estimate the sum.

$$\begin{array}{r} ②8.75 \longrightarrow 30 \\ +①6.5 \longrightarrow +20 \\ \hline 50 \end{array}$$

Lisa ordered about 50 kg of soil.

■ The arboretum has 11.47 km of self-guided trails. There are guided tours of 3.89 km of trails. About how many more kilometers of trails are self-guided?

To find about how many more, estimate the difference.

Circle the first digit in each number. Round each number to the circled place. Subtract to estimate the difference.

$$\begin{array}{r} ①1.47 \longrightarrow 10 \\ - ③.89 \longrightarrow - 4 \\ \hline 6 \end{array}$$

There are about 6 km more of self-guided trails.

Try These

Estimate each answer.

1. 4.83 +1.18	**2.** 6.32 −2.76	**3.** 19.693 − 8.041	**4.** 63.6 +29.58	**5.** 75.04 −16.9

6. 92.16 + 29.51   **7.** 9.664 − 3.2   **8.** 83.45 − 64.09

Exercises

Estimate each answer.

1. $\begin{array}{r} 41.5 \\ -\ 6.2 \\ \hline \end{array}$		**2.** $\begin{array}{r} 29.6 \\ +\ 8.1 \\ \hline \end{array}$		**3.** $\begin{array}{r} 7.52 \\ -3.76 \\ \hline \end{array}$		**4.** $\begin{array}{r} 24.6 \\ +83.78 \\ \hline \end{array}$		**5.** $\begin{array}{r} 49.45 \\ -12.67 \\ \hline \end{array}$	

6. $\begin{array}{r} 57.83 \\ +10.49 \\ \hline \end{array}$		**7.** $\begin{array}{r} 12.55 \\ -\ 9.06 \\ \hline \end{array}$		**8.** $\begin{array}{r} 24.27 \\ +38.01 \\ \hline \end{array}$		**9.** $\begin{array}{r} 63.62 \\ -32.48 \\ \hline \end{array}$		**10.** $\begin{array}{r} 2.7 \\ +9.478 \\ \hline \end{array}$	

11. $\begin{array}{r} 84.502 \\ -17.759 \\ \hline \end{array}$		**12.** $\begin{array}{r} 4.789 \\ +28.018 \\ \hline \end{array}$		**13.** $\begin{array}{r} 44.3 \\ +37.935 \\ \hline \end{array}$		**14.** $\begin{array}{r} 190.3 \\ -\ 86.95 \\ \hline \end{array}$		**15.** $\begin{array}{r} 814.91 \\ +156.33 \\ \hline \end{array}$	

16. $4.27 + 8.8$ **17.** $4.82 - 3.75$ **18.** $31.493 + 82.761$

19. $21.8 - 5.2$ **20.** $28.31 + 9.58$ **21.** $814.6 - 56.89$

 Estimate. Use a calculator to find the exact answer.

22. $\begin{array}{r} 5.8 \\ +9.14 \\ \hline \end{array}$		**23.** $\begin{array}{r} 3.7 \\ -1.2 \\ \hline \end{array}$		**24.** $\begin{array}{r} 14.007 \\ +89.59 \\ \hline \end{array}$		**25.** $\begin{array}{r} 73.62 \\ +19.4 \\ \hline \end{array}$		**26.** $\begin{array}{r} 284.8 \\ -187.77 \\ \hline \end{array}$	

27. $8.72 + 29.06$ **28.** $36.578 - 18.14$ **29.** $5.24 + 6.9 + 8.619$

Decide if you need an estimate or an exact answer. Then solve.

30. Lisa prepares a liquid plant food for the hibiscus. She has 1.56 L of liquid plant food. She mixes it with 4.4 L of water. About how much solution does she have?

31. Margaret is the horticulturist for the arboretum. She has 9.2 L of plant food solution for the ferns. She uses 4.8 L. About how much solution is left?

32. Margaret attends a special class on tropical plants at the university. She drives 28.8 km to class. Then she drives 44.2 km to her home. How far does she drive altogether?

33. The arboretum is reseeding the north lawn. Lisa mixes 4.5 kg of rye grass seed, 11.25 kg of fescue, and 1.8 kg of blue grasses. How much seed does she have?

★ **34.** Jeff waters the first greenhouse in 1.2 h, the second greenhouse in 2.8 h, and the third greenhouse in the same time as the first. About how long does it take him to water all the greenhouses?

★ **35.** Jeff is repairing pipes in the first greenhouse. He has a pipe 4.2 m long. He cuts off three pieces, each measuring 0.75 m. Does he have enough left to cut a 1-m piece?

Problem Solving: Applications

READ
PLAN
DO
CHECK

USING DECIMALS

Steve is buying a new tent. A four-person tent weighs 6.35 kg. A three-person tent weighs 3.68 kg. How much heavier is the four-person tent?

Subtract to find the difference.

```
        12
    5  2 15
    6. 3  5   ←—— four-person tent
  − 3. 6  8   ←—— three-person tent
    2. 6  7
```

Add to check.

```
    2.67   ←—— difference in weight
  +3.68   ←—— weight of three-person tent
    6.35 ✔ ←—— weight of four-person tent
```

The four-person tent is 2.67 kg heavier than the three-person tent.

Try These

Solve each problem.

1. Hugo and Steve spent 2.5 h shopping for camping supplies in the morning. They continued shopping for 3.4 h in the afternoon. How many hours of shopping is this?

2. Hugo and Steve bought a three-person tent for $79.97. They also bought a flashlight for $9.69 and a cooler for $14.94. How much money did they spend?

3. Hugo's backpack weighs 1.35 kg. Steve's backpack weighs 1.6 kg. How much more does Steve's backpack weigh?

4. On Saturday, Steve and Hugo hiked 4.8 km. On Sunday, they hiked 6.75 km. How far did the boys hike altogether?

Exercises

Solve each problem.

1. The boys owed the campsite manager $15.75 for their campsite. Steve paid for this with a $20 bill. What was his change?

2. Steve's canteen holds 0.95 L of water. Hugo's canteen holds 1.5 L of water. How much more water does Hugo's canteen hold?

3. Steve bought a new tackle box. The box weighs 2.475 kg. He places 0.9 kg of equipment in the box. How much does Steve's tackle box weigh now?

4. Hugo and Steve paddled a canoe from Savoy Landing to Chad's Cove by way of Pine Island. Pine Island is 4.2 km from Savoy Landing and 1.8 km from Chad's Cove. How far did they travel?

★ 5. Hugo's 1.5-L canteen is full. He fills two 250-mL cups with water from his canteen. How much water is left in the canteen?

★ 6. Steve has a piece of string 8 m long. He cuts off two pieces. One is 3.3 m long. The other is 1.5 m long. Does he have enough left to cut another 3.3-m piece?

Use the information and the map of the Niangua River to plan a canoe trip.

Here are the conditions:

> The river flows north.
> You want to travel about 2 km per hour.
> You want to put the canoe in at 9 A.M.
> You want to take the canoe out at about 3 P.M.

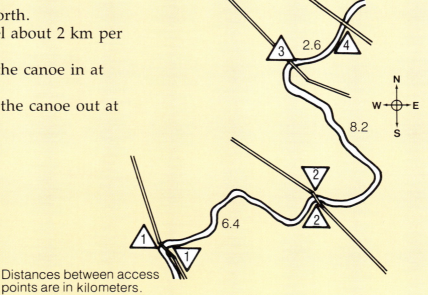

△ Access Points
① Moon Valley
② Sand Spring
③ Corkery
④ Prosperine

Distances between access points are in kilometers.

7. Decide where you will put the canoe in.

8. Decide where you will take the canoe out.

9. Decide whether you will have time to stop for lunch.

CHAPTER CHECKPOINT

Write a decimal to tell how much is shaded. (pp. 238–241)

1. 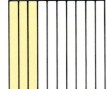   2. 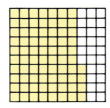   3.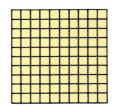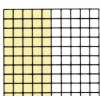

Write as a decimal. (pp. 238–243)

4. $\frac{6}{10}$ 5. $\frac{9}{100}$ 6. $2\frac{1}{10}$ 7. $3\frac{7}{10}$ 8. $2\frac{47}{100}$ 9. $35\frac{99}{100}$

10. 826 and 315 thousandths   11. 54 and 70 hundredths

12. thirty-seven and forty-five hundredths

13. five and six hundred seventy-eight thousandths

What does the digit 6 mean in each number? (pp. 238–243)

14. 6.402   15. 27.465   16. 30.836   17. 68.429   18. 7.64

Write >, <, or =. (pp. 244–245)

19. 0.4 ▧ 0.6   20. 0.43 ▧ 0.42   21. 36.49 ▧ 36.5

22. 4.30 ▧ 4.3   23. 8.7 ▧ 8.698   24. 25.4 ▧ 25.40

Write in order from least to greatest. (pp. 244–245)

25. 5.768   4.986   5.678   5.786

26. 21.269   20.968   21.368   21.296

Round to the nearest whole number. (pp. 246–247)

27. 5.1   28. 8.5   29. 26.37   30. 71.09   31. 54.881

Round to the nearest tenth. (pp. 246–247)

32. 6.14   33. 9.35   34. 24.079   35. 84.324   36. 75.924

Round to the nearest hundredth. (pp. 246–247)

37. 5.091   38. 16.246   39. 39.008   40. 154.042   41. 19.379

Add. (pp. 248–249)

42. 3.4
   + 2.3

43. 0.78
   + 0.15

44. 6.581
   + 2.394

45. 31.32
   + 17.533

46. 38.096
   + 79.4

47. 2.5
   + 3.2

48. 0.36
   + 0.47

49. 3.273
   + 1.584

50. 5.04
   + 6.835

51. 37.19
   9.07
   + 18.94

52. 0.3 + 0.86

53. 5.26 + 1.486

54. 27.5 + 16 + 9.37

Subtract. (pp. 250–251)

55. 7.4
   − 3.2

56. 0.64
   − 0.27

57. 16.54
   − 1.237

58. 8.345
   − 0.28

59. 38.016
   − 19.75

60. 5.6
   − 2.3

61. 0.73
   − 0.38

62. 7.6
   − 1.341

63. 36.227
   − 10.19

64. 84.24
   − 37.964

65. 0.5 − 0.3

66. 8.914 − 3.76

67. 82.091 − 54.37

Estimate each answer. (pp. 254–255)

68. 5.75
   + 2.14

69. 7.86
   − 2.04

70. 36.14
   + 24.97

71. 16.19
   − 9.78

72. 160.8
   + 67.34

73. 4.24 + 8.7

74. 31.32 − 8.794

75. 204.58 + 64.12

Decide if you need an estimate or an exact answer. Then solve. (pp. 238–257)

76. Joan drove 12.7 km in the morning. She drove 9.5 km in the afternoon. How far did she drive in all?

77. Joan had 29.5 L of fuel in her tank. She used 9.8 L on a trip to her grandmother's. About how much fuel is left?

78. How far is it from Hatford to Center City by way of Wallington?

79. How much farther is it to go from Hatford to Center City by way of Wallington than directly?

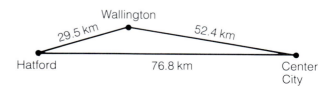

Wallington

29.5 km   52.4 km

Hatford   76.8 km   Center City

COMPUTERS AND PROBLEM SOLVING

■ Your computer has a Logo command to allow it to round any decimal number to the nearest whole number. Here is how the computer works with the ROUND command.

You type:
The computer prints:

```
? PRINT ROUND 4.8
5
? ▤
```

```
? PRINT ROUND 4.4
4
? ▤
```

■ You can program the computer to tell whether a number has been rounded correctly. This flow chart shows the steps your procedure might follow.

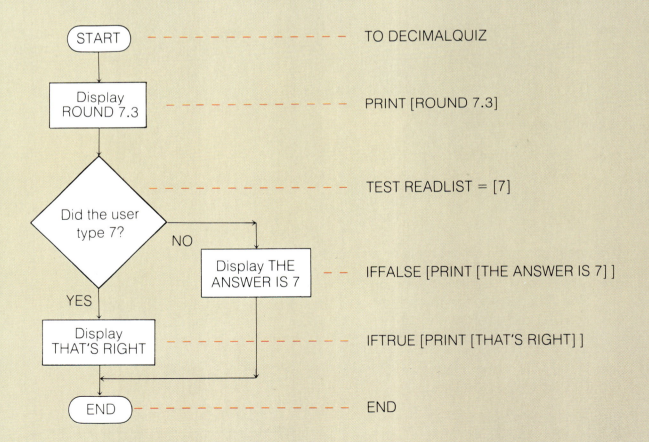

Flow chart	Procedure
START	TO DECIMALQUIZ
Display ROUND 7.3	PRINT [ROUND 7.3]
Did the user type 7?	TEST READLIST = [7]
NO → Display THE ANSWER IS 7	IFFALSE [PRINT [THE ANSWER IS 7]]
YES → Display THAT'S RIGHT	IFTRUE [PRINT [THAT'S RIGHT]]
END	END

The flow chart helped you write the correct procedure.

Now, look at the procedure on page 260 once more. How is each command used?

DECIMALQUIZ is the name of the procedure.

PRINT [ROUND 7.3] tells the computer to display the characters inside the brackets.

READLIST tells the computer to wait for an input.

TEST READLIST = [7] compares the user's input with 7.

IFFALSE tells the computer what to do if the input does not equal 7.

IFTRUE tells the computer what to do if the input equals 7.

Solve each problem.

1. What will the computer display if you type 8 in the DECIMALQUIZ procedure?

2. Change this procedure so the computer will display CORRECT! if your answer is right and YOU NEED TO STUDY MORE if it is wrong.

3. Suppose you changed the line TEST READLIST = [7] to TEST READLIST = [8]. What would the computer's display be if your reply to ROUND 7.3 were 7?

DECIMAL SQUARES

Draw and cut out 16 circles.

1. Write 2.6 on four of the circles.

2. Write 5.2 on four circles.

3. Write 7.8 on four circles.

4. Write 10.4 on four circles.

Place the 16 circles on the square below. Make a magic square. A number can appear in a row, column, or diagonal only once.

The magic sum is 26.

OPENING A JUICE STAND

You are opening a juice stand. You have a loan of $10 to buy frozen juice and other supplies. At the end of 2 days, you must pay back the loan and have made at least $5. What is your plan?

Some Questions to Explore
- How much juice should you buy?
- How many cups can you sell in 2 days?
- What will be the selling price of a cup of juice?

Some Strategies to Explore

Consider the first question. Start with the strategy of finding information on a label.

- Decide what size cans of juice you will buy.
- Find out how much juice you can make with each can.
- Decide what size cups you will use.
- Decide how many servings each can will make.

What strategies will you use to answer the other questions above? List other questions and strategies you need to explore. Use them to solve the problem.

SKILLS CHECK

Choose the correct answer.

1. Which is the number for 789 thousand 26?

a. 78,926
b. 789,026
c. 789,260
d. 789,000,026

2. 143 + 485

a. 528
b. 618
c. 628
d. NG

3. 4,681
− 2,735

a. 1,946
b. 1,956
c. 2,154
d. 2,946

4. 47
× 50

a. 2,070
b. 2,350
c. 3,645
d. 4,750

5. 2,456
× 231

a. 14,736
b. 212,236
c. 445,136
d. 567,336

6. 900 ÷ 3

a. 3
b. 10
c. 30
d. 300

7. $24\overline{)49,152}$

a. 2,048
b. 2,163
c. 2,897
d. 3,418

8. 5 km = ■ m

a. 50
b. 500
c. 5,000
d. NG

9. $\frac{2}{3} + \frac{3}{9}$

a. $\frac{5}{9}$
b. $\frac{7}{12}$
c. $1\frac{1}{3}$
d. NG

10. A shipment of 4 heavy-duty hoses costs $63.44. How much does each hose cost?

a. $14.64
b. $15.86
c. $188.46
d. $253.76

11. Beth buys a frame for $18.50 and a print for $9.79. How much money does Beth spend?

a. $8.71
b. $18.54
c. $27.39
d. $28.29

12. Alison has a string that is $\frac{3}{4}$ yd long. She uses $\frac{5}{8}$ yd to tie up a package for mailing. How much string is left?

a. $\frac{1}{8}$ yd
b. $\frac{1}{4}$ yd
c. $1\frac{1}{8}$ yd
d. NG

9

DECIMALS:
MULTIPLICATION AND DIVISION

Multiplying Decimals

■ Shawn travels 6.8 mi to work. Her boss, Mr. Tobias, drives 3 times as far. How far does Mr. Tobias drive to work?

Multiply 3 and 6.8 to find how far.

Multiply decimals as you would whole numbers.

$$
\begin{array}{r}
6.8 \\
\times\ \ 3 \\
\hline
2\,0\,4
\end{array}
$$

Estimate to help place the decimal point.

$$
\begin{array}{r}
6.8 \longrightarrow\ \ 7 \\
\times\ \ 3 \longrightarrow \times 3 \\
\hline
21
\end{array}
$$
←— So, the decimal product is about 21.

Place the decimal point in the product.

$$
\begin{array}{r}
6.8 \\
\times\ \ 3 \\
\hline
2\,0.4
\end{array}
$$

Mr. Tobias drives 20.4 mi to work.

■ You can count the number of decimal places in the factors to place the decimal point in the product.

Multiply: 5.3×6.43

$$
\begin{array}{r}
6.4\,3 \\
\times\ \ 5.3 \\
\hline
1\,9\,2\,9 \\
3\,2\,1\,5\,0 \\
\hline
3\,4.0\,7\,9
\end{array}
$$
6.43 ←— 2 decimal places
× 5.3 ←— 1 decimal place
34.079 ←— 3 decimal places

Count off as many decimal places in the product as there are in the two factors.

$$2 + 1 = 3$$

Then check by estimating.
5.3×6.43 is about 5×6, or 30.
34.079 seems reasonable.

Multiply: 0.8×5.4

$$
\begin{array}{r}
5.4 \\
\times 0.8 \\
\hline
4.32
\end{array}
$$
5.4 ←— 1 decimal place
×0.8 ←— 1 decimal place
4.32 ←— 2 decimal places

Check: $1 \times 5 = 5$
4.32 seems reasonable.

Multiply: 3×1.6

$$
\begin{array}{r}
1.6 \\
\times\ \ 3 \\
\hline
4.8
\end{array}
$$
1.6 ←— 1 decimal place
× 3 ←— 0 decimal places
4.8 ←— 1 decimal place

Check: $3 \times 2 = 6$
4.8 seems reasonable.

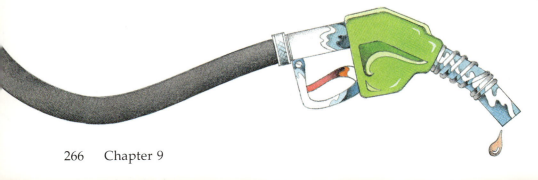

Try These

Multiply. Estimate to check.

1. 12.8
   × 4

2. 3.6
   × 4.8

3. 8.2
   × 3.7

4. 0.87
   × 5.2

5. 4.54
   × 0.3

6. 7.9 × 8

7. 3.8 × 1.6

8. 3.2 × 0.7

Exercises

Multiply.

1. 24.6
   × 5.8

2. 75.2
   × 2.3

3. 0.73
   × 0.4

4. 1.23
   × 4.5

5. 64.3
   × 9.2

6. 2.36
   × 0.6

7. 6.54
   × 5.2

8. 6.28
   × 4.3

9. 0.26
   × 0.7

10. 2.46
   × 16

11. 30.7
   × 14

12. 78
   × 1.9

13. 0.49
   × 2

14. 0.2
   × 5

15. 325
   × 2.2

16. 3.8 × 36.7

17. 0.03 × 12

18. 2.12 × 0.2

19. 0.07 × 9

20. 8.5 × 3.7

21. 6.3 × 4.25

Solve each problem.

22. The gas tank of a car holds 18 gal. It averages 23.6 mpg. About how far will the car travel on a full tank of gasoline?

23. A car was traveling at an average speed of 54.6 mph. The gas tank holds 22 gal. How far did the car go in 1.5 hours?

24. The gas tank in Rebecca's car holds 16 gal when full. Her car averages 26.3 mpg. Rebecca fills her car and drives to the beach. When she stops at the beach for gas, she needs 3 gal. About how far was it to the beach?

25. The gas tank of a medium car holds 18 gal. The car averages 24.2 mpg. A smaller car has a tank that holds 14 gal. The car averages 29.7 mpg. Which of the cars goes farther on one tank of gasoline? How much farther?

26. Mrs. Chung used 8.07 gal of gasoline for her trip. Mr. Dexter used 5.3 gal for the same trip. How much more gasoline did Mrs. Chung use?

27. Mr. Tobias has an income of $21,500. He uses 0.03 of his income for repairs on his car and 0.07 of his income for gasoline. How much does Mr. Tobias spend on his car and gasoline?

More Multiplying Decimals

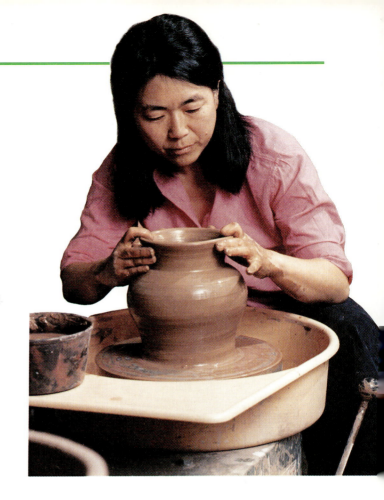

■ Sometimes you need to write a 0 in the product in order to place the decimal point.

Multiply: 0.4 × 0.23

$$
\begin{array}{r}
0.23 \quad \longleftarrow \text{2 decimal places} \\
\times \; 0.4 \quad \longleftarrow \text{1 decimal place} \\
\hline
0.092 \quad \longleftarrow \text{3 decimal places}
\end{array}
$$

■ Sometimes you need to write more than one 0 in the product in order to place the decimal point.

Multiply: 0.2 × 0.04

$$
\begin{array}{r}
0.04 \quad \longleftarrow \text{2 decimal places} \\
\times \; 0.2 \quad \longleftarrow \text{1 decimal place} \\
\hline
0.008 \quad \longleftarrow \text{3 decimal places}
\end{array}
$$

Try These

Multiply.

1. 0.8 ×0.09	**2.** 0.03 × 0.6	**3.** 0.02 × 0.3	**4.** 1.5 ×0.05	**5.** 0.03 × 0.3

6. 1.25 × 0.04   **7.** 0.04 × 0.9   **8.** 0.07 × 0.83

Exercises

Multiply.

1. 0.07 × 0.8	**2.** 0.13 × 0.4	**3.** 0.49 × 0.2	**4.** 0.2 ×0.05	**5.** 0.07 × 0.9
6. 0.03 × 0.2	**7.** 0.05 × 35	**8.** 3.8 ×0.02	**9.** 0.73 × 0.1	**10.** 4.9 ×0.5

11. 0.07
× 0.3

12. 85.9
× 0.3

13. 1.2
×0.06

14. 0.86
× 0.1

15. 1.5
×0.02

16. 1.6
×0.03

17. 0.08
× 0.6

18. 0.24
× 0.4

19. 25.6
×0.12

20. 3.5
×0.2

21. 1.4 × 8.3

22. 0.06 × 0.4

23. 0.3 × 6.2

24. 0.76 × 0.1

25. 0.6 × 1.7

26. 0.17 × 0.5

 Multiply.

27. 9.6 × 4.7

28. 35.6 × 42.8

29. 17.6 × 3.7

30. 3.5 × 4.8

31. 7.2 × 6.5

32. 4.5 × 8.6

33. There are tenths and hundredths in the answers to exercises 27–29. Why does the calculator show only tenths in the answers to exercises 30–32?

Solve each problem. You may choose paper and pencil or a calculator.

34. Betty used 10.75 kg of clay on Mrs. Finch's pottery order. Betty needs 2.5 times that much clay for the craft fair. How much clay does she need?

35. Betty bought 4.5 kg of clay at the Country Store. She bought 2.8 kg of clay at Brady's Craft Supply. How much clay did Betty buy?

36. Betty makes a sugar and creamer set. She uses 0.46 kg of clay to make the sugar bowl. She uses 0.54 kg of clay to make the creamer. How much clay does Betty use to make the set?

37. Betty teaches a craft class every Monday night. She drives 19.2 km from her studio to the class. Then she drives 41.6 km to her home. How far does Betty travel each Monday night?

38. Betty uses 2.2 kg of clay to make a large pitcher. She uses 0.78 kg of clay to make a small pitcher. How much more clay does Betty use to make the large pitcher?

39. A large ceramic plate can be made from 2.25 kg of clay. A small ceramic plate can be made from 0.5 times as much clay. How much clay is needed for the small plate?

40. A gift shop places an order for 8 of Betty's bowls. Betty charges them $9.50 for each bowl. How much does the gift shop order total?

41. Betty orders 3 cases of glaze. Each case contains 12 jars. Each jar contains 0.25 L of glaze. How many liters of glaze does Betty order?

Dividing a Decimal by a Whole Number

■ Angelita has a rope that is 8.4 m long. She wants to cut it into 2 pieces of the same length. How long will each piece be?

Divide 8.4 by 2 to find the length of each piece.

Divide decimals as you would whole numbers.

```
  4 2
2)8.4
  8
  4
  4
  0
```

Estimate to place the decimal point.

```
         4  ← So, the decimal
2)8.4 → 2)8     quotient is
         8      about 4.
         0
```

Place the decimal point in the quotient.

```
  4.2
2)8.4
  8
  4
  4
  0
```

Each piece will be 4.2 m long.

■ When dividing a decimal by a whole number, you can place the decimal point in the quotient above the decimal point in the dividend.

Divide: 12)37.92

Place the decimal point.

```
      .
12)37.92
```

Divide.

```
    3.1 6
12)37.9 2
   36
    1 9
    1 2
      7 2
      7 2
        0
```

Check.

```
    3.1 6
  ×   1 2
    6 3 2
  3 1 6
  3 7.9 2 ✔
```

Try These

Divide. Check each answer.

1. 3)12.45   **2.** 2)96.4   **3.** 5)25.10   **4.** 8)65.6

5. 1.54 ÷ 7   **6.** 126.4 ÷ 4   **7.** 76.5 ÷ 15

Exercises

Divide.

1. $4\overline{)8.4}$ **2.** $6\overline{)24.6}$ **3.** $8\overline{)73.6}$ **4.** $4\overline{)13.68}$

5. $3\overline{)1.35}$ **6.** $7\overline{)2.954}$ **7.** $3\overline{)739.8}$ **8.** $9\overline{)31.059}$

9. $6\overline{)1,003.2}$ **10.** $2\overline{)69.58}$ **11.** $9\overline{)1.935}$ **12.** $8\overline{)38.104}$

13. $12\overline{)49.2}$ **14.** $21\overline{)12.6}$ **15.** $34\overline{)244.8}$ **16.** $16\overline{)41.6}$

17. $5\overline{)\$70.70}$ **18.** $8\overline{)\$58.08}$ **19.** $42\overline{)\$9.66}$ **20.** $25\overline{)\$8.75}$

21. $3.71 \div 7$ **22.** $8.28 \div 9$ **23.** $58.8 \div 21$

24. $98.6 \div 29$ **25.** $18.72 \div 52$ **26.** $6.804 \div 21$

27. $\$43.96 \div 7$ **28.** $\$35.88 \div 26$ **29.** $\$29.12 \div 52$

Find each answer.

30. $39.6 + 13.62$ **31.** 2.9×4 **32.** $26.7 - 12.426$

33. $87.12 \div 66$ **34.** $83.5 + 2.634$ **35.** $9.92 \div 8$

36. 9.1×4.7 **37.** $9.52 \div 56$ **38.** $0.6 - 0.379$

39. $77.36 + 9.24$ **40.** $52 - 36.41$ **41.** 8.3×1.6

Solve each problem.

42. The lumber yard delivers $76.51 worth of supplies to Fred's house. Fred gives the driver $80. What is Fred's change?

43. Fred has a board 13.5 m long. He cuts it into 3 pieces of the same length. How long is each piece?

★ **44.** Fred wants to place some boards around his garden. The garden has four sides. Each side is 1.6 m long. He has a board 7 m long to cut. Will the board be long enough? How much is left?

★ **45.** Fred and his brother are sharing equally the cost of building a playhouse. They buy 2 pieces of plywood. Each piece costs $16.96. Tools cost $9.78. Paint costs $6.42. How much does each pay?

Zeros in Division

■ Jerome Blake is a chemist. He is weighing sodium chloride for an experiment. He has 0.297 g. He wants to divide it equally into 3 test tubes. How much should Jerome put in each test tube?

To find how much in each, divide 0.297 by 3.

Place the decimal point.

$$3\overline{)0.297}$$

There are not enough tenths to divide.

$$\begin{array}{r} .0 \\ 3\overline{)0.297} \end{array}$$

Write a 0 in the tenths place.

Divide.

$$\begin{array}{r} 0.099 \\ 3\overline{)0.297} \\ \underline{27} \\ 27 \\ \underline{27} \\ 0 \end{array}$$

Jerome should put 0.099 g of sodium chloride in each test tube.

■ Sometimes you can continue to divide by writing a 0 in the dividend.

Divide: $15\overline{)34.8}$

Place the decimal point.

$$15\overline{)34.8}$$

Divide.

$$\begin{array}{r} 2.3 \\ 15\overline{)34.8} \\ \underline{30} \\ 4\,8 \\ \underline{4\,5} \\ 3 \end{array}$$

Write a 0 in the dividend. Continue dividing.

$$\begin{array}{r} 2.32 \\ 15\overline{)34.80} \\ \underline{30} \\ 4\,8 \\ \underline{4\,5} \\ 30 \\ \underline{30} \\ 0 \end{array}$$

◄—— 34.80 is equivalent to 34.8.

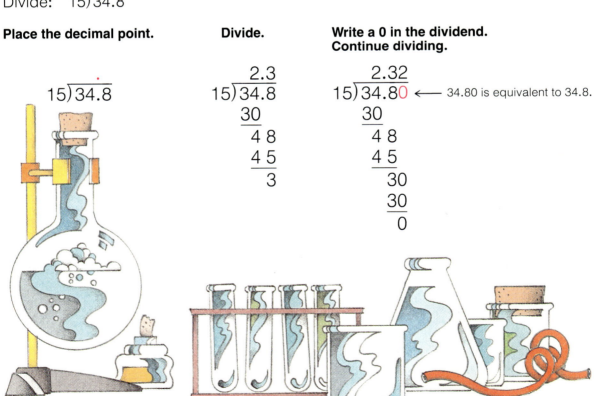

Try These

Divide. Check each answer.

1. $3\overline{)0.156}$ **2.** $24\overline{)3.6}$ **3.** $9\overline{)0.567}$ **4.** $2\overline{)8.3}$

5. $0.256 \div 4$ **6.** $4.2 \div 35$ **7.** $61.5 \div 25$

Exercises

Divide.

1. $4\overline{)1.34}$ **2.** $12\overline{)4.2}$ **3.** $5\overline{)21.46}$ **4.** $4\overline{)8.56}$

5. $18\overline{)0.198}$ **6.** $32\overline{)0.64}$ **7.** $7\overline{)99.05}$ **8.** $6\overline{)3.57}$

9. $12\overline{)0.144}$ **10.** $6\overline{)527.4}$ **11.** $25\overline{)5.5}$ **12.** $5\overline{)0.015}$

13. $21\overline{)0.126}$ **14.** $77\overline{)2.31}$ ★ **15.** $8\overline{)0.006}$ ★ **16.** $50\overline{)26}$

17. $5.6 \div 16$ **18.** $2.315 \div 5$ **19.** $2.84 \div 8$

20. $2.6 \div 20$ ★ **21.** $0.013 \div 4$ ★ **22.** $52 \div 8$

Solve each problem.

23. Jerome has 24.6 g of calcium carbonate. He wants to divide it into 12 equal parts. How much will be in each part?

24. This week Jerome spent 3 h teaching a new lab assistant on Monday and 2.5 h on Thursday. How many hours of teaching is that?

25. Jerome estimates that 0.05 of his experiments will have errors. If Jerome does 100 experiments, about how many will have errors?

★ **26.** It is 7.35 km to the lab. Jerome rode to the lab and back on his bicycle. It took him 35 min. What was his rate in kilometers per minute?

KEEPING IN SHAPE

1. $\begin{array}{r} 36 \\ \times\ 9 \\ \hline \end{array}$ **2.** $\begin{array}{r} 84 \\ +96 \\ \hline \end{array}$ **3.** $\begin{array}{r} 400 \\ -176 \\ \hline \end{array}$ **4.** $\begin{array}{r} 216 \\ \times\ 29 \\ \hline \end{array}$ **5.** $\begin{array}{r} 2,458 \\ +9,297 \\ \hline \end{array}$

6. $468 + 97$ **7.** $2,014 - 967$ **8.** 400×56

9. $218 \div 17$ **10.** $74 + 26 + 15$ **11.** $12,974 + 37,096$

Writing Fractions as Decimals

Carole is practicing for a dance program. She uses decimals to record her practice time. What decimal will Carole write for $\frac{3}{4}$ hour?

Here are two ways to change a fraction to a decimal.

THINK OF FRACTIONS

Find a fraction equivalent to $\frac{3}{4}$  with 100 as the denominator.

$$\frac{3}{4} = \frac{3 \times 25}{4 \times 25} = \frac{75}{100} = 0.75$$

$$\frac{3}{4} = 0.75$$

THINK OF DIVISION

$\frac{3}{4}$ means $3 \div 4$, or $4\overline{)3}$.
Remember that 3 is equivalent to 3.0, 3.00, or 3.000.

Place the decimal point. Write a 0 in the dividend. Divide.

$$\begin{array}{r} 0.7 \\ 4\overline{)3.0} \\ \underline{2\,8} \\ 2 \end{array}$$

↖ There is a remainder.

Write another 0 in the dividend. Continue dividing.

$$\begin{array}{r} 0.75 \\ 4\overline{)3.00} \\ \underline{2\,8} \\ 20 \\ \underline{20} \\ 0 \end{array}$$

Carole practiced for 0.75 hour.

Try These

Write each fraction as a decimal.

1. $\frac{3}{5}$ **2.** $\frac{4}{5}$ **3.** $\frac{9}{20}$ **4.** $\frac{5}{4}$ **5.** $\frac{7}{4}$ **6.** $\frac{3}{50}$

Exercises

Write each fraction as a decimal.

1. $\frac{3}{20}$ **2.** $\frac{6}{10}$ **3.** $\frac{1}{25}$ **4.** $\frac{85}{100}$ **5.** $2\frac{1}{4}$ **6.** $\frac{7}{20}$

7. $\frac{2}{5}$ **8.** $\frac{27}{50}$ **9.** $1\frac{1}{2}$ **10.** $\frac{2}{100}$ **11.** $\frac{11}{20}$ **12.** $\frac{9}{50}$

13. $4\frac{1}{5}$ **14.** $\frac{17}{20}$ **15.** $1\frac{4}{5}$ **16.** $\frac{4}{25}$ **17.** $\frac{3}{25}$ **18.** $\frac{8}{5}$

19. $2\frac{1}{2}$ **20.** $9\frac{1}{4}$ **21.** $\frac{12}{16}$ ★ **22.** $\frac{39}{50}$ ★ **23.** $\frac{7}{8}$ ★ **24.** $\frac{13}{40}$

 You can use a calculator to write a fraction as a decimal.

Write $\frac{7}{50}$ as a decimal. Press ⟨7⟩ ⟨÷⟩ ⟨5⟩ ⟨0⟩ ⟨=⟩

Write each fraction as a decimal.

25. $\frac{9}{25}$ **26.** $\frac{17}{25}$ **27.** $\frac{29}{40}$ **28.** $\frac{19}{20}$ **29.** $\frac{3}{10}$ **30.** $\frac{9}{8}$

Write each fraction as a decimal.
Then write >, <, or =.

31. $\frac{4}{5}$ ▣ 0.9 **32.** 0.45 ▣ $\frac{2}{5}$ **33.** $\frac{11}{25}$ ▣ 0.5 **34.** 0.85 ▣ $\frac{7}{8}$

Solve each problem. You may choose paper and pencil or a calculator.

35. Carole practices her leap for $\frac{3}{5}$ h. What decimal should Carole use for $\frac{3}{5}$ h?

36. The director orders 4 benches. The total cost is $146.36. How much does each bench cost?

37. The costume Carole wears in this performance costs $56.70. The costume she wore in last year's performance cost $19.00 less. How much did last year's costume cost?

38. One week, the choreographer spent 1.5 h taping music, 2.4 h with the director, and 6.1 h with the dancers. How long did the choreographer work that week?

★ **39.** Carole practices for the program 1.5 h each day. She practices 4 days each week. How many hours does she practice in 3 weeks?

★ **40.** It is 12.9 km from Carole's house to the theater. She makes 4 round-trips each week. How many kilometers does she travel in 3 weeks?

Problem Solving: Strategies

FINDING INFORMATION

A **line graph** shows information. It shows change over time. A line graph can help you solve problems.

This line graph shows the amount of rain that fell in 6 hours. A rain gauge was used to measure the rainfall. The gauge was read every hour for 6 hours.

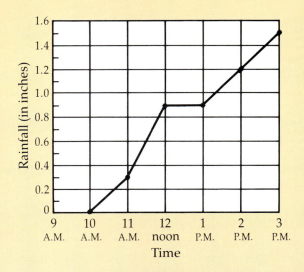

The time is along the bottom of the graph. The amount of rainfall in inches is along the left side of the graph. A dot shows where the time and the measurement meet. Then the dots are connected to make a line.

How much rain had fallen by 11 A.M.?

  Find the dot above 11 A.M.
  Read across to the
  amount of rainfall.

0.3 in. of rain had fallen by 11 A.M.

Using the Strategy

Use the line graph to find the amount of rainfall at each of these times.

1. 12 noon

2. 1 P.M.

3. 2 P.M.

4. 3 P.M.

5. 9 A.M.

6. 10 A.M.

7. Between which hours did it start raining?

8. Between which hours did it stop raining?

9. How does the line graph show that it stopped raining?

10. Between which hours did the most rain fall?

This graph shows the average monthly rainfall in Honolulu, Hawaii.

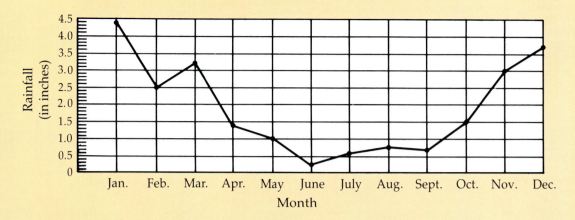

11. What is the average rainfall in March?

12. What is the average rainfall in August?

13. Which month has the most rainfall?

14. Which month has the least rainfall?

15. Which season, summer or winter, has the most rain?

16. Which month, May or September, has the least rain?

17. What is the average rainfall altogether during the first 3 months of the year?

18. What is the average rainfall altogether during June, July, and August?

19. How much more rain falls in January than in December?

20. What is the average yearly rainfall in Honolulu?

ACTIVITY

MAKING A RAIN GAUGE
You can make your own rain gauge.

1. Tape a ruler to the outside of a wide-mouthed jar. Be sure the 0 measurement is at the bottom of the jar.

2. Wait for the next time the weather forecaster predicts rain. Put your rain gauge outside in a clear area.

3. Read and record the amount of rainfall each hour.

4. Make a line graph of the hourly rainfall.

Multiplying and Dividing by 10, by 100, and by 1,000

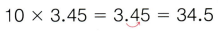

■ Multiply by 10. Look for a pattern.

$$\begin{array}{r} 3.45 \\ \times\ \ 10 \\ \hline 34.50 \end{array} \qquad \begin{array}{r} 34.5 \\ \times\ \ 10 \\ \hline 345.0 \end{array}$$

There is one 0 in 10. Move the decimal point in the other factor one place to the *right*.

$10 \times 3.45 = 3.45 = 34.5$

$10 \times 34.5 = 34.5 = 345$

Multiply by 100.

There are two 0s in 100. Move the decimal point in the other factor two places to the *right*.

$100 \times 0.124 = 0.124 = 12.4$

$100 \times 1.24 = 1.24 = 124$

Multiply by 1,000.

There are three 0s in 1,000. Move the decimal point in the other factor three places to the *right*.

$1{,}000 \times 0.247 = 0.247 = 247$

$1{,}000 \times 2.47 = 2.470 = 2{,}470$

■ Divide by 10. Look for a pattern.

$$\begin{array}{r} 2.46 \\ \hline 10\overline{)24.60} \end{array} \qquad \begin{array}{r} 0.246 \\ \hline 10\overline{)2.460} \end{array}$$

Move the decimal point in the dividend one place to the *left*.

$24.6 \div 10 = 24.6 = 2.46$

$2.46 \div 10 = 2.46 = 0.246$

Divide by 100.

Move the decimal point in the dividend two places to the *left*.

$347 \div 100 = 347. = 3.47$

$34.7 \div 100 = 34.7 = 0.347$

Divide by 1,000.

Move the decimal point in the dividend three places to the *left*.

$2{,}750 \div 1{,}000 = 2{,}750. = 2.750$

$275 \div 1{,}000 = 275. = 0.275$

Try These

Multiply.

1. 10×2.56

2. 100×5.4

3. $1,000 \times 0.76$

4. 100×2.3

5. $1,000 \times 35.2$

6. 10×0.28

Divide.

7. $0.05 \div 10$

8. $540 \div 10$

9. $1,276 \div 1,000$

10. $1.8 \div 100$

11. $72.5 \div 10$

12. $0.9 \div 1,000$

Exercises

Multiply.

1. $1,000 \times 3.4$

2. 100×0.08

3. 10×172

4. 100×10.4

5. $1,000 \times 0.005$

6. 100×2.56

7. 10×75.9

8. 100×0.96

9. $1,000 \times 86.23$

Divide.

10. $56.4 \div 100$

11. $93 \div 1,000$

12. $1.5 \div 10$

13. $2.75 \div 100$

14. $49 \div 100$

15. $18.5 \div 1,000$

16. $20.6 \div 10$

17. $19.76 \div 10$

18. $9.6 \div 100$

Multiply or divide. Do as many as you can mentally.

19. 100×1.38

20. $7.9 \div 100$

21. 10×1.98

22. $7.33 \div 10$

23. $672 \div 1,000$

24. $87.2 \div 100$

25. $1,000 \times 0.46$

26. 100×146.3

27. $37 \div 10$

28. 10×927.86

29. $8 \div 1,000$

30. $3.48 \div 100$

Solve each problem mentally or with paper and pencil.

31. Mary Ebner is an interior designer. She orders 65 m of fabric to reupholster 10 chairs. How much fabric is needed for each chair?

32. A piece of fabric is 17.2 m long. Mary used 11.8 m to reupholster a sofa. How many meters of fabric are left?

33. Mary is having 100 dining chairs reupholstered for a restaurant. She needs 0.75 m of fabric for each chair. How many meters of fabric should she order?

★ **34.** Mary needs 8 lengths of fabric to make some draperies. 4 of the lengths will be 2.1 m long, and 4 will be 1.3 m long. What is the total length of the fabric needed?

Changing Metric Measurements

■ Review the metric equivalents:

length: 1 cm = 10 mm
         1 m = 100 cm
         1 km = 1,000 m
capacity: 1 L = 1,000 mL
weight: 1 kg = 1,000 g

To give the same measurement in a smaller unit, multiply by 10, by 100, or by 1,000.

To give the same measurement in a larger unit, divide by 10, by 100, or by 1,000.

■ Jimmy and Debbie are making 10 bows for party decorations. Each bow uses 150 cm of ribbon. How many meters of ribbon do they need?

Multiply to find how many centimeters of ribbon.

$$10 \times 150 = 1,500 \text{ cm}$$

To give the answer in meters, divide by 100.

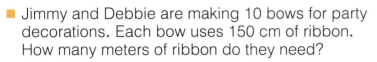

$$1,500 \text{ cm} = \blacksquare \text{ m}$$
$$1,500 \div 100 = 15 \text{ m}$$

Jimmy and Debbie need 15 m of ribbon.

■ There will be 10 people at the party. Jimmy and Debbie have 4.5 L of juice. How many milliliters of juice are there for each person?

Divide to find how many liters of juice for each person.

$$4.5 \div 10 = 0.45 \text{ L}$$

To give the answer in milliliters, multiply by 1,000.

$$0.45 \text{ L} = \blacksquare \text{ mL}$$
$$1,000 \times 0.450 = 450 \text{ mL}$$

There are 450 mL of juice for each person.

Try These

Copy and complete.

1. 50 mm = ■ cm
2. 3 cm = ■ mm
3. 3.7 mm = ■ cm
4. 12 km = ■ m
5. 800 cm = ■ m
6. 2,000 m = ■ km
7. 4,000 mL = ■ L
8. 1.5 cm = ■ mm
9. 0.26 cm = ■ mm

Exercises

Copy and complete.

1. 2.5 km = ■ m
2. 1,500 mL = ■ L
3. 0.35 m = ■ cm
4. 3,000 g = ■ kg
5. 0.5 km = ■ m
6. 1.25 L = ■ mL
7. 1.45 km = ■ m
8. 300 cm = ■ m
9. 0.8 cm = ■ mm
10. 70 mm = ■ cm
11. 1.54 m = ■ cm
12. 35 mm = ■ cm
13. 0.756 L = ■ mL
14. 3,500 m = ■ km
15. 450 cm = ■ m

Change to the same units. Write >, <, or =.

16. 0.5 m ■ 5 cm
17. 3.4 L ■ 3,400 mL
18. 2.75 cm ■ 27.5 mm
19. 1.5 kg ■ 150 g
20. 0.36 kg ■ 3,600 g
21. 450 mL ■ 0.45 L

Solve each problem.

22. Susan buys a box of crackers. It is labeled 0.675 kg. How many grams of crackers did she buy?

23. A package of 100 party mints weighs 220 g. About how much does each mint weigh?

24. Debbie makes 0.85 kg of potato salad. Lena makes 900 g of potato salad. Who makes more potato salad?

★ 25. A can holds 355 mL of frozen juice. It is to be mixed with 3 cans of water. How many liters of liquid will this make?

THINK AND TRY

USING MEASUREMENT

1. A dime is about 0.1 cm thick. How many dimes would it take to make a stack 1 m high?

2. How much money would you have if you had a "meter" of dimes?

3. Would a "meter" of nickels be worth half as much? Compare a dime and a nickel. Then answer.

4. 6 quarters are 0.01 m high. What is the value of a "meter" of quarters?

Estimating Products and Quotients

■ The Jackson family is taking a trip to Massachusetts. They drive 354.25 km each day. It takes them 3.5 days to get to Boston. About how many kilometers did the Jackson family travel?

To find about how many kilometers, estimate the product.

Circle the first digit in each factor. Round each factor to the circled place. Multiply to estimate the product.

$$
\begin{array}{r}
③54.25 \longrightarrow 400 \\
\times \quad ③.5 \longrightarrow \times \quad 4 \\
\hline
1{,}600
\end{array}
$$

The Jackson family traveled about 1,600 km.

■ The Jackson family drove 299.75 km as they traveled throughout Massachusetts. They used 32 L of gasoline. About how many kilometers per liter did the Jackson family average?

To find about how many, estimate the quotient.

Round the divisor to the nearest ten. Change the dividend to a whole number that is easy to divide by the rounded divisor. Then divide to estimate the quotient.

Round the divisor. 32 rounds to 30.	Change the dividend.	Estimate the quotient.
$30)\overline{299.75}$	$30)\overline{300}$	$\begin{array}{r} 10 \\ 30)\overline{300} \\ \underline{300} \\ 0 \end{array}$

The Jackson family averaged 10 kilometers per liter.

Try These

Estimate each answer.

1. 4.8×3.1

2. 37.2×8.6

3. 50.9×7.2

4. 154.35×3.8

5. 256.98×34.2

6. $4 \overline{)9.96}$

7. $8 \overline{)65.88}$

8. $63 \overline{)180.27}$

9. $27 \overline{)299.76}$

Exercises

Estimate each answer.

1. 3.9×6

2. 4.25×2.7

3. 6.98×8.1

4. 37.8×6.2

5. 56.18×5.5

6. 104.87×8.9

7. 91.375×4.1

8. 134.8×2.8

9. 456.08×3.5

10. 72.09×6.6

11. $5 \overline{)9.5}$

12. $3 \overline{)19.91}$

13. $73 \overline{)489.7}$

14. $81 \overline{)720.32}$

15. $48 \overline{)150.2}$

16. $2 \overline{)85.78}$

17. $6 \overline{)56.64}$

18. $93 \overline{)269.74}$

19. 141.8×2.8

20. 96.58×4.4

21. $15.25 \div 5$

 Estimate. Use a calculator to find the exact answer.

22. 4.1×1.8

23. 4.2×17.9

24. $24.16 \div 8$

25. $43.8 \div 6$

26. 25×2.25

27. $299.88 \div 49$

Decide if you need an estimate or an exact answer. Then solve.

28. There are 3 Jackson children. Each child has $34.50 to spend on souvenirs. About how much money can be spent altogether?

29. There are 5 members of the Jackson family. Mr. Jackson spends $36.95 for lunches. About how much did each lunch cost?

30. The Jackson family spent 4 h on a walking tour of Old Sturbridge Village. They walked 8.2 km. How many kilometers did they walk each hour?

31. The Jackson family returned home using another route. They drove 426.5 km each day. It took them 2.5 days. About how many kilometers did they travel to get home?

Problem Solving: Applications

USING A LINE GRAPH

Whales are marine mammals. They are warm-blooded and breathe air through lungs. This means that whales cannot breathe underwater as fish do. One kind of whale, the blue whale, is the largest animal ever known to live on earth.

This line graph shows the average growth of a baby blue whale. Whale babies are called calves.

How much does a whale calf grow during its first month of life?

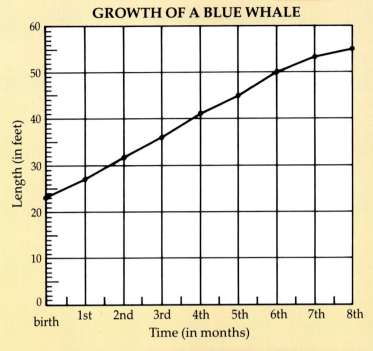

GROWTH OF A BLUE WHALE

$$
\begin{array}{r}
27 \leftarrow \begin{bmatrix} \text{length after} \\ \text{1 month} \end{bmatrix} \\
-23 \leftarrow \text{length at birth} \\
\hline
4
\end{array}
$$

A whale calf grows 4 ft during its first month of life.

Try These

Solve each problem.

1. How much does a calf grow from its first month to its second month of life?

2. How many inches does a calf grow from its first month to its second month of life?

3. How long is a calf that is $4\frac{1}{2}$ months old?

4. How much does a calf grow from birth to its sixth month?

5. What is the average monthly growth of a calf from birth to its sixth month?

6. An adult blue whale is about 100 ft long. About how much more will a calf grow after its eighth month?

Exercises

Solve each problem.

This graph shows the average weight gain of a blue whale calf.

1. How much does a calf weigh at birth?

2. How many pounds does a calf weigh at birth?

3. How much weight does a calf gain during its first month of life?

4. How many pounds does a calf gain during its first month of life?

5. How many pounds does a calf gain each day during its first month of life? (Hint: There are an average of 30 days in a month.)

6. An adult blue whale weighs about 100 tons. About how much weight does a calf gain after its sixth month?

7. How much does a $3\frac{1}{2}$ month old calf weigh?

8. The tail fluke of a blue whale is about 21 ft wide. How many yards wide is the tail fluke?

9. The growth of a calf slows down after its sixth month. Its weight gain is about 2 tons each month. About how much does a year-old calf weigh?

10. A blue whale eats about 8,000 lb of krill each day. How many tons of krill does a blue whale eat in a week?

11. Blue whales have baleen plates instead of teeth. Blue whales were hunted for their baleen plates. Baleen plates vary from 23 in. to 41 in. in length. What is the average length of a baleen plate?

★ 12. A blue whale has about 700 baleen plates. Estimate how many feet of baleen the hunters got from one whale. (Hint: Use the average length of a baleen plate.)

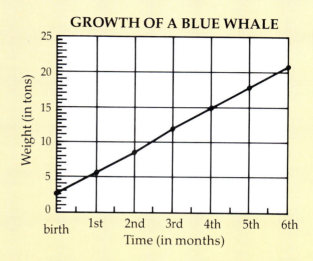

GROWTH OF A BLUE WHALE

Weight (in tons) / Time (in months)

birth 1st 2nd 3rd 4th 5th 6th

Problem Solving: Applications

READ
PLAN
DO
CHECK

MULTISTEP PROBLEMS

■ Some cities and states charge **sales tax**. The sales tax is paid when you buy certain items.

To find the amount of sales tax, multiply the cost of the item by the rate of tax.

Find the sales tax on a puzzle that costs $12.95 if the sales tax is $.06 on a dollar.

$$\begin{array}{r} \$12.95 \\ \times\ \ 0.06 \\ \hline \$.7770 \end{array}$$

Round $.7770 to the nearest cent. $.7770 rounded to the nearest cent is $.78.

The sales tax is $.78.

■ Jennifer bought a card for $1.25 and wrapping paper for $2.10. There is a sales tax of $.05 on a dollar. How much did Jennifer spend altogether?

Step 1　Add to find the cost of the card and the wrapping paper.

$$\begin{array}{r} \$1.25 \\ +\ 2.10 \\ \hline \$3.35 \end{array}$$

Step 2　Multiply by $.05 to find the tax on $3.35.

$$\begin{array}{r} \$3.35 \\ \times\ 0.05 \\ \hline \$.1675 \end{array}$$

Round $.1675 to the nearest cent. $.1675 rounded to the nearest cent is $.17.

Step 3　Add the cost of the items and the sales tax to find the total cost.

$$\begin{array}{r} \$3.35 \\ +\ \ \ .17 \\ \hline \$3.52 \end{array}$$

Jennifer spent $3.52 altogether.

Try These

Solve each problem.

1. Mrs. Ames bought paper plates for $2.80 and napkins for $1.25. There is a sales tax of $.06 on a dollar. How much does Mrs. Ames spend altogether?

2. Parker bought a pen and pencil set for $14.60. There is a sales tax of $.05 on a dollar. How much change should Parker receive from a $20 bill?

Exercises

Solve each problem. Explain the way you solved each problem.

1. Gerald bought a birthday card for $.95 and 3 candles for $1.45 each. There is a sales tax of $.04 on a dollar. How much did Gerald spend altogether?

2. Louise works at the card shop in the mall 6 h each day. She earns $4.25 per hour. How much money does she earn in 5 days?

3. The card shop receives a shipment of 24 cartons of gift wrap. There are 36 rolls of gift wrap in each carton. How many rolls of gift wrap were in the shipment?

4. Mrs. Brewster bought a $7.69 item. There was a sales tax of $.05 on a dollar. She returns the item for credit. What is the total amount of her credit?

5. Mr. Diaz bought 4 cards. Each card costs $1.25. He also bought a poster for $3.59. There is a sales tax of $.05 on a dollar. How much does Mr. Diaz spend altogether?

6. Kate bought 3 m of ribbon at $1.85 per meter. There is a sales tax of $.07 on a dollar. How much change does she receive from $10?

7. There are 3 full-time employees at the card shop earning $9,800 each. 4 part-time employees earn $4,200 each. The manager earns $16,350. How much does the card shop spend each year for salaries?

8. There is a $20,000 budget to remodel the card shop. The carpeting will cost $3,000, display racks will cost $4,500, and counters will cost $7,800. How much will be left for painting and lighting?

9. On Thursday, $2,038 worth of items were sold at a card shop. Each customer paid a sales tax of $.06 on a dollar. How much sales tax did the card shop collect?

10. The original price of a statue was $32.50. During a sale, the price was reduced by $9.75. Christine bought 2 of them. If there was a sales tax of $.06 on a dollar, what was the total cost?

Multiply. (pp. 266–269, 278–279)

1. 2.3 × 5	**2.** 0.6 ×1.7	**3.** 45.8 × 2.3	**4.** 9.75 × 4.8	**5.** 26.3 × 2.1
6. 0.7 ×0.06	**7.** 0.36 × 0.2	**8.** 0.64 × 0.1	**9.** 0.08 ×0.09	**10.** 0.17 × 0.4

11. 5.8 × 0.3   **12.** 0.03 × 0.3   **13.** 7.56 × 4.7
14. 10 × 6.4   **15.** 100 × 0.25   **16.** 1,000 × 4.6

Divide. (pp. 270–273, 278–279)

17. $3\overline{)37.26}$ **18.** $21\overline{)8.631}$ **19.** $42\overline{)84.588}$ **20.** $18\overline{)0.198}$

21. $4\overline{)17.4}$ **22.** $5\overline{)0.425}$ **23.** $13\overline{)0.169}$ **24.** $6\overline{)0.372}$

25. 49.44 ÷ 4   **26.** 738.3 ÷ 23   **27.** 12.6 ÷ 5
28. 12.7 ÷ 10   **29.** 135.2 ÷ 100   **30.** 64.3 ÷ 1,000

Write each fraction as a decimal. (pp. 274–275)

31. $\frac{1}{5}$ **32.** $\frac{9}{20}$ **33.** $\frac{3}{4}$ **34.** $6\frac{1}{2}$ **35.** $\frac{1}{4}$

Copy and complete. (pp. 280–281)

36. 0.18 cm = ▧ mm   **37.** 6.75 m = ▧ cm   **38.** 1.37 km = ▧ m
39. 400 mL = ▧ L   **40.** 360 cm = ▧ m   **41.** 3,000 mL = ▧ L
42. 2,500 m = ▧ km   **43.** 64 mm = ▧ cm   **44.** 950 g = ▧ kg

Estimate each answer. (pp. 282–283)

45. 6.8 × 4	**46.** 5.25 × 3.8	**47.** 7.96 × 7.2	**48.** 38.1 × 8.8	**49.** 126.42 × 5.5

50. $4\overline{)14.6}$ **51.** $53\overline{)100.1}$ **52.** $9\overline{)26.73}$ **53.** $84\overline{)719.68}$

54. 74.68 × 4.4   **55.** 439.7 ÷ 68   **56.** 24.328 ÷ 8

Decide if you need an estimate or an exact answer. Then solve. (pp. 266–287)

57. The gas tank of a car holds 20 gal. The car averages 19.8 mpg. About how far will the car travel on a full tank of gasoline?

58. Jerome spends a total of 20.7 h teaching a new lab assistant over a period of 6 days. That is an average of how many hours per day?

59. Cindy practices the piano for $\frac{1}{2}$ h. What decimal should Cindy use for $\frac{1}{2}$ h?

60. 0.252 L of solution fills 3 bottles. How much does 1 bottle hold?

61. The largest wasp is the North American ichneumon. It can be as long as 11.43 cm. How many millimeters is that?

62. Anne bought a dress for $36.49. There is a sales tax of $.06 on a dollar. How much did Anne spend altogether?

63. Sue has a board that is 3.4 m long. She cuts it in 4 equal parts. How long is each part in centimeters?

64. The total restaurant bill for 5 people is $23.75. About how much does each meal cost?

This graph shows the average monthly temperatures in Brookby Village.

65. Which 2 months are the warmest?

66. For which months are the temperatures lower than 16 degrees?

67. How much does the temperature change between March and April?

68. How much does the temperature change between January and June?

69. What is the difference between the high and low temperatures?

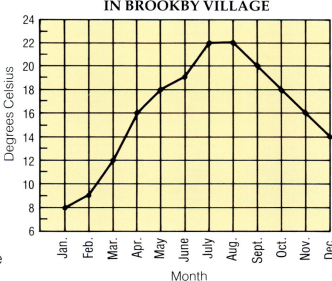

AVERAGE MONTHLY TEMPERATURES IN BROOKBY VILLAGE

COMPUTERS AND PROBLEM SOLVING

■ Your computer can change a fraction to a decimal.

You type:
The computer prints:

```
?PRINT 3/4
.75
?▤
```

How did the computer solve this problem?

The computer read the slash (/) as a division symbol.

The computer found the value of $\frac{3}{4}$.

$$4\overline{)3.00}\ \ ^{.75}$$

The computer printed .75

This procedure works to give one correct answer.

■ There is a way to allow the user more than one chance to get the correct answer. Read this flow chart.

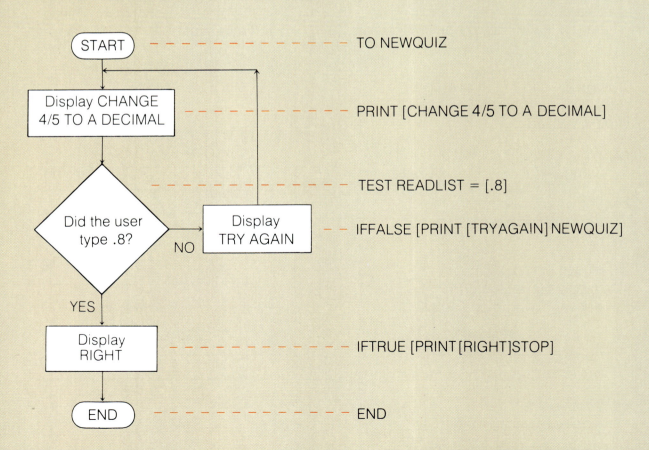

START — — — — — — — — — — TO NEWQUIZ

Display CHANGE 4/5 TO A DECIMAL — — — — — — — PRINT [CHANGE 4/5 TO A DECIMAL]

— — — — — — TEST READLIST = [.8]

Did the user type .8? — NO — Display TRY AGAIN — — IFFALSE [PRINT [TRYAGAIN] NEWQUIZ]

YES

Display RIGHT — — — — — — — IFTRUE [PRINT[RIGHT]STOP]

END — — — — — — — — — END

Solve each problem.

This is what the computer displayed when Zach tried the procedure.

```
?NEWQUIZ
CHANGE 4/5 TO A
  DECIMAL
.1
TRY AGAIN
CHANGE 4/5 TO A
  DECIMAL
▤
```

This is what the computer displayed when Lisa tried the procedure.

```
?NEWQUIZ
CHANGE 4/5 TO A
  DECIMAL
.8
RIGHT
?▤
```

1. How many times did the computer wait for Lisa to type an answer?

2. Why didn't the computer display the words TRY AGAIN when Lisa tried the procedure?

3. How many more times could Zach type an answer?

4. How can Zach stop the procedure?

5. Change the procedure to display CHANGE 2/8 TO A DECIMAL. What other line in the procedure will you have to change?

6. What does the command STOP in the statement IFTRUE [PRINT [RIGHT] STOP] tell the computer?

7. What does the second NEWQUIZ command in the procedure tell the computer?

ENRICHMENT

REPEATING DECIMALS

Write $\frac{1}{3}$ as a decimal.

$\frac{1}{3} = 1 \div 3$

$$\begin{array}{r} 0.3333 \\ 3\overline{)1.0000} \\ 9 \\ \overline{10} \\ 9 \\ \overline{10} \\ 9 \\ \overline{10} \\ 9 \\ \overline{1} \end{array}$$

← The 3 in the quotient repeats.

← There is never a remainder of 0.

0.333. . . is a **repeating decimal**.

To show that a digit or digits repeat, write a bar over the repeating digit or digits.

$\frac{1}{3} = 0.\overline{3}$

Write $\frac{2}{11}$ as a decimal.

$\frac{2}{11} = 2 \div 11$

$\frac{2}{11} = 0.\overline{18}$

$$\begin{array}{r} 0.1818 \\ 11\overline{)2.0000} \\ 1\,1 \\ \overline{90} \\ 88 \\ \overline{20} \\ 11 \\ \overline{90} \\ 88 \\ \overline{2} \end{array}$$

Write each fraction as a decimal. Use a bar to show repeating digits.

1. $\frac{4}{9}$
2. $\frac{1}{6}$
3. $\frac{2}{3}$
4. $\frac{4}{11}$
5. $\frac{5}{27}$
6. $\frac{7}{15}$

7. $\frac{1}{11}$
8. $\frac{1}{15}$
9. $\frac{7}{12}$
10. $\frac{1}{33}$
11. $\frac{29}{45}$
12. $\frac{7}{27}$

Write each fraction as a decimal. Round each quotient to the nearest hundredth.

13. $\frac{1}{8}$
14. $\frac{5}{6}$
15. $\frac{1}{9}$
16. $\frac{7}{22}$
17. $\frac{3}{16}$
18. $\frac{7}{11}$

Write a fraction for the shaded part.

1.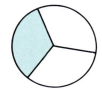

2.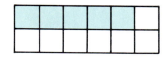

3.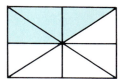

Copy and complete.

4. $\frac{1}{2} = \frac{\blacksquare}{6}$

5. $\frac{4}{9} = \frac{12}{\blacksquare}$

6. $\frac{2}{3} = \frac{\blacksquare}{6}$

7. $\frac{3}{5} = \frac{9}{\blacksquare}$

Write >, <, or =.

8. $\frac{3}{5} \;\blacksquare\; \frac{1}{2}$

9. $\frac{4}{5} \;\blacksquare\; \frac{1}{3}$

10. $\frac{3}{4} \;\blacksquare\; \frac{15}{20}$

11. $\frac{1}{4} \;\blacksquare\; \frac{3}{5}$

Add or subtract. Write each answer in lowest terms.

12.
$$\begin{array}{r} \frac{1}{8} \\ +\frac{5}{8} \\ \hline \end{array}$$

13.
$$\begin{array}{r} \frac{7}{10} \\ -\frac{3}{10} \\ \hline \end{array}$$

14.
$$\begin{array}{r} \frac{3}{4} \\ -\frac{1}{8} \\ \hline \end{array}$$

15.
$$\begin{array}{r} \frac{5}{6} \\ +\frac{1}{4} \\ \hline \end{array}$$

16. $\frac{1}{2} + \frac{1}{3}$

17. $\frac{3}{4} + \frac{1}{6}$

18. $\frac{2}{3} - \frac{5}{8}$

19. $\frac{3}{4} + \frac{1}{12}$

20. $\frac{2}{6} + \frac{5}{12}$

21. $\frac{2}{3} + \frac{1}{3}$

22. $\frac{4}{5} + \frac{2}{3}$

23. $\frac{93}{100} - \frac{7}{10}$

24. $\frac{5}{6} - \frac{7}{9}$

Write as a decimal.

25. $\frac{8}{10}$

26. $2\frac{15}{100}$

27. $\frac{68}{1,000}$

28. $3\frac{9}{10}$

29. $\frac{359}{1,000}$

Write >, <, or =.

30. $0.5 \;\blacksquare\; 0.7$

31. $0.62 \;\blacksquare\; 0.26$

32. $18.46 \;\blacksquare\; 18.5$

33. $5.6 \;\blacksquare\; 5.60$

34. $92.1 \;\blacksquare\; 9.209$

35. $47.8 \;\blacksquare\; 47.80$

(Continued)

Add or subtract.

36. $\begin{array}{r} 0.69 \\ +1.46 \\ \hline \end{array}$

37. $\begin{array}{r} 4.2 \\ -1.87 \\ \hline \end{array}$

38. $\begin{array}{r} 82.9 \\ -56.47 \\ \hline \end{array}$

39. $\begin{array}{r} 71.90 \\ +\ 6.973 \\ \hline \end{array}$

40. $\begin{array}{r} 50.62 \\ -18.97 \\ \hline \end{array}$

41. $\begin{array}{r} 10.64 \\ +\ 2.59 \\ \hline \end{array}$

42. $\begin{array}{r} 37.4 \\ +\ 6.809 \\ \hline \end{array}$

43. $\begin{array}{r} 80.92 \\ -17.3 \\ \hline \end{array}$

44. $\begin{array}{r} 27.35 \\ +\ 9.7 \\ \hline \end{array}$

45. $\begin{array}{r} 43.65 \\ -35.9 \\ \hline \end{array}$

46. $0.72 - 0.68$

47. $7.25 + 9 + 3.658$

48. $156.9 - 89.75$

Multiply.

49. $\begin{array}{r} 36.4 \\ \times\ \ \ \ 3 \\ \hline \end{array}$

50. $\begin{array}{r} 1.23 \\ \times\ 1.6 \\ \hline \end{array}$

51. $\begin{array}{r} 0.03 \\ \times\ 0.2 \\ \hline \end{array}$

52. $\begin{array}{r} 0.21 \\ \times\ 0.4 \\ \hline \end{array}$

53. $\begin{array}{r} 4.68 \\ \times\ \ 10 \\ \hline \end{array}$

54. 2.86×4.2

55. 16.78×100

56. 97.4×0.6

Divide.

57. $7\overline{)29.4}$

58. $15\overline{)186.75}$

59. $3\overline{)0.288}$

60. $4\overline{)17.8}$

61. $15.36 \div 6$

62. $5.2 \div 40$

63. $21.8 \div 100$

Solve each problem.

64. Maureen had $\frac{7}{8}$ yd of ribbon. She used $\frac{5}{8}$ yd to wrap a package. How much ribbon did she have left?

65. Leo drove 26.9 km in the morning. He drove 58.6 km in the afternoon. How far did Leo drive in all?

66. The round trip to the park is 3.9 km. Jackie walks to the park and back every day. About how far does she walk in 7 days?

67. Lena weighs 40 kg. Maura weighs 42,000 g. Who weighs more, Lena or Maura?

68. A rope 12.36 m long is cut into 4 jump ropes of the same length. How long is each one?

69. A stack of 10 pennies is about 15 mm high. About how thick is 1 penny?

10

GEOMETRY AND MEASUREMENT

Lines and Segments

■ A **line** goes on and on in both directions.
A **line segment** is part of a line.
The **endpoints** show where the line segment begins
and ends.

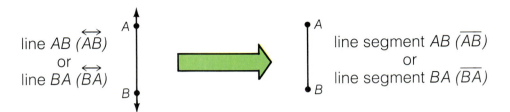

line AB $(\overleftrightarrow{AB})$
or
line BA $(\overleftrightarrow{BA})$

line segment AB $(\overline{AB})$
or
line segment BA $(\overline{BA})$

■ These lines lie on a **plane**. A plane is a
flat surface that goes on and on in all
directions.

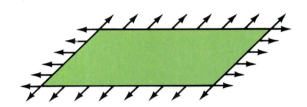

■ Lines can cross, or **intersect**.

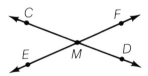

$\overleftrightarrow{CD}$ intersects $\overleftrightarrow{EF}$ at point M.

Lines that never intersect are **parallel**.

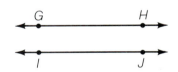

$\overleftrightarrow{GH}$ is parallel to $\overleftrightarrow{IJ}$.

■ Line segments are **congruent** if they have the same
measurement. Here are two ways to check segments that
look congruent.

1. Use a ruler.

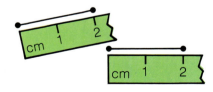

The length of each line segment
is 2 cm.

The line segments are congruent.

2. Use a compass.

Open it to match
one line segment.

Try that opening
on the other line
segment.

The openings are the
same.

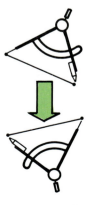

The line segments are congruent.

Try These

Write two names for each line or line segment.

1.

2.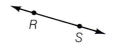

3.

Write whether the lines are *parallel* or *intersect*.

4.

5.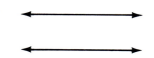

6.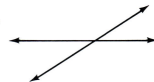

7. Are line segments *CD* and *EF* congruent? Use a ruler or a compass to check.

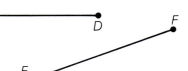

Exercises

Write two names for each line or line segment.

1.

2.

3.

Write whether the lines are *parallel* or *intersect*.

4.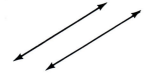

5.

6.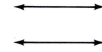

Do the line segments look congruent? Write *yes* or *no*. Use a ruler or a compass to check.

7.

8.

9.

Use this figure to answer exercises 10–12.

10. Name two lines that look parallel.

11. Name two lines that intersect.

12. Name three line segments.

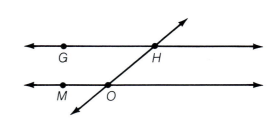

Rays and Angles

■ A **ray** is part of a line. It has only one
endpoint. To name a ray, write the
endpoint first.

ray SG ($\overrightarrow{SG}$)

■ When two rays have the same endpoint,
they form an **angle**. The endpoint is the
vertex of the angle. The rays are the
sides of the angle.

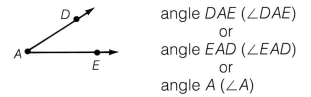

angle DAE (∠DAE)
or
angle EAD (∠EAD)
or
angle A (∠A)

■ A **protractor** is used to measure angles. It is
marked in units of measure called **degrees**.

To measure ∠CBF, place the protractor as shown.

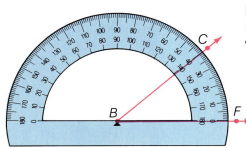

Place the center of the
protractor at vertex B.

Read from the outside scale.
Read: 40 degrees
Write: 40°

Place the protractor edge on one side of
the angle. The side must be at 0°.

■ Angles are congruent if they have the same measure. Is
angle PRQ congruent to angle TSU? Use a protractor to
measure each angle.

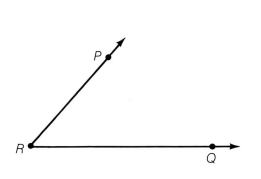

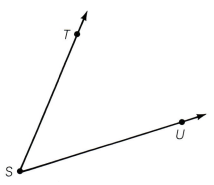

Try These

Name each ray.

1.

2.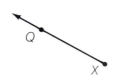

3.

Write three names for each angle.

4.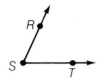

5.

6.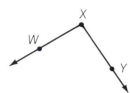

Find the measure of each angle.

7.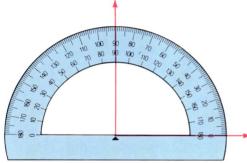

8.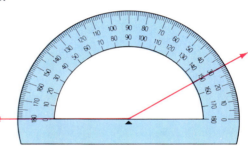

Exercises

Name the rays in each angle. Then write three names for each angle.

1.

2.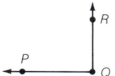

3.

Trace each angle. Use a protractor to measure it. Draw longer sides if necessary.

4.

5.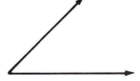

6.

7.

8.

9.

10. Which two angles in exercises 4–9 are congruent?

Right, Acute, and Obtuse Angles

■ Angle *GFE* is a **right** angle. Its measure is 90°.

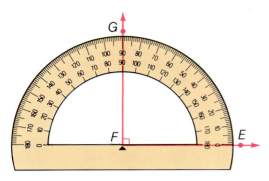

The measure of angle *GFE* is 90°.

┐ *means right angle.*

Angle *RDS* is an **acute** angle. Its measure is less than 90°.

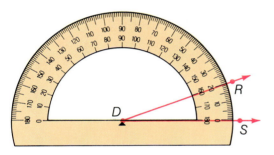

The measure of angle *RDS* is 20°.

Angle *PMT* is an **obtuse** angle. Its measure is greater than 90°.

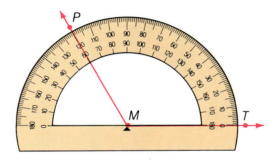

The measure of angle *PMT* is 120°.

■ You can draw an angle using a ruler and a protractor. To draw angle *B* with a measure of 50°:

1. Draw a ray. Label the endpoint *B*.
2. Place center ▲ at *B*. Place the edge of the protractor at 0° on the ray.
3. Count to 50 on the scale. Mark a dot.
4. From endpoint *B*, draw a ray through the dot.

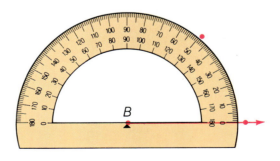

■ Lines that intersect and form right angles are **perpendicular lines**.

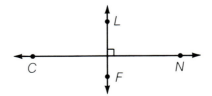

$\overleftrightarrow{CN}$ is perpendicular to $\overleftrightarrow{LF}$.

Try These

Use these figures to answer exercises 1–3.

1. Which angle is a right angle?
2. Which angle is an acute angle?
3. Which angle is an obtuse angle?

Are the intersecting lines perpendicular? Write *yes* or *no*.

4.

5.

6.

Draw each angle.

7. 65°   8. 90°   9. 130°   10. 45°   11. 160°

Exercises

Use these figures to answer exercises 1–3.

1. Which angle is a right angle?

2. Which angles are acute angles?

3. Which angles are obtuse angles?

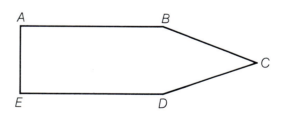

Use this figure to answer exercises 4–6.

4. Name two right angles.

5. Name an acute angle.

6. Name two obtuse angles.

Use this figure to answer exercises 7–10.

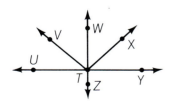

7. Name two perpendicular lines.
8. Name four right angles.
9. Name four acute angles.
10. Name four obtuse angles.

Draw each angle.

11. 30°   12. 150°   13. 55°   14. 145°   15. 95°

Polygons

■ These figures are **polygons**. Each side is a line segment. The line segments meet at a vertex to form an angle.

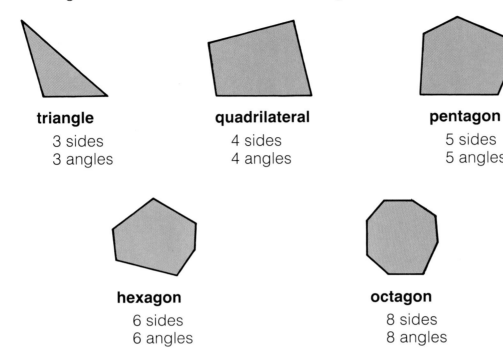

triangle
3 sides
3 angles

quadrilateral
4 sides
4 angles

pentagon
5 sides
5 angles

hexagon
6 sides
6 angles

octagon
8 sides
8 angles

■ Some triangles have special names.

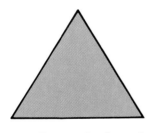  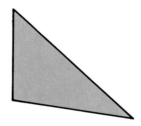

equilateral triangle
All sides have the same length.

isosceles triangle
At least two sides have the same length.

scalene triangle
No sides have the same length.

■ A **diagonal** of a polygon is a line segment whose endpoints are vertices (plural of *vertex*), but the line segment is not a side.

$\overline{JM}$ and $\overline{LK}$ are diagonals of quadrilateral *JKML*.

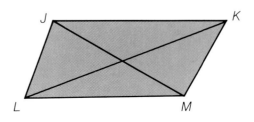

Try These

Name each polygon.

1.
2.
3.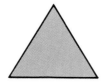
4.

Write the special name for each triangle.

5.
6.
7.
8.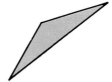

9. Name all the diagonals of pentagon *EFGHI*.

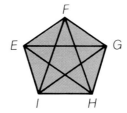

Exercises

Match the letter of each figure to its description.

1. an equilateral triangle

2. an octagon with all sides the same length

3. a hexagon with two acute angles

4. a pentagon with three diagonals

5. an isosceles triangle

6. a quadrilateral with four right angles

7. a hexagon with three diagonals

8. a quadrilateral with two obtuse angles

9. a scalene triangle

10. a pentagon with all sides the same length

a.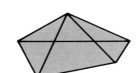
b.
c.
d.
e.
f.
g.
h.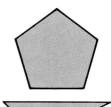
i.
j.

Congruent Polygons

Polygons are congruent if they have the same size and shape.

■ Is triangle *ABC* congruent to triangle *DEF*?

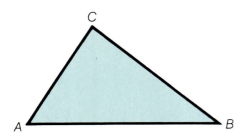 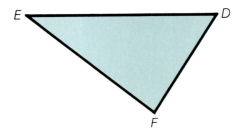

Trace triangle *ABC* on your paper.

Turn and **slide** the paper to see if triangle *ABC* matches triangle *DEF*.

The triangles match. Triangle *ABC* is congruent to triangle *DEF*.

When polygons are congruent, their matching parts are also congruent.

Angle *A* is congruent to angle *D*. Which angle is congruent to angle *E*? Angle *F*?

$\overline{AB}$ is congruent to $\overline{DE}$. Which side is congruent to $\overline{DF}$? $\overline{FE}$?

■ Is triangle *MNO* congruent to triangle *PQR*?

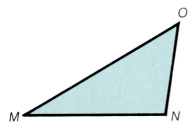 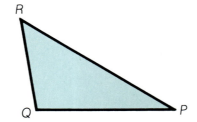

Trace triangle *MNO* on your paper. Can you turn and slide it to match triangle *PQR*?

Flip your tracing over.

Now do the triangles match?

Triangle *MNO* is congruent to triangle *PQR*.

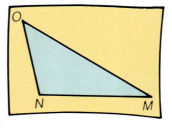 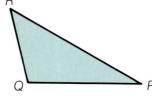

Which angles are congruent? Which sides are congruent?

Try These

Are the polygons congruent? Write *yes* or *no*.

1.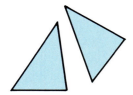

2.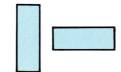

3.

Copy and complete.

Triangle *SVT* is congruent to triangle *WYX*.

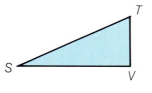
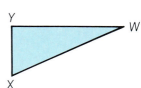

4. Angle *S* is congruent to angle ▓.
5. Angle *V* is congruent to angle ▓.
6. $\overline{VT}$ is congruent to ▓.
7. $\overline{TS}$ is congruent to ▓.

Exercises

Are the polygons congruent? Write *yes* or *no*.

1.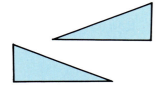

2.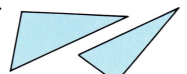

3.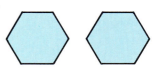

Copy and complete.

Pentagon *ABCDE* is congruent to pentagon *FGHIJ*.

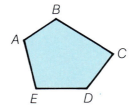
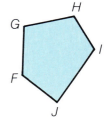

4. Angle *A* is congruent to angle ▓.
5. Angle *C* is congruent to angle ▓.
6. Angle *E* is congruent to angle ▓.
7. $\overline{BC}$ is congruent to ▓.
8. $\overline{DE}$ is congruent to ▓.
9. $\overline{EA}$ is congruent to ▓.

10. Which figures are congruent?

a.
b.
c.
d.

e.
f.
g.
h.

Quadrilaterals

■ Some quadrilaterals have special names.

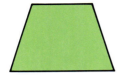

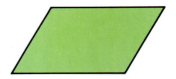

trapezoid
One pair of sides is parallel.

parallelogram
Opposite sides are parallel. Opposite sides are congruent.

■ Some parallelograms have special names.

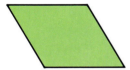

rhombus
All sides are congruent.

rectangle
All four angles are right angles.

square
All angles are right angles. All sides are congruent.

Try These

Write the special name for each quadrilateral.

1.

2.

3.

4.

Use this figure to answer exercises 5–7.

5. Name a pair of opposite sides.

6. Name a pair of congruent sides.

7. Name a pair of parallel sides.

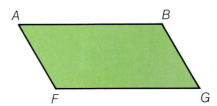

Exercises

Use these figures to answer exercises 1–6.

a.  b.   c.  d.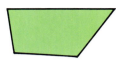

e.  f.  g. 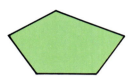 h.

1. Which figures are quadrilaterals?

2. Which figure is a trapezoid?

3. Which figures are parallelograms?

4. Which figures are rhombuses?

5. Which figures are rectangles?

6. Which figures are squares?

Use this figure to answer exercises 7–10.

7. Name a pair of parallel sides.

8. Name the side opposite $\overline{ML}$.

9. Name a pair of congruent sides.

10. Name four right angles.

Use this figure to answer exercises 11–15.

11. Name a pair of parallel sides.

12. Name two right angles.

13. Name an obtuse angle.

14. Name the side opposite $\overline{RU}$.

15. Name an acute angle.

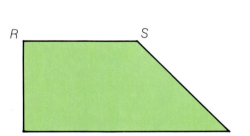

Write *yes* or *no*.

16. All rectangles are parallelograms.

17. All parallelograms are rectangles.

18. All trapezoids are quadrilaterals.

19. All rectangles are squares.

20. All squares are parallelograms.

21. All squares are rectangles.

Circles

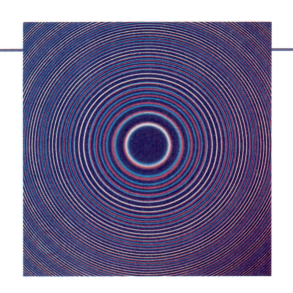

Circles are sometimes used in art.
There are many circles in this design.
This art was drawn by a computer.

■ This is circle O. Point O is the **center** of
the circle. Points A, B, C, and D are *on*
the circle. All points on the circle are the
same distance from the center.

Line segments connect points on the
circle. A **radius** is a line segment from
the center to a point on the circle.

$\overline{OA}$, $\overline{OC}$, and $\overline{OB}$ are radii (plural of
radius) of circle O.

A **chord** is a line segment from a point
on the circle to another point on the
circle.

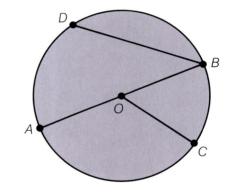

$\overline{DB}$ and $\overline{AB}$ are chords of circle O.

A **diameter** is a chord that passes
through the center of the circle.

$\overline{AB}$ is a diameter of circle O.

■ The **circumference** of a circle is the
distance around the circle. The
circumference is about 3 times the
diameter.

The diameter of circle O is about 5 cm.
The circumference of circle O is about
3 × 5, or 15, cm.

■ You can use a compass to draw a circle.
Put the metal tip on a point. Move the
pencil around to draw the circle.

Try These

Use this circle to answer exercises 1–7.

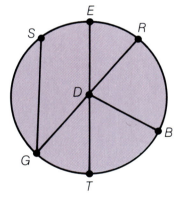

1. Name the center.
2. Name three radii.
3. Name two chords.
4. Name a diameter.
5. Is $\overline{EH}$ a diameter? Why?
6. Find the length of each radius to the nearest centimeter. Are they all the same length?
7. Find the length of the diameter to the nearest centimeter. Estimate the circumference.
8. Draw a circle with the following.
   a. point K as the center
   b. $\overline{EF}$ as the diameter
   c. $\overline{KG}$ as a radius
   d. $\overline{HG}$ as a chord

Exercises

Use this circle to answer exercises 1–11.

1. Name the center.
2. Name five radii.
3. Name three chords.
4. Name two diameters.
5. Name four radii that are part of a diameter.
6. Find the length of $\overline{GR}$. Is it longer or shorter than $\overline{SG}$?
7. Is $\overline{DR}$ congruent to $\overline{DB}$?
8. Find the length of each radius to the nearest centimeter.
9. Find the length of each diameter to the nearest centimeter.
10. How does the length of a radius compare to the length of a diameter?
11. Estimate the circumference.
12. Draw a circle with the following.
    a. point P as the center
    b. $\overline{RS}$ as a diameter
    c. $\overline{PT}$ as a radius
    d. $\overline{ET}$ as a chord
13. Draw a 3-cm line segment. Set the compass to match the segment. Draw a circle with the compass. What is the length of a radius? Of a diameter?
14. Draw a circle. Draw a diameter of the circle. Draw other line segments connecting points on the circle. What is the longest segment that connects two points on a circle?

Symmetry

■ When a figure is folded along a **line of symmetry,** the two parts match.

Is the red line a line of symmetry?

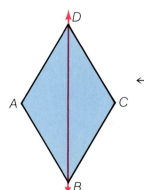

← Trace quadrilateral *ABCD*.

Fold along the red line. ⟶

Triangle *BAD* matches triangle *BCD*.

The red line is a line of symmetry.

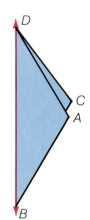

On the figure you traced, draw a line through *A* and *C*.

Fold along the line.

Do the two parts match?

Quadrilateral *ABCD* has two lines of symmetry.

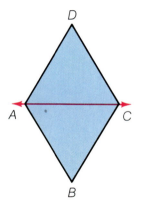

■ Sometimes a figure does not have a line of symmetry.

Trace the quadrilateral.

Does it have a line of symmetry?

Check by folding the tracing.

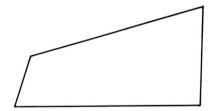

Try These

Is the red line a line of symmetry? Write *yes* or *no*.

1.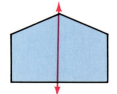

2.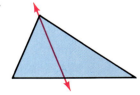

3.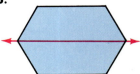

4.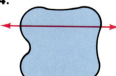

Exercises

Trace each figure. Draw as many lines of symmetry as you can. Tell how many lines of symmetry each figure has.

1.

2.

3.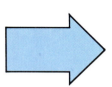

4.

5.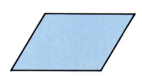

6.

7.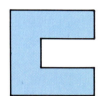

★ **8.**

Some letters have lines of symmetry.
    A has a line of symmetry.
    B has a line of symmetry.
    H has two lines of symmetry.

 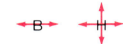

Is the red line a line of symmetry? Write *yes* or *no*.

9.

10.

11.

12.

13.

14.

15.

16.

17. MOM

18. ←WEEK→

19. ←BOX→

20. DAD

 KEEPING IN SHAPE

1. $\begin{array}{r} 2.4 \\ +6.3 \\ \hline \end{array}$

2. $\begin{array}{r} 5.7 \\ -4.5 \\ \hline \end{array}$

3. $\begin{array}{r} 9.5 \\ -3.48 \\ \hline \end{array}$

4. $\begin{array}{r} 6.2 \\ \times\ 4 \\ \hline \end{array}$

5. $\begin{array}{r} 13.44 \\ +\ 9.38 \\ \hline \end{array}$

6. $\begin{array}{r} 0.74 \\ \times\ 0.6 \\ \hline \end{array}$

7. $\begin{array}{r} 2.09 \\ +6.135 \\ \hline \end{array}$

8. $\begin{array}{r} 2.54 \\ \times\ 6.1 \\ \hline \end{array}$

9. $\begin{array}{r} 24.46 \\ -10.39 \\ \hline \end{array}$

10. $\begin{array}{r} 0.17 \\ \times\ 0.2 \\ \hline \end{array}$

11. $0.7 + 0.45$

12. $0.9 - 0.24$

13. 9.4×0.6

14. $8.061 - 5.32$

15. $25.28 \div 8$

16. $3.64 + 8 + 5.2$

Space Figures

■ Each of these objects is shaped like a **space figure**.

cube

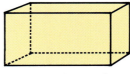

rectangular prism

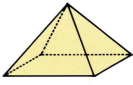

rectangular pyramid

cone

cylinder

sphere

■ The cube, prism, and pyramid have **faces** that are shaped like squares, rectangles, or triangles. The **edges** are line segments. The edges meet at vertices.

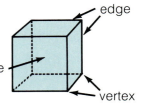

■ The cone and cylinder have faces that are flat or curved. The edges are curved.

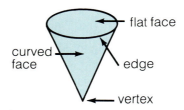

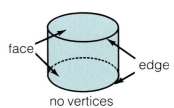

Try These

Name the shape of each object.

1.

2.

3.

4.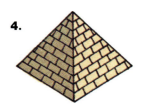

Copy and complete.

5. A cube has ■ faces, ■ edges, and ■ vertices.

6. A cone has ■ faces, ■ edge, and ■ vertex.

Exercises

Name the shape of each object.

1.

2.

3.

4.

5.

6.

7.

⭐ 8.

How would each figure look from the bottom?
Write *rectangle*, *square*, or *circle*.

9.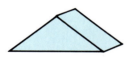

10.

11.

12.

Count the number of faces, vertices, and edges for each figure listed. Copy and complete the table.

Figure	13.	14.	15.	16.	17.	18.
Number of Faces	▨	▨	▨	▨	▨	▨
Number of Edges	12	▨	▨	▨	▨	▨
Number of Vertices	8	▨	▨	▨	▨	▨

⭐ **19.** Look for a pattern that relates the number of faces, the number of vertices, and the number of edges for each space figure. What is the pattern?

⭐ **20.** Write a formula that shows the pattern. Let *F* be the number of faces. Let *V* be the number of vertices. Let *E* be the number of edges.

Perimeter

■ **Perimeter** is the distance around a figure. To find the perimeter, add the lengths of the sides.

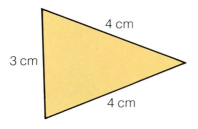

3 + 4 + 4 = 11

The perimeter is 11 cm.

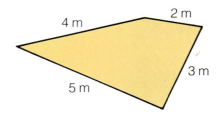

4 + 5 + 3 + 2 = 14

The perimeter is 14 m.

■ Find the perimeter of this rectangle.

Think: Opposite sides of a rectangle are congruent.

Two sides are 28 m long.
Two sides are 42 m long.

Perimeter = 28 + 42 + 28 + 42
= 140

The perimeter is 140 m.

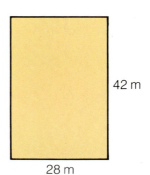

Try These

Find the perimeter of each polygon.

1.

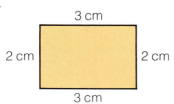

2.

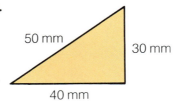

3.

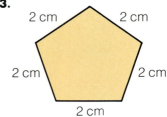

4.

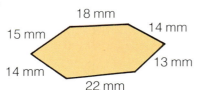

5.

6.

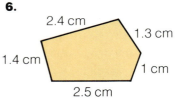

Exercises

Find the perimeter of each polygon.

1.
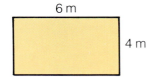
6 m
4 m

2.
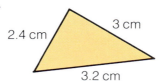
2.4 cm
3 cm
3.2 cm

3.
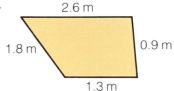
2.6 m
1.8 m
0.9 m
1.3 m

4. Find the perimeter of the square.

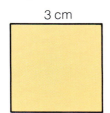
3 cm

5. Find the perimeter of the equilateral triangle.

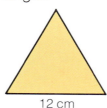
12 cm

★ **6.** Find the missing measure. The perimeter is 28 cm.

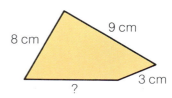
8 cm
9 cm
3 cm
?

Find the perimeter of a polygon with these measurements.

7. 24 cm, 12 cm, 24 cm, 28 cm

8. 3.5 m, 7 m, 2.6 m, 4.8 m

9. 16.3 cm, 12.9 cm, 18.4 cm

10. 43 mm, 29 mm, 12 mm, 35 mm, 26 mm

★ **11.** 78 mm, 3.7 cm, 6.1 cm

★ **12.** 75 cm, 1.3 m, 46 cm, 0.8 m

Solve each problem.

13. The park workers put a fence around the garden. How much fencing did they use?

14. The town is planning to build a tennis court at the park. The tennis court is a rectangle 23.7 m long and 10.9 m wide. What is the perimeter of the tennis court?

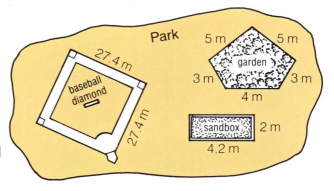
Park
5 m   5 m
garden
3 m   3 m
4 m
27.4 m
baseball diamond
27.4 m
sandbox   2 m
4.2 m

15. The park workers are putting a wood railing around the sandbox. How much railing will they need?

16. Justin was playing baseball at the park. He hit a home run. How far did he run around the baseball diamond?

17. Draw a rectangle with a perimeter of 24 centimeters. Can you draw several rectangles with the same perimeter that are different shapes?

★ **18.** The perimeter of an equilateral triangle is 51 cm. What is the length of a side?

Area: Rectangle and Right Triangle

Area is the number of square units needed to cover a region. A **square centimeter (cm^2)** is a unit used to measure area.

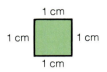

1 square centimeter (1 cm^2)

■ Find the area of the rectangle.

Count the number of square centimeters. There are 12 square centimeters. The area is 12 square centimeters.

You can multiply to find the area of the rectangle.

Think: 3 rows
         4 square centimeters in each row

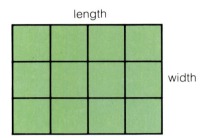

length

width

$$3 \times 4 = 12$$
$$\text{Area} = 12 \text{ cm}^2$$

> *To find the area of a rectangle, multiply the length (l) by the width (w). The formula for the area of a rectangle is:*
>
> $$A = l \times w$$

■ A **right triangle** has one right angle. The area of a right triangle is half the area of a rectangle.

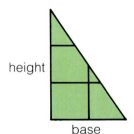

height

base

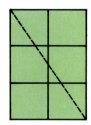

Find the area of the rectangle.

$$A = l \times w$$
$$= 2 \times 3$$
$$= 6 \text{ cm}^2$$

Find the area of the right triangle.

$$6 \div 2 = 3$$
$$\text{Area} = 3 \text{ cm}^2$$

> *To find the area of a right triangle, multiply the base (b) by the height (h). Then divide by 2. The formula for the area of a right triangle is:*
>
> $$A = (b \times h) \div 2$$

Try These

Find the area of each figure.

1.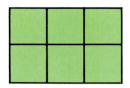

2.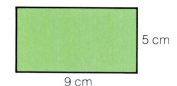
5 cm
9 cm

3.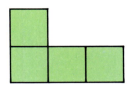

4.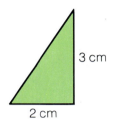
3 cm
2 cm

5.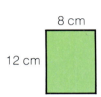
8 cm
12 cm

6.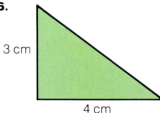
3 cm
4 cm

Exercises

Find the area of each figure.

1.
4.8 cm
1.2 cm

2.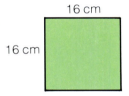
16 cm
16 cm

3.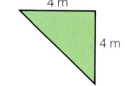
4 m
4 m

4. a rectangle with length of 30 cm and width of 16 cm

5. a right triangle with base of 5 cm and height of 8 cm

6. a rectangle with length of 4.1 m and width of 2.7 m

7. a right triangle with base of 3.5 cm and height of 1.2 cm

★ **8.** a rectangle with length of 1.6 m and width of 54 cm

Solve each problem.

9. Adrian's living room is 6 m long and 4 m wide. How many square meters of carpeting are needed to cover the floor?

10. The base of a triangular piece of tile Adrian is using in the bathroom is 91 mm. Its height is 122 mm. What is its area?

★ **11.** The guest room in Adrian's house is in the shape of a square. One wall is 5 m long. Find the perimeter and the area of the room.

★ **12.** Adrian is using cork on one wall. The area of a rectangular piece of cork is 900 cm². It is 25 cm long. How wide is each piece of cork?

Problem Solving: Strategies

ORGANIZING INFORMATION

Sometimes **making a diagram** is a strategy that can help you solve a problem.

Mike is planning a pen for his dog. He wants the pen to be at least 45 m². He can use his toolshed as one post. He draws this diagram of a possible pen.

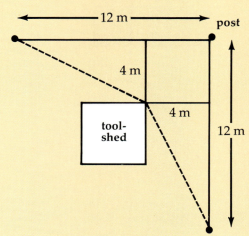

Mike divides the diagram into parts to find the area of this dog pen. The pen is divided into one square and two right triangles.

Find the area of the square.

$$A = l \times w$$
$$= 4 \times 4 = 16 \text{ m}^2$$

Find the area of the right triangles.

Think: Each triangle has one side that is 4 m long. The other side is 12 m − 4 m = 8 m.

$$A = (b \times h) \div 2$$
$$= (4 \times 8) \div 2$$
$$= 32 \div 2 = 16 \text{ m}^2$$

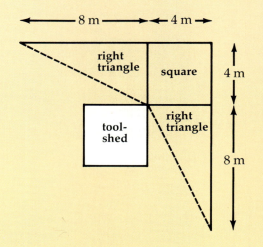

Add the areas of the three parts.

square	16 m²
right triangle	16 m²
right triangle	+16 m²
	48 m²

The area of this dog pen is 48 m². The pen is large enough.

Using the Strategy

Solve each problem.

1. Mike could use this plan. His new fence is the dotted line. The toolshed is a square 4 m on a side. What is the area of this dog pen?

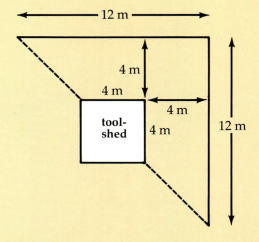

2. Which figure has the greatest area? Which figures have the same area?

a.

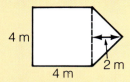

b.

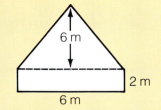

c.

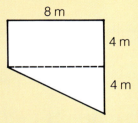

d.

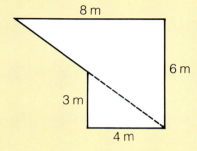

Draw a diagram to find the area of each figure.

3. A figure divided into:
   a. a square that is 4 m by 4 m
   b. a triangle whose base is one side of the square and whose height is 5 m

4. A figure divided into:
   a. a rectangle that is 2 m by 6 m
   b. a square that is 5 m by 5 m

ACTIVITY

EXPERIMENTING WITH SHAPES

1. Cut eight strips of cardboard.

2. Put three of them together with a brass tack at each corner.

3. Can you change the shape without bending the cardboard?

4. Put four strips together. Can you change the shape?

5. Why do you think engineers use triangles as supports?

6. Use another strip to form a diagonal of the quadrilateral.

7. Can you change the shape now?

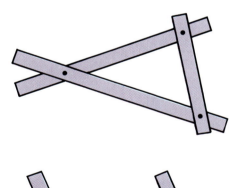

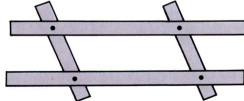

Volume

Volume is the number of cubic units needed to fill a space. A **cubic centimeter (cm³)** is a unit used to measure volume.

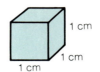

1 cubic centimeter (1 cm³)

Find the volume of the rectangular prism.

Count the number of cubic centimeters. Be sure to count the hidden cubes. There are 24 cubic centimeters. The volume is 24 cubic centimeters.

You can multiply to find the volume of a rectangular prism.

Think: Each layer is 4 × 3, or 12, cubic centimeters.
There are 2 layers.

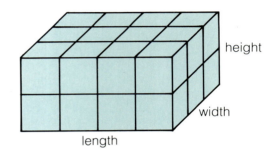

2 × 12 = 24
Volume = 24 cm³

> *To find the volume of a rectangular prism, multiply the length (l) by the width (w) and then by the height (h).*
>
> $V = l \times w \times h$

Try These

Find the volume of each rectangular prism.

1.

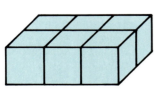

2.

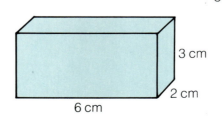

6 cm · 2 cm · 3 cm

3. 3.6 cm

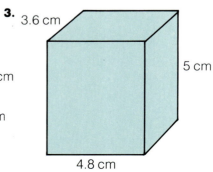

4.8 cm · 5 cm

Exercises

Find the volume of each rectangular prism.

1.
9 cm 5 cm 2 cm

2.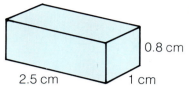
2.5 cm 1 cm 0.8 cm

3.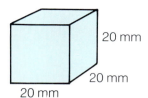
20 mm 20 mm 20 mm

4.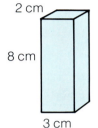
2 cm 8 cm 3 cm

5.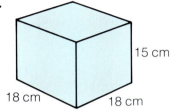
18 cm 18 cm 15 cm

6.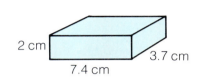
2 cm 7.4 cm 3.7 cm

7. a box 6 cm long, 5 cm wide, and 3 cm high

8. a box 3.8 cm long, 4.5 cm wide, and 1.1 cm high

9. a box 13 mm long, 26 mm wide, and 10 mm high

10. a box 7 cm long and wide and 2.2 cm high

★ **11.** a box 4 cm long, 35 mm wide, and 1.7 cm high

Solve each problem.

12. An aquarium is 60 cm long, 30 cm wide, and 25 cm high. What is the volume of the aquarium?

13. A box of fish food is 50 mm long, 35 mm wide, and 60 mm high. What is the volume of the box?

14. A storage cabinet is 1.5 m long, 0.8 m wide, and 2 m high. What is the volume of the storage cabinet?

15. A rectangular tabletop is 1.3 m long and 0.9 m wide. What is the perimeter of the tabletop?

16. A square rug is 4.2 m long. What is the area of the rug?

Geometry and Measurement   321

Using Customary Units

■ You can use the **square inch (in.²)**, the **square foot (ft²)**, and the **square yard (yd²)** to measure area.

Find the area of a patio that is 16 ft long and 12 ft wide.

$$A = l \times w$$
$$= 16 \times 12$$
$$= 192 \text{ ft}^2$$

The area of the patio is 192 ft².

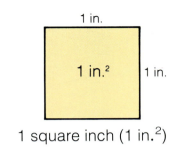

1 square inch (1 in.²)

■ You can use the **cubic inch (in.³)**, the **cubic foot (ft³)**, and the **cubic yard (yd³)** to measure volume.

Find the volume of a swimming pool that is 30 yd long, 15 yd wide, and 3 yd deep.

$$V = l \times w \times h$$
$$= 30 \times 15 \times 3$$
$$= 1{,}350 \text{ yd}^3$$

The volume of the swimming pool is 1,350 yd³.

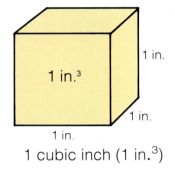

1 cubic inch (1 in.³)

Try These

Find the area of each figure.

1.

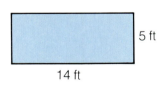

5 ft

14 ft

2.

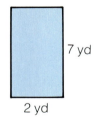

7 yd

2 yd

3.

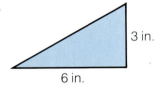

3 in.

6 in.

Find the volume of each rectangular prism.

4.

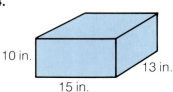

10 in.

13 in.

15 in.

5.

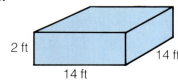

2 ft

14 ft

14 ft

6.

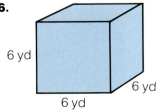

6 yd

6 yd

6 yd

Exercises

Find the perimeter and the area of each figure.

1.
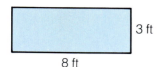
3 ft
8 ft

2.
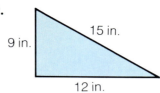
9 in.   15 in.
12 in.

3.
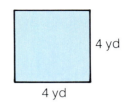
4 yd
4 yd

Find the volume of each rectangular prism.

4.
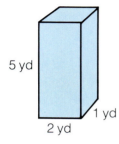
5 yd
1 yd
2 yd

5.
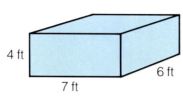
4 ft
7 ft
6 ft

6.
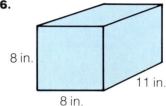
8 in.
8 in.
11 in.

Find the area of each figure.

7. a rectangle with a length of 12 ft and a width of 5 ft

8. a rectangle with a length of 9 in. and a width of 16 in.

9. a right triangle with a base of 6 yd and a height of 8 yd

10. a right triangle with a base of 8 ft and a height of 9 ft

Find the volume of each rectangular prism.

11. a box 10 in. long, 7 in. wide, and 5 in. high

12. a tank 6 ft long, 4 ft wide, and 3 ft deep

13. a box 9 in. long, 6 in. wide, and 3 in. high

14. a carton 2 yd long and wide and 5 yd high

THINK AND TRY

EXPLORING VOLUME

1. A lunch box is 12 in. long, 8 in. wide, and 4 in. deep. Find its volume.

2. A sandwich is 4 in. by 4 in. by 2 in. Find the volume of the sandwich.

3. The lunch box is how many times larger than the sandwich?

4. How many sandwiches can be packed in the lunch box?

Problem Solving: Applications

READ
PLAN
DO
CHECK

READING A BLUEPRINT

This is a **blueprint**. It is a map of a house. Architects work from a blueprint when they are building a house.

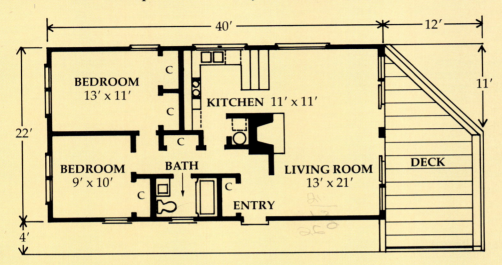

What is the area of this house?

Study the blueprint.

The length of the house, according to the blueprint, is 40 ft. (40' means 40 ft.)

The width of the house, according to the blueprint, is 22 ft.

Find the area.

$$A = l \times w$$
$$= 40 \times 22$$
$$= 880 \text{ ft}^2$$

The area of this house is 880 ft².

Try These

Solve each problem.

1. How many rooms are in this house? List the rooms.

2. What is the area of the living room?

3. What is the area of the larger bedroom? What is the area of the smaller bedroom?

4. The owners of the house want to carpet both bedrooms. How many square feet of carpeting are needed altogether?

Exercises

Solve each problem.

1. The owner wants to buy lumber to build the deck. Find the area of the deck.

2. What is the area of the land occupied by the house and the deck?

3. The owner wants to buy an air conditioner for the large bedroom. The ceilings are 8 ft high. How many cubic feet must the air conditioner be able to cool?

4. The unbroken wall in the small bedroom will be covered with wallpaper. How many square feet of wallpaper will be needed for the wall?

5. The refrigerator is 60 in. high, 30 in. wide, and 26 in. deep. What is its volume?

6. How much space, in feet, is between the top of the refrigerator and the ceiling?

7. ▭ is the blueprint symbol for a window.
How many windows are in the house? (Do not count the sliding doors that open onto the deck.)

★ 8. The kitchen floor will be tiled. Each tile is 6 in. on a side. How many tiles will be needed to cover the kitchen floor? (Hint: Change the kitchen measurements to inches first.)

This is a map of the lot and the position of the house.

9. What is the area of this plot of land?

10. A pool is planned for the yard. The pool is 15 ft in diameter. Where on the lot is there room for the pool?

11. The owner wants to put a fence around the property. How many yards of fencing are needed?

★ 12. How much of the lot is not taken up by the house and the deck?

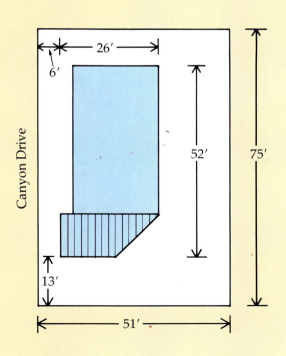

Graphing Ordered Pairs

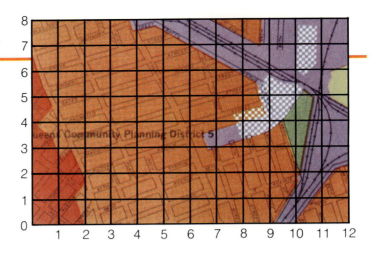

Barry Miller is a city planner. He puts numbered squares on his maps. To locate a building, Barry uses an **ordered pair** of numbers.

■ (5, 3) is an ordered pair. It gives the location of the post office.

The 5 tells how many units to the right of 0.

The 3 tells how many units up.

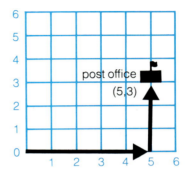

■ The order of the numbers is important.

(3, 5) is different from (5, 3).

Graph (3, 5).
Start at 0.
Count 3 units to the right.
Count 5 units up.

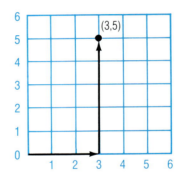

Try These

Name the point for each ordered pair.

1. (1, 3)   2. (3, 2)   3. (4, 4)

4. (5, 1)   5. (0, 3)   6. (5, 0)

Name the ordered pair for each point.

7. C   8. H   9. L

10. F   11. A   12. E

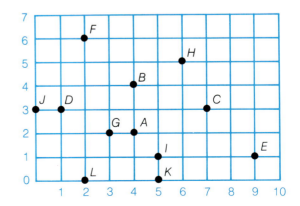

Exercises

Name the point for each ordered pair.

1. (3, 5) **2.** (6, 3) **3.** (2, 2)

4. (0, 1) **5.** (8, 4) **6.** (4, 0)

Name the ordered pair for each point.

7. J **8.** R **9.** N

10. S **11.** Q **12.** L

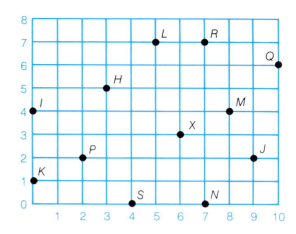

Use graph paper. Copy this graph.

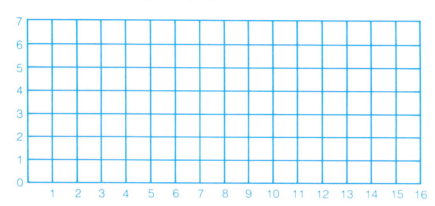

13. Locate these points. Label each with its letter.

A(1, 6)	E(1, 4)	I(3, 2)	M(7, 6)	Q(3, 2)
B(3, 4)	F(3, 6)	J(13, 6)	N(9, 2)	R(11, 2)
C(5, 6)	G(5, 2)	K(15, 2)	O(11, 6)	S(14, 6)
D(7, 2)	H(9, 6)	L(1, 2)	P(15, 6)	

14. Riddle: What falls often but *never* gets hurt? Draw these segments on your graph. Then read the answer.

$\overline{FA}$	$\overline{CG}$	$\overline{HN}$	$\overline{JQ}$
$\overline{AE}$	$\overline{CD}$	$\overline{NR}$	$\overline{QS}$
$\overline{EB}$	$\overline{MD}$	$\overline{RO}$	$\overline{SK}$
$\overline{BI}$		$\overline{OH}$	$\overline{KP}$
$\overline{IL}$			

★ **15.** Make up your own riddle or message. Write a code using ordered pairs. Give it to a friend to solve.

CHAPTER CHECKPOINT

Find the measure of each angle. Then write whether the angle is *right, acute,* or *obtuse.* (pp. 298–301)

1. 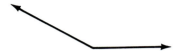   **2.**    **3.**

Write whether the lines are *parallel, perpendicular,* or *intersecting* but not perpendicular. (pp. 296–297, 300–301)

4.    **5.**    **6.**

Name each polygon. Give the special name for each triangle. (pp. 302–303)

7. 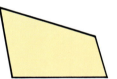   **8.** 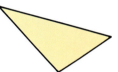   **9.**    **10.**

Are the figures congruent? Write *yes* or *no.* (pp. 296–297, 304–305)

11.    **12.** 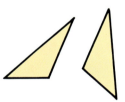   **13.**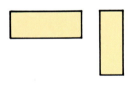

Write the special name for each quadrilateral. (pp. 306–307)

14.   **15.** 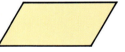   **16.** 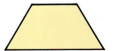   **17.**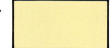

Use this circle to answer exercises 18–21. (pp. 308–309)

18. Name three radii.
19. Name a chord.
20. Name a diameter.
21. Estimate the circumference.

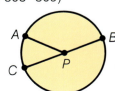

Is the red line a line of symmetry? Write _yes_ or _no_. (pp. 310–311)

22.

23.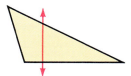

24.

25.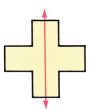

Name the shape of each object. (pp. 312–313)

26.

27.

28.

29.

Find the perimeter and the area of each figure. (pp. 314–317, 322–323)

30. a rectangle with a length of 2.4 cm and a width of 3.3 cm

31. a square with a length of 7.1 m

32. a rectangle with a length of 8 yd and a width of 5 yd

33. a right triangle with a base of 8 in., a height of 6 in., and a side of 10 in.

Find the volume of each rectangular prism. (pp. 320–323)

34. a box 4.2 cm long, 3.8 cm wide, and 2 cm high

35. a cabinet 4 m long, 2 m wide, and 3 m high

36. a carton 5 ft long, 3 ft wide, and 2 ft high

37. a box 8 in. long, 14 in. wide, and 14 in. high

Name the point for each ordered pair. (pp. 326–327)

38. (1, 3) **39.** (6, 2) **40.** (4, 0)

Name the ordered pair for each point. (pp. 326–327)

41. *B* **42.** *E* **43.** *G*

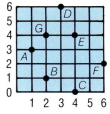

Solve each problem. (pp. 296–327)

44. A rectangular lawn is 7 m long and 6.5 m wide. What is the perimeter of the lawn? What is the area of the lawn?

45. Find the area of this figure.

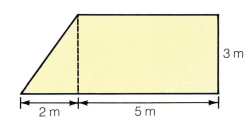

COMPUTERS AND PROBLEM SOLVING

Study this grid.

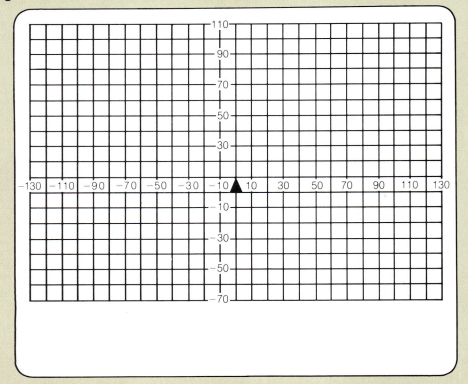

■ The turtle's home position is at the 0,0 point of the grid. How many units will the turtle travel in a straight line from:

> HOME to the top of the grid?
> > the top to the bottom of the grid?
> HOME to the right side of the grid?
> > the right side to the left side of the grid?

You can teach the turtle to draw shapes and designs by typing commands that will move it around the grid.

Read this command.

SETPOS [100 100]

SETPOS tells the turtle to set its new position at the point named by the ordered pair (100, 100).

If you look for (100, 100) on the grid, you will see that the turtle would travel toward the top right corner.

Solve each problem.

1. Put your finger on the turtle in its HOME position. Trace the path the turtle would travel if it followed this procedure:

   TO TURTLEPATH
   SETPOS [50 50]
   SETPOS [50 −50]
   SETPOS [−50 −50]
   SETPOS [0 0]
   END

2. Draw a picture of the design the turtle will display.

■ You can also use the PENUP, PU, and PENDOWN, PD, commands in teaching the turtle to create designs and shapes.

This procedure will teach the turtle to draw a rectangle·

   TO RECTANGLE
   PU SETPOS [60 40] PD
   SETPOS [60 −40]
   SETPOS [−60 −40]
   SETPOS [−60 40]
   SETPOS [60 40]
   END

Solve each problem.

1. Write the missing lines to teach the turtle to make a triangle.

   TO TRIANGLE
   PU SETPOS [100 100]PD

   SETPOS [0 0]

   END

2. What picture will the turtle display with this procedure?

   TO MINE
   PU SETPOS [0 70] PD
   SETPOS [70 0]
   SETPOS [0 −70]
   SETPOS [−70 0]
   SETPOS [0 70]
   END

3. Write a procedure to teach the turtle to write the first letter of your name. Use the commands PU, PD, and SETPOS in the procedure.

4. Rewrite the procedure in problem 3 using the commands FD, BK, RT, and LT.

5. What do you type to get any procedure to run?

6. Write a procedure with the SETPOS command to teach the turtle to draw a square with the perimeter of 80 units.

ENRICHMENT

VENN DIAGRAMS

This **Venn diagram** shows the members of two clubs. Each circle contains a **set** of names. Set A shows the fifth graders in the Bicycle Club. Set B shows the fifth graders in the Bowling Club.

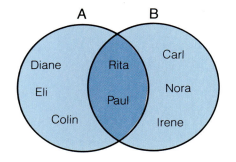

You can list the members of each set.

A = {Diane, Eli, Colin, Rita, Paul}
B = {Carl, Nora, Irene, Paul, Rita}

Two students are in both clubs. Their names are in both circles. They form the **intersection** of set A and set B.

You can show the intersection of sets A and B with the symbol ∩.

A ∩ B = {Rita, Paul}

Read: the intersection of A and B

The students who are in either the Bicycle Club or the Bowling Club form the **union** of set A and set B.

You can show the union of sets A and B with the symbol ∪.

A ∪ B = {Diane, Eli, Colin, Rita, Paul, Nora, Carl, Irene}

Read: the union of A and B

Use the Venn diagrams to solve each problem.

C is the set of factors of 28.
D is the set of factors of 42.

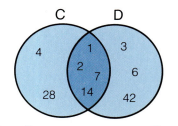

List the factors in each set.

1. C

2. D

3. C ∩ D

4. C ∪ D

Draw a Venn diagram to show the factors of 48 and 60. Make E the set of factors of 48. Make F the set of factors of 60.

5. Which numbers form the intersection of E and F?

Add, subtract, multiply, or divide.

1. 258 + 17 + 406

2. 73,124 − 6,059

3. 8,112 × 45

4. 732 ÷ 19

5. 604 × 875

6. 3,648 ÷ 48

Copy and complete.

7. 40 mm = ▥ cm

8. 2,000 g = ▥ kg

9. 3 L = ▥ mL

10. 70 cm = ▥ mm

11. 8,000 mL = ▥ L

12. 4 kg = ▥ g

13. 12 yd = ▥ ft

14. 3 lb = ▥ oz

15. 16 qt = ▥ gal

Write >, <, or =.

16. $\frac{3}{4}$ ▥ $\frac{2}{3}$

17. $\frac{4}{5}$ ▥ $\frac{1}{2}$

18. $\frac{1}{3}$ ▥ $\frac{1}{2}$

19. $\frac{6}{8}$ ▥ $\frac{3}{4}$

20. 0.2 ▥ 0.5

21. 1.25 ▥ 1.26

22. 3.7 ▥ 3.70

23. 2.4 ▥ 2.39

Add or subtract. Write each answer in lowest terms.

24. $\frac{2}{3}$
$+\frac{1}{4}$

25. $\frac{5}{6}$
$-\frac{2}{3}$

26. $\frac{1}{2}$
$+\frac{3}{5}$

27. $\frac{7}{8}$
$-\frac{5}{6}$

28. $\frac{3}{4}$
$+\frac{3}{8}$

Estimate each answer.

29. 635 + 47

30. 3,149 − 1,845

31. 76 × 3

32. 27,942 + 43,156

33. 195 × 31

34. 52,973 − 1,068

Add, subtract, or multiply.

35. 24.09
+ 18.63

36. 7.5
− 0.83

37. 11.2
× 6.1

38. 39.02
− 8.15

39. 0.47
× 0.03

Solve each problem.

40. Karen had $\frac{3}{4}$ yd of ribbon. She used $\frac{2}{5}$ yd to make a sock puppet. How much ribbon was left?

41. Jason needs 6 pieces of rope to make a macrame belt. Each piece has to be 0.95 m long. How much rope does Jason need to make the belt?

SKILLS CHECK

Choose the correct answer.

1. $7.48
     1.06
  + 3.50

 a. $1.24
 b. $10.24
 c. $11.94
 d. $12.04

2. 5,070 − 868

 a. 4,202
 b. 4,278
 c. 4,862
 d. NG

3.   361
     × 49

 a. 4,693
 b. 17,689
 c. 18,689
 d. 19,399

4. 32)‾800‾

 a. 20
 b. 25
 c. 30
 d. NG

5. Write the fraction $\frac{17}{5}$ as a mixed number.

 a. $2\frac{2}{5}$ b. $2\frac{7}{15}$

 c. $3\frac{2}{17}$ d. $3\frac{2}{5}$

6. $\frac{7}{12} + \frac{1}{3} = \frac{\blacksquare}{12}$

 a. 4
 b. 8
 c. 15
 d. NG

7. $\frac{9}{10} - \frac{2}{5}$

 a. $\frac{1}{3}$ b. $\frac{2}{5}$

 c. $\frac{1}{2}$ d. $\frac{7}{5}$

8. Write a decimal for $8\frac{3}{100}$.

 a. 0.83
 b. 8.003
 c. 8.03
 d. 8.3

9.   3.317
     − 1.890

 a. 1.427
 b. 1.537
 c. 2.587
 d. 25.27

10. A city budget was cut from $426 million to $389 million. How much money was cut from the budget?

 a. $23 million
 b. $37 million
 c. $48 million
 d. $63 million

11. John bowls 5 games. His scores are 138, 159, 206, 174, and 198. What is his average score?

 a. 168
 b. 175
 c. 199
 d. NG

12. In 2 days, you walked 10.4 km. The first day you walked 5.5 km. How far did you walk the second day?

 a. 4.9 km
 b. 5.1 km
 c. 5.9 km
 d. 15.9 km

MORE ABOUT FRACTIONS

11

Mixed Numbers

■ Remember the two ways to write a fraction as a mixed number.

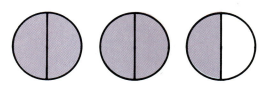

Write $\frac{5}{2}$ as a mixed number.

One way:

$$\frac{5}{2} = \frac{4}{2} + \frac{1}{2}$$

$$= 2\frac{1}{2}$$

$$\frac{5}{2} = 2\frac{1}{2}$$

Another way:

$\frac{5}{2}$ means $5 \div 2$.

$$\begin{array}{r} 2 \text{ R1, or } 2\frac{1}{2} \leftarrow \text{remainder} \\ \qquad\qquad \leftarrow \text{divisor} \\ 2\overline{)5} \\ \underline{4} \\ 1 \end{array}$$

$$\frac{5}{2} = 2\frac{1}{2}$$

■ You can also write a mixed number as a fraction.

Write $1\frac{3}{4}$ as a fraction.

$$1\frac{3}{4} = 1 + \frac{3}{4}$$

$$= \frac{4}{4} + \frac{3}{4}$$

$$= \frac{7}{4}$$

Write $3\frac{1}{3}$ as a fraction.

$$3\frac{1}{3} = 3 + \frac{1}{3}$$

$$= \frac{3}{1} + \frac{1}{3} \leftarrow \text{Find a common denominator.}$$

$$= \frac{9}{3} + \frac{1}{3}$$

$$= \frac{10}{3}$$

■ You can use a shortcut to write a mixed number as a fraction.

Write $2\frac{3}{5}$ as a fraction.

Multiply to find the number of fifths in 2.

$$5 \times 2 = 10$$

Add to find the total number of fifths.

$$10 + 3 = 13$$

$$2\frac{3}{5} = \frac{13}{5}$$

$10 + 3 = 13$

$$2 \overset{+}{\underset{\times}{\frown}} \frac{3}{5}$$

$5 \times 2 = 10$

Try These

Write each fraction as a mixed number or as a whole number.

1. $\frac{5}{4}$
2. $\frac{7}{3}$
3. $\frac{15}{5}$
4. $\frac{23}{4}$
5. $\frac{8}{4}$
6. $\frac{14}{3}$

Write each mixed number as a fraction.

7. $1\frac{1}{3}$
8. $1\frac{2}{5}$
9. $2\frac{1}{2}$
10. $2\frac{3}{5}$
11. $1\frac{7}{10}$
12. $3\frac{4}{9}$

Exercises

Write each fraction as a mixed number or as a whole number.

1. $\frac{33}{5}$
2. $\frac{49}{8}$
3. $\frac{18}{6}$
4. $\frac{24}{7}$
5. $\frac{11}{8}$
6. $\frac{27}{8}$

7. $\frac{9}{2}$
8. $\frac{21}{3}$
9. $\frac{16}{3}$
10. $\frac{11}{10}$
11. $\frac{9}{5}$
12. $\frac{23}{10}$

Write each mixed number as a fraction.

13. $1\frac{5}{8}$
14. $2\frac{3}{7}$
15. $3\frac{2}{3}$
16. $7\frac{1}{2}$
17. $6\frac{1}{5}$
18. $5\frac{1}{4}$

19. $3\frac{3}{4}$
20. $8\frac{1}{4}$
21. $3\frac{9}{10}$
22. $2\frac{4}{5}$
23. $1\frac{3}{100}$
24. $4\frac{5}{7}$

25. $4\frac{1}{2}$
26. $6\frac{3}{8}$
27. $5\frac{7}{10}$
28. $1\frac{3}{4}$
29. $3\frac{5}{8}$
30. $2\frac{3}{7}$

Solve each problem. Write each answer in lowest terms.

31. Pam used $2\frac{1}{2}$ pieces of fabric to make curtains for her dollhouse. Write the number of pieces Pam used as a fraction.

32. Brad spent $\frac{2}{3}$ h cutting wallpaper. Then he spent $\frac{3}{4}$ h pasting it on the walls. How much time did he spend wallpapering in all?

33. Pam has 14 pieces of dollhouse furniture. She uses 10 pieces in the living room. What part of the pieces are for the living room?

34. Brad spent $\frac{16}{3}$ h painting the dollhouse. Write the number of hours as a mixed number.

Adding Mixed Numbers

■ Dr. Victoria Mullin is a veterinarian. She spent $4\frac{1}{6}$ hours in her office. She also spent $2\frac{3}{6}$ hours operating on patients. How many hours did Dr. Mullin work that day?

To find how many hours, add $4\frac{1}{6}$ and $2\frac{3}{6}$.

Add the fractions.	Add the whole numbers.	Write the sum in lowest terms.
$4\frac{1}{6}$ $+2\frac{3}{6}$ $\overline{\frac{4}{6}}$	$4\frac{1}{6}$ $+2\frac{3}{6}$ $\overline{6\frac{4}{6}}$	$4\frac{1}{6}$ $+2\frac{3}{6}$ $\overline{6\frac{4}{6}=6\frac{2}{3}}$

Dr. Mullin worked $6\frac{2}{3}$ hours.

■ Add: $3\frac{1}{4} + 5\frac{1}{6}$

Remember: To add fractions with different denominators, first write equivalent fractions with the same denominator.

Find the least common denominator. Write equivalent fractions.

$$3\frac{1}{4} = 3\frac{3}{12}$$
$$+5\frac{1}{6} = +5\frac{2}{12}$$

Add.

$$3\frac{1}{4} = 3\frac{3}{12}$$
$$+5\frac{1}{6} = +5\frac{2}{12}$$
$$\overline{8\frac{5}{12}}$$

Try These

Add. Write each sum in lowest terms.

1. $5\frac{1}{5}$ $+2\frac{3}{5}$

2. $1\frac{1}{6}$ $+2\frac{1}{2}$

3. 7 $+2\frac{3}{4}$

4. $5\frac{1}{12}$ $+\frac{5}{12}$

5. $6\frac{1}{2}$ $+2\frac{1}{3}$

6. $2\frac{1}{12} + 1\frac{1}{6}$

7. $9\frac{1}{5} + 6\frac{1}{2}$

8. $9\frac{1}{4} + 3\frac{1}{4}$

Exercises

Add. Write each sum in lowest terms.

1. $3\frac{1}{3}$
$+2\frac{1}{3}$

2. $4\frac{1}{5}$
$+2\frac{3}{10}$

3. 6
$+3\frac{1}{2}$

4. $5\frac{1}{6}$
$+7\frac{1}{6}$

5. $1\frac{2}{3}$
$+2\frac{1}{4}$

6. $4\frac{1}{6}$
$+2\frac{1}{2}$

7. $2\frac{7}{10}$
$+3\frac{1}{10}$

8. $3\frac{4}{9}$
$+5\frac{2}{9}$

9. $7\frac{3}{8}$
$+4$

10. $3\frac{2}{5}$
$+4\frac{1}{2}$

11. 8
$+5\frac{6}{7}$

12. $4\frac{2}{5}$
$+1\frac{1}{3}$

13. $5\frac{3}{8}$
$+4\frac{1}{4}$

14. $9\frac{1}{10}$
$+8\frac{4}{5}$

15. $2\frac{3}{8}$
$+6\frac{1}{8}$

16. $8\frac{5}{12} + 6\frac{1}{3}$

17. $7\frac{7}{10} + 16\frac{1}{10}$

18. $11\frac{3}{14} + 6\frac{2}{7}$

19. $5\frac{3}{7} + 3\frac{3}{7}$

20. $9\frac{3}{7} + 6$

21. $6\frac{1}{4} + 8\frac{5}{8}$

Solve each problem. Write each answer in lowest terms.

22. Meg works for Victoria Mullin $\frac{3}{4}$ h on Monday. She works 2 h on Tuesday. How many hours does she work in all?

23. On a busy week, Meg worked extra hours. She worked $1\frac{3}{4}$ h on Thursday and 2 h on Friday. How many extra hours did she work that week?

24. A fawn weighed $29\frac{1}{5}$ lb. It gained $3\frac{1}{2}$ lb. How much does the fawn weigh now?

25. Meg typed bills for $1\frac{1}{6}$ h on Tuesday and $3\frac{3}{4}$ h on Wednesday. How many hours did Meg spend typing bills?

★ **26.** A fawn weighs 30 lb. That is about $\frac{1}{5}$ its adult weight. About what will it weigh as an adult?

★ **27.** To prepare for a presentation at the zoo, Dr. Mullin worked $3\frac{3}{4}$ h in the morning and $2\frac{1}{4}$ h in the afternoon. What fraction of the day did she work on the presentation?

Renaming Sums

■ Melinda read $6\frac{3}{4}$ pages of a book before supper. She read $8\frac{1}{2}$ pages before she went to bed. How many pages did Melinda read altogether?

Add $6\frac{3}{4}$ and $8\frac{1}{2}$ to find how many altogether.

Find the least common denominator. Write an equivalent fraction.	**Add.**	**Rename the sum.**
$6\frac{3}{4} = 6\frac{3}{4}$ $+8\frac{1}{2} = +8\frac{2}{4}$	$6\frac{3}{4} = 6\frac{3}{4}$ $+8\frac{1}{2} = +8\frac{2}{4}$ $\phantom{+8\frac{1}{2} = } 14\frac{5}{4}$	$14\frac{5}{4} = 14 + \frac{5}{4}$ $= 14 + 1\frac{1}{4}$ $= 15\frac{1}{4}$

Melinda read $15\frac{1}{4}$ pages.

■ Add: $2\frac{4}{8} + 5\frac{2}{3}$

Find the least common denominator. Write equivalent fractions.	**Add.**	**Rename the sum.**
$2\frac{4}{8} = 2\frac{12}{24}$ $+5\frac{2}{3} = +5\frac{16}{24}$	$2\frac{4}{8} = 2\frac{12}{24}$ $+5\frac{2}{3} = +5\frac{16}{24}$ $\phantom{+5\frac{2}{3} = } 7\frac{28}{24}$	$7\frac{28}{24} = 7 + \frac{28}{24}$ $= 7 + 1\frac{4}{24}$ $= 8\frac{4}{24}$ $= 8\frac{1}{6}$

Try These

Add. Write each sum in lowest terms.

1. $\begin{array}{r} 2\frac{5}{12} \\ +1\frac{1}{4} \\ \hline \end{array}$

2. $\begin{array}{r} 3\frac{1}{2} \\ +2\frac{3}{4} \\ \hline \end{array}$

3. $\begin{array}{r} 5\frac{2}{3} \\ +1\frac{5}{6} \\ \hline \end{array}$

4. $\begin{array}{r} 6\frac{3}{4} \\ +2\frac{1}{3} \\ \hline \end{array}$

5. $\begin{array}{r} 3\frac{5}{6} \\ +2\frac{5}{6} \\ \hline \end{array}$

6. $3\frac{4}{5} + 4\frac{7}{10}$

7. $1\frac{4}{5} + 2\frac{3}{5}$

8. $9\frac{1}{2} + 7\frac{3}{4}$

Exercises

Add. Write each sum in lowest terms.

1. $4\frac{1}{2}$
$+2\frac{1}{3}$

2. $3\frac{5}{8}$
$+1\frac{7}{8}$

3. $3\frac{4}{5}$
$+\ \ \frac{3}{10}$

4. $3\frac{1}{12}$
$+1\frac{1}{6}$

5. $1\frac{7}{10}$
$+\ \ \frac{1}{2}$

6. $4\frac{1}{4}$
$+2\frac{5}{12}$

7. $5\frac{2}{5}$
$+5\frac{1}{3}$

8. $3\frac{5}{6}$
$+1\frac{3}{4}$

9. $6\frac{1}{4}$
$+3\frac{4}{5}$

10. $7\frac{3}{4}$
$+1\frac{11}{12}$

11. $1\frac{1}{2}$
$+3\frac{5}{8}$

12. $2\frac{2}{3}$
$+1\frac{5}{6}$

13. $7\frac{4}{5}$
$+6\frac{7}{10}$

14. $4\frac{9}{10}$
$+7\frac{3}{5}$

15. $6\frac{1}{2}$
$+4\frac{1}{6}$

16. $6\frac{5}{8} + 1\frac{3}{8}$

17. $5\frac{1}{6} + 2\frac{1}{2}$

18. $12\frac{7}{10} + 13\frac{6}{10}$

19. $3\frac{5}{6} + 4\frac{3}{4}$

20. $\frac{7}{8} + 3\frac{4}{5}$

21. $18\frac{1}{6} + 3\frac{4}{9}$

22. $7\frac{11}{12} + 4\frac{1}{3}$

★ **23.** $6\frac{4}{5} + 3 + 4\frac{7}{10}$

★ **24.** $3\frac{1}{4} + 8\frac{2}{5} + 5\frac{1}{4}$

Solve each problem. Write each answer in lowest terms.

Melinda keeps a record of the number of pages she reads each day.

How many pages did Melinda read each day?

25. Monday
26. Tuesday
27. Wednesday
28. Thursday
29. Friday

Week of March 20		
	Pages Read	
Day	before supper	at bedtime
Monday	10	$6\frac{1}{2}$
Tuesday	$4\frac{3}{4}$	$25\frac{1}{2}$
Wednesday	$20\frac{1}{3}$	8
Thursday	$15\frac{3}{4}$	$9\frac{1}{4}$
Friday	$8\frac{1}{2}$	$3\frac{1}{2}$

★ **30.** What is the total number of pages Melinda read before supper this week?

★ **31.** What is the total number of pages Melinda read at bedtime this week?

Subtracting Mixed Numbers

■ Nancy works in a crafts shop. There were $8\frac{3}{4}$ lb of clay on the shelf. She sold $2\frac{1}{4}$ lb to a customer. How much clay is left?

Subtract $2\frac{1}{4}$ from $8\frac{3}{4}$ to find how much is left.

Subtract the fractions.	**Subtract the whole numbers.**	**Write the difference in lowest terms.**
$8\frac{3}{4}$	$8\frac{3}{4}$	$8\frac{3}{4}$
$-2\frac{1}{4}$	$-2\frac{1}{4}$	$-2\frac{1}{4}$
$\frac{2}{4}$	$6\frac{2}{4}$	$6\frac{2}{4} = 6\frac{1}{2}$

There are $6\frac{1}{2}$ lb of clay left.

■ Subtract: $6\frac{5}{6} - 4\frac{3}{8}$

Remember: To subtract fractions with different denominators, first write equivalent fractions with the same denominator.

Find the least common denominator. Write equivalent fractions.	**Subtract.**
$6\frac{5}{6} = \ 6\frac{20}{24}$	$6\frac{5}{6} = \ 6\frac{20}{24}$
$-4\frac{3}{8} = -4\frac{9}{24}$	$-4\frac{3}{8} = -4\frac{9}{24}$
	$2\frac{11}{24}$

Try These

Subtract. Write each difference in lowest terms.

1. $3\frac{7}{10}$
   $-2\frac{3}{10}$

2. $7\frac{3}{5}$
   $-5\frac{3}{10}$

3. $3\frac{7}{8}$
   $-\ \ \frac{5}{8}$

4. $4\frac{1}{2}$
   $-2\frac{3}{10}$

5. $6\frac{5}{6}$
   $-1\frac{1}{6}$

6. $3\frac{1}{2} - 1\frac{1}{6}$

7. $6\frac{2}{3} - 4$

8. $6\frac{1}{2} - 1\frac{1}{5}$

Exercises

Subtract. Write each difference in lowest terms.

1. $4\frac{5}{6}$
$-4\frac{1}{3}$

2. $3\frac{3}{4}$
$-1\frac{1}{2}$

3. $6\frac{4}{5}$
$-2\frac{3}{10}$

4. $9\frac{3}{4}$
$-6\frac{1}{4}$

5. $7\frac{7}{10}$
$-3\frac{1}{5}$

6. $7\frac{1}{3}$
$-1\frac{1}{6}$

7. $3\frac{2}{3}$
-3

8. $4\frac{1}{2}$
$-1\frac{1}{6}$

9. $3\frac{1}{2}$
$-1\frac{1}{5}$

10. $4\frac{6}{7}$
$-2\frac{2}{3}$

11. $6\frac{15}{16} - 5\frac{5}{8}$

12. $7\frac{5}{12} - 3\frac{1}{4}$

13. $9\frac{5}{6} - 2\frac{3}{4}$

★ **14.** $7\frac{3}{4} - \blacksquare = 5\frac{1}{2}$

★ **15.** $10\frac{4}{9} - \blacksquare = 2\frac{1}{3}$

★ **16.** $6\frac{5}{6} - \blacksquare = 4\frac{2}{3}$

Add or subtract. Write each answer in lowest terms.

17. $3\frac{5}{6}$
$-2\frac{2}{3}$

18. 6
$+1\frac{1}{2}$

19. $7\frac{3}{4}$
$-3\frac{3}{8}$

20. $4\frac{2}{3}$
$+3\frac{2}{3}$

21. $9\frac{5}{10}$
$-3\frac{3}{10}$

22. $3\frac{1}{6}$
$+1\frac{1}{2}$

23. $6\frac{5}{6}$
$-2\frac{1}{6}$

24. $3\frac{1}{12}$
$+2\frac{1}{6}$

25. $12\frac{1}{2}$
$-7\frac{1}{4}$

26. $3\frac{7}{10}$
$+6\frac{6}{10}$

27. $8\frac{5}{8} + 2\frac{3}{8}$

28. $6\frac{2}{3} - 4$

29. $7\frac{2}{3} + 1\frac{5}{6}$

Solve each problem. Write each answer in lowest terms.

30. Jim used yarn to weave a mat. He used $8\frac{1}{2}$ yd of red yarn. He used $4\frac{1}{4}$ yd of blue yarn. How much yarn did he use in all?

31. Meg bought $3\frac{1}{2}$ yd of rope. She used $1\frac{1}{3}$ yd of rope to make a halter for her horse. How much rope did she have left?

32. Rose is making a quilt for her bed. She bought $6\frac{1}{2}$ yd of fabric to back the quilt. Rose used $5\frac{1}{3}$ yd of the fabric. How much fabric is left?

★ **33.** Joe sold fabric to 3 customers. There were 20 yd of fabric on the bolt. He sold $3\frac{1}{2}$ yd, $2\frac{1}{4}$ yd, and $5\frac{2}{3}$ yd. How many yards of fabric are left on the bolt?

Renaming in Subtraction

■ Sometimes you must rename the mixed number to subtract.

Subtract: $6\frac{1}{4} - 2\frac{3}{4}$

Because $\frac{3}{4} > \frac{1}{4}$, rename $6\frac{1}{4}$ to subtract.

$$6\frac{1}{4} = 5 + 1 + \frac{1}{4}$$
$$= 5 + \frac{4}{4} + \frac{1}{4}$$
$$= 5\frac{5}{4}$$

Subtract.

$$\begin{array}{r} 6\frac{1}{4} = 5\frac{5}{4} \\ -2\frac{3}{4} = -2\frac{3}{4} \\ \hline 3\frac{2}{4} = 3\frac{1}{2} \end{array}$$

■ To subtract a fraction or a mixed number from a whole number, rename the whole number.

Subtract: $3 - 1\frac{1}{6}$

Because $\frac{1}{6} > \frac{0}{6}$, rename 3 to subtract.

$$3 = 2 + 1$$
$$= 2 + \frac{6}{6}$$
$$= 2\frac{6}{6}$$

Subtract.

$$\begin{array}{r} 3 = 2\frac{6}{6} \\ -1\frac{1}{6} = -1\frac{1}{6} \\ \hline 1\frac{5}{6} \end{array}$$

■ Sometimes you must rename more than once to subtract.

Subtract: $9\frac{1}{2} - 5\frac{4}{5}$

Find the least common denominator. Write equivalent fractions.

$$\begin{array}{r} 9\frac{1}{2} = 9\frac{5}{10} \\ -5\frac{4}{5} = -5\frac{8}{10} \\ \hline \end{array}$$

Because $\frac{8}{10} > \frac{5}{10}$, rename $9\frac{5}{10}$ to subtract.

$$9\frac{5}{10} = 8 + 1 + \frac{5}{10}$$
$$= 8 + \frac{10}{10} + \frac{5}{10}$$
$$= 8\frac{15}{10}$$

Subtract.

$$\begin{array}{r} 9\frac{1}{2} = 8\frac{15}{10} \\ -5\frac{4}{5} = -5\frac{8}{10} \\ \hline 3\frac{7}{10} \end{array}$$

Try These

Subtract. Write each difference in lowest terms.

1. $6\frac{1}{3}$
   $-2\frac{2}{3}$

2. 9
   $-1\frac{1}{8}$

3. $4\frac{1}{3}$
   $-1\frac{1}{2}$

4. $3\frac{1}{4}$
   $-2\frac{3}{4}$

5. $12\frac{3}{5}$
   $-4\frac{4}{5}$

6. $8\frac{3}{7} - 7\frac{5}{7}$

7. $3\frac{1}{10} - 1\frac{3}{5}$

8. $4\frac{1}{4} - 1\frac{2}{3}$

Exercises

Subtract. Write each difference in lowest terms.

1. $3\frac{1}{2}$
   $-1\frac{5}{6}$

2. $6\frac{2}{5}$
   $-2\frac{9}{10}$

3. $9\frac{4}{5}$
   $-3\frac{1}{5}$

4. $5\frac{1}{6}$
   $-2\frac{2}{3}$

5. $3\frac{2}{3}$
   $-2\frac{3}{4}$

6. $2\frac{1}{2}$
   $-\frac{3}{4}$

7. $7\frac{1}{3}$
   $-\frac{2}{3}$

8. 6
   $-4\frac{3}{10}$

9. $8\frac{3}{4}$
   $-2\frac{1}{2}$

10. $9\frac{1}{2}$
    $-5\frac{2}{3}$

11. $7\frac{3}{8} - 5\frac{7}{8}$

12. $8\frac{1}{2} - \frac{1}{2}$

13. $4\frac{3}{4} - 2\frac{1}{10}$

Add or subtract. Write each answer in lowest terms.

14. $3\frac{1}{10} - 1\frac{4}{5}$

15. $9\frac{1}{2} + 3\frac{1}{2}$

16. $5\frac{1}{2} + 3\frac{2}{3}$

17. $5 - 4\frac{5}{16}$

18. $5\frac{3}{4} + 7\frac{1}{2}$

19. $16\frac{9}{10} - 9\frac{7}{10}$

Solve each problem. Write each answer in lowest terms.

20. You plan to practice your music for $1\frac{1}{4}$ h. You have practiced for $\frac{1}{2}$ h. How much longer do you need to practice?

21. Mildred practiced her solo for $1\frac{1}{2}$ h in the morning and $\frac{3}{4}$ h in the afternoon. How long did she practice in all?

★ 22. Eva practiced for 6 h in 3 days. She practiced for $2\frac{1}{2}$ h on Monday and $1\frac{3}{4}$ h on Wednesday. How long did she practice on Friday?

★ 23. Emile has 3 packages of balloons. He used $1\frac{1}{2}$ packages to practice his magic act. Does he have enough left to practice again?

Problem Solving: Strategies

FINDING INFORMATION

A **circle graph** shows information. It can help you solve problems. A circle graph is divided into sections. The size of each section is important.

Kurt and Dolores took a survey. They asked their classmates to name their favorite team sport. Kurt and Dolores made this circle graph to show the results of the survey.

Favorite Team Sport

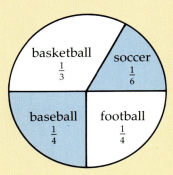

What team sport is the favorite of the most students?

> Find the largest section in the circle graph. The largest section is for basketball.

Basketball is the favorite team sport of the most students.

What fraction of the students named basketball as their favorite team sport?

> Find the section for basketball. The basketball section is $\frac{1}{3}$ of the circle.

$\frac{1}{3}$ of the students named basketball as their favorite team sport.

Using the Strategy

Use the circle graph to solve each problem.

1. What fraction of the students named baseball as their favorite team sport?

2. Which team sport is the favorite of the least number of students?

3. Which two sports were the favorites of an equal number of students?

4. What fraction of the students named baseball and football?

This circle graph shows the favorite individual sports of some fifth graders.

FAVORITE INDIVIDUAL SPORT

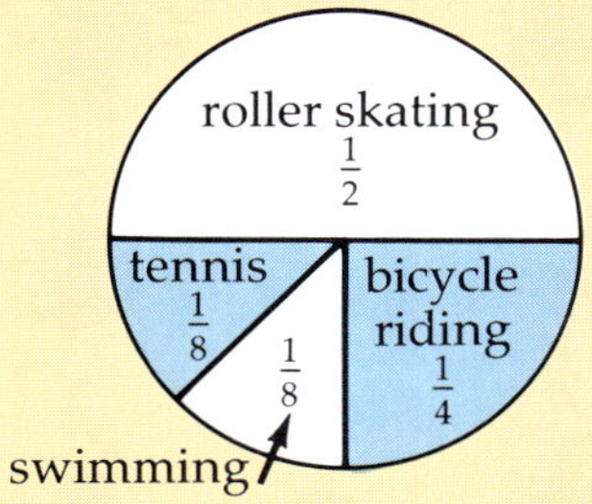

5. What individual sport is the favorite of the most students?

6. What fraction of the students named bicycle riding as their favorite individual sport?

7. Which two sports were the favorites of an equal number of students?

8. What fraction of the students named tennis and swimming as their favorite individual sport?

9. What fraction of the students named tennis, swimming, and bicycle riding?

10. Which sport was named twice as often as bicycle riding?

ACTIVITY

MAKING A CIRCLE GRAPH

Pat and Chris took a survey of the favorite team sports among their classmates. This is a tally of the results.

1. Copy and complete the table.

2. How many students answered the survey?

3. Write a fraction for the total number who chose each sport.

4. Use a compass to draw a circle.

5. Divide the circle into sections according to the fractions in exercise 3.

6. Label each section with the sport and fraction.

FAVORITE TEAM SPORT

Sport	Tally	Total
baseball	卌 卌	
football	卌	
basketball	卌	

Make a survey of the favorite sports among your classmates. Then make a circle graph of the results.

Fraction of a Number

■ David bought a dozen eggs. He used $\frac{1}{6}$ of the eggs for breakfast. How many eggs did David use for breakfast?

To find the answer, find $\frac{1}{6}$ of 12.

Divide by 6 to find $\frac{1}{6}$ of 12.

Think: $\frac{1}{6}$ of 12 = 2

David used 2 eggs for breakfast.

1 dozen = 12

■ David used $\frac{2}{3}$ of the dozen eggs during the week. How many eggs did David use during the week?

To find the answer, find $\frac{2}{3}$ of 12.

Divide by 3 to find $\frac{1}{3}$ of 12.

$\frac{1}{3}$ of 12 = 4

Then multiply by 2 to find $\frac{2}{3}$ of 12.

$$2 \times 4 = 8$$

David used 8 eggs during the week.

Try These

Find the fraction of each number. Do as many as you can mentally.

1. $\frac{1}{3}$ of 6

2. $\frac{3}{4}$ of 12

3. $\frac{2}{9}$ of 18

4. $\frac{1}{4}$ of 16

5. $\frac{5}{6}$ of 24

6. $\frac{2}{3}$ of 9

7. $\frac{1}{8}$ of 32

8. $\frac{3}{5}$ of 10

Exercises

Find the fraction of each number. Do as many as you can mentally.

1. $\frac{1}{2}$ of 8

2. $\frac{1}{8}$ of 16

3. $\frac{2}{3}$ of 21

4. $\frac{5}{9}$ of 18

5. $\frac{3}{4}$ of 16

6. $\frac{5}{9}$ of 27

7. $\frac{1}{3}$ of 6

8. $\frac{3}{8}$ of 24

9. $\frac{1}{6}$ of 36

10. $\frac{4}{5}$ of 20

11. $\frac{1}{2}$ of 10

12. $\frac{2}{7}$ of 14

13. $\frac{3}{5}$ of 25

14. $\frac{5}{8}$ of 40

15. $\frac{3}{4}$ of 24

16. $\frac{8}{9}$ of 27

17. $\frac{3}{7}$ of 21

18. $\frac{7}{8}$ of 16

19. $\frac{7}{10}$ of 100

20. $\frac{19}{25}$ of 75

Solve each problem. Write each answer in lowest terms.

21. Laurette bought 10 sweet potatoes. She used $\frac{3}{5}$ of them for a casserole. How many sweet potatoes did Laurette use for the casserole?

22. A recipe calls for $1\frac{3}{8}$ lb of chopped pork and $1\frac{3}{4}$ lb of chopped beef. How much meat is needed in all?

23. Laurette's casserole has been baking for $\frac{1}{4}$ h. It must bake for $\frac{3}{4}$ h. How much longer should the casserole bake?

★ **24.** David bought 2 dozen eggs. He used $\frac{2}{3}$ of them for salads. He used the rest in omelettes. How many eggs did he use in omelettes?

KEEPING IN SHAPE

Find the perimeter of a polygon with these measurements.

1. 6 cm, 12 cm, 6 cm, 8 cm, 8 cm

2. 16.8 m, 7.6 m, 16.8 m, 7.6 m

Find the area of each figure.

3. a rectangle with a length of 19 cm and a width of 12 cm

4. a square with each side 6.4 m

Find the volume of each rectangular prism.

5. a box 8 cm long, 4 cm wide, and 3 cm high

6. a cabinet 5.2 m long, 3 m wide, and 2 m high

Multiplying Fractions

■ What fraction names $\frac{1}{2}$ of $\frac{1}{3}$?

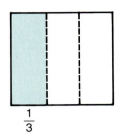 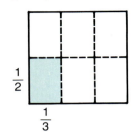

$\frac{1}{3}$ $\frac{1}{2}$ $\frac{1}{3}$

Each of the smallest rectangles is $\frac{1}{6}$ of the figure.

$\frac{1}{2}$ of $\frac{1}{3}$ is $\frac{1}{6}$ of the figure.

$\frac{1}{2}$ of $\frac{1}{3}$ is $\frac{1}{2} \times \frac{1}{3}$.

To multiply fractions:

1. Multiply the numerators. $\frac{1}{2} \times \frac{1}{3} = \frac{1 \times 1}{} = \frac{1}{}$

2. Multiply the denominators. $\frac{1}{2} \times \frac{1}{3} = \frac{1 \times 1}{2 \times 3} = \frac{1}{6}$

■ Multiply: $\frac{3}{4} \times \frac{2}{7}$

$$\frac{3}{4} \times \frac{2}{7} = \frac{3 \times 2}{4 \times 7}$$
$$= \frac{6}{28}$$
$$= \frac{3}{14}$$

■ When one factor is a whole number, first write it as a fraction.

Multiply: $7 \times \frac{1}{4}$

Think: $7 = \frac{7}{1}$

$$7 \times \frac{1}{4} = \frac{7}{1} \times \frac{1}{4}$$
$$= \frac{7 \times 1}{1 \times 4}$$
$$= \frac{7}{4}$$
$$= 1\frac{3}{4}$$

Multiply: $\frac{3}{5} \times 25$

Think: $25 = \frac{25}{1}$

$$\frac{3}{5} \times 25 = \frac{3}{5} \times \frac{25}{1}$$
$$= \frac{3 \times 25}{5 \times 1}$$
$$= \frac{75}{5}$$
$$= 15$$

Try These

Study each figure. Then complete to find each product.

1.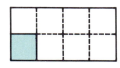

$$\frac{1}{2} \times \frac{1}{4} = \frac{\blacksquare}{\blacksquare}$$

2.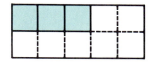

$$\frac{1}{2} \times \frac{3}{5} = \frac{\blacksquare}{\blacksquare}$$

3.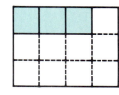

$$\frac{1}{3} \times \frac{3}{4} = \frac{\blacksquare}{\blacksquare}$$

Multiply. Write each product in lowest terms.

4. $\frac{1}{3} \times \frac{3}{4}$

5. $\frac{1}{2} \times \frac{6}{7}$

6. $10 \times \frac{3}{5}$

7. $\frac{4}{5} \times \frac{3}{4}$

8. $\frac{1}{2} \times 9$

Exercises

Multiply. Write each product in lowest terms.

1. $\frac{2}{3} \times \frac{4}{5}$
2. $\frac{3}{4} \times \frac{1}{2}$
3. $\frac{1}{3} \times \frac{5}{6}$
4. $\frac{1}{5} \times \frac{3}{4}$
5. $\frac{3}{4} \times 6$

6. $\frac{3}{8} \times \frac{3}{4}$
7. $\frac{1}{2} \times \frac{3}{7}$
8. $\frac{1}{10} \times \frac{3}{10}$
9. $\frac{1}{5} \times \frac{2}{5}$
10. $\frac{1}{3} \times \frac{2}{3}$

11. $\frac{3}{4} \times \frac{2}{3}$
12. $\frac{2}{5} \times \frac{1}{4}$
13. $3 \times \frac{1}{2}$
14. $\frac{1}{5} \times 2$
15. $\frac{1}{8} \times \frac{1}{2}$

16. $\frac{5}{6} \times \frac{3}{4}$
17. $\frac{3}{10} \times \frac{2}{9}$
18. $\frac{1}{3} \times \frac{3}{5}$
19. $9 \times \frac{2}{3}$
20. $\frac{4}{5} \times \frac{1}{10}$

21. $\frac{2}{3} \times \frac{2}{3}$
22. $\frac{1}{2} \times \frac{7}{8}$
23. $\frac{1}{2} \times \frac{3}{8}$
24. $\frac{2}{5} \times \frac{5}{8}$
25. $\frac{2}{3} \times \frac{1}{4}$

Solve each problem. Write each answer in lowest terms.

26. It rained $\frac{3}{10}$ in. on Monday. On Tuesday, it rained 5 times as much. How many inches did it rain on Tuesday?

27. The town of Montoya had $\frac{3}{4}$ in. of rain yesterday. In Everest, there was $\frac{1}{2}$ as much rain. How much rain fell in Everest?

28. Dr. Blake wrote an article for the newspaper. He spent $\frac{3}{4}$ h studying weather maps and $1\frac{1}{2}$ h writing his article. How much time did Dr. Blake spend on the article?

★ 29. It takes Dr. Blake 2 h to travel to the weather station at Point Breeze. $\frac{1}{3}$ of this time is spent riding a train. How many minutes does he spend on the train?

Problem Solving: Applications

BUDGETS

Marcia earns $6 a week delivering newspapers. She earns $6 a week baby-sitting. Her parents give her $4 a week allowance. She has a total of $16 a week to spend.

Marcia makes a circle graph to show how she budgets her money.

How much money does Marcia spend on lunches each week?

Study the graph. Marcia spends $\frac{1}{2}$ of her money on lunches.

Find $\frac{1}{2}$ of $16.

$$\frac{1}{2} \times 16 = \frac{16}{2}$$
$$= 8$$

Marcia spends $8 on lunches each week.

Marcia's Weekly Budget

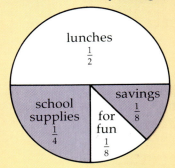

Try These

Solve each problem.

1. What fraction of her income does Marcia spend on school supplies?

2. How much money does Marcia spend on school supplies?

3. How much money does Marcia spend for fun each week?

4. How much money does Marcia save each week?

5. What fraction of her income does Marcia spend on lunches and for fun?

Exercises

Solve each problem. Write each answer in lowest terms.

Marcia's allowance is increased to $6 a week. She plans a new budget.

1. What is Marcia's income now?

2. How much money does Marcia spend on lunches each week?

3. What fraction of her income does Marcia save each week?

4. How much money does Marcia spend on school supplies? For fun?

5. How much money does Marcia spend on lunches and school supplies altogether?

6. What fraction of her income does Marcia spend on lunches and school supplies?

7. Marcia wants to buy a bicycle that costs $84. How many weeks will it take her to save enough money to buy the bicycle?

★ 8. Marcia receives $15. She decides to save it toward the bicycle. How many fewer weeks will it take for her to get her bicycle?

Marcia's Weekly Budget

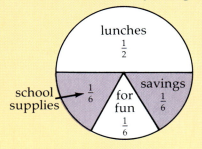

Joe works in a supermarket. He earns $45 a week. This graph shows how he budgets his money.

9. How much money does Joe spend on lunches each week?

10. How much money does Joe spend on transportation?

11. How much money does Joe save each week?

12. Joe buys a record. From which section of his budget does he take the money?

13. How much money does Joe spend on lunches and school supplies altogether?

14. What fraction of his income does Joe spend on transportation and entertainment?

15. Does Joe put less money toward savings or entertainment? What fraction less?

16. Joe wants to go to a concert. The tickets for the concert are $22. How many weeks will it take to pay for the tickets?

17. Joe spent $4 on transportation, $5 on food, and $9 on a T-shirt. What fraction of his budget did Joe spend at the concert?

Joe's Weekly Budget

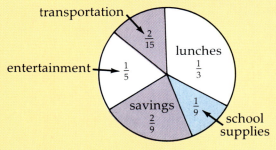

Problem Solving: Applications

CONSUMER MATHEMATICS

Stores often have sales. They offer **discounts** on items they carry. The consumer can save money by buying items at discount prices.

■ A bracelet regularly sells for $18. How much can you save at this sale?

Find $\frac{1}{3}$ of $18 to find how much you can save.

$$\frac{1}{3} \times 18 = \frac{18}{3}$$
$$= 6$$

You can save $6 at this sale.

■ What is the sale price of the bracelet?

Subtract the amount saved from the regular price to find the sale price.

$$\$18 - \$6 = \$12$$

The sale price is $12.

Try These

Solve each problem.

1. How much money can you save if you buy a ring on sale?

2. How much money can you save if you buy earrings on sale?

3. How much money can you save if you buy a watch on sale? What is the sale price?

4. How much money can you save if you buy pearls on sale? What is the sale price?

Exercises

The tags show the regular prices. Find the amount saved and the sale price for the item.

1. gold pin

2. pearl earrings

3. cuff links

$60   ¼ OFF

$58   ½ OFF

$45   ⅕ OFF

Find the amount saved and the sale price.

4. a pendant: regular price $16, $\frac{1}{4}$ off

5. a necklace: regular price $90, $\frac{1}{10}$ off

6. earrings: regular price $125, $\frac{1}{5}$ off

7. a ring: regular price $54, $\frac{1}{6}$ off

Which is the better buy?

8. a silver charm: **a.** regular price $9, $\frac{1}{3}$ off   **b.** regular price $10, $\frac{1}{2}$ off

9. a ruby ring: **a.** regular price $80, $\frac{1}{2}$ off   **b.** regular price $90, $\frac{1}{3}$ off

10. a jogger's watch: **a.** regular price $56, $\frac{1}{4}$ off   **b.** regular price $60, $\frac{1}{5}$ off

Solve each problem.

11. Alice buys a pearl necklace for $85 and a pair of pearl earrings for $35. There is a sale of $\frac{1}{4}$ off. How much does Alice spend on the necklace and earrings?

12. A watch regularly sells for $75. Fred buys it when there is a sale of $\frac{1}{3}$ off. The sales tax is $.06 on each dollar. How much change should Fred receive from $60?

★ 13. The sale price of a ring is $150. The original price was $200. How much is the saving? What fraction of the original price is saved?

★ 14. Jeff has saved $100 toward a watch costing $240. He sees this ad. His father says he will lend him the rest of the money if Jeff pays it back after 1 year with $\frac{1}{10}$ interest. Explain what you think Jeff should do and why.

ALARM WATCH

REGULARLY $240

SALE $\frac{1}{6}$ OFF

Multiplying Mixed Numbers

■ The farthest Janice swam last month was $2\frac{1}{4}$ lengths of the pool. Today she swam 3 times that far. How far did she swim?

To find how far, multiply 3 times $2\frac{1}{4}$.

Write both numbers as fractions.

$$3 = \frac{3}{1}$$
$$2\frac{1}{4} = \frac{9}{4}$$

Multiply. Rename the product.

$$\frac{3}{1} \times \frac{9}{4} = \frac{27}{4}$$
$$= 6\frac{3}{4}$$

Janice swam $6\frac{3}{4}$ lengths today.

■ Multiply: $3\frac{1}{2} \times \frac{1}{3}$

Write the mixed number as a fraction.

$$3\frac{1}{2} = \frac{7}{2}$$

Multiply. Rename the product.

$$\frac{7}{2} \times \frac{1}{3} = \frac{7}{6}$$
$$= 1\frac{1}{6}$$

■ Multiply: $2\frac{3}{5} \times 1\frac{2}{3}$

Write the mixed numbers as fractions.

$$2\frac{3}{5} = \frac{13}{5}$$
$$1\frac{2}{3} = \frac{5}{3}$$

Multiply. Rename the product.

$$\frac{13}{5} \times \frac{5}{3} = \frac{65}{15}$$
$$= 4\frac{5}{15}$$
$$= 4\frac{1}{3}$$

Try These

Multiply. Write each product in lowest terms.

1. $3 \times 2\frac{3}{4}$

2. $\frac{3}{4} \times 2\frac{1}{2}$

3. $1\frac{1}{2} \times \frac{3}{5}$

4. $2\frac{1}{2} \times 1\frac{3}{4}$

5. $\frac{1}{5} \times 2\frac{1}{2}$

6. $1\frac{1}{4} \times 1\frac{1}{4}$

7. $3\frac{1}{2} \times 2$

8. $\frac{1}{3} \times 2\frac{1}{2}$

Exercises

Multiply. Write each product in lowest terms.

1. $7 \times 1\frac{1}{2}$

2. $3 \times 2\frac{1}{5}$

3. $1\frac{1}{3} \times 5$

4. $1\frac{1}{4} \times 2\frac{1}{2}$

5. $\frac{1}{2} \times 1\frac{1}{5}$

6. $2\frac{1}{10} \times \frac{1}{2}$

7. $\frac{3}{4} \times 1\frac{1}{4}$

8. $3\frac{3}{4} \times 1\frac{3}{5}$

9. $1\frac{3}{5} \times \frac{3}{5}$

10. $3\frac{1}{2} \times \frac{3}{10}$

11. $2\frac{1}{3} \times 3$

12. $2\frac{4}{5} \times 1\frac{1}{7}$

13. $3\frac{1}{2} \times 2\frac{1}{4}$

14. $1\frac{1}{3} \times 2\frac{1}{2}$

15. $1\frac{2}{3} \times 1\frac{3}{4}$

16. $\frac{1}{4} \times \frac{2}{3}$

17. $2\frac{1}{2} \times 1\frac{1}{10}$

18. $1\frac{4}{5} \times 2\frac{1}{2}$

★ **19.** $3\frac{1}{3} \times 15 \times 1\frac{2}{5}$

★ **20.** $1\frac{1}{3} \times \frac{3}{4} \times 3\frac{1}{2}$

Solve each problem. Write each answer in lowest terms.

21. The school track is $\frac{1}{4}$ mi long. Juan jogs $5\frac{1}{4}$ times around the track. How far does he jog?

22. Janice swam $\frac{3}{4}$ h before lunch. Then she swam $\frac{2}{3}$ h after lunch. How long did she swim in all?

23. Juan spent 3 h using equipment and swimming at the gym. He spent $1\frac{3}{4}$ h using the equipment. How much time did he spend swimming?

★ **24.** Ramon swims $\frac{3}{5}$ mi each day. He spends $1\frac{1}{2}$ h in the pool. How many yards does Ramon swim?

THINK AND TRY

USING PARENTHESES AND BRACKETS

Solve. Write each answer in lowest terms.

1. $4 \times \left(\frac{1}{3} + \frac{3}{4}\right)$

2. $\left(2\frac{1}{2} \times \frac{2}{3}\right) - 1\frac{1}{6}$

3. $\left[\left(\frac{3}{4} \times \frac{1}{2}\right) + 2\frac{5}{8}\right] - 1\frac{1}{2}$

4. $\left[\left(2\frac{1}{2} - 1\frac{2}{3}\right) \times 3\frac{1}{8}\right] - 1\frac{3}{4}$

5. $3 \times \left[\left(\frac{1}{3} + 2\frac{1}{2}\right) + \left(6\frac{1}{2} \times \frac{3}{4}\right)\right]$

6. $2\frac{3}{4} - \left[\left(\frac{1}{5} \times \frac{2}{3} \times \frac{1}{8}\right) + 1\frac{1}{5}\right]$

Dividing by a Fraction

■ How many $\frac{1}{3}$s are in 2?

Divide: $2 \div \frac{1}{3}$

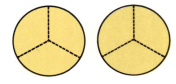

$$2 \div \frac{1}{3} = 6$$
$$2 \times 3 = 6$$

There are six $\frac{1}{3}$s in 2.

■ How many $\frac{1}{6}$s are in $\frac{2}{3}$?

Divide: $\frac{2}{3} \div \frac{1}{6}$

$$\frac{2}{3} \div \frac{1}{6} = 4$$
$$\frac{2}{3} \times 6 = 4$$

There are four $\frac{1}{6}$s in $\frac{2}{3}$.

■ How many $\frac{3}{4}$s are in $1\frac{1}{2}$?

Divide: $1\frac{1}{2} \div \frac{3}{4}$

$$1\frac{1}{2} \div \frac{3}{4} = 2$$
$$\frac{3}{2} \times \frac{4}{3} = 2$$

There are two $\frac{3}{4}$s in $1\frac{1}{2}$.

Try These

Study each figure. Then complete to find each quotient.

1.

$$2 \div \frac{1}{4} = \blacksquare$$

2.

$$\frac{3}{4} \div \frac{1}{12} = \blacksquare$$

3.

$$1\frac{2}{3} \div \frac{1}{6} = \blacksquare$$

Exercises

Study each figure. Then complete to find each quotient.

1.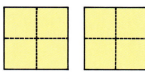

$$2 \div \frac{1}{4} = \blacksquare$$

2.

$$\frac{2}{3} \div \frac{1}{9} = \blacksquare$$

3.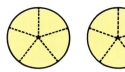

$$2 \div \frac{2}{5} = \blacksquare$$

4.

$$1\frac{1}{2} \div \frac{1}{4} = \blacksquare$$

5.

$$\frac{1}{2} \div \frac{1}{8} = \blacksquare$$

6.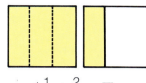

$$1\frac{1}{3} \div \frac{2}{3} = \blacksquare$$

7.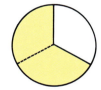

$$\frac{2}{3} \div \frac{1}{3} = \blacksquare$$

8.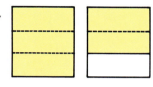

$$1\frac{2}{3} \div \frac{1}{3} = \blacksquare$$

9.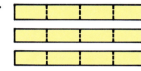

$$3 \div \frac{1}{4} = \blacksquare$$

10.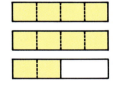

$$2\frac{1}{2} \div \frac{1}{4} = \blacksquare$$

11.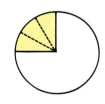

$$\frac{1}{4} \div \frac{1}{12} = \blacksquare$$

★ **12.**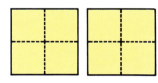

$$2 \div \frac{3}{4} = \blacksquare$$

Solve each problem. Write each answer in lowest terms.

13. John spent 3 h working in Mr. Reed's yard. He spent $1\frac{1}{2}$ h mowing the lawn and the rest of the time trimming bushes. How long did he spend trimming bushes?

14. Manuel spends $1\frac{3}{4}$ h pulling weeds in Mr. Albert's garden. Then he spends $\frac{2}{3}$ h fertilizing the garden. How much time does Manuel work in Mr. Albert's garden?

★ **15.** Manuel earned $6 mowing the lawn for his father. He spent $\frac{3}{4}$ of it at the hardware store. How much did he spend?

★ **16.** John has 6 c of plant food. He wants to give each plant $\frac{3}{4}$ c of plant food. How many plants can receive plant food?

More about Fractions   359

CHAPTER CHECKPOINT

Write each fraction as a mixed number or as a whole number. (pp. 336–337)

1. $\frac{11}{3}$　　　2. $\frac{15}{5}$　　　3. $\frac{14}{6}$　　　4. $\frac{21}{7}$　　　5. $\frac{22}{4}$　　　6. $\frac{17}{3}$

Write each mixed number as a fraction. (pp. 336–337)

7. $3\frac{1}{4}$　　　8. $1\frac{2}{3}$　　　9. $4\frac{5}{6}$　　　10. $2\frac{2}{9}$　　　11. $1\frac{7}{8}$　　　12. $3\frac{5}{7}$

Add. Write each sum in lowest terms. (pp. 338–341)

13. $2\frac{1}{5}$
  $+3\frac{2}{5}$

14. $1\frac{1}{2}$
  $+3\frac{1}{4}$

15. $6\frac{5}{12}$
  $+\ \frac{1}{12}$

16. $4\frac{3}{4}$
  $+2$

17. $8\frac{3}{14}$
  $+1\frac{2}{7}$

18. $1\frac{3}{4}$
  $+2\frac{3}{4}$

19. $1\frac{1}{2}$
  $+1\frac{1}{2}$

20. $2\frac{2}{3}$
  $+1\frac{3}{4}$

21. $6\frac{2}{3}$
  $+\ \frac{5}{6}$

22. $\frac{5}{8}$
  $+1\frac{3}{4}$

Subtract. Write each difference in lowest terms. (p. 342–345)

23. $2\frac{5}{7}$
  $-1\frac{2}{7}$

24. $3\frac{1}{2}$
  $-1\frac{1}{3}$

25. $3\frac{4}{5}$
  $-1\frac{2}{5}$

26. $4\frac{3}{4}$
  $-1\frac{1}{2}$

27. $5\frac{1}{4}$
  $-2\frac{3}{4}$

28. 3
  $-1\frac{1}{3}$

29. $6\frac{1}{3}$
  $-1\frac{1}{2}$

30. $4\frac{2}{3}$
  -3

31. 5
  $-2\frac{1}{2}$

32. $8\frac{1}{2}$
  $-3\frac{4}{5}$

Find the fraction of each number. (pp. 348–349)

33. $\frac{1}{2}$ of 6　　　34. $\frac{3}{4}$ of 16　　　35. $\frac{2}{9}$ of 18　　　36. $\frac{1}{4}$ of 12

37. $\frac{2}{3}$ of 9　　　38. $\frac{4}{5}$ of 10　　　39. $\frac{3}{8}$ of 40　　　40. $\frac{5}{9}$ of 27

Multiply. Write each product in lowest terms. (pp. 350–351, 356–357)

41. $\frac{1}{2} \times \frac{3}{5}$

42. $\frac{1}{3} \times \frac{2}{5}$

43. $\frac{3}{4} \times 2$

44. $2 \times \frac{5}{6}$

45. $\frac{1}{2} \times \frac{4}{7}$

46. $6 \times 1\frac{1}{2}$

47. $3\frac{1}{2} \times \frac{2}{3}$

48. $1\frac{1}{2} \times 2\frac{2}{3}$

49. $2\frac{1}{2} \times 1\frac{1}{3}$

50. $\frac{1}{5} \times 1\frac{1}{2}$

Study each figure. Then complete to find each quotient. (pp. 358–359)

51.

$2 \div \frac{1}{8} = \blacksquare$

52.

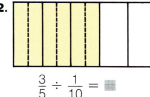

$\frac{3}{5} \div \frac{1}{10} = \blacksquare$

53.

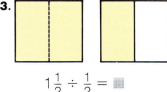

$1\frac{1}{2} \div \frac{1}{2} = \blacksquare$

Solve each problem. Write each answer in lowest terms.
(pp. 336–357)

54. Jeff worked $2\frac{1}{4}$ h on Monday. He worked $1\frac{1}{2}$ h on Tuesday. How many hours did he work in all?

55. Each Saturday Eva works $5\frac{2}{3}$ h. Fred works $4\frac{1}{2}$ h longer. How long does Fred work each Saturday?

56. Mr. Ward went to the main store for $4\frac{1}{2}$ h. He spent $\frac{1}{3}$ of his time with the supervisors. How long did he spend with the supervisors?

57. A shirt regularly sells for $20. It is marked $\frac{1}{5}$ off the regular price. What is the amount saved? What is the sale price?

This graph shows the items sold at the Clothes Barn.

58. Which item has the greatest number of sales?

59. What part of the sales are coats?

60. There are 80 sales on Saturday. About how many of the sales were shirts?

Clothes Barn Sales

COMPUTERS AND
PROBLEM SOLVING

■ Programmers say Garbage In, Garbage Out. It means that if the procedure you give the computer is wrong, the information you get from the computer will be wrong.

Read the procedure and the screen below.

```
TO MATHQUIZ
PR [SOLVE: 2.3 + 3.2]
TEST READLIST = [4.4]
IFTRUE [PR [RIGHT]]
IFFALSE [PR [THAT'S WRONG] ]
END
```

```
?MATHQUIZ
SOLVE: 2.3 + 3.2
5.5
THAT'S WRONG
?▮
```

The user typed MATHQUIZ to start the procedure. After the computer displayed SOLVE: 2.3 + 3.2 the user typed 5.5, the right answer. But the computer then displayed THAT'S WRONG.

Look at the procedure again. The TEST READLIST line tells the computer that the correct answer is 4.4, but the correct answer is 5.5. The programmer gave the computer the wrong answer. Garbage in, garbage out.

Solve each problem.

1. Correct this line from the procedure above:

TEST READLIST = [▮.▮]

3. Using the corrected procedure in problem 2, what would the computer display if you typed 7.3 as the answer?

2. Find and correct the error in this procedure.

```
TO MATHQUIZ
PR [SOLVE: 4.2 + 3.1]
TEST READLIST = [7.3]
IFTRUE [PR [TRY AGAIN] STOP]
IFFALSE [PR [GOOD THINKING] ]
MATHQUIZ
END
```

4. What would the computer display if you typed 6.3?

■ Using a flow chart can help you to avoid errors when you write a procedure.

Read the flow chart.
Find the errors.

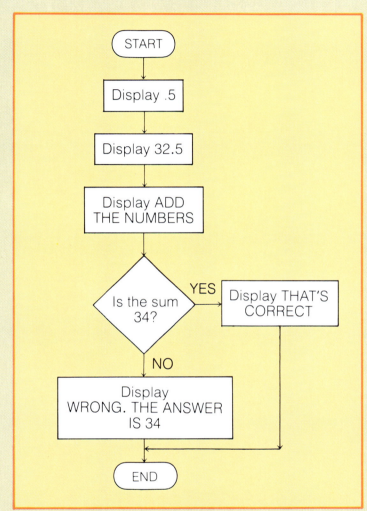

Solve each problem.

1. Rewrite the flow chart to correct the errors.

3. Rewrite the procedure in problem 2 to display WRONG. TRY AGAIN and give the user another chance.

2. Rewrite this procedure to put it in the correct order.

TO MATHQUIZ
PR [SOLVE: 3.6 + 4.1]
IFTRUE [PR [RIGHT]]
IFFALSE [PR [WRONG]]
TEST READLIST = [7.7]
END

ENRICHMENT

FRACTIONS AND DECIMALS

Sometimes it is easier to use a fraction than a decimal when multiplying.

Multiply: 0.25×36

$$
\begin{array}{r}
36 \\
\times 0.25 \\
\hline
1\ 80 \\
7\ 20 \\
\hline
9.00
\end{array}
$$

But 0.25 is the same as $\frac{25}{100}$, and $\frac{25}{100} = \frac{1}{4}$.
So 0.25×36 is the same as $\frac{1}{4} \times 36$.

$$\frac{1}{4} \times 36 = \frac{36}{4}$$
$$= 9$$

To multiply by $\frac{1}{4}$ mentally, divide by 4.

Try these without paper and pencil. Think of 0.25 as $\frac{1}{4}$.
Write each product.

1. 0.25×48 **2.** 0.25×24 **3.** $0.25 \times \$12$ **4.** 0.25×28

Write each decimal as a fraction.

5. 0.5   **6.** 0.2   **7.** 0.125

Use fractions to do these mentally. Write each product.

8. 0.5×16 **9.** 0.2×45 **10.** 0.125×32 **11.** 0.25×40
12. 0.2×75 **13.** $0.5 \times \$86$ **14.** 0.25×60 **15.** 0.125×64

$0.75 = \frac{3}{4}$
To multiply by $\frac{3}{4}$, multiply by 3 and divide by 4.

Find these products mentally. Write each product.

16. 0.75×8 **17.** 0.75×12 **18.** 0.75×36 **19.** 0.75×48

DESIGNING A CHILDREN'S PLAYGROUND

You have been asked to design a playground for children. The playground will be a rectangle that is 300 feet long and 200 feet wide. How will you plan the playground?

Some Questions to Explore
- What will the playground look like?
- How much will the equipment cost?
- What will be the cost of installing the equipment?

Some Strategies to Explore

Consider the first question. One strategy you might use is to make a drawing of the playground.

- Determine how the playground will be sectioned and where the equipment will be located.
- Determine the area of each section.
- Determine how the equipment will be placed in each section.

Decide what strategies you will use to answer the other questions above. What other questions and strategies do you need to explore? List them. Then use them to solve the problem.

SKILLS CHECK

Choose the correct answer.

1. Round 1,978 to the nearest hundred.

   a. 1,000
   b. 1,900
   c. 1,980
   d. 2,000

2. 1,924 + 5,086

   a. 6,982
   b. 7,010
   c. 7,064
   d. 7,110

3. $104.00
   −   68.79

   a. $34.31
   b. $35.21
   c. $44.31
   d. $64.79

4.   832
   ×647

   a. 496,714
   b. 527,926
   c. 532,818
   d. 538,304

5. Find the greatest common factor of 15 and 25.

   a. 5
   b. 10
   c. 50
   d. 75

6. 100 ÷ 40

   a. 2
   b. 2 R20
   c. 5 R2
   d. 20 R2

7. Find a decimal equivalent to 17.90.

   a. 1.790
   b. 17.09
   c. 179.0
   d. NG

8. 6,000 g = ▦ kg

   a. 6
   b. 10
   c. 60
   d. 600

9. Find the area.

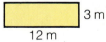 3 m
   12 m

   a. 30 m^2
   b. 36 m^2
   c. 72 m^2
   d. 120 m^2

10. Each magazine costs $2.75. Faith buys 9 magazines. How much money does she spend?

   a. $18.95
   b. $23.85
   c. $24.75
   d. NG

11. A fork is 7 in. long. A spoon is $5\frac{3}{4}$ in. long. How much longer is the fork than the spoon?

   a. $1\frac{1}{4}$ in.   **b.** $1\frac{1}{2}$ in.

   c. $2\frac{3}{4}$ in.   **d.** NG

12. A suitcase is priced at $48. A special sale gives you $\frac{1}{4}$ off. How much do you pay for the suitcase on sale?

   a. $12
   b. $18
   c. $36
   d. $40

RATIO AND PERCENT

12

Ratio

■ A **ratio** is used to compare two numbers.

The ratio of cats to dogs is 3 to 5.
The ratio of dogs to cats is 5 to 3.
The ratio of dogs to animals is 5 to 8.
The ratio of cats to animals is 3 to 8.

■ Here are two ways you can write a ratio.

Write: 3 to 5   or $\frac{3}{5}$
Read: three to five

3 is the first term of the ratio.
5 is the second term of the ratio.

■ The ratio of goldfish to zebra fish is 6 to 4, or $\frac{6}{4}$.

The ratio of zebra fish to goldfish is 4 to 6, or $\frac{4}{6}$.

The ratio of goldfish to angelfish is 6 to 3, or $\frac{6}{3}$.

What is the ratio of angelfish to zebra fish?

What is the ratio of goldfish to all the fish?

What is the ratio of all the fish to angelfish?

Try These

Write each ratio.

1. parrots to parakeets

2. parakeets to canaries

3. canaries to parakeets

4. parrots to canaries

5. parakeets to all the birds

6. all the birds to parrots

Exercises

Write each ratio.

1. owls to eagles

2. eagles to crows

3. crows to eagles

4. eagles to all the birds

5. all the birds to owls

This chart shows the inventory at Harold's Pet Shop.

fox terrier	🐕🐕
poodle	🐩🐩🐩🐩🐩
St. Bernard	🐕🐕🐕
husky	🐕🐕🐕🐕🐕🐕
cocker spaniel	🐕🐕🐕🐕
German shepherd	🐕🐕🐕🐕🐕🐕🐕

Write each ratio.

6. poodles to cocker spaniels

7. huskies to fox terriers

8. St. Bernards to German shepherds

9. fox terriers to cocker spaniels

10. poodles to all the dogs

11. huskies to all the dogs

★ 12. cocker spaniels to St. Bernards to poodles

★ 13. German shepherds to fox terriers to huskies

14. Harold's Pet Shop receives 2 more fox terriers. What is the ratio of fox terriers to all the dogs now?

15. Harold sells all the fox terriers and 2 poodles. What is the ratio of the remaining poodles to all the dogs now?

Ratio and Percent   369

Equal Ratios

■ Wanda is making a granola snack. The recipe calls for 8 oz of raisins and 4 oz of wheat germ.

The ratio of raisins to wheat germ is 8 to 4, or $\frac{8}{4}$.

Wanda has 16 oz of raisins. How many ounces of wheat germ does she need to make granola?

Multiply to find the amount of wheat germ.

$$\text{raisins} \longrightarrow \frac{8}{4} = \frac{8 \times 2}{4 \times 2} = \frac{16}{8} \longleftarrow \text{wheat germ}$$

Wanda needs 8 oz of wheat germ.

$\frac{8}{4}$ and $\frac{16}{8}$ are **equal ratios**.　　$\frac{8}{4} = \frac{16}{8}$

■ Wanda has 2 oz of wheat germ left. How many ounces of raisins does she need to make granola?

Divide to find the amount of raisins.

$$\text{raisins} \longrightarrow \frac{8}{4} = \frac{8 \div 2}{4 \div 2} = \frac{4}{2} \longleftarrow \text{wheat germ}$$

Wanda needs 4 oz of raisins.

$\frac{8}{4}$ and $\frac{4}{2}$ are equal ratios.　　$\frac{8}{4} = \frac{4}{2}$

Try These

Copy and complete to make equal ratios.

1. $\frac{7}{8} = \frac{3 \times 7}{3 \times 8} = \frac{\blacksquare}{24}$

2. $\frac{3}{4} = \frac{4 \times 3}{4 \times 4} = \frac{12}{\blacksquare}$

3. $\frac{4}{6} = \frac{4 \div 2}{6 \div 2} = \frac{\blacksquare}{3}$

4. $\frac{4}{7} = \frac{8}{\blacksquare}$

5. $\frac{12}{15} = \frac{\blacksquare}{5}$

6. $\frac{5}{6} = \frac{10}{\blacksquare}$

7. $\frac{6}{12} = \frac{\blacksquare}{2}$

Exercises

Copy and complete to make equal ratios.

1. $\dfrac{3}{10} = \dfrac{\blacksquare}{20}$

2. $\dfrac{24}{28} = \dfrac{\blacksquare}{7}$

3. $\dfrac{7}{9} = \dfrac{21}{\blacksquare}$

4. $\dfrac{1}{3} = \dfrac{6}{\blacksquare}$

5. $\dfrac{8}{10} = \dfrac{\blacksquare}{5}$

6. $\dfrac{5}{8} = \dfrac{20}{\blacksquare}$

7. $\dfrac{4}{9} = \dfrac{\blacksquare}{36}$

8. $\dfrac{20}{30} = \dfrac{2}{\blacksquare}$

9. $\dfrac{8}{9} = \dfrac{24}{\blacksquare}$

10. $\dfrac{14}{20} = \dfrac{\blacksquare}{10}$

11. $\dfrac{8}{56} = \dfrac{\blacksquare}{7}$

12. $\dfrac{6}{10} = \dfrac{\blacksquare}{100}$

13. $\dfrac{9}{12} = \dfrac{18}{\blacksquare}$

14. $\dfrac{16}{48} = \dfrac{\blacksquare}{12}$

15. $\dfrac{5}{9} = \dfrac{\blacksquare}{36}$

16. $\dfrac{14}{35} = \dfrac{2}{\blacksquare}$

Solve each problem.

17. The ratio of raisins to walnuts is 3 to 1. There are 12 oz of raisins. How many ounces of walnuts are there?

18. The ratio of wheat germ to rice is 1 to 5. There are 15 oz of rice. How many ounces of wheat germ are there?

THINK AND TRY

USING RATIOS

The poodle's height is 200 mm. The German shepherd's height is 60 cm. To compare the heights, both heights must be in the *same* unit.

100 mm = 10 cm, so 200 mm = 20 cm

The ratio of the heights is $\dfrac{20}{60}$.

In lowest terms, the ratio is $\dfrac{20}{60} = \dfrac{20 \div 20}{60 \div 20} = \dfrac{1}{3}$.

The poodle's height is $\dfrac{1}{3}$ of the German shepherd's height.

Change the measures to the same unit. Then write the ratio as a fraction in lowest terms.

1. 5 m to 100 cm

2. 100 g to 1 kg

3. 1 L to 200 mL

4. 50 mm to 2 cm

5. 40 cm to 1 m

6. 6 m to 100 cm

Cross Products

■ If two ratios are equal, their **cross products** are equal.

Are the ratios $\frac{5}{2}$ and $\frac{10}{4}$ equal? Find the cross products.

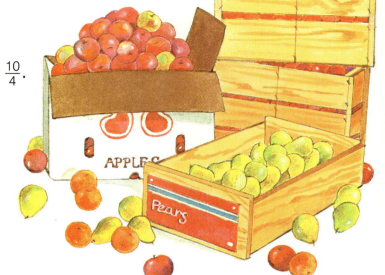

$$\frac{5}{2} \diagdown\!\!\!\diagup \frac{10}{4}$$

$$5 \times 4 \qquad 2 \times 10$$
$$20 = 20$$

The cross products are equal, so $\frac{5}{2} = \frac{10}{4}$.

■ Are the ratios $\frac{7}{3}$ and $\frac{21}{6}$ equal?
Find the cross products.

$$\frac{7}{3} \diagdown\!\!\!\diagup \frac{21}{6}$$

$$7 \times 6 \qquad 3 \times 21$$
$$42 \ne 63$$

└── **is not equal to**

The cross products are not equal, so $\frac{7}{3} \ne \frac{21}{6}$.

■ Are the ratios $\frac{8}{14}$ and $\frac{4}{6}$ equal? Find the cross products.

$$\frac{8}{14} \diagdown\!\!\!\diagup \frac{4}{6}$$

$$8 \times 6 \qquad 14 \times 4$$
$$48 \ne 56$$

The cross products are not equal, so $\frac{8}{14} \ne \frac{4}{6}$.

Try These

Are the ratios equal? Use cross products to check.

1. $\frac{3}{4}$ and $\frac{9}{12}$ **2.** $\frac{7}{8}$ and $\frac{3}{4}$ **3.** $\frac{10}{8}$ and $\frac{5}{4}$ **4.** $\frac{5}{8}$ and $\frac{6}{10}$

5. $\frac{5}{2}$ and $\frac{15}{10}$ **6.** $\frac{16}{12}$ and $\frac{8}{4}$ **7.** $\frac{15}{20}$ and $\frac{3}{4}$ **8.** $\frac{7}{8}$ and $\frac{14}{16}$

Exercises

Are the ratios equal? Use cross products to check.

1. $\frac{3}{5}$ and $\frac{60}{100}$

2. $\frac{3}{8}$ and $\frac{15}{25}$

3. $\frac{1}{8}$ and $\frac{125}{100}$

4. $\frac{6}{9}$ and $\frac{16}{24}$

5. $\frac{3}{4}$ and $\frac{15}{22}$

6. $\frac{4}{5}$ and $\frac{18}{25}$

7. $\frac{5}{7}$ and $\frac{25}{35}$

8. $\frac{3}{5}$ and $\frac{21}{35}$

9. $\frac{1}{2}$ and $\frac{6}{12}$

10. $\frac{7}{10}$ and $\frac{54}{80}$

11. $\frac{1}{5}$ and $\frac{4}{20}$

12. $\frac{1}{3}$ and $\frac{16}{51}$

13. $\frac{5}{10}$ and $\frac{4}{8}$

14. $\frac{1}{3}$ and $\frac{33}{100}$

15. $\frac{7}{21}$ and $\frac{3}{9}$

16. $\frac{6}{5}$ and $\frac{24}{30}$

17. $\frac{15}{24}$ and $\frac{10}{16}$

18. $\frac{4}{4}$ and $\frac{16}{32}$

19. $\frac{5}{10}$ and $\frac{3}{6}$

20. $\frac{4}{6}$ and $\frac{5}{8}$

Solve each problem.

21. A supermarket buys fruit by the crate. 2 crates of apples weigh 90 lb. 4 crates of oranges weigh 180 lb. Write a ratio of crates to pounds. Are the ratios equal?

22. The supermarket pays $16 for 2 crates of apples. It pays $36 for 4 crates of pears. Write a ratio of dollars to crates. Are the ratios equal?

★ **23.** 2 crates of apples contain about 180 apples. How many apples are in 6 crates? (Hint: Write a ratio of crates to apples.)

★ **24.** 4 crates of pears contain about 720 pears. How many pears are in 8 crates? (Hint: Write a ratio of crates to pears.)

 KEEPING IN SHAPE

1. $\frac{1}{2}$ $+\frac{1}{3}$

2. $3\frac{1}{4}$ $-1\frac{5}{8}$

3. $9\frac{1}{2}$ $+3$

4. 8 $-2\frac{3}{5}$

5. $4\frac{2}{9}$ $+3\frac{7}{9}$

6. $5\frac{2}{5}$ $-2\frac{1}{2}$

7. $\frac{1}{2} \times 6$

8. $1\frac{1}{2} \times \frac{1}{3}$

9. $3\frac{1}{8} - 2\frac{5}{8}$

10. $11\frac{2}{3} + 6\frac{5}{9}$

11. $9\frac{1}{3} - 4\frac{5}{6}$

12. $6\frac{1}{2} \times 4\frac{1}{3}$

Scale Drawings

This is a **scale drawing** of a cafeteria and its kitchen. 1 cm on the drawing stands for 4 m in the actual room.

The **scale** is 1 cm to 4 m, or $\frac{1}{4}$.

centimeters $\longrightarrow 1$
meters $\longrightarrow 4$

The scale shows the ratio between distances on the drawing and actual distances.

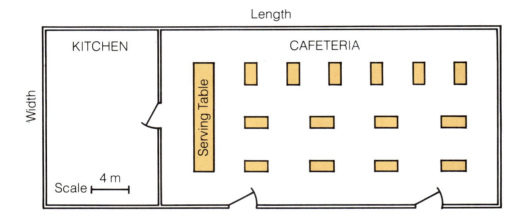

How long is the actual serving table?

Use equal ratios to find the actual length of the serving table. In the drawing, it is 3 cm long.

$$\frac{1}{4} = \frac{1 \times 3}{4 \times 2} = \frac{3}{12} \begin{array}{l} \leftarrow \text{ length on drawing} \\ \leftarrow \text{ actual length} \end{array}$$

The serving table is 12 m long.

Try These

Solve each problem.

1. Measure the length of the cafeteria. Use the scale to find the actual length.

2. Measure the length of the kitchen. Use the scale to find the actual length.

3. Measure the width of the kitchen. Use the scale to find the actual width.

4. The serving table is 0.5 cm wide in the drawing. What is the actual width?

Exercises

This is a scale drawing of the state of Colorado. The scale is 1 cm to 90 km.

Measure the map distance to the nearest centimeter. Then find the actual distance.

1. Find the actual length of Colorado.

2. Find the actual width of Colorado.

3. What is the perimeter of Colorado in kilometers?

4. What is the area of Colorado in square kilometers?

5. Find the road distance from Denver to Pueblo. Why is this hard to do?

6. Find the distance across Colorado on the highway shown in red. Compare it to your answer in exercise 1.

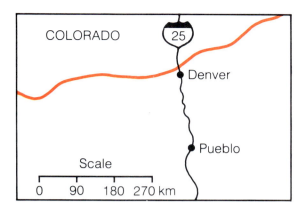

Some United States cities are shown on this map. 1 cm on the map stands for 160 km.

Measure the map distance to the nearest centimeter. Then find the actual distance.

7. New York City to Syracuse

8. Washington, D.C., to Pittsburgh

9. Pittsburgh, through Harrisburg, to Philadelphia

10. Buffalo to New York City by way of Syracuse

11. Which distance is farther?
   a. Buffalo to New York City by way of Harrisburg and Philadelphia
   b. Buffalo to New York City by way of Syracuse

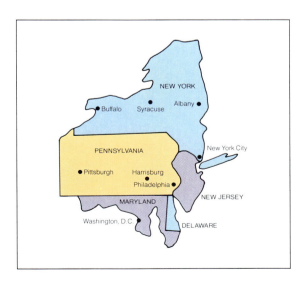

Problem Solving: Strategies

GENERALIZING

Sometimes **finding and extending a pattern** can help you solve problems.

Some numbers can be shown as geometric shapes. The shapes are drawn using dots. Some numbers can be drawn as triangles. These numbers are **triangular numbers**.

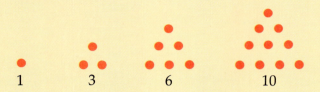

1   3   6   10

The first four triangular numbers are 1, 3, 6, and 10.

Find the fifth triangular number.
Look for a pattern to help you find the number.

$$1 \quad\overset{2}{\searrow\nearrow}\quad 3 \quad\overset{3}{\searrow\nearrow}\quad 6 \quad\overset{4}{\searrow\nearrow}\quad 10$$

← This is the difference between pairs of numbers.

The pattern shows that the difference between pairs of triangular numbers is one greater each time.

To find the fifth triangular number, add 5 to the fourth triangular number.

$$1 \quad\overset{2}{\searrow\nearrow}\quad 3 \quad\overset{3}{\searrow\nearrow}\quad 6 \quad\overset{4}{\searrow\nearrow}\quad 10 \quad\overset{5}{\searrow\nearrow}\quad 15$$

The fifth triangular number is 15.

Using the Strategy

Use the pattern to solve each problem.

1. Find the sixth triangular number. Draw it using dots.

2. Find the seventh triangular number. Draw it using dots.

Some numbers are **square numbers**.

1   4   9   16

3. What is the pattern to find the next square number?

4. What is the fifth square number? Draw it using dots.

5. What is the sixth square number?

6. What is the seventh square number?

Find and complete each pattern.

7. 1, 3, 7, 13, ▨, ▨

8. 2, 4, 3, 5, 4, ▨, ▨

9. 1, 2, 4, 8, 16, ▨, ▨

10. 3, 7, 5, 9, 7, ▨, ▨

11. A, B, B, C, D, D, ▨, ▨

12. AB, DE, GH, ▨

ACTIVITY

FINDING A PATTERN

Draw a large circle. Keep a record as you complete each step.

1. Draw a straight line through the circle. The line divides the circle into 2 parts.

2. Draw another straight line. The line must intersect the first line. How many parts is the circle divided into?

Number of Lines	Number of Parts
0	1
1	2
2	▨
3	▨
4	▨
5	▨

3. Draw another straight line that intersects the first lines. It must not pass through the point of intersection of the first lines. How many parts is the circle divided into now?

4. Continue drawing straight lines and counting the number of parts until you complete the table.

5. Look for a pattern. How many parts will the circle be divided into when 6 lines are drawn? 7 lines? 8 lines?

Percents and Fractions

■ **Percent** means per hundred, or hundredths. The symbol for percent is %. Think of a percent as a ratio of some number to 100.

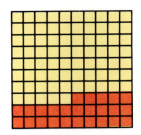

This large square is divided into 100 squares.

There are 25 red squares.
The ratio of red squares to all the squares is 25 to 100.

$$\text{red squares} \longrightarrow \frac{25}{100}$$
$$\text{all the squares} \longrightarrow$$

25% of the squares are red.

There are 75 yellow squares.
The ratio of yellow squares to all the squares is 75 to 100.

$$\text{yellow squares} \longrightarrow \frac{75}{100}$$
$$\text{all the squares} \longrightarrow$$

75% of the squares are yellow.

■ It is easy to write a fraction that names hundredths as a percent.

$$\frac{3}{100} = 3\%$$

If the denominator does not name hundredths, rename the fraction.

Write $\frac{2}{5}$ as a percent.

First, write $\frac{2}{5}$ as hundredths.

$$\frac{2}{5} = \frac{2 \times 20}{5 \times 20} = \frac{40}{100}$$

Then, write $\frac{40}{100}$ as a percent.

$$\frac{2}{5} = \frac{40}{100} = 40\%$$

■ You can also write a percent as a fraction.
Write 70% as a fraction.

First, write 70% as hundredths.

$$70\% = \frac{70}{100}$$

Then, write $\frac{70}{100}$ in lowest terms.

$$\frac{70}{100} = \frac{70 \div 10}{100 \div 10} = \frac{7}{10}$$

Try These

Copy and complete the ratio of red squares to all the squares.

1.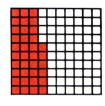

⬛ to 100, or $\frac{⬛}{100}$
⬛% are red.

2.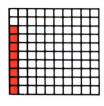

⬛ to 100, or $\frac{⬛}{100}$
⬛% are red.

3.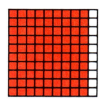

⬛ to 100, or $\frac{⬛}{100}$
⬛% are red.

Write each fraction as a percent.

4. $\frac{39}{100}$ **5.** $\frac{1}{5}$ **6.** $\frac{3}{10}$ **7.** $\frac{45}{100}$ **8.** $\frac{4}{5}$ **9.** $\frac{7}{20}$

Write each percent as a fraction in lowest terms.

10. 5% **11.** 30% **12.** 55% **13.** 60% **14.** 2% **15.** 12%

Exercises

Write each fraction as a percent.

1. $\frac{42}{100}$ **2.** $\frac{1}{2}$ **3.** $\frac{2}{5}$ **4.** $\frac{14}{100}$ **5.** $\frac{1}{4}$ **6.** $\frac{1}{10}$

7. $\frac{9}{10}$ **8.** $\frac{1}{25}$ **9.** $\frac{83}{100}$ **10.** $\frac{3}{50}$ **11.** $\frac{8}{25}$ **12.** $\frac{75}{100}$

13. $\frac{9}{20}$ **14.** $\frac{26}{100}$ **15.** $\frac{3}{4}$ **16.** $\frac{17}{100}$ **17.** $\frac{3}{25}$ **18.** $\frac{17}{50}$

Write each percent as a fraction in lowest terms.

19. 40% **20.** 99% **21.** 75% **22.** 1% **23.** 4% **24.** 60%

25. 85% **26.** 68% **27.** 23% **28.** 30% **29.** 21% **30.** 95%

31. 18% **32.** 44% **33.** 74% **34.** 50% **35.** 65% **36.** 7%

Solve each problem.

37. There are 100 squares. 78 of them are red. What percent of the squares are red?

★ **38.** There are 100 squares. 50 are blue. 20 are green. What percent of the squares are neither blue nor green?

Percents and Decimals

A sales tax is often written as a percent. A tax of $.04 on a dollar is a ratio of 4 cents to 100 cents.

■ It is easy to write a decimal that names hundredths as a percent.

$$0.04 = 4 \text{ hundredths}$$
$$= 4 \text{ hundredths} = 4\%$$

A tax of 4 cents on $1 is a 4% tax.

Write 0.6 as a percent.

First, write tenths as hundredths.

$$0.6 = 0.60$$

Then, write hundredths as a percent.

$$0.60 = 60\%$$

■ You can also write a percent as a decimal.

Write 47% as a decimal.
47% means 47 hundredths.

$$47\% = 0.47$$

Write 5% as a decimal.
5% means 5 hundredths.

$$5\% = 0.05$$
└─ Remember the 0.

Try These

Write each decimal as a percent.

1. 0.75   **2.** 0.30   **3.** 0.8   **4.** 0.13   **5.** 0.32   **6.** 0.6

Write each percent as a decimal.

7. 37%   **8.** 5%   **9.** 63%   **10.** 1%   **11.** 2%   **12.** 45%

Exercises

Write each decimal as a percent.

1. 0.05   **2.** 0.17   **3.** 0.99   **4.** 0.3   **5.** 0.1   **6.** 0.15

7. 0.01   **8.** 0.8   **9.** 0.2   **10.** 0.70   **11.** 0.50   **12.** 0.07

13. 0.11   **14.** 0.10   **15.** 0.54   **16.** 0.09   **17.** 0.16   **18.** 0.9

Write each percent as a decimal.

19. 14%   **20.** 92%   **21.** 85%   **22.** 67%   **23.** 65%   **24.** 75%

25. 3%   **26.** 7%   **27.** 1%   **28.** 5%   **29.** 9%   **30.** 6%

31. 18%   **32.** 4%   **33.** 38%   **34.** 2%   **35.** 98%   **36.** 47%

 You can use a calculator to write a fraction as a percent.

Write $\frac{3}{5}$ as a percent.

$\frac{3}{5}$ means $3 \div 5$. Press .

The display shows 0.6. $0.6 = 0.60$

Write: $0.60 = 60\%$.

Write each fraction as a percent.

37. $\frac{3}{4}$ **38.** $\frac{4}{25}$ **39.** $\frac{11}{20}$ **40.** $\frac{49}{50}$ **41.** $\frac{24}{25}$ **42.** $\frac{9}{20}$

43. Try the same method for $\frac{1}{3}$.
To the nearest hundredth, 0.3333333 rounds to ▇.
0.3333333 is about ▇%.

Estimate the percent.

44. $\frac{2}{3}$ **45.** $\frac{1}{6}$ **46.** $\frac{3}{8}$ **47.** $\frac{7}{8}$ **48.** $\frac{1}{9}$ **49.** $\frac{4}{9}$

Solve each problem. You may choose paper and pencil or a calculator.

50. Wilma's dress shop collects a sales tax of $.05 on a dollar. What percent is the sales tax?

★ **51.** Wilma receives a shipment of 16 blazers. 12 of them are wool. What percent of the blazers are not wool?

Finding a Percent of a Number

■ A chain of bicycle stores has 15 stores. 80% of the stores are in shopping malls. How many of the bicycle stores are in shopping malls?

Find 80% of 15.

Write the percent as a decimal.

$$80\% = 0.80$$

Multiply.

$$
\begin{array}{r}
15 \\
\times 0.80 \\
\hline
12.00
\end{array}
$$

← number of stores
← percent in shopping malls

12 of the stores are in shopping malls.

■ Shoppers often use percents. Bicycles are regularly $95. They are on sale for 25% off. How much money can be saved?

Find 25% of $95.

Write the percent as a decimal.

$$25\% = 0.25$$

Multiply.

$$
\begin{array}{r}
\$\ \ \ \ 95 \\
\times\ \ \ 0.25 \\
\hline
4\ 75 \\
19\ 00 \\
\hline
\$23.75
\end{array}
$$

← regular price
← percent saved

$23.75 can be saved.

What is the sale price of the bicycle?

$$
\begin{array}{r}
\$95.00 \\
-\ \ 23.75 \\
\hline
\$71.25
\end{array}
$$

← regular price
← amount saved

The sale price is $71.25.

Try These

Solve.

1. 20% of 65
4. 15% of 300

2. 10% of 50
5. 5% of 100

3. 50% of 12
6. 12% of $200

Exercises

Solve.

1. 75% of 48
2. 8% of 50
3. 40% of 1,000
4. 35% of $200
5. 90% of $50
6. 80% of $75
7. 40% of $5
8. 35% of $160
9. 3% of $25
10. 5% of $30
11. 2% of 370
12. 99% of $100

Find and complete each pattern.

13. 2, 4, 8, 10, 14, ▧, ▧
14. 22, 21, 19, 16, 12, ▧, ▧
15. A, C, E, G, I, ▧, ▧
16. AB, ZY, CD, XW, EF, ▧, ▧

Solve each problem.

17. A shipment of 45 bicycles arrives. $\frac{2}{5}$ of them are for the Westerly branch. The rest are for the Newbury branch. How many bicycles are for the Newbury branch?

18. A bicycle regularly sells for $180. Walt buys it for 30% off. The sales tax is $.07 on each dollar. How much change should Walt receive from $150?

19. A customer orders a bicycle for $74, an auto carrier for $14.75, and a foot pump for $12.25. There is a sales tax of $.07 on each dollar. What is the total cost of the order?

20. The Cycle Shops pay $106.32 for a carton of bicycle locks. There are 12 locks in each carton. What is the cost of each lock?

21. Stan works at the Bradley branch. He works 25 hours each week. He earns $4.85 each hour. How much does Stan earn each week?

22. The ratio of tricycles sold to bicycles sold is 2 to 9. 28 tricycles are sold. How many bicycles are sold?

This circle graph shows the Cycle Shops' advertising budget. The yearly budget is $18,000.

23. What fraction of the money is used on television advertisements?

24. How much money is spent on newspaper advertisements?

★ 25. Which kind of advertising costs the Cycle Shops $4,500 each year?

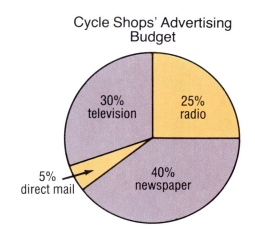

Cycle Shops' Advertising Budget

30% television
25% radio
40% newspaper
5% direct mail

Problem Solving: Applications

CONSUMER MATHEMATICS

■ People can save money by putting it in a savings account at a bank. The bank pays a fee. The fee is called **interest**.

David has $183 in his savings account. The bank pays interest at a rate of 6% per year. How much interest will David's money earn in 1 year?

Find 6% of $183.

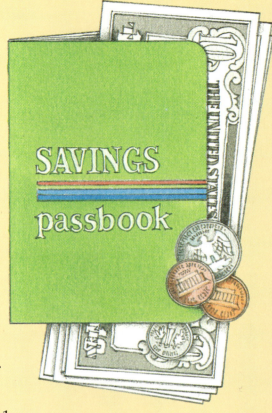

Write the percent as a decimal.　　**Multiply.**

$$6\% = 0.06$$

$$\begin{array}{r} \$183 \\ \times\ \ 0.06 \\ \hline \$10.98 \end{array}$$

David's money earns $10.98 in interest.

■ People sometimes borrow money from banks. They pay the bank a fee for the use of the money. This fee is also called interest.

Helen borrowed $2,000. She paid 12% interest for 1 year. Find the amount of the interest.

Multiply to find 12% of $2,000.

$$\begin{array}{r} \$\ 2,000 \\ \times\ \ \ \ \ 0.12 \\ \hline \$240.00 \end{array}$$ ← amount borrowed
← percent of interest

Helen paid $240 interest.

What was the total amount she owed at the end of the year?

$$\begin{array}{r} \$2,000 \\ +\ \ \ \ 240 \\ \hline \$2,240 \end{array}$$ ← amount borrowed
← amount of interest

She owed a total of $2,240.

Try These

Solve each problem.

1. Elliot has $450 in his savings account. The bank pays interest at a rate of 7%. How much interest will Elliot's money earn in 1 year?

2. Robin borrowed $500. She paid 13% interest for 1 year. What was the total amount she owed at the end of the year?

Exercises

Solve each problem.

1. Gary has $2,500 in his savings account. The bank pays interest at a rate of 8%. How much interest will Gary's money earn in 1 year?

2. Joe borrowed $1,000. He paid 12% interest for 1 year. What was the total amount he owed at the end of the year?

3. Anna had a balance of $356.12 in her checking account. She deposited $185.95. What is the total amount in Anna's account now?

4. Jay has $1,400 in his savings account. He withdrew 30% of his money to make a down payment on a car. How much money is left in his account?

5. Allan has $9,800 in a Golden Savings Account. It earns 9% interest in 1 year. He makes no deposits. How much money will Allan have in this account in 1 year?

6. Jacques had $1,465 in his savings account. He deposited 25% of his paycheck into this account. His paycheck was $800. What is the total amount in his savings account now?

7. 70% of the people who have checking accounts also have savings accounts. 2,680 people have checking accounts. How many of these people have savings accounts?

8. Kim has $560 in her savings account. She deposits a $265 paycheck and $60 in cash. How much money is in her savings account now?

★ **9.** Lee put $600 in a savings account earning 5% interest in 1 year. He left the interest in his account at the end of each year and made no other deposits. How much money did he have in his account at the end of 2 years?

★ **10.** In 1 year, Theresa earned $25 in interest on a savings account. Theresa had $500 in the account. What was the rate of interest?

12 CHAPTER CHECKPOINT

Write each ratio. (pp. 368–369)

1. tubes of red paint to tubes of blue paint

2. tubes of blue paint to tubes of green paint

3. tubes of green paint to all the tubes of paint

Copy and complete to make equal ratios. (pp. 370–371)

4. $\frac{9}{21} = \frac{3}{\blacksquare}$

5. $\frac{1}{3} = \frac{\blacksquare}{12}$

6. $\frac{2}{5} = \frac{8}{\blacksquare}$

7. $\frac{8}{12} = \frac{\blacksquare}{3}$

Are the ratios equal? Use cross products to check. (pp. 372–373)

8. $\frac{2}{5}$ and $\frac{6}{15}$

9. $\frac{3}{5}$ and $\frac{9}{25}$

10. $\frac{3}{4}$ and $\frac{9}{11}$

11. $\frac{4}{18}$ and $\frac{1}{9}$

12. $\frac{3}{4}$ and $\frac{6}{8}$

13. $\frac{5}{10}$ and $\frac{6}{12}$

14. $\frac{3}{9}$ and $\frac{5}{20}$

15. $\frac{8}{12}$ and $\frac{18}{27}$

Write each fraction as a percent. (pp. 378–379)

16. $\frac{25}{100}$

17. $\frac{3}{100}$

18. $\frac{1}{2}$

19. $\frac{3}{4}$

20. $\frac{2}{5}$

21. $\frac{9}{20}$

Write each percent as a fraction in lowest terms. (pp. 378–379)

22. 13%

23. 10%

24. 20%

25. 80%

26. 15%

27. 25%

Write each decimal as a percent. (pp. 380–381)

28. 0.75

29. 0.01

30. 0.35

31. 0.05

32. 0.8

33. 0.48

34. 0.07

35. 0.56

36. 0.9

37. 0.14

38. 0.2

39. 0.85

Write each percent as a decimal. (pp. 380–381)

40. 35%

41. 20%

42. 3%

43. 42%

44. 10%

45. 4%

46. 6%

47. 84%

48. 12%

49. 99%

50. 76%

51. 8%

Copy and complete. Write >, <, or =. (pp. 380–381)

52. 0.64 ▨ 0.46

53. 56% ▨ 0.56

54. 0.70 ▨ 0.7

55. 50% ▨ 5%

56. 0.04 ▨ 0.40

57. 0.9 ▨ 90%

Solve. (pp. 382–383)

58. 3% of 10

59. 20% of 50

60. 80% of 40

61. 4% of $10

62. 25% of $12

63. 90% of $200

Find and complete each pattern. (pp. 376–377)

64. 6, 8, 7, 9, 8, ▨, ▨

65. 8, 16, 4, 8, 2, ▨, ▨

66. A, N, B, O, C, ▨, ▨

67. A, A, B, C, C, ▨, ▨

Solve each problem. (pp. 368–385)

68. The ratio of students to teachers is 15 to 2. There are 8 teachers. How many students are there?

69. The Caruso School bought 8 packages of poster board for $50. How much would 16 packages cost?

70. There were 100 questions on a test. Anna answered 85 of them correctly. What percent did she answer correctly?

71. There are 25 students in a class. 20% of the class was absent on Monday. How many students were absent?

72. Bruce has $259 in his savings account. The bank pays interest at the rate of 6%. How much interest will Bruce earn in 1 year?

73. Juanita borrowed $400. She paid 14% interest for 1 year. What was the total amount she owed at the end of the year?

1 cm on this drawing stands for 3 m in the actual room.

74. Measure the length of the conference room. Use the scale to find the actual length.

75. Measure the width of the conference room. Use the scale to find the actual width.

Conference Room

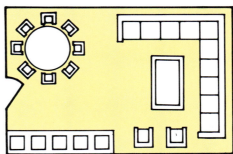

COMPUTERS AND PROBLEM SOLVING

■ You can solve many types of problems by looking for a pattern. Find the pattern in the table below, and fill in the blanks.

Regular Polygons

Name of polygon	Number of sides	Number of angles	Total number of degrees in shape	Size of each turn
square	4	4	360	90
pentagon	5	▦	360	72
hexagon	▦	6	360	60
octagon	8	▦	▦	45
nonagon	9	▦	▦	▦
decagon	▦	10	▦	▦

■ You can use the table to program the turtle to draw regular polygons. For example:

```
TO PENTAGON
REPEAT 5[FD 60 RT 72]
END
```

There is an easier way. You can write one procedure that will tell the turtle to draw any polygon for you. The computer must find the number of degrees the turtle must turn to make the shape. Look at this procedure.

```
TO POLYGONS :ANGLES
REPEAT :ANGLES [FD 40 RT 360/ :ANGLES]
END
```

:ANGLES is a variable. To run the procedure, POLYGONS :ANGLES, you must give :ANGLES a value. Do this by replacing :ANGLES with a number.

For example, type POLYGONS 5. The computer will use the 5 wherever :ANGLES appears in the procedure.

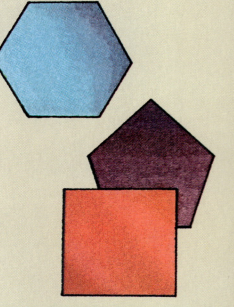

Now the computer knows its directions are:

REPEAT 5 [FD 40 RT 360/5]

The computer will find the value of 360/5 and follow this direction:

REPEAT 5 [FD 40 RT 72]

Which polygon will the turtle draw?

■ Now that you have taught the turtle the **subprocedure**, POLYGONS :ANGLES, you can use it as part of a larger procedure. The larger procedure is called a **superprocedure**.

```
TO MANYSHAPES
PU SETPOS [− 80 0] PD
POLYGONS 6
PU RT 90 FD 60 PD LT 90
POLYGONS 5
PU RT 90 FD 60 PD LT 90
POLYGONS 4
END
```

The procedure above used MANYSHAPES as the superprocedure. POLYGONS :ANGLES was the subprocedure.

Solve this problem.

In the procedure above, the commands PU RT 90 FD 60 PD LT 90 could be written as a procedure named MOVE. Rewrite the superprocedure to include MOVE as a subprocedure.

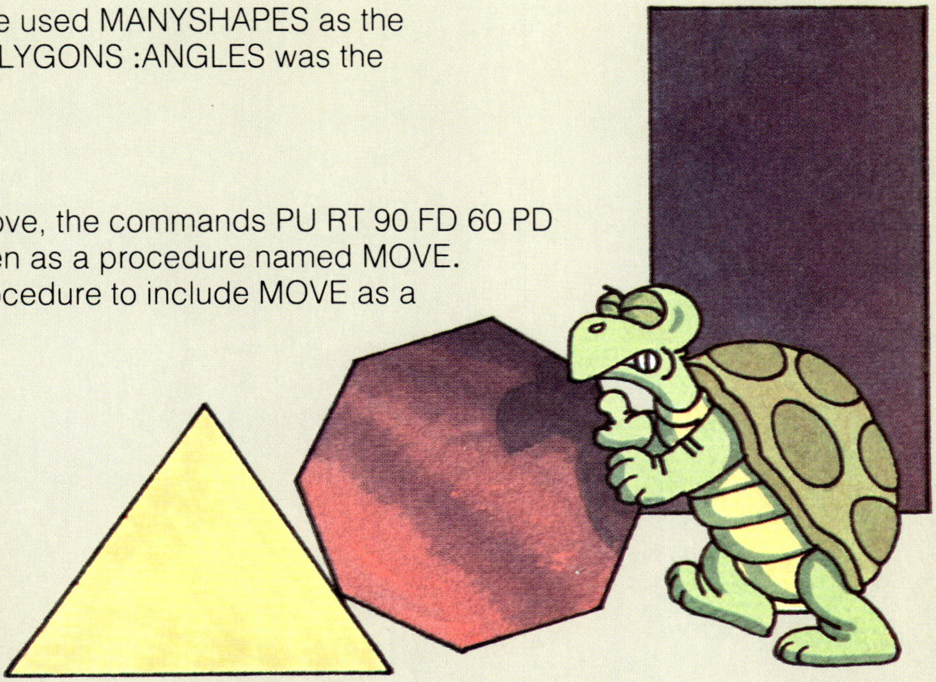

ENRICHMENT

PROPORTIONS

■ Are $\frac{7}{21}$ and $\frac{3}{9}$ equal ratios?

Find the cross products.

$$\frac{7}{21} \times \frac{3}{9}$$

$$7 \times 9 \qquad 21 \times 3$$
$$63 = 63$$

The cross products are equal, so $\frac{7}{21} = \frac{3}{9}$.

A statement that two ratios are equal is called a **proportion**.

■ You can use cross products to find a missing term in a proportion.

Find the value of n.

$$\frac{3}{4} = \frac{9}{n}$$

The n means a number is unknown. Use cross products to solve for n.

$$3 \times n = 4 \times 9$$

$3n$ means $\rightarrow 3n = 36$
$3 \times n$

$$\frac{3n}{3} = \frac{36}{3}$$

Divide both sides of the equal sign by 3.

$$n = 12$$

Solve for n.

1. $\frac{4}{6} = \frac{14}{n}$ **2.** $\frac{6}{8} = \frac{n}{12}$ **3.** $\frac{3}{4} = \frac{n}{20}$ **4.** $\frac{6}{9} = \frac{8}{n}$

5. $\frac{3}{15} = \frac{n}{40}$ **6.** $\frac{9}{21} = \frac{6}{n}$ **7.** $\frac{n}{35} = \frac{4}{7}$ **8.** $\frac{9}{42} = \frac{3}{n}$

9. $\frac{n}{10} = \frac{72}{80}$ **10.** $\frac{2}{5} = \frac{n}{20}$ **11.** $\frac{n}{16} = \frac{15}{20}$ **12.** $\frac{9}{5} = \frac{108}{n}$

13. $\frac{6}{4} = \frac{n}{10}$ **14.** $\frac{10}{n} = \frac{15}{18}$ **15.** $\frac{21}{15} = \frac{14}{n}$ **16.** $\frac{n}{18} = \frac{4}{12}$

CUMULATIVE REVIEW

Write as a decimal.

1. $\frac{3}{10}$ **2.** $\frac{6}{100}$ **3.** $2\frac{7}{10}$ **4.** $13\frac{56}{100}$ **5.** $84\frac{98}{100}$ **6.** $53\frac{9}{10}$

7. twenty-six and thirty-eight hundredths

8. thirteen and seven tenths

9. four hundred ten and fifty-seven thousandths

10. five hundredths

11. two hundred and six thousandths

Write in order from least to greatest.

12. 6.798   5.321   4.987   6.978

13. 93.241   93.142   93.314   93.214

Add or subtract.

14. $\begin{array}{r} 4.8 \\ +2.6 \\ \hline \end{array}$ **15.** $\begin{array}{r} 6.3 \\ -1.827 \\ \hline \end{array}$ **16.** $\begin{array}{r} 5.734 \\ +0.789 \\ \hline \end{array}$ **17.** $\begin{array}{r} 25.0 \\ -\ 0.68 \\ \hline \end{array}$ **18.** $\begin{array}{r} 84.24 \\ +37.876 \\ \hline \end{array}$

Add or subtract. Write each answer in lowest terms.

19. $\begin{array}{r} \frac{2}{5} \\ +\frac{1}{3} \\ \hline \end{array}$ **20.** $\begin{array}{r} \frac{3}{4} \\ -\frac{1}{2} \\ \hline \end{array}$ **21.** $\begin{array}{r} \frac{7}{8} \\ -\frac{2}{3} \\ \hline \end{array}$ **22.** $\begin{array}{r} \frac{2}{3} \\ +\frac{1}{2} \\ \hline \end{array}$ **23.** $\begin{array}{r} 5\frac{3}{10} \\ +2\frac{1}{10} \\ \hline \end{array}$

24. $\begin{array}{r} 6\frac{5}{12} \\ -3\frac{1}{4} \\ \hline \end{array}$ **25.** $\begin{array}{r} 9\frac{5}{6} \\ +\ \frac{3}{4} \\ \hline \end{array}$ **26.** $\begin{array}{r} 6\frac{1}{4} \\ +3\frac{4}{5} \\ \hline \end{array}$ **27.** $\begin{array}{r} 8\frac{1}{3} \\ -3\frac{1}{2} \\ \hline \end{array}$ **28.** $\begin{array}{r} 6 \\ -4\frac{3}{10} \\ \hline \end{array}$

Multiply. Write each answer in lowest terms.

29. $\frac{1}{2} \times \frac{2}{3}$ **30.** $\frac{2}{5} \times \frac{5}{8}$ **31.** $\frac{5}{6} \times \frac{1}{2}$ **32.** $\frac{3}{4} \times 12$

33. $2\frac{1}{2} \times 3$ **34.** $3\frac{1}{6} \times 2\frac{1}{2}$ **35.** $2\frac{1}{2} \times 3\frac{3}{4}$ **36.** $\frac{1}{5} \times 6\frac{2}{3}$

(Continued)

Multiply.

37. 4.7
  × 6

38. 2.5
  ×0.6

39. 34.5
  × 1.2

40. 0.765
  × 29

41. 0.31
  × 0.2

42. 10 × 8.35

43. 100 × 0.46

44. 1,000 × 9.7

Divide.

45. 4)‾16.8‾

46. 9)‾0.891‾

47. 28)‾0.8624‾

48. 42)‾$9.66‾

49. 42.7 ÷ 10

50. 257.8 ÷ 100

51. 91.3 ÷ 1,000

Find the perimeter and the area of each figure.

52. a rectangle with a length of 15 cm and a width of 8.6 cm

53. a square with a length of 9.2 m

Write each fraction as a percent.

54. $\frac{19}{100}$

55. $\frac{3}{4}$

56. $\frac{2}{5}$

57. $\frac{1}{2}$

58. $\frac{38}{100}$

59. $\frac{9}{10}$

Write each percent as a decimal.

60. 35%

61. 9%

62. 86%

63. 7%

64. 20%

65. 40%

Solve.

66. 8% of $10

67. 75% of 36

68. 40% of 60

Solve each problem.

69. Jason spent $3\frac{1}{2}$ h repairing the fence. Then he spent $2\frac{1}{4}$ h painting the fence. How long did Jason work on the fence?

70. The regular price of a set of wrenches is $72. The sale price is 30% less than that. Find the sale price of the set of wrenches.

71. A storage area is 3 m long, 1.6 m wide, and 2 m high. What is the volume of the storage area?

72. Alicia paid $27.90 for 6 pieces of board. How much did each piece of board cost?

To the student:

In each chapter of this book, you studied a new problem solving strategy. These pages of Problem Solving: Extensions give you a chance to use those strategies to solve challenging real-life problems and interesting problems. There may be many ways to solve each problem. It is up to you to decide which strategy or strategies to use.

For some problems, you will have to conduct an experiment and do some measurements to get the data you need. For other problems, you may have to find necessary information in reference books.

We hope you find these Extensions interesting.

Good luck!

The authors

Problem Solving: Extensions

ORGANIZING DATA

Read the story. Organize the information by making a table. Then solve each problem.

The people of Hudson County held an arts and crafts fair. People displayed many handmade objects. Six exhibitors had handmade pottery for sale. Jenny sold 6 bowls, 12 mugs, 8 candlesticks, and 3 vases. Paul sold 16 candlesticks, 9 lamps, and 5 vases. Steve sold 16 mugs, 3 vases, and 22 lamps. Cathy sold 7 bowls, 4 vases, and 15 mugs. Richard sold 7 vases, 10 mugs, 6 candlesticks, 5 lamps, and 4 bowls. Susan sold 5 bowls, 4 candlesticks, 9 mugs, and 5 vases.

1. Who sold the most vases?

2. Which object was sold by all the exhibitors?

3. Which exhibitors did not sell bowls?

4. Which objects were sold by both Paul and Jenny?

5. How many lamps were sold altogether?

6. How many objects did Susan sell?

7. Who sold more mugs, Jenny or Cathy? How many more?

8. Which object was sold the most often?

Problem Solving: Extensions

USING LOGIC

Bill, Kate, and Joe each have a notebook. The notebooks are red, blue, and green.

Bill said, "Kate's notebook is not blue."
Joe said, "Somebody else's red notebook is on my desk."
Kate said, "It's not Bill's. His notebook is green."

Use the clues to decide which notebook belongs to each student.

A table may help you organize the information. The first clue tells you that Kate's notebook is not blue. Put an X in the table. The X shows that the blue notebook cannot be Kate's.

	Notebook		
	red	blue	green
Bill			
Kate		X	
Joe			

1. Complete the table. Which notebook belongs to each student?

2. Jan, Louis, and Ellen each have a pet. Their pets are a dog, a cat, and a rabbit.

   Louis said, "Neither Ellen nor I owns a rabbit." Jan said, "Louis's pet barks."

   What kind of pet does each person have?

3. Fred, Sue, Emily, and Peggy each take part in an after-school activity. They belong to the swimming club, the bowling club, the basketball team, and the student council.

   Sue and Emily are afraid of water.
   Fred missed the last team practice.
   Two-thirds of her classmates voted for Sue.

   In what activity does each student take part?

Problem Solving: Extensions

EXPLORING LARGE NUMBERS

Bob's father made him this offer:

"I will give you an allowance
of $20 a month for 1 year.
Or I will give you $1 the first
month, $2 the second month,
$4 the third month, and so on,
doubling your allowance each
month until the end of the
year."

If you were Bob, which offer
would you take?

To decide which offer to take, find
how much Bob would receive with
each plan.

a. Find the amount Bob would get if he received $20 a
   month for 1 year.

b. Find the amount Bob would get each month under the
   second plan. Then find the total for the year.

The problem above is like an ancient problem. A king
agreed to give an amount of grain equal to 1 grain of
wheat on the first square of a chessboard, 2 grains of
wheat on the second square, 4 grains on the third square,
and so on, doubling for each square. There are 64 squares
on a chessboard.

1. How many grains of wheat would be on the
   21st square? Round the number to the nearest
   million.

2. Use the rounded number to find the number of
   millions on the 41st square.

3. A million millions is a trillion. About how many
   trillions would be on the 61st square?

4. Do you think the king could keep his promise? Why or why not?

Problem Solving: Extensions

EXPERIMENTING WITH MEASUREMENTS

About how many sheets are there in 1 ton of paper?

One way to solve this problem is to weigh 1 package of paper. Use standard $8\frac{1}{2}$-inch by 11-inch paper.

a. About how many pounds does 1 package weigh?
b. About how many packages would weigh 1 ton?
c. How many sheets are in each package?

Solve each problem.

1. About how much would the ton of paper cost? (Find the cost of 1 package first.)

2. Suppose you weighed 1 ton of mathematics books like this one. About how many books would that be?

3. Suppose you placed new pencils end to end around your classroom. About how many pencils would it take? (Measure a new pencil to the nearest inch.)

4. 120 new pencils fit end to end along the length of a cafeteria. About how many feet long is the cafeteria?

Problem Solving: Extensions

ANALOGIES

Study this example.

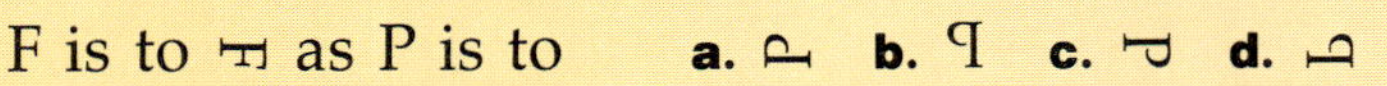

F is to ⊣ as P is to   **a.** ⌐ **b.** � **c.** �┙ **d.** ⊏

In the first pair, F has been turned to make ⊣. Which figure shows P turned the same way?

Choose the correct answer to complete each analogy.

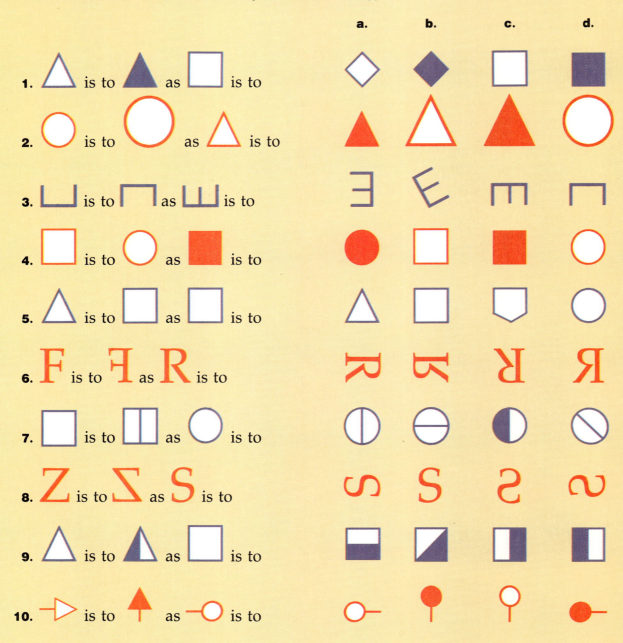

398   Problem Solving: Extensions (use after Chapter 5)

Problem Solving: Extensions

USING REFERENCES

Suppose each person in your state gave you a penny.
How many dollars would you have?

To solve this problem, you must do some research.

a. What information do you need?
b. Where can you get it?
c. How do you express a number of cents in dollars?

How many dollars would you have if each person in your state gave you the following?

1. a dime   **2.** a $1 bill   **3.** a $10 bill

How many dollars would you have if each person in the world gave you the following?

4. a penny   **5.** a dime   **6.** a $10 bill

7. Suppose every person in the United States gave you a
$1 bill. Placed end to end, would the bills reach around
the equator?

Problem Solving: Extensions

PLANNING THE USE OF SPACE

A class bought 2 boxes of tomato plants. There were 8 plants in each box. The class has a garden that is 8 feet by 8 feet.

Each tomato plant must be at least 2 feet from every other plant. The outside plants must be 1 foot from the edge of the garden.

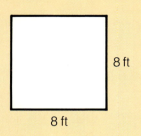

8 ft

8 ft

Decide the best way to space the plants in the garden. Draw a picture to help you plan.

The class decides to enlarge the garden. Some students dig up 2 more feet on one side of the garden. The garden is now 10 feet by 8 feet.

1. How many more tomato plants can be planted? Draw a picture of this plan.

Plan a garden to plant each given number of tomato plants.

There must be 2 feet between plants and 1 foot between a plant and the edge of the garden. Make the garden as small as you can.

2. 25 plants
3. 9 plants
4. 12 plants

Problem Solving: Extensions

SOLVING NUMBER PUZZLES

Here are some number sequences. Find a pattern. Then write the next number in each sequence.

1. 6, 12, 18, 24, 30, ▦

2. 2, 4, 8, 16, 32, ▦

3. 50, 40, 31, 23, 16, ▦

4. 10, 15, 13, 18, 16, ▦

5. 0, 1, 3, 6, 10, 15, ▦

6. 1, 2, 6, 24, 120, ▦

Use the clues to find the number in each puzzle.

7. This number is a 3-digit number. All three digits are the same. If it is divided by 2, by 3, by 4, by 6, or by 8, there is a zero remainder. What is the number?

8. This is a 1-digit number. If you multiply it by 3, the result is 4 more than the result when you multiply it by 2. What is the 1-digit number?

9. This number is a 3-digit number. When it is divided by 3, the quotient is 94 more than when it is divided by 5. What is the number?

10. Round this number to the nearest ten and the result is 430. The sum of its digits is 9. What is the number?

11. This number is a 4-digit number. When it is multiplied by 4, the product is a number with the same digits exactly reversed. What is the number?

12. Both digits of this number are the same. The sum of the digits is less than 10. If you add 16 to the number or subtract 16 from the number, the result will be a multiple of 4. What is the number?

13. This number is a 1-digit number. When it is multiplied by 5, the sum of the digits in the product is 1 more than the number. What is the number?

14. This is a 4-digit number. Each digit is 1 more than the digit before. The number formed by the middle 2 digits is twice the product of the first and last digits. What is the number?

Problem Solving: Extensions

EXPERIMENTING WITH COINS

About how many millimeters high is a stack of 100 pennies?

One way to begin this problem is to make a stack of 10 pennies. Measure the height of the stack to the nearest millimeter.

a. How high is the stack?
b. How many stacks like this will 100 pennies make?

Solve each problem.

1. About how high would a stack of 1,000 pennies be?

2. About how thick is 1 penny?

3. About how many millimeters high is a stack of 10 nickels?

4. About how thick is 1 nickel?

One stack contains 90 pennies. Another stack contains 90 nickels.

5. Which stack is higher? About how much higher?

6. Which stack is worth more? How much more?

7. Suppose a stack of pennies reached the ceiling of your classroom. About what would the stack be worth?

Problem Solving: Extensions

EXPERIMENTING WITH SHAPES

A **pentomino** is a flat figure made with 5 congruent squares. At least one side of each square must match a side of another square. How many different pentominoes are there?

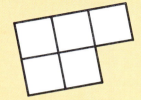

One way to solve this problem is to use graph paper. Draw as many different pentominoes as you can. Then cut them out. (Two pentominoes are different if you cannot match them by turning and flipping.)

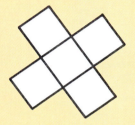

Solve each problem.

1. A **triomino** is a flat figure made with 3 congruent squares. How many different triominoes are there?

2. A **tetromino** is made with 4 congruent squares. How many different tetrominoes are there?

3. Cut an open-ended cube from a milk carton. Guess which pentominoes could be made by cutting certain edges and unfolding. (Count only those pentominoes that would be in one piece after the cutting.)

4. Actually cut several cubes made from milk cartons. Check your answers to exercise 3.

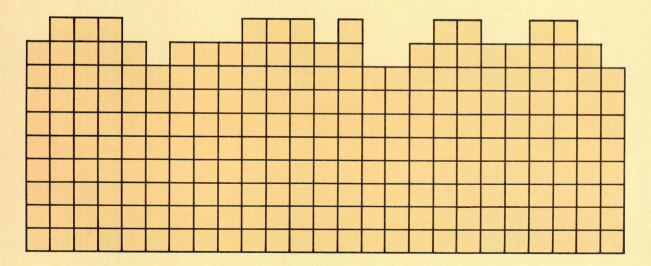

Problem Solving: Extensions

Suppose everyone in your state lined up around the state border. If the people were spaced equally, how far apart would they be from each other?

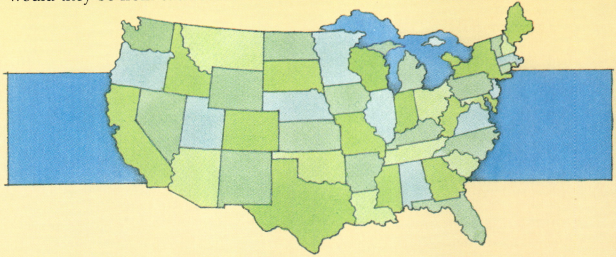

To solve this problem, you must do some research.

a. What information do you need?
b. Where can you get that information?
   (In using a map, use the scale and estimate the perimeter. Include shorelines as well as land borders.)

Solve each problem.

1. Name a state in which the residents around the border would be far apart. What two facts are important in making your choice?

2. Name a state in which the residents would be close together.

3. 24 girls are spaced equally around a square with 12-ft sides. 24 boys are spaced equally around a triangle with three 18-ft sides. Which are closer, the boys or the girls?

4. Suppose all the students in your class lined up around the classroom. If they were evenly spaced, about how far apart would they be? Do you think they could hold hands?

Problem Solving: Extensions

EXPERIMENTING WITH VOLUME

About how many grains of rice does this box hold? Guess first. Then experiment.

One way to solve this problem is to make a paper cube 1 centimeter on each edge. (There is a 1-cm cube on page 215. You can trace it.)

a. How many grains of rice will the cube hold?
b. What is the volume of the box?

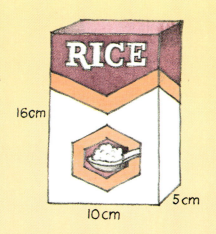

Solve each problem.

1. About how many grains of rice would fit in this box?

2. A cube measures 10 centimeters on each edge. About how many grains of rice would fit in it?

3. 512 sunflower seeds fit in a cube. There are about 8 sunflower seeds in each cubic centimeter. What is the volume of the cube in cubic centimeters?

More Practice

SET 1 (pp. 2–5)

Write each number.

1. 17 thousand 17

2. 46 thousand 515

3. two hundred thirty thousand, five hundred sixty-one

What does the digit 8 mean in each number?

4. 678,123   **5.** 2,481   **6.** 543,821   **7.** 386,790   **8.** 814,569

SET 2 (pp. 6–7)

Write >, <, or =.

1. 7,721 ▧ 7,834   **2.** 989 ▧ 989   **3.** 25,961 ▧ 25,691

Write in order from least to greatest.

4. 7,083   783   8,730   8,703   **5.** 46,512   45,216   4,865   45,215

SET 3 (pp. 8–11)

Round to the nearest hundred.

1. 658   **2.** 36,502   **3.** 8,274   **4.** 27,563   **5.** 149,736

Round to the nearest thousand.

6. 12,637   **7.** 8,490   **8.** 37,516   **9.** 143,859   **10.** 694,073

SET 4 (pp. 14–17)

What does the digit 5 mean in each number?

1. 25,396,271   **2.** 65,902,743,001   **3.** 357,600,428   **4.** 503,762,148,907

Write each number.

5. 47 million 72 thousand 635

6. 18 million 59 thousand 74

7. 84 billion 76 million 410

8. 31 billion 276 thousand 458

SET 5 (pp. 18–19)

Solve each problem.

1. Which city has the most telephones?

2. Which city has the fewest telephones?

3. Which cities have between 1,100,000 and 1,150,000 telephones?

4. Write the cities in order from fewest to greatest number of telephones.

City	Number of Telephones
Baltimore, Maryland	1,456,284
Phoenix, Arizona	1,131,519
Houston, Texas	1,496,626
Miami, Florida	1,129,870
San Diego, California	1,161,954

SET 6 (pp. 28–33)

Add.

1.
$$\begin{array}{r} 6 \\ +0 \\ \hline \end{array}$$

2.
$$\begin{array}{r} 50 \\ +75 \\ \hline \end{array}$$

3.
$$\begin{array}{r} 39 \\ +64 \\ \hline \end{array}$$

4.
$$\begin{array}{r} 78 \\ +67 \\ \hline \end{array}$$

5.
$$\begin{array}{r} 876 \\ +459 \\ \hline \end{array}$$

6.
$$\begin{array}{r} \$3.74 \\ +\ 1.32 \\ \hline \end{array}$$

7. $(2 + 4) + 9$

8. $61 + 94$

9. $625 + 275$

10. $356 + 93$

SET 7 (pp. 34–37)

Add. Estimate to check.

1.
$$\begin{array}{r} 201 \\ 49 \\ +189 \\ \hline \end{array}$$

2.
$$\begin{array}{r} 367 \\ 856 \\ +124 \\ \hline \end{array}$$

3.
$$\begin{array}{r} 61 \\ 238 \\ +479 \\ \hline \end{array}$$

4.
$$\begin{array}{r} 15,237 \\ +\ 3,965 \\ \hline \end{array}$$

5.
$$\begin{array}{r} 397,452 \\ 198,843 \\ +\ 92,105 \\ \hline \end{array}$$

6. $55 + 302 + 27 + 421$

7. $8,736 + 3,694$

8. $27,468 + 315,409$

SET 8 (pp. 40–45)

Subtract.

1.
$$\begin{array}{r} 17 \\ -\ 9 \\ \hline \end{array}$$

2.
$$\begin{array}{r} 45 \\ -22 \\ \hline \end{array}$$

3.
$$\begin{array}{r} 65 \\ -29 \\ \hline \end{array}$$

4.
$$\begin{array}{r} 76 \\ -18 \\ \hline \end{array}$$

5.
$$\begin{array}{r} \$8.48 \\ -\ 1.78 \\ \hline \end{array}$$

6.
$$\begin{array}{r} 366 \\ -231 \\ \hline \end{array}$$

7. $13 - 8$

8. $38 - 19$

9. $458 - 297$

10. $942 - 67$

SET 9 (pp. 46–49)

Subtract.

1. 607 −245	**2.** 720 −381	**3.** 209 − 78	**4.** 500 −493	**5.** 340 − 69	**6.** 800 −642

Use the bar graph on page 48 to solve each problem.

7. How much more is the root growth of Delicious compared to the root growth of Grow Home?

8. Cathy has an America's Best tomato plant. It is 65 centimeters tall. How much more should the plant grow?

SET 10 (pp. 50–57)

Subtract. Estimate to check.

1. 3,736 −1,539	**2.** 1,732 − 853	**3.** 46,823 − 9,847	**4.** 607,050 −245,879	**5.** 488,307 − 49,318

Solve each problem.

6. Ann spent $1.69. She paid with a $5 bill. The cash register shows that Ann should receive $3.31 in change. Count out Ann's change.

7. Joe spent $4.30 on magazines. He paid with a $10 bill. Count up to find the change Joe should receive.

8. A store sold 119 birthday cards, 12 travel cards, and 26 get-well cards. About how many cards were sold altogether?

9. A store sold 126 morning newspapers, 84 afternoon newspapers, and 36 magazines. How many newspapers were sold?

SET 11 (pp. 66–73)

Multiply.

1. 1 ×4	**2.** 71 × 3	**3.** 64 × 5	**4.** 58 × 7	**5.** 128 × 6	**6.** $2.47 × 8

7. 6 × 0 **8.** 2 × 39 **9.** 4 × $1.73 **10.** 9 × 578

Find the least common multiple (other than 0).

11. 2 and 15 **12.** 4 and 8 **13.** 3 and 12 **14.** 6 and 4

SET 12 (pp. 74–77)

Multiply. Estimate to check.

1. $\begin{array}{r} 9{,}736 \\ \times \quad\; 9 \\ \hline \end{array}$

2. $\begin{array}{r} 35{,}127 \\ \times \quad\;\; 4 \\ \hline \end{array}$

3. $\begin{array}{r} 276{,}210 \\ \times \qquad 5 \\ \hline \end{array}$

4. $\begin{array}{r} 31{,}402 \\ \times \quad\;\; 7 \\ \hline \end{array}$

5. $\begin{array}{r} 6 \\ \times 1{,}578 \\ \hline \end{array}$

Solve each problem.

6. At a sale, Barbara bought a plant for $2.95 and a pot for $1.60. How much change did she receive from $10?

7. At the sale, roses cost $1.75 each and orchids cost $5.95 each. How much will 2 roses and 1 orchid cost?

SET 13 (pp. 78–83)

Multiply.

1. $\begin{array}{r} 431 \\ \times \;\; 40 \\ \hline \end{array}$

2. $\begin{array}{r} 37 \\ \times 52 \\ \hline \end{array}$

3. $\begin{array}{r} 7{,}809 \\ \times \quad\; 26 \\ \hline \end{array}$

4. $\begin{array}{r} 4{,}127 \\ \times \quad\; 78 \\ \hline \end{array}$

5. $\begin{array}{r} \$28.74 \\ \times \qquad 37 \\ \hline \end{array}$

6. $3{,}782 \times 20$

7. $63 \times \$5.32$

8. 41×527

9. $5{,}063 \times 84$

SET 14 (pp. 86–95)

Multiply. Estimate to check.

1. $\begin{array}{r} 4{,}203 \\ \times \quad\; 600 \\ \hline \end{array}$

2. $\begin{array}{r} 619 \\ \times 324 \\ \hline \end{array}$

3. $\begin{array}{r} 5{,}087 \\ \times \quad\; 268 \\ \hline \end{array}$

4. $\begin{array}{r} 815 \\ \times 170 \\ \hline \end{array}$

5. $\begin{array}{r} 729 \\ \times 608 \\ \hline \end{array}$

Solve each problem.

6. There are about 125 fish in each fish tank. There are 37 fish tanks. About how many fish are there altogether?

7. Mae works 3 hours in the morning. She works 4 hours in the afternoon. She works 18 days per month. How many hours does Mae work each month?

SET 15 (pp. 104–105, 108–113)

Divide.

1. $8\overline{)48}$

2. $6\overline{)27}$

3. $8\overline{)75}$

4. $5\overline{)59}$

5. $3\overline{)68}$

6. $6\overline{)93}$

7. $9 \div 9$

8. $51 \div 7$

9. $19 \div 5$

10. $83 \div 8$

11. $98 \div 9$

12. $74 \div 3$

13. $92 \div 4$

14. $88 \div 7$

SET 16 (pp. 116–117, 120–129)

Divide.

1. $5\overline{)767}$ 2. $2\overline{)157}$ 3. $3\overline{)317}$ 4. $7\overline{)705}$ 5. $6\overline{)124}$ 6. $3\overline{)6,438}$

7. $298 \div 4$ 8. $7,532 \div 9$ 9. $\$49.25 \div 5$

Solve each problem.
If information is missing, tell what you need to know.

10. Brian has 61 records. 9 records fit in each box. How many boxes does he need for all the records?

11. Karen has 125 stamps. She can put 8 stamps on a page. How many pages can she fill?

12. Vincent bought a record album for $6.95, sheet music for $3.50, and 2 guitar picks. How much did he spend altogether?

13. Ellen's weekly paychecks for 1 month were $124, $137, $116, and $143. What were her average weekly earnings?

SET 17 (pp. 138–145)

Divide.

1. $20\overline{)90}$ 2. $50\overline{)724}$ 3. $40\overline{)8,365}$ 4. $84\overline{)924}$ 5. $67\overline{)8,240}$

6. $81\overline{)2,837}$ 7. $27\overline{)2,405}$ 8. $78\overline{)709}$ 9. $52\overline{)1,975}$ 10. $76\overline{)8,917}$

11. $909 \div 39$ 12. $2,354 \div 67$ 13. $263 \div 35$

14. $756 \div 21$ 15. $7,015 \div 56$ 16. $997 \div 79$

SET 18 (pp. 146–147, 150–155)

Estimate each quotient. Then divide.

1. $36\overline{)74,211}$ 2. $84\overline{)68,701}$ 3. $27\overline{)81,108}$ 4. $53\overline{)16,472}$

Solve each problem.

5. There are 48 rolls in a basket. 3 boxes of rolls are delivered. Each box contains 24 rolls. Write a question. Then answer it.

6. Which is a better buy: 9 ounces of peanuts for $1.69 or 16 ounces of peanuts for $2.89?

SET 19 (pp. 164–167)

What time is it?

1. 2 hours 45 minutes after 11:15 A.M.

2. 4 hours 9 minutes before 7:32 P.M.

Copy and complete.

3. 128 hours = ■ days ■ hours

4. 2 days = ■ hours

5. 3 minutes 39 seconds = ■ seconds

6. 4 weeks 6 days = ■ days

SET 20 (pp. 170–179)

Choose the sensible measurement.

1. The height of a room is about ■. **a.** 30 cm **b.** 3 m **c.** 9 m
2. Mount Everest is about ■ high. **a.** 800 m **b.** 8 km **c.** 80 km
3. A pin is about ■ long. **a.** 34 mm **b.** 34 cm **c.** 3 mm
4. A cup holds about ■ of water. **a.** 1 L **b.** 20 mL **c.** 200 mL
5. A horse weighs about ■. **a.** 545 kg **b.** 5 kg **c.** 500 g

Solve each problem.

6. A pharmacist has a 1-L bottle of medicine. She pours out 125 mL of medicine. How much medicine is left in the bottle?

7. A nurse has a 20-m roll of gauze. He cuts off two 75-cm-long pieces. How much gauze is left on the roll?

SET 21 (pp. 182–193)

Choose the sensible measurement.

1. A table is about ■ high. **a.** 3 yd **b.** 3 ft **c.** 30 ft
2. The grandfather clock is ■ high. **a.** 2 ft **b.** 6 yd **c.** 2 yd
3. A bottle holds ■ of shampoo. **a.** 16 pt **b.** 1 pt **c.** 1 c
4. A cat weighs about ■. **a.** 10 lb **b.** 10 oz **c.** 5 lb

Solve each problem.

5. Mark bought 3 lb of meat. He used 1 lb 9 oz in a recipe. How much meat is left?

6. Use the graph on page 193. Find the range of the number of birds seen in the park.

SET 22 (pp. 202–203)

Write a fraction for the shaded part.

1.

2.

3.

SET 23 (pp. 204–209)

Copy and complete.

1. $\frac{2}{3} = \frac{\blacksquare}{15}$

2. $\frac{4}{5} = \frac{20}{\blacksquare}$

3. $\frac{7}{21} = \frac{1}{\blacksquare}$

4. $\frac{30}{40} = \frac{\blacksquare}{4}$

Write each fraction as a whole number or as a mixed number in lowest terms.

5. $\frac{15}{3}$

6. $\frac{12}{5}$

7. $\frac{35}{5}$

8. $\frac{50}{8}$

9. $\frac{32}{6}$

10. $\frac{27}{3}$

SET 24 (pp. 210–221)

Add or subtract. Write each answer in lowest terms.

1. $\frac{3}{10} + \frac{5}{10}$

2. $\frac{7}{8} + \frac{5}{8}$

3. $\frac{7}{9} - \frac{4}{9}$

4. $\frac{35}{50} - \frac{15}{50}$

5. $\frac{5}{12} + \frac{2}{6}$

6. $\frac{7}{9} + \frac{2}{6}$

7. $\frac{3}{4} - \frac{1}{12}$

8. $\frac{6}{8} - \frac{2}{3}$

Write >, <, or =.

9. $\frac{1}{3} \ \blacksquare \ \frac{1}{2}$

10. $\frac{4}{5} \ \blacksquare \ \frac{6}{5}$

11. $\frac{3}{4} \ \blacksquare \ \frac{9}{12}$

12. $\frac{4}{2} \ \blacksquare \ \frac{8}{7}$

SET 25 (pp. 222–229)

Solve each problem.

1. Jim built $\frac{2}{8}$ of a model one day. He built $\frac{2}{6}$ of the model the next day. How much of the model has he built?

2. A spinner has 12 sections. The sections are numbered from 1 through 12. What is the probability of spinning an even number?

SET 26 (pp. 238–243)

Write as a decimal.

1. $\frac{5}{10}$ **2.** $\frac{1}{10}$ **3.** $3\frac{7}{10}$ **4.** $\frac{6}{100}$ **5.** $65\frac{37}{100}$ **6.** $3\frac{2}{100}$

7. five and forty-two thousandths

8. twenty-six and seven hundred three thousandths

9. eighteen and nine hundredths

What does the digit 5 mean in each number?

10. 40.512   **11.** 3.005   **12.** 62.157   **13.** 15.32   **14.** 23.145

SET 27 (pp. 244–247)

Write >, <, or =.

1. 0.62 ▦ 0.612   **2.** 5.47 ▦ 5.46   **3.** 0.41 ▦ 0.5

4. 0.7 ▦ 0.70   **5.** 81.43 ▦ 8.143   **6.** 5.37 ▦ 53.7

Round to the nearest whole number.

7. 3.452   **8.** 12.908   **9.** 24.69   **10.** 7.5   **11.** 6.09

SET 28 (pp. 248–251, 254–257)

Estimate each answer. Then add or subtract.

1. 6.7
+3.13

2. 8.761
+2.3

3. 28.16
+ 5.2

4. 2.132
−1.17

5. 6.532
−2.575

6. 9.206 + 13.8   **7.** 2.5 + 2.761   **8.** 13.7 + 4.625

9. 2.98 − 1.872   **10.** 77.54 − 8.041   **11.** 6.914 − 4.7

Solve each problem.

12. Kathy and Joanne bicycled 2.6 km in the morning. They rode 3.5 km in the afternoon. How far did they bicycle altogether?

13. Tim and Eric want to jog 6.5 km. They have already jogged 2.9 km. How much farther do they have to jog?

SET 29 (pp. 266–269)

Multiply.

1. $\begin{array}{r} 20.5 \\ \times\ 13 \\ \hline \end{array}$
2. $\begin{array}{r} 3.2 \\ \times 1.1 \\ \hline \end{array}$
3. $\begin{array}{r} 4.25 \\ \times\ 4.5 \\ \hline \end{array}$
4. $\begin{array}{r} 0.57 \\ \times\ 0.3 \\ \hline \end{array}$
5. $\begin{array}{r} 0.6 \\ \times 0.07 \\ \hline \end{array}$

6. 2.1×0.5 7. 0.4×0.16 8. 0.13×0.5

SET 30 (pp. 270–275)

Divide.

1. $3\overline{)8.22}$ 2. $5\overline{)0.935}$ 3. $16\overline{)49.92}$ 4. $8\overline{)0.752}$
5. $62.97 \div 73$ 6. $0.186 \div 31$ 7. $3.375 \div 5$

Write each fraction as a decimal.

8. $\frac{16}{20}$ 9. $\frac{36}{100}$ 10. $\frac{43}{50}$ 11. $7\frac{1}{4}$ 12. $\frac{8}{25}$ 13. $\frac{7}{8}$

SET 31 (pp. 278–281)

Multiply or divide.

1. 10×5.8 2. $1,000 \times 0.268$ 3. $8.89 \div 10$
4. $73.24 \div 100$ 5. 100×0.761 6. $924 \div 1,000$

Copy and complete.

7. $0.5 \text{ cm} = \blacksquare \text{ mm}$ 8. $4,500 \text{ m} = \blacksquare \text{ km}$ 9. $0.257 \text{ L} = \blacksquare \text{ mL}$
10. $0.2 \text{ kg} = \blacksquare \text{ g}$ 11. $350 \text{ mL} = \blacksquare \text{ L}$ 12. $0.7 \text{ km} = \blacksquare \text{ m}$

SET 32 (pp. 282–287)

Estimate each answer.

1. 24×31.6 2. 3.3×7.91 3. 47.2×6.48
4. $26.9 \div 5$ 5. $378.2 \div 93$ 6. $496.4 \div 57$

Solve each problem.

7. Use the graph on page 285. How much weight does a whale calf gain from birth to its sixth month?

8. Jim bought an iron for $41.75 and an ironing board for $27.50. The sales tax is $.06 on a dollar. How much did Jim spend in all?

**Name and measure each angle. Then write whether the angle
is *right, acute,* or *obtuse*.**

1.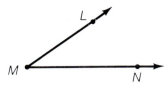

2.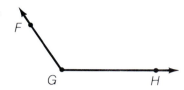

3.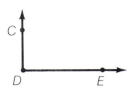

SET 34   (pp. 302–307)

**Name each polygon. Give the special name for each triangle
and quadrilateral.**

1.

2.

3.

4.

5.

6.

7.

8.

9. Which figures in exercises 1–8 are congruent?

SET 35   (pp. 308–311)

Use the circle to answer exercises 1–4.

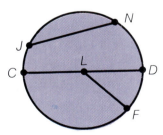

1. Name three radii.
2. Name a chord.
3. Name a diameter.
4. Estimate the circumference.

Is the red line a line of symmetry? Write *yes* or *no*.

5.

6.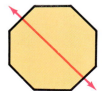

7.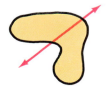

8.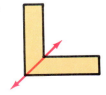

SET 36 (pp. 312–317, 320–325)

Use this figure to answer exercises 1–4.

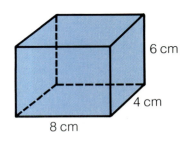

1. Name the shape of the figure.
2. Find the perimeter of the front face.
3. Find the area of the top face.
4. Find the volume of the figure.

6 cm

4 cm

8 cm

Solve each problem.

5. A room is 12 ft long, 8 ft wide, and 8 ft high. How much carpeting is needed to cover the floor?

6. Use the blueprint on page 324. C stands for a closet. How many closets are there in this house?

SET 37 (pp. 336–345)

Write each mixed number as a fraction.

1. $5\frac{2}{3}$ 2. $3\frac{1}{2}$ 3. $2\frac{5}{8}$ 4. $1\frac{7}{10}$ 5. $4\frac{3}{5}$ 6. $6\frac{1}{4}$

Add or subtract. Write each answer in lowest terms.

7. $7\frac{2}{4}$ $+2\frac{1}{3}$

8. $3\frac{2}{9}$ $+4\frac{2}{3}$

9. $5\frac{1}{2}$ $+2\frac{3}{6}$

10. $1\frac{6}{8}$ $+1\frac{2}{3}$

11. $3\frac{5}{8}$ $-2\frac{3}{8}$

12. $8\frac{3}{4} - 1\frac{3}{6}$

13. $9 - 4\frac{3}{5}$

14. $11\frac{1}{3} - 7\frac{5}{6}$

SET 38 (pp. 348–357)

Multiply. Write each product in lowest terms.

1. $\frac{3}{4} \times \frac{2}{5}$

2. $\frac{1}{2} \times \frac{3}{8}$

3. $\frac{3}{5} \times \frac{5}{3}$

4. $\frac{7}{10} \times \frac{1}{7}$

5. $8 \times 2\frac{1}{2}$

6. $1\frac{1}{5} \times \frac{2}{3}$

7. $2\frac{1}{4} \times 1\frac{1}{2}$

8. $2 \times 3\frac{1}{6}$

Solve each problem.

9. Use the graph of Joe's weekly budget on page 353. How much money does Joe spend on entertainment?

10. A toaster regularly sells for $36. It is on sale for $\frac{1}{4}$ off. How much can be saved at this sale? What is the sale price?

SET 39 (pp. 358–359)

Study each figure. Then complete to find each quotient.

1.

$\frac{2}{3} \div \frac{1}{9} = $ ▦

2.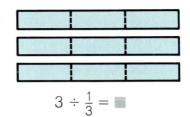

$3 \div \frac{1}{3} = $ ▦

3.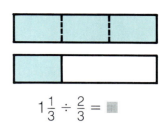

$1\frac{1}{3} \div \frac{2}{3} = $ ▦

SET 40 (pp. 368–373)

Write each ratio.

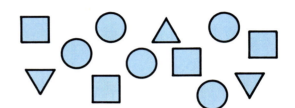

1. triangles to squares

2. circles to squares

3. triangles to all the shapes

Are the ratios equal? Write *yes* or *no*.

4. $\frac{3}{4}$ and $\frac{75}{100}$

5. $\frac{3}{9}$ and $\frac{5}{12}$

6. $\frac{20}{12}$ and $\frac{5}{4}$

7. $\frac{4}{10}$ and $\frac{6}{15}$

SET 41 (pp. 378–381)

Write as a percent.

1. $\frac{79}{100}$　　**2.** $\frac{1}{2}$　　**3.** $\frac{13}{20}$　　**4.** 0.7　　**5.** 0.85　　**6.** 0.01

Write each percent as a decimal.

7. 67%　　**8.** 45%　　**9.** 10%　　**10.** 2%　　**11.** 98%　　**12.** 8%

SET 42 (pp. 374–375, 382–385)

Solve.

1. 20% of $75　　**2.** 50% of 250　　**3.** 6% of 35　　**4.** 5% of $400

Solve each problem.

5. On a map, 1 cm stands for 50 km. What is the actual distance between two cities that are 2.5 cm apart on the map?

6. Kiome has $1,500 in an account. The bank pays 8% interest per year. How much interest will she earn in 1 year?

Glossary

addition An operation that gives the total number, or amount in all.

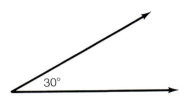

$$45 + 21 = 66$$

addends   sum

angle When two rays have the same endpoint, they form an angle.

30°

A *degree (°)* is a unit used for measuring angles. A *right angle* has a measure of 90°. An *acute angle* has a measure less than 90°. An *obtuse angle* has a measure greater than 90°.

area The number of square units needed to cover a region. *Square centimeters* and *square meters* are units used to measure area in the metric system. *Square inches*, *square feet*, and *square yards* are units used to measure area in the customary system.

The formula for the area of a rectangle is:

Area = length × width.

capacity Capacity is the amount of a substance that a container can hold.

circle A simple closed curve. All of the points are an equal distance from the center.

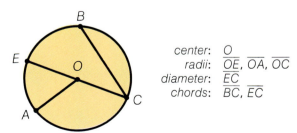

center: O
radii: $\overline{OE}$, $\overline{OA}$, $\overline{OC}$
diameter: $\overline{EC}$
chords: $\overline{BC}$, $\overline{EC}$

circumference The distance around a circle. The circumference is about 3 times the diameter.

common factor *See* greatest common factor.

common multiple *See* least common denominator.

cone A space figure with 1 curved face, 1 flat face, 1 curved edge, and 1 vertex.

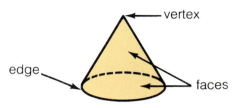

vertex

edge

faces

congruent Figures that have the same size and shape are congruent. Two angles or two line segments are congruent if they have the same measurement. Two polygons are congruent if they can be made to coincide by sliding, turning, or flipping.

cross products If two ratios are equal, their cross products are equal.

$$\frac{2}{8} \diagup\!\!\!\!\diagdown \frac{3}{12}$$

2 × 12   8 × 3
24 = 24

The cross products are equal.

cube A space figure with 6 square faces, 12 edges, and 8 vertices.

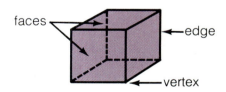

faces

edge

vertex

customary system A system of measurement used primarily in the United States. The *inch*, the *foot*, the *yard*, and the *mile* are units used to measure length. The *fluid ounce*, the *cup*, the *pint*, the *quart*, and the *gallon* are units used to measure capacity. The *ounce*, the *pound*, and the *ton* are units used to measure weight.

cylinder   A space figure with 2 flat faces, 1 curved face, 2 curved edges, and no vertices.

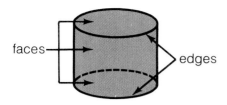

faces— edges

decimal   A whole number, fraction, or mixed number that is expressed using a decimal point.

digit   Any of the symbols: 0, 1, 2, 3, 4, 5, 6, 7, 8, 9.

division   An operation that gives the quotient of two numbers or amounts.

$$\overset{quotient \longrightarrow}{\underset{divisor \ \rightarrow}{}} 5\overline{)23} \overset{4 \text{ R}3 \leftarrow remainder}{\underset{\longleftarrow dividend}{}}$$

equivalent decimals   Decimals that name the same number. 0.7 and 0.70 are equivalent decimals.

equivalent fractions   Fractions that name the same number. $\frac{1}{2}$, $\frac{2}{4}$, and $\frac{3}{6}$ are equivalent fractions.

estimate   To find an approximate answer mentally by rounding the numbers before solving the problem.

even number   A number that has 2 as a factor.

expanded form   A form in which a whole number is written as the sum of the values of its digits.

$$3,476 = 3,000 + 400 + 70 + 6$$

fraction   A number such as $\frac{3}{5}$. A fraction may name part of a region or part of a set.

$\frac{3}{5}$ ← numerator
← denominator

The numerator and the denominator are the *terms* of a fraction.

greater than (>)   A way to compare numbers.

$$20 > 15 \qquad \frac{4}{6} > \frac{1}{6} \qquad 1.3 > 1.2$$

greatest common factor   The largest number that is a common factor of two or more numbers.

factors of 12:   1, 2, 3, 4, 6, 12
factors of 18:   1, 2, 3, 6, 9, 18
common factors of 12 and 18:   1, 2, 3, 6
greatest common factor of 12 and 18:   6

hexagon   A polygon with 6 sides and 6 angles.

intersect   Lines that cross at one point intersect.

least common denominator   The *least common multiple* of the denominators of two or more fractions. The least common multiple of 4 and 6 is 12, so 12 is the least common denominator of $\frac{3}{4}$ and $\frac{5}{6}$.

least common multiple   *See* least common denominator.

less than (<)   A way to compare numbers.

$$35 < 39 \qquad \frac{1}{4} < \frac{3}{4} \qquad 2.4 < 2.9$$

line   A line goes on and on in both directions.

line *AB* ($\overleftrightarrow{AB}$) or
line *BA* ($\overleftrightarrow{BA}$)

line segment   A line segment is part of a line. The *endpoints* show where a line segment begins and ends.

line segment *AB* ($\overline{AB}$) or
line segment *BA* ($\overline{BA}$)

line of symmetry   A line that divides a figure into two parts that match.

lowest terms   A fraction is in lowest terms when the numerator and the denominator have no common factor other than 1.

mean   Mean is another name for average. It is a single number used to represent a set of numbers.

metric system A system of measurement used throughout the world. The *millimeter*, the *centimeter*, the *meter*, and the *kilometer* are units used to measure length. The *liter* and the *milliliter* are units used to measure capacity. The *gram* and the *kilogram* are units used to measure weight.

mixed number A number such as $2\frac{1}{2}$, which has a whole number part (2) and a fraction part $\left(\frac{1}{2}\right)$.

multiplication An operation that gives the product of two numbers or amounts.

$$\begin{array}{r} 9 \\ \times 8 \\ \hline 72 \end{array} \; \text{factors}$$
$$72 \leftarrow \text{product}$$

$$8 \times 9 = 72$$
$$\text{factors} \quad \text{product}$$

octagon A polygon with 8 sides and 8 angles.

odd number A number that is not a multiple of 2.

ordered pair A pair of numbers that locates a point on a grid. (2, 6) is an ordered pair. The 2 tells how many units to the right of 0. The 6 tells how many units up.

parallel Two lines in a plane that do not meet are parallel.

parallelogram A quadrilateral in which the opposite sides are parallel and congruent.

pentagon A polygon with 5 sides and 5 angles.

percent (%) A ratio that compares a number to 100. 9% means 9 hundredths.

$$9\% = \frac{9}{100} = 0.09$$

perimeter The distance around a figure. To find the perimeter, add the lengths of the sides. The formula for the perimeter of a rectangle is: Perimeter = (2 × length) + (2 × width).

perpendicular Two lines that intersect to form right angles are perpendicular.

plane A flat surface that goes on and on in all directions.

polygon A closed figure with sides that are line segments. The line segments meet at a vertex to form an angle.

probability The chance that a certain event will happen. A fraction can be used to show a probability.

quadrilateral A polygon with 4 sides and 4 angles.

range The difference between the least and the greatest numbers of given information.

ratio A way to compare two numbers.

ray A part of a line. It has one endpoint and extends without end in one direction.

ray AB $(\overrightarrow{AB})$

rectangle A parallelogram with 4 right angles.

rectangular prism A space figure with 6 faces, 12 edges, and 8 vertices. A prism is named for the shape of its base.

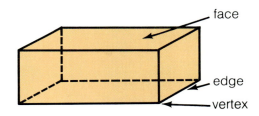

rectangular pyramid A space figure with 4 triangular faces, 1 rectangular face, 8 edges, and 5 vertices. The triangular faces meet at a point.

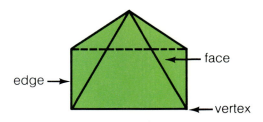

rhombus A parallelogram in which all sides are congruent.

scale drawing A figure drawn using equal ratios of lines in the figure to actual lengths. A map is a scale drawing of a region.

space figure A three-dimensional figure. The sides of a space figure are called *faces*. Faces can be flat or curved. The faces of a space figure meet at an *edge*. Edges can be straight or curved. The corner of a space figure is called the *vertex* (plural, *vertices*).

sphere A space figure that has the shape of a ball.

square A rectangle with 4 right angles and 4 congruent sides.

subtraction An operation that gives the difference between two numbers or amounts.

$$12 - 5 = 7$$

$$\begin{array}{r} 12 \\ -\ 5 \\ \hline 7 \end{array} \leftarrow difference$$

$difference$

time The *second*, the *minute*, the *hour*, the *day*, the *week*, the *month*, and the *year* are units used to measure time.

trapezoid A quadrilateral with a pair of parallel sides.

triangle A polygon with 3 sides and 3 angles. An *equilateral triangle* has all sides the same length. An *isosceles triangle* has at least 2 sides of the same length. A *scalene triangle* has no sides of the same length. A *right triangle* has 1 right angle.

unit price The price per item or per unit of weight, volume, or capacity.

volume The number of cubic units needed to fill a space figure. *Cubic centimeters* and *cubic meters* are units used to measure volume in the metric system. *Cubic inches*, *cubic feet*, and *cubic yards* are units used to measure volume in the customary system.

The formula for the volume of a rectangular prism is:

Volume = length $\times$ width $\times$ height.

whole numbers The set of numbers 0, 1, 2, 3, 4, 5, . . . This is the set consisting of 0 and all the numbers used in counting.

Computer Terms

asterisk (∗) A symbol that means multiplied by.

BACK (BK) A Logo command to move the turtle a certain number of steps.

BASIC (Beginner's All-Purpose Symbolic Instruction Code) A computer language.

command (BASIC) An instruction to a computer that gets it ready to or starts it doing work for you.

command (Logo) A single instruction to the computer.

CONTROL-C A computer command that instructs the computer to interrupt any program that is in progress.

display Any text or graphics that appear on the screen.

END The last statement performed by a computer program.

ERASE A Logo command that removes a procedure from the computer's memory.

flow chart A diagram that shows the step-by-step procedures of a program.

FOR...NEXT A pair of BASIC statements used to create a loop in a program.

FORWARD (FD) A Logo command to move the turtle a certain number of steps.

GOTO A BASIC statement to instruct the program to go directly to a stated line number.

graphics Pictures and designs generated by the computer.

hardware The equipment that you use in computing: computer, disk drives, printers, monitor, etc.

HOME In BASIC, this command moves the cursor to the top left corner of the video screen. In Logo, this command places the turtle in the center of the screen.

IF...THEN A BASIC statement. IF sets up a comparison of two data items; THEN specifies an action to be taken should that comparison be true.

IFFALSE A Logo command that tells the computer to look at the most recent test and, if false, to take a given action.

IFTRUE A Logo command that tells the computer to look at the most recent test and, if true, to take a given action.

INPUT A BASIC statement that asks for information from the user and assigns that information to a variable.

INT A BASIC function that removes any decimal part of a number: INT(123.454) would equal 123.

LEFT (LT) A Logo command to turn the turtle a certain number of degrees.

LET A BASIC statement that tells what piece of data a variable will stand for.

Logo A computer language generally used to tell a turtle how to draw shapes on the screen.

loop Part of a computer program that repeats.

NEW A BASIC command used to clear the computer's memory of any stored program.

PENDOWN A Logo command that restores the turtle's drawing capability after a PENUP.

PENUP A Logo command that allows the turtle to move without drawing a line.

PRINT A computer statement to display the data that follows it.

PRINT RUN READLIST A Logo command that tells the computer to display the answer to a math problem you type in.

procedure A set of Logo instructions that tells the computer how to do a specific job.

program A set of BASIC instructions that tells the computer how to do a specific job.

REPEAT A Logo command that causes a procedure to happen a specified number of times.

RIGHT (RT) A Logo command to turn the turtle a certain number of degrees.

RUN A computer command to start a program.

SAVE A computer command to store a program on a disk or cassette for later use.

SETPOS A Logo command that uses ordered pairs to send the turtle to a given position on the screen.

software Computer programs and procedures.

statement A BASIC instruction that gets a computer to do a specific piece of work for you.

STOP A Logo command that halts the procedure that is running and returns control to the user.

string variable A variable ending with a "$" symbol that stands for a group of letters, digits, or symbols; e.g. A$ = "WOW". String variables can never be used for math.

TEST READLIST This Logo command compares the user's response to a predetermined answer and sets up a true-or-false condition for the IF commands to detect.

user The person operating the computer.

variable A name that is assigned by the user to a number or data item. BASIC variables must be a letter or begin with one. Logo variables begin with a colon. Variables are used for math.

Index

Boldface indicates the page on which the term is defined.)

PHOTO CREDITS